# Village Echoes

# Village Echoes

## The Fiction of Wu Zuxiang

Philip F. Williams

Westview Press

BOULDER • SAN FRANCISCO • OXFORD

To my parents,
Franklin Springer Williams
Elizabeth Bassett Williams

Copyright © 1993 by Westview Press, Inc.

Published in 1993 in the United States of America by Westview Press, Inc., 5500 Central Avenue, Boulder, Colorado 80301-2877, and in the United Kingdom by Westview Press, 36 Lonsdale Road, Summertown, Oxford OX2 7EW

Library of Congress Cataloging-in-Publication Data
Williams, Philip F.
    Village echoes : the fiction of Wu Zuxiang / Philip F. Williams.
        p.   cm.
    Includes bibliographical references and index.
    ISBN 0-8133-1600-6
    1. Wu, Tsu-hsiang—Criticism and interpretation.   I. Title.
PL2921.T72Z95   1993
895.1'35—dc20                                                               92-20075
                                                                                CIP

Printed and bound in the United States of America

The paper used in this publication meets the requirements
∞ of the American National Standard for Permanence of Paper
for Printed Library Materials Z39.48-1984.

10     9     8     7     6     5     4     3     2     1

# Contents

*Acknowledgments*                                                    vii

Introduction                                                          1

### PART ONE:
### FORMATIVE AND CREATIVE YEARS

1   Origins and Literary Stirrings Up to 1930                         13

2   A Vision of Contrasts: Rural Versus Urban, 1931–1932              32

3   Contrasts Within the Village: Past Equilibrium
    Versus Present Decline, 1933–1934                                 61

4   Portraits of Rural Recovery at the Grassroots Level, 1934–1936    91

5   Wartime Visions of Infectious Nationalism, 1937–1943             121

### PART TWO:
### TECHNICAL PROCLIVITIES

6   Dramatization and Typicality in Characterization                 145

7   Variegated Narrative Voice and Minimalist Plot
    Structure                                                        158

8   Central Patterns of Metaphor Usage                               167

### PART THREE:
### PULLBACK FROM CONTEMPORANEITY

9   From Dramatizing the Present to Reclaiming
    the Heritage                                                      183

*v*

Conclusion 196

*Notes* 201
*Western-Language Works Cited* 249
*Chronological List of Wu's Creative Works* 257
*Selected Bibliography of Other Writings by Wu* 263
*Selected Bibliography of Other East Asian Source Materials* 271
*Glossary* 285
*About the Book and Author* 293
*Index* 295

# Acknowledgments

As the subject of this book, Wu Zuxiang kindly agreed to several lengthy interviews in his Beijing University campus apartment. Perry Link and Timothy Cheek offered meticulous critiques of earlier drafts of this study, as did Jeffrey Kinkley and Hoyt Tillman with later drafts. Fang Xide, C. T. Hsia, Vera Schwarcz, Randolph Trumbull, and Yan Jiayan had valuable suggestions to make about source materials. At Westview Press, Susan McEachern, Martha Robbins, Alison Auch, and an anonymous reader provided expert assistance during the final stages of manuscript preparation in the winter of 1991–1992. Thanks are also due to the many individuals who kindly lent a hand during my May 1983 visit to Wu's old home village in southeastern Anhui.

I owe much to the organizations that helped fund this project: the National Academy of Sciences Committee for Scholarly Communication with the People's Republic of China, the National Endowment for the Humanities Summer Stipend Program, the Arizona State University Graduate Humanities Fellowship Committee, and the University of Vermont Committee on Research and Scholarship. The Department of Chinese at Beijing University provided a generous measure of administrative assistance.

Libraries at Harvard, U.C.L.A., Arizona State, Stanford, Berkeley, and other U.S. universities furnished source materials, as did the Beijing Municipal, Beijing University, the Chinese Academy of Social Sciences, Hong Kong University, the Chinese University of Hong Kong, the Shanghai Public, and Tokyo University.

Unless noted otherwise, translated excerpts are the author's own renderings.

*Philip F. Williams*

# Introduction

Maolin, a village in southeastern Anhui only a few hours' bus ride southwest from Nanjing [Nanking], today appears all but cut off from history. A formerly brightly-hued propaganda wall painting of Mao Zedong has weathered into a greyish shadow-like figure, causing the viewer to ponder over the eventual fate of today's heads of state. Far more enduring is a scene just outside the village: behind a water buffalo trudges a wiry peasant, clad in a hand-woven reed raincoat and leaning on a plow identical to a design invented two millennia ago. Similarly sturdy, ancient ancestral temples still stand in these luxuriantly green hills and valleys, even if their ceremonial functions have given way to storing grain or providing office space for cadres.[1]

Hard though it may be to believe, this quiet and remote village has provided the backdrop for two occasions of international import during this century. It was here in Maolin that the uneasy wartime alliance between the Nationalists and the Communists came to split irreparably in 1941 with the New Fourth Army Incident: the Communist New Fourth Army had tarried south of the Yangtze River beyond the deadline Chiang Kai-shek had decreed for them to move back north, and thus was summarily surrounded and annihilated by KMT troops encircling Maolin. Although both political parties would make numerous perfunctory gestures of cooperation before the onset of civil war later in the decade, they were set on an unavoidable collision course from that point on. Half a century afterwards, the bitter and often deadly rivalry between the two parties still shows no signs of ending.

Turning back to the first decades of this century—and from the military [wu] to the cultural [wen] arena—the highest roof among Maolin's scores of wall-enclosed dwellings sheltered a young man destined to become one of the nation's top half-dozen writers in the 1930s. Wu Zuxiang (1908– ) would grow up to write almost exclusively about this locale, even long after taking permanent leave of his village in favor of various urban residences. After all, the overwhelmingly urban Chinese readership had

*1*

A few miles outside of Maolin, a peasant plows a paddy just as his ancestors did 2,000 years ago. (*Photo by the author*)

much to learn from his gripping fictional dramatizations of the concerns and hardships of villagers long neglected by a government bent on urban industrial development. Wu felt himself duty-bound to help bridge the gap in understanding between villager and urbanite within his nation—a gap no less formidable than the cultural barrier between urban Chinese and urban Westerner. Aiming to clear the air of stereotyped views of countryside life, Wu studiously avoided the melodramatic excesses of self-styled proletarian writers like his fellow Anhui literatus, Jiang Guangci, whose rural-based scenes typically included monstrous land-lords running roughshod over seraphic but powerless peasants. Himself a scion of Maolin's local elite, Wu knew that rural class stratification was immeasurably more complex, and could not be grasped by means of any hastily sketched Manichaean conceptual scheme.

However sound Wu's understanding of Maolin's social structure was, his writings would not have won acclaim had it not been for an excellent literary apprenticeship at Beijing's Qinghua University from 1929 to 1934. Many literature professors he studied under were every bit as interested in creative writing as in literary criticism, and strongly encouraged Wu to develop his aptitude for fiction. His stories and novellas, overall bulking somewhat larger than Lu Xun's fictional output, soon made their way from the pages of university magazines to China's foremost literary monthlies and quarterlies. By 1935, his first two collections of fiction had already come off the press from a leading publisher in Shanghai: both maintained the highest standards for tightly structured plots, smooth and true-to-life dialogue, and imaginative explorations of the human psyche under enormous pressures.

Wu Zuxiang was simultaneously typical and unique among the Chinese writers of his age. He comes across as typical in his general adherence to the tenets of nineteenth-century European literary realism; his strong affinities with Turgenev were considerably more representative of his generation than was Lu Xun's kinship with Andreyev. Moreover, Wu's view of the writer as primarily a social critic and conscience for his society resonates with key nineteenth-century European masters of the novel (e.g., G. Eliot, Tolstoy, and Zola), as well as with traditional Chinese views about moral imperatives in serious writing. Furthermore, as in the novels and stories of so many of his May Fourth peers, father figures are strangely absent from Wu's fiction, suggesting that a crisis in authority was challenging China's strongly patriarchal traditional social structure. Wu's fatherless societal landscape, indicative of the vacuum of legitimate authority at the foundation of rural Chinese society, was ripe for the influx of a new organizational structure aggressive enough to finish off the loosely amalgamated local elite that had superceded the defunct traditional gentry. As it turned out, the Japanese invasion and Chiang Kai-shek's ineffectual rural policies combined to provide the Communist Party with a golden opportunity to regroup and systematically overwhelm the transitional local elite. Wu subsequently joined the bulk of his May Fourth peers in withdrawing from the perilous front line of the Maoist literary scene to the safer climes of academe and the ponderous Party cultural bureaucracy. In retrospect, the numerous representative features in his career could even provide the grist for an outline biography of his entire generation of novelists.

On the other hand, Wu's literary career exhibits many flashes of uniqueness and the unexpected. With "Little Lord Guanguan's Tonic" (1932), he takes Lu Xun's unprecedented vernacular Chinese experiments with presentational irony and unreliable narrators to a new level of complexity and acerbic wit. "Splay-petaled Honeysuckle" (1933) reveals a Proustean psychological insight into the recovery of dormant childhood memories that makes Lu Xun's "My Old Home" seem rather mechanical by comparison. In "The Verdant Bamboo Hermitage" (1933), Wu's odd takeoff on the Chinese Gothic tale, he anticipates rhetorically self-reflexive, aesthetically self-parodying works of "meta-fiction" like Vladimir Nabokov's *Pale Fire* and John Barth's *Lost in the Funhouse*. Furthermore, none of his peers wrote a novella closer in structure to a play than "1800

Bushels" (1934), nor did any of them surpass the extent to which the art of dialogue dominated the visual imagination throughout his *oeuvre*. And in terms of subject matter, no other major May Fourth writer so thoroughly urbanized in lifestyle and outlook wrote so exclusively about village society.

Perhaps the very anomalies which made Wu stand out from his peers set the stage for the Shanghai-based doyens, Mao Dun and Lu Xun, to marginalize him during the mid-1930s under the label of "petty bourgeois" academic writer. His literary standing within Beijing academic circles hardly put him in good stead with the Shanghai-headquartered League of Left-wing Writers, a combative, faction-ridden organization he preferred not to join. What is beyond question is that these incongruities rendered him unfit to pen fiction for decades after the mid-century point. Under Mao Zedong's rule, the conformity of the tractable camp follower became the new and vigorously enforced norm for Chinese writers.

Rather than diminishing Wu Zuxiang's standing, the distinctive features of his narrative style and thematic range justify his ranking among the very top echelon of China's 1930s story writers.[2] What Shen Congwen achieved for the previously anonymous provincials of the Sino-Miao borderland culture of West Hunan, Wu carried out on a more austere scale for the upland villagers along the more rugged outcroppings of the Han Chinese heartland in the lower Yangzi. As insiders intimate with the entire spectrum of social classes in their locales, both authors gave voice to regional constituencies that other writers had either ignored or else described in sketchy terms. Neither Wu nor Shen was willing to march in lock-step with influential literary elders like Lu Xun or Mao Dun, whose portraits of peasants like Runtu ("My Old Home") and Lao Tongbao ("Spring Silkworms") betray the urban outsider's schematization of the rustic personality as basically passive, or at most reactive, in nature.[3] Instead, these younger writers of rural upbringing tended to mold rustic protagonists with initiative and an inner life that runs on more than the mere one or two tracks that townsman writers allot to such "deprived" minds. The typicality of a memorable village character in Wu's fiction resides not in a bundle of predictable traits exhibited by a caricatured or allegorical figure, but in the complexly and plausibly drawn interplay between the inner psyche and outer behavior of the flesh-and-blood rustic with a regional identity.

This dynamic quality in Wu's vision of rural society and its individual members comes across most clearly in his changing portrayal of the solidarity among Maolin's laboring masses. From the start of Wu's literary career through its midpoint of 1934, the rural masses usually amounted to little more than a hapless and fragmented lot, wholly ineffectual in molding itself into a constituency capable of serving as a countervailing force to the power of the local elite. On the sole occasion in which the masses acted in unison, it was to aid and abet the barbaric arrest and execution of one of their own kind in "Little Lord Guanguan's Tonic." However, beginning in 1934 and continuing until the outbreak of the War in 1937, a new tendency towards coalescence among the masses led first to their coercive insistence on the right to subsistence ("1800 Bushels"), and eventually the successful defense of hard-won gains against local elite intimidation tactics ("A Certain Day"/1936). In Wu's final period of creative writing during the Second World War, rural coalescence extended to envelop the local elite in a united and non-class-specific effort to defend the homeland from foreign invaders (*Mountain Torrent*/1943). By the twilight of Wu's twenty-year writing career in the 1940s, his fiction was thus portraying a startling amount of solidarity among the rural masses, if compared with his early stories.

While the early War years definitely witnessed a temporary boost in morale among Chinese citizens newly united by a common enemy, one also senses a strongly personal component in Wu's increasingly heady optimism about the resurgent masses of his home locale.[4] Unable to carry out any first-hand observation of life in Maolin for several years following 1934, Wu had to rely more and more heavily upon his memory and imagination in order to design the rural settings of his later fiction. As the recollections from many a summer's residence in Maolin began to fade, the conceptualizing faculty of his imagination—hopeful as it was about the prospects for grassroots coalescence—stepped in to fill in many of the inevitable gaps in memory. The result was a gradual skewing towards a decided optimism in his vision of rural development. Of course, Wu's pen was not alone in growing "fonder" by virtue of lengthy absence from its preferred literary setting: Shen Congwen's sunniest pastoral vision of his remote rural homeland in West Hunan took shape during several years of uninterrupted city living, while a subsequent visit to his provincial home in 1933 resulted in a pessimistic turn in his rural fiction.[5]

Memories of a faraway provincial homeland can grow even fonder if one's immediate living and working conditions in the city take a turn for the worse. Upon leaving graduate school at Qinghua in 1934, Wu became unhappy with the way that his new job responsibilities left him with little time or energy for writing. Dissatisfied with the impediments to literary creation stemming from his occupation of secretary in the entourage of General Feng Yuxiang, Wu compensated for some of his personal frustrations by imagining that the lower-class rural figures with whom he had long sympathized were now making great strides towards economic and political self-reliance. In the 1934 preface to *West Willow*, Wu's first short-story anthology, he mentions that "the bad state of the family finances" contributed to the necessity of leaving his literary haven in academe for outside employment; it comes as little surprise that he would subsequently delight in writing of the resurgent peasantry in "A Certain Day," who have the power and panache to ward off a threat to their self-reliant lifestyle by would-be exploiters from the local elite.

T. A. Hsia once noted a common tendency among May Fourth intellectuals to work off their frustrations with society through the vicarious manner of imagining the lower classes striking back at their social betters.[6] As a psychological mechanism which allows success in one endeavor to overshadow failure in another, compensation typically takes on a social or political coloring in the less affluent developing countries like China that had often been manhandled by the industrialized world powers.[7] In what H. Ernest Lewald calls "a compensatory reaction that makes abundant use of the emotive powers inherent in national feeling," a developing-country intellectual like Wu Zuxiang could overcome personal frustrations and disappointments by imagining how his country has become strengthened through the regeneration of the economically self-reliant rural masses ("A Certain Day"), or through a new civil ethic of active peasant cooperation with the reformed army (*Mountain Torrent*).[8]

Not all Chinese writers found the rural interior of the late 1930s and early 1940s quite so brimming with solidarity, however. The high level of social coalescence portrayed in *Mountain Torrent* and his other later works stands in stark contrast with the smoldering tensions between the masses and soldiers in various other prominent fictional works of that time. In Xu Dishan's "Yuguan" (1939), the "rice Christian" heroine has a very difficult time protecting herself and other local village women from both rape and forced labor on the part of rampaging Chinese soldiers.[9] Similarly, in Ai Wu's *Qiu shou* [Autumn Harvest] (1941), a young village woman whose husband was fighting at the front grows to fear and resent the presence of wounded soldiers recuperating in her village.[10] A few of the more mischievous of these soldiers have made a point of singing bawdy limericks within earshot of the village women laundering clothes by the riverside; the women respond with a blanket mistrust and contempt for all of the men in uniform.[11] They even go so far as to strike back by grossly overcharging the army men for local foodstuffs, and gruffly refuse the more well-mannered soldiers' offers to lend a hand with the local harvest. These well-meaning soldiers in turn grow to resent the local women's undeservedly sweeping rejection of their friendly overtures, complaining, "Wretched creatures! We've been spilling our blood in the fight against Japan for the likes of them!"[12] Although the tensions between the soldiers and the local women would eventually abate somewhat, at story's end the well-meaning soldiers still feel disillusioned about the gulf of mistrust separating them from the villagers. On the whole, whether in "Yuguan" or

"Autumn Harvest," the reader searches in vain for the sort of amity between soldier and villager that infuses *Mountain Torrent*.

The contemporary reader cannot help but feel ambivalent when confronted with the relatively gilded portrayal of rural Chinese society in Wu's later fiction. In defense of this approach to writing, the production of such optimistic literature could arguably be considered the proper duty of a nationalistic intellectual whose own land is being invaded and partially colonized. On the other hand, the internal promptings to write such fiction often derive from intense emotions such as rage and guilt, which tend to cloud the writer's perspicacity in making moral and aesthetic judgments. For example, Wu's sense of guilt over having accomplished little and risked nothing on behalf of the war effort, combined with his anger at the enemy invaders, created the "side effect" in which his novel exaggerated the degree to which the old class divisions and patriarchal social traditions of his homeland had withered away in the face of wartime grassroots solidarity. In contrast, Wu's gloomier vision of rural impoverishment and anomie before the mid-1930s strikes the reader as relatively free of personal remorse: he felt that he shared the fate of the impoverished protagonists of this period, for he saw himself as but another victim of the rural Depression, which was gradually reducing his formerly well-to-do family to a condition little better than genteel poverty.[13]

A pair of informal essays by Wu from the early 1940s suggest how remorseful he had eventually grown over his self-perceived inability to contribute anything substantial to society or the war effort. In a short piece entitled "The Back Street" [*Hou jie*], Wu recounts a dream in which a hungry little street urchin and his mangy dog rush to attack the author as he sits at a resplendent open-air feast.[14] Without pausing to take so much as a moment's thought on the matter, Wu casually kicks out at the boy and dog, booting both of them head over heels into a nearby river. When he realizes what he has just done, he feels too ashamed to continue with his meal, instead castigating himself as a callous glutton. A similar sense of falling short in the service of society comes across in an undramatized, discursive essay from the same period entitled "Facing My Lamp" [*Dui deng*].[15] Much as Qu Qiubai's death-row memoirs contain the *mea culpa* of a cerebral "superfluous man," Wu berates himself as a sort of Chinese Rudin (from Turgenev's novel of the same title) who can impress other people with his eloquence, but does nothing that could be deemed socially constructive.[16] Wu himself has interpreted "Facing My Lamp" as a personal confession that he had contributed too little to the national welfare in a time of crisis.[17] Such repeated confessions of inadequacy as a meliorist during the early 1940s suggest that the high level of social coalescence in his later fiction may have stemmed from a deep-seated conviction that overrode his adherence to the iconoclastic May Fourth legacy—a conviction that his reformist duty was to spur society forward by any means whatsoever, even if that meant portraying the current social order as far more humane and integrated than it actually was. This sense of duty was coupled with the psychological need to compensate for a disappointing post-1934 creative life by portraying the condition of rural society, and especially the laboring masses at its foundation, as improving both spiritually and materially.

Free of this nagging conflict between social duty and authenticity of literary portrayal, Wu's fiction from his Qinghua days in the early 1930s stands out as the finest collective achievement of his career. Instead of compromising his commitment to the quasi-Nietzschean May Fourth spirit for the sake of bolstering wartime morale, during this period he felt free to tell the whole harsh truth about provincial Chinese society, at least as he had come to know it through first-hand observation in his home village. In writing out these dark-hued visions, he did not have to face the pressures of bucking an influential intellectual trend, as he surely would have during the War, had he refused to gild his portrayal of rural society at that time. On the contrary, the global Depression had sent shock waves of doubt about the stability of the global socio-economic status quo among writers from the Western Hemisphere to China and Southeast Asia; the result was a kind of mainstream standing for 1930s *engagé* leftism.[18] Indeed, the Great Depression seemed to bolster the sense of urgency with which his generation of May Fourth intellectuals had long been calling for a thoroughgoing re-evaluation of all traditional cultural values.

At the same time that Wu felt comfortably situated within the worldwide literary *zeitgeist* of delving remorselessly into the socio-economic crisis of the early 1930s, he was able to enjoy the psychological benefits of a growing self-confidence in his own originality and outspokenness. A polemical essay he wrote in 1931 takes his fellow Qinghua writers to task for focusing too narrowly on topics related to their own elite educated class and atypically comfortable socio-political milieu, as well as neglecting broader social problems such as rural anomie.[19] While challenging the merits of Zhou Zuoren's influential advocacy of the personalistic Ming *gongan* school of prose writing, Wu's essay noticeably refrains from citing a counter-authority like Lu Xun in his call for a more committed type of literature. Therefore, by the age of twenty-three, Wu was already self-assured enough about the soundness of his literary leanings to recommend them to his peers—and without bothering to cite a respected authority in support of his bold contentions. At the same time that he sensed a strong affinity between his own fiction and that of other *engagé* writers in his own land and around the world, the spirit of independence with which he stated his credo of literary commitment reveals that he felt beholden to no particular individual or faction for his special orientation. Instead, it was his remote home region, rich personal history, and inquiring mind that impelled him to write as he did. Indeed, the key strand running through the entirety of Wu's fiction is not his meticulous attention to dialogue-based diction or tightly knit plot structure—excellent though they may be—but his indefatigable delving into sensitive contemporary social issues. In a comment on Ivan Turgenev, whose rural fiction bears a strong affinity with the Anhui author's efforts at the peak of his career, Henry James has captured something of the importance attached to social engagement in Wu's *oeuvre*: "A matter which filled his existence a great deal more than the consideration of how a story should be written was his hopes and fears on behalf of his native land."[20] It thus seems inaccurate to describe a modern Chinese *engagé* writer like Wu as a "critical realist,"[21] for this term has strong associations with Western realists like Flaubert, whose choice of literary realism arose more from an aesthetic conscience than from the social conscience motivating writers like Turgenev, Shaw, and Tolstoy.[22] Wu Zuxiang and his fellow writers of social conscience might be better characterized as "melioristic realists" than "critical realists." As Ellman and Feidelson define it, melioristic realism emphasizes the power of literature to infect readers with ethical insights into bettering society and the human condition.[23] I will simply refer to Wu as a meliorist, for the realist basis of his work is obvious and has never been at issue.[24]

Meliorist writers of realist fiction are rarely prone to either the fatalist proclivities of a Chekhov, or the adamant pessimism and *impassibilité* of a Flaubert.[25] Instead, no matter how dark a mood Wu and other meliorists may have fallen into from time to time, they remain mindful of the redeeming humane qualities in their cultural traditions, the power of reason to influence the course of history, and the capacity for benevolence and resiliency in the human spirit. In the meliorists' concern to awaken their brethren to various social conditions or viewpoints, they are too intent upon morally edifying the reader to conjure forth the sort of thoroughly disinterested descriptions of social reality that can be found in the true critical realist. It thus comes as little surprise that Wu Zuxiang has emphatically objected to Mao Dun's labeling of him as a "purely objectivist writer," particularly since most other critics commenting on the issue have noticed Wu's deft and yet unmistakable partisanship for the underprivileged in rural society.[26]

On the other hand, no matter how sincere, well-informed, and insightful a meliorist writer may be, something less tangible is also needed if the works in question are not to wind up flat and insipid. As Bonnie McDougall has noted, the "solemn self-consciousness" of many *engagé* May Fourth writers erected "a barrier between them and their potential audience: it is hard to think of even a reform-minded student reader of the 1920s being content with an unrelieved diet of May Fourth writing."[27]

Much in the manner of Zhou Zuoren, Wu Zuxiang has pointed to *quwei* [piquancy] as the intuitive and evocative quality in literature which counteracts flatness by imparting a special flavor to a work.[28] The concept of piquancy includes both what the reader absorbs from his reading and what the author imparts to his writing: it points to an aesthetic situation wherein the reader's expectations are violated in a stimulating and evocative way. An analogy related directly to the sensation of taste would be an unusual but pleasingly seasoned dish, which can only be properly appreciated if the chef's flair for combining the flavors and textures is matched by the banquet-goer's sensitivity of palate. By marshalling the pleasing asymmetries in character and incident that are humorous, novel, or unexpected, piquancy prevents the meliorist *zhi*, or "substance," of a literary work from slipping into a ponderous, owlish solemnity.[29] Through such techniques as the seamless interweaving of serious and farcical scenes, as well as abrupt shifts between waking consciousness and dreaming, Wu evokes the *quwei* of his literary situations as skillfully as any of his meliorist contemporaries. It is precisely Wu's adeptness at balancing the meliorist substance of his fiction with piquant crosscurrents that enables his readers to partake of a proper Horatian blend of pleasure and instruction.[30]

PART ONE

# Formative
# and Creative Years

# 1

## Origins and Literary Stirrings
## Up to 1930

### Clan Ancestry

Wu Zuxiang's clan originally came from the North China Plain, whence they fled invading Jurchen armies in the twelfth century. The Wu clan settled down in the hilly and lightly populated region of southeastern Anhui called Wannan, which lies to the south of the Yangzi River and from 200 to 350 miles upriver from the seacoast. The abundance of greenery at the site they cleared for the village resulted in the place-name "Maolin" [lit., "lush forest"]. When Wu Zuxiang was born there in 1908, over 90% of his fellow villagers were surnamed Wu. Even today, close to half of Maolin's residents share that surname.

The founders of Maolin village chose a sound agricultural site: creeks from hills ringing a spacious tract of tableland provided adequate irrigation for rice farming. Complementing the economic backbone of rice farming were sideline forest industries like bamboo handicrafts, papermaking, and woodcutting.[1] Huizhou and other regional mercantile hubs buttressed Maolin's prosperity by means of wealthy merchants' travels and investments throughout the locale. Yet the pinnacle of success in traditional Chinese society was to obtain high office via the civil service examination system, and Wu's home region held to the centuries-long pattern in which southeastern China was the densest regional incubator of scholarly talent throughout the nation. One lintel plaque still standing in a Maolin residence reads "A family that plows and studies" [geng du renjia], thus voicing the local commitment to maintaining an economic base in agriculture while investing in education for sons bright enough to have a reasonable chance of passing the government service exams and thereby gaining a coveted official appointment.[2]

The Wu clan at Maolin produced more scholars of fame than what might be expected from an upland village. Perhaps the most eminent ancestor was a seventeenth-century "renowned official" [ming huan] named Wu Shangmo, whose contributions to the state included bolstering the

13

From the outskirts of Maolin, a view of the low mountains ringing the village. (*Photo by the author*)

coastal defenses against attacks from Japanese pirates, allying with the Donglin political group to counter the baleful influences of the powerful eunuch clique leader Wei Zhongxian, and running a large granary relief program.[3] A more recent ancestor who served as a high official was Wu Fangpei, who held a prestigious post at the Hanlin Academy in the capital.[4] The county gazetteer records a large assemblage of other scholarly Qing dynasty forbears from Maolin and their collections of literary and philosophical writings.[5] This Confucianist legacy of scholarship and service to society established by Wu Zuxiang's clan in Maolin helped set the stage for his eventual development into an *engagé* writer.

### Family Background

Wu Zuxiang's recollections of recent family history extend to the time of his great-grandfather Wu Shifan, whose life spanned the first two-thirds of the nineteenth century.[6] Wu Shifan was a patriarch of the Wu clan's seventh branch [*qifang*], a clan subdivision consisting of several families living within a single residential compound. While Wu Shifan was a "high official and large-scale landowner," his extensive upland holdings suffered less damage from the Taiping Rebellion (1851–1864) than did the property of southern Chinese gentry located in vulnerable

low-lying areas. He nevertheless opposed the Taipings, as did his eldest
son and fellow scholar-official Wu Shaolie, who served under the anti-Tai-
ping Qing Restorationist Zeng Guofan (1811–1872).[7] Family prosperity
continued to batten under Wu Shifan's second son, Wu Yanglie, who established himself in commerce rather than officialdom.[8] With such a degree of involvement in officialdom and commerce, it is little wonder that
the seventh branch of the Wu clan has earned the epithet of an "eminent
local family" [*da hu renjia*] from various Maolin villagers.[9]

Economic positions of a moderate or humble nature also existed within
the affluent seventh branch. One of these was occupied by Wu Shifan's
youngest son and Wu Zuxiang's paternal grandfather, Wu Jixin (1838–
1911). Wu Jixin worked as an entrepreneur of modest means, managing
the clan's various oilseed-press shops as well as operating some shops of
his own. Unable or unwilling to gain financial backing from his wealthy
elder brothers,[10] Wu Jixin procured investment capital by borrowing small
parcels of savings from numerous clan members.[11] Rental income from
nearly five acres of farmland his father gave him complemented his modest entrepreneurial income; if Wu Jixin had to live more frugally than his
elder brother Wu Yanglie, at least he avoided the humbled circumstances
of Yanglie's descendants, who had to fall back on bamboo handicrafting
when no longer able to make a living through commerce.[12]

Of Wu Jixin's five sons, the only ones to survive bouts of illness during
young adulthood followed their father's line of work in managerial and
entrepreneurial enterprises. The youngest son became the clan's business
manager, while the next to youngest—and the father of Wu Zuxiang—Wu
Qingyu (1864–1928) mixed small-scale landholding with entrepreneur-
ship.

Wu Zuxiang associates his father's choice of occupation with socio-political idealism. Among the five sons of Wu Jixin, it seems that only Wu
Qingyu refused to take the government service examinations; the very examination system itself seems to have met with Qingyu's disapproval.[13]
Yet the socio-political theorists whom Wu Qingyu admired were the reformist proponents of a Westernized constitutional monarchy for China,
namely Kang Youwei (1858–1921) and Liang Qichao (1873–1929); far from
urging a boycott of the obviously flawed examination system, they had
passed through that system themselves and hoped to reform it from the
inside rather than undermine it from the outside.[14] Wu Qingyu's decision
not to embark on an official career probably depended on personal factors
no less than philosophical convictions, much as the Qing novelist Wu
Jingzi's failure to take a set of civil service exams in 1736 was more likely a
result of his having contracted a serious illness that year than the sort of
deep-seated revulsion for "feudalism" that a few politically-minded modern scholars have ascribed to him.[15]

A more reliable indication of Wu Qingyu's enlightened attitude about the necessity for fundamental social change in China was his encouragement of his sons to pursue foreign subjects along with traditional Chinese areas of learning. At first personally supervising the elementary education of his two sons, he later funded their secondary schooling at urban boarding schools, where they picked up the sort of training in social sciences and foreign languages necessary for a successful showing in the highly competitive university entrance exams. Wu Qingyu may have been highly accomplished in the age-old art of calligraphy, but he knew that the sort of extended apprenticeship in calligraphy he had undertaken during his own youth would not be an appropriate path for his sons to follow.

Wu Qingyu nevertheless insisted that his children gain a basic foundation in traditional learning before going away to pursue modern subjects. Wu Zuxiang remembers his father as a stern instructor of calligraphy who would tolerate no deviations from the prescribed stroke order on the part of his young sons. Not surprisingly, Zuxiang's few warm reminiscences of his parents are limited to his mother.[16] In an essay published during the budding writer's teens, he complains at length about the Confucian hardliner's fear that a father might spoil a son unless he maintained an air of stern formality in their relationship.[17] A shortage of warmth in the father-son relationship is also evident in Wu's boyhood chagrin when relatives over for a visit would take their leave; he found the atmosphere at home chilly without them, especially since his father seemed more intent on instructing him than establishing a rapport at the emotional level.[18]

The benefits of Wu Qingyu's severity were not lost upon Wu Zuxiang, however, for he absorbed his father's aesthetic teachings on the ideals of symmetry of composition and scrupulous attention to detail. However much Wu Zuxiang's fictional leanings may owe to his iconoclastic peers or Western antecedents like Maupassant, he insists that his stylistic preference for the concise rendering of detail and balanced, tightly-knit composition derive from traditional Chinese aesthetics that he first began to assimilate under his father.[19]

His mother Feng Suzhu (1862–1944), the daughter of a well-to-do landlord in the neighboring village of Fengcun, was illiterate, so it is little wonder that her son looked on her more as a nurturer than a stern headmaster. Her ministrations to Wu Zuxiang's childhood illnesses such as malaria were all the more circumspect in light of the fact that ten of his twelve elder siblings had died from disease during childhood.[20] He still remembers the scrupulous manner in which she prayed to the Boddhisattva Guanyin for his recovery, and dosed him with quinine to calm his fevers.

Feng Suzhu's instruction of the children was mostly focused on the toddler period, when she kept them on a regimen of rising promptly at dawn to listen to story recitations and sing folk ditties. According to Wu

Zuxiang, this is beneficial to a toddler's memory retention: even at the age of nearly eighty, he could still clearly remember scenes dating back to when he was only three or four years old.[21] The precocious cultivation of Wu's memory capacity probably had an impact on his creative methodology: instead of working from a written outline and revising heavily as many authors are wont to do, he would plot out the whole story in his mind over a matter of weeks or months before writing it all down within a relatively short duration.[22]

Wu Zuxiang wrote too little domestic autobiographical fiction for his parents to have played much of a direct literary role as thinly disguised characters.[23] Their impact on his career was more diffuse in nature, enmeshed as it was with the upbringing they gave him. Both of them cultivated his fondness for learning and instilled a sense of discipline and regularity in the pursuit of studies. Furthermore, his mother's warmth and empathy made up for his father's shortcomings as a nurturer, while his father's encouragement to study modern subjects compensated for his illiterate mother's thoroughgoing provinciality of outlook. As a result, Wu Zuxiang received a well-rounded upbringing both modern enough to aid his eventual integration into the urban intelligentsia, as well as traditionally provincial enough to imbue him with a strong sense of his native place—a native place that so dominated the setting of his fiction as to become a virtual trademark of it.

### Childhood in the Hills: Maolin Village

Born on 5 April 1908, Wu Zuxiang was the youngest of his parents' three surviving children. His older sister, Wu Runbao, who lived from 1892 to 1960, was practically a generation above him. The young man whom she married at age sixteen died within the year, and the inflexible code of Qing dynasty Confucian propriety forbade that she remarry on pain of shunning by the clan.[24] Wu Zuxiang remembers her as often depressed by her fate, most specifically whenever she watched a kind of southern Chinese popular drama called "Yellow-plum opera" [*huang mei xi*] that features romances between lovesick characters.[25] Partly as a result of frequent contact with his sister and other more distant female relatives, his fiction would eventually address a number of issues involving women in rural China. He was particularly sensitive to the passive sufferings that Qing Confucian rules of propriety inflicted on the southern Chinese women of genteel background among whom he had grown up. Practically the only women in his fiction who achieve a higher level of independence and self-reliance hail from the lower social strata, and often from the poorer rural areas north of the Yangzi River where the luxuries of women's economic inactivity and its accoutrements like footbinding were simply unaffordable for most people.

The elementary schoolhouse in Maolin, in which Wu studied as a boy. (*Photo by the author*)

Wu Zuxiang's only surviving brother, Wu Zuguang, was four years his senior and a model in many ways.[26] As a boy, Wu Zuguang often practiced penmanship and composition by writing down many of the lively stories and folk ballads that clan members would gather to exchange during festivals and other times of leisure; Zuxiang naturally followed his brother's lead.[27] In a general way, Wu Zuxiang would later follow in his brother's footsteps through various secondary schools and the entrance examinations for Qinghua University in Beijing, where the younger brother first majored in Zuguang's field of economics. Yet Zuxiang's subsequent switch to literature may have been foreshadowed by his early behavior pattern of taciturn bookishness, which one contemporary recalls as distinguishing the younger from the more gregarious elder.[28] Zuguang later settled into an active career in commerce, while Zuxiang got bored with his college roommates' conversations about business and withdrew from the economics department by the beginning of his sophomore year in college.[29]

Among non-relatives in Wu's rural homeland, he was probably closest to various members of the Pan clan in nearby Pan Village; he was particularly fond of the local primary school teacher from that clan, and corresponded with him for many years after leaving Maolin. Wu also grew up with servants in his gentry household: one of his earliest childhood memories is being escorted by a maid to a clan storytelling session that amused her but left him uncomprehending and listless.

As the transformation from toddler to boy took place, Wu gradually came to view the periodic gatherings of clan relatives to exchange stories and news as a welcome relief from the drudgery of everyday rural life. His clan's general preference for ghost stories like those collected in *The Strange Tales of Liaozhai* [*Liaozhai zhi yi*] is detectable in one of Wu's stories from the 1930s, "The Verdant Bamboo Hermitage" [*Luzhu shanfang*], a work with a Gothic flavor very rare in *engagé* fiction of the day.[30]

Wu Zuxiang's earliest schooldays were more of a family affair than a clan affair, however. By the time he was seven in 1915, he was practicing calligraphy under his father's supervision for an average of two to three hours daily. From 1915 to 1917, his father hired a teacher and organized a household private school [*sishu*] with only four pupils. Among the subjects he studied was parallel sentence structure in composition, a highly stylized type of prose that appears in his canon only once in full-blown form.[31]

In 1918 at the age of eleven, Wu Zuxiang enrolled in an upper-level elementary school in Maolin. It was called Instruct-the-Valorous Elementary School [*Yu ying xiaoxue*], and was run partly with clan funds. Wu completed his studies there in 1920, which was his final year of continuous residence in the village except for a long "village honeymoon" in 1927. From that time on, he would visit Maolin only during vacation from urban schools or employment, but the emotional attachment he felt for life in his village was already so firmly established as to make southeastern Anhui village life the center stage of his literary edifice.

### To Boarding Schools in Cities Downstream

Wu Zuxiang's first residence outside of Maolin was Xuancheng, a county seat larger than any town in Wu's home county and approximately three-quarters of the distance north to the large Yangzi riverport of Wuhu.[32] From February to July 1921 he roomed and studied at Xuancheng's Number Eight Provincial Middle School, whose program emphasized readings from standard texts in Classical Chinese.[33] Since Wu was one of many youths who were encouraged by the May Fourth New Culture Movement to read controversial new vernacular-language materials, he looked for a chance to test into a school where vernacular writings formed at least part of the curriculum. Wu found such an institution at Wuhu's Number Five Provincial Middle School, where he studied from January 1922 to December 1923. Situated on a forested hilltop above the bustle of an inland Yangzi treaty port, the middle school at Wuhu was a hotbed of new-culture activities, at least in comparison to anything Wu had previously encountered. Instructors encouraged students to take an

The hilltop middle school in Wuhu, the town in which Wu studied and lived during the early 1920s (currently used to house literature faculty from the local university). (*Photo by the author*)

interest in not only their daily coursework, but also controversial issues of the day like the Chinese boycott of imported Japanese merchandise. Progressive school administrators like the principal, Liu Xiping, urged students to discuss problems related to China's future that had been raised via the New Culture Movement.[34]

One medium through which the students in Wuhu could voice their ideas was the local school journal *Sienna Mountain* [*Zhe shan*], which Wu Zuxiang took a hand in running while still in his teens. No copies of this journal appear to have survived the Cultural Revolution, but a piece of Wu's writing from the same period has been preserved in a newspaper literary supplement of the *Minguo ribao* [*Republic Daily*] known as "The Awakening" [*Juewu*].[35]

This first published piece of any note by Wu appeared on 7 October 1923 toward the end of his two-year stay at the Wuhu middle school.[36] A plot summary of the sophomoric maiden work, entitled "The Ill-fated Little Plant" [*Buxing de xiao cao*], reveals its nature as fable rather than fiction proper. A small plant growing near the sea yearns to venture out of its little nook and have an impact on the world. When its wish is granted by the currents of wave and wind, it discovers that the world's hazards prove to be much more powerful than its allures. Thrown about by currents too overpowering to navigate amidst, the plant realizes that it cannot achieve its ambitions and subsequently dies from battering atop a briny reef.

The structure of the story is highly symmetrical, even rigidly so. The plant is growing with vitality during springtime at the story's outset, while it is a lifeless blob of torn and wilted fibers by autumn at the story's conclusion. Aside from the plant, there are only two characters personified with the ability to speak: the wind-blown sands lead the plant in flight through the sky above, while at another point the sea turtles lead the plant through the churning ocean waves below.

Above all, the fable is an allegory of rebellion. Even though spring's bounty has arrived, the plant is dissatisfied with both its environment and its own limitations, particularly its rooted immobility. It resolutely struggles to detach itself from its familiar environment by withdrawing its roots from the soil and casting itself on the currents of water and wind. Like the young writer himself, the restless plant turns its back on the secure and familiar place of its origin to embark on an adventure into the unknown.

The sentence structure of the story reveals a limit to the rebelliousness of the author, however, for the work's ornate parallelism reflects his adherence at that time to a formal style of writing that had been drilled into him since the age of seven:[37] "This ill-fated little plant was born by the shores of a vast ocean, and in the corridor of rumbling storms. Never had it ever seen the resplendent sun or the limpid moon."[38] A specialist in the decorative couplet has described the sort of early training a child of Wu's generation would receive:

> Not too long ago, Chinese children were still taught the art of writing couplets as soon as they had some idea of the four tones. The initial stage of the training consisted of such exercises as setting single words against each other antithetically, like "heaven" against "earth," "mountain" against "stream," and "river" against "sea." After this, the pupil would go on to devising suitable matches to two-character phrases, as in pairing "white teeth" with "red lips" and coupling "nine classics" with "three histories." Soon the pupil advanced to combinations of three characters. Phrases like "three-foot sword" [*san chi jian*] would be placed side by side with "five cartloads of books" [*wu che shu*]; "sing old songs" [*ge jiu qu*] with "distill new wine" [*niang xin pei*] and so on . . .[39]

Wu's early instruction in writing was nearly all in Classical Chinese. Even in Wuhu, the most progressive of the schools he had thus far attended, the teachers of Chinese language and literature still used the classical idiom as the basis of instruction. For his study of vernacular narrative and dialogue, Wu Zuxiang had to draw on his spare time, during which he looked up to his copy of the Qing novel *Dream of the Red Chamber* as his "teacher" of vernacular prose.[40] However far he may have advanced with his personal study of *Dream of the Red Chamber*, by the time Wu wrote "The Ill-fated Little Plant," his prose style was still encumbered by an overdependence on the sort of florid parallelism which sounds natural in the classical idiom, but comes across as awkward, obtrusive, and contrived in the vernacular.

The slightly incompatible sentiments of impetuosity and timorousness which the plant exhibits in its losing struggle against large-scale forces beyond its comprehension surely reveal one side of Wu's own writing career. Throughout his career, he would dare to address controversial issues like the government's alarming inadequacy to deal with rural social deterioration, yet he would hesitate to get embroiled in the kind of oppositional political activism (e.g., membership in the League of Left-wing Writers) that was liable to elicit harsh retaliation from the authorities.

Since the ambivalence the young writer expressed through his story could have been rendered via a realistic social setting and ordinary human protagonists, why would Wu turn to the fable as the genre for his maiden work? Apparently, by 1923 he had not yet fully emerged from his childhood associations of literature with a performative occasion redolent with folklore and fanciful, non-naturalistic motifs. As a child, he had enjoyed listening to fabular folk tales, some collections of which contain stories quite similar to "The Ill-fated Little Plant."[41] One such collection of regional folk tales draws its materials solely from the southeastern Anhui region around the famous Huangshan ["Yellow Mountains"] range, which is only a few dozen miles from Wu's home village.[42] A fable in this collection entitled "The Golden Tortoise Straddles a Sea Turtle" [*Aoyu tuo jin gui*] features a villainous giant sea turtle out to devour a benevolent plant with magical properties, the *lingzhicao*. Unlike Wu's melancholy fable, this folk fable ends in comic fashion with the Chinese equivalent of a European dragon-slayer charging on the scene to kill the giant sea turtle, which hardens to form a curiously shaped crag the locals now call "The Golden Tortoise Straddles a Sea Turtle." And yet one is struck by the similarity of this fable with Wu's—the personified characters from Wu's fable all appear in some form here, including the "flying sands" [*fei sha*] which had followed in the earlier sea turtle's wake.[43]

Wu Zuxiang would soon discard the fanciful folklorist motifs from his initial sources in regionalist oral literature. Not so transient, however, was the regionalist sensibility implicit in his maiden work; it would endure throughout the entire twenty years of his writing career.

### The Late 1920s: On to Shanghai and Contemporaneity

Only two months after Wu published his first work in the fall of 1923, the firing of most of the progressive school officials in Wuhu led to ex-

Principal Liu Xiping's move to Nanjing, where he founded the Renovate-the-People Middle School [*Xin min zhongxue*]. Wu was one of the many pupils who quit school in Wuhu in order to follow Liu Xiping to Nanjing.

The Nanjing school managed to stay in operation for only one semester before closing its doors in July 1924.[44] Wu Zuxiang decided to return to his family residence in Maolin for a stay of several months. He soon realized that this was decidedly not the place to continue his preparations for the college entrance exams, so with family backing he left in February 1925 for Shanghai, China's largest metropolis.

Wu spent most of the latter half of the 1920s in Shanghai, first completing middle school and then beginning college coursework. He lived in a small apartment upstairs from a storefront in the Japanese concession of the treaty port. The private school he attended was a combination of a liberal arts institution, Perseverance College [*Chi zhi daxue*], and its attached middle school of the same name, *Chi zhi daxue fushu zhongxue*.[45] Shortly after beginning coursework here in 1925, Wu wrote and published his second work of fiction.

"Soaring Hawks and Plunging Fish" [*Yuan fei yu yue*] emerged as Wu's first attempt at his mainstream fictional approach of filling a contemporary setting with basically naturalistic, life-like characters.[46] The narrator's young uncle is on the eve of venturing afar from his rural gentry family compound, which is known by its auspicious namesake of "Soaring Hawks and Plunging Fish," when his frank and assertive young wife offends her domineering grandmother. The growing wrath of the old matron extends to the uncle when he humbly attempts to defend his wife. Not even the old matron's husband can soothe her august fury. Shamed by the matron's shrill rebukes, the uncle and his wife both secretly commit suicide. Momentarily shaken by the discovery of the two corpses, the matron is soon comforted by her old friend from the local nunnery, who dismisses the whole sad affair as an inscrutable twist of fate.

Similar in length to "The Ill-fated Little Plant," "Soaring Hawks and Plunging Fish" contains only about 1500 words, yet is even more maudlin in tone, containing over twice as many exclamatory utterances as found in the earlier story. The most significant point in common between the two is the mood of rebellion; the later story repeatedly debunks the traditional auspicious sentiments expressed by the phrase on the front entrance's lintel plaque, "Soaring Hawks and Plunging Fish."

To fathom what Wu Zuxiang is debunking, one must turn to the literary and biographical contexts of this particular phrase. Within the literary context, a poem entitled "Drought-stricken Foothills" [*Han lu*] in *The Book of Odes* [*Shi jing*] first coins this phrase in the third stanza:

The hawk soars into the heavens [*yuan fei li tian*],
The fish plunges into the depths [*yu yue yu yuan*].

Glad and at ease is the ruler;
He can't help encouraging others.[47]

According to the preface of this paean to a benevolent feudal lord, the subject of the poem is "the blessing received from the ancestors."[48] The ruler's fitness to encourage others by his model bearing is likened to the natural affinity hawks have for the skies and fish have for the depths; he achieves this fitness as Nature's reward for his maintenance of the ancestral sacrifices repeatedly alluded to throughout the poem.[49] The "soaring hawks" and "plunging fish" are auspiciously juxtaposed to the idealized ruler who cannot help but reign in a benevolent manner. In contrast, Wu Zuxiang's story portrays the exact opposite, in that its most powerful figure, the matron, is the true villain of the piece. It is not the matron at the top of the age hierarchy but the doomed uncle and aunt in the lower levels of that hierarchy who are associated with the virtues of soaring hawks and plunging fish. As the narrator remarks in a refrain at both the beginning and end of the story, "The hawks have soared off and fish have plunged away, leaving the whole household forlorn and abandoned . . ."[50]

Aside from debunking the literary associations of awe for one's ancestors and elders that are connoted by the story's title phrase, Wu uses the title to make a rebellious statement about his own familial milieu in Maolin. Homes in his remote village tended to be identified not by a house number, but by their most prominent lintel plaque; until 1935 Wu's summer mailing address was "'Soaring Hawks and Plunging Fish' Study [*Yuan fei yu yue zhai*], Maolin, Anhui."[51] Though the lintel plaque from the Wu family residence has been lost in recent decades, one long-time resident of Maolin still remembers its exact appearance, noting that it was engraved after the style of the renowned Qing calligrapher He Shaoji.[52] Wu Zuxiang was thus adopting his own rather placid village home as the setting for the calamitous events of this story, just as in his longest pre-war work ("1800 Bushels") he would later use the Maolin ancestral temple as the fictional setting for a food riot that never actually occurred in his normally peaceful village.[53]

The theme of "Soaring Hawks and Plunging Fish" coalesces around an objectionable archaic feature found within Wu's own family milieu, namely the rigid age hierarchy that concentrates so much power in the hands of a domineering grandparent.[54] To contrive a couple's suicide as a reaction to mere harsh words of a matron, however, is obviously an exaggerated way of expressing opposition to this hierarchy, and the two critics who have discussed this story have briefly taken Wu to task for his unconvincing hyperbole.[55]

Regardless of the story's various crudities of execution, in many ways it marks a promising new beginning in Wu's career as a writer. Many of the vivid characters in Wu's mature 1930s fiction roughly follow certain prototypical characters that first appeared in "Soaring Hawks and Plunging Fish." In particular, the narrator who elegizes the fate of a peer ill-treated by older relatives recurs in a number of later stories.[56]

The diction and phrasing of "Soaring Hawks and Plunging Fish" shows a remarkable development away from the stiff parallelism and trite refrains of "The Ill-fated Little Plant." A smooth and natural-sounding vernacular prose has replaced the antithetical extravagances of the earlier fable. Moreover, the sense of irony that informs much of Wu's later work surfaces for the first time in the very title of "Soaring Hawks and Plunging Fish." Unlike his earlier fable's title, which informs the reader at the very outset of the protagonist's unfortunate circumstances, the auspicious title of "Soaring Hawks" suggests that the story would be far less melancholy than it finally turns out to be. In fact, the title's auspicious connotations eventually serve to highlight the story's tone of doom by force of contrast.

After completing a year and a half of middle-school coursework in Shanghai, Wu graduated in July 1926. By the following September, he had enrolled in Perseverance College itself, where he majored in English.

During a summer interlude in Maolin shortly before entering college in 1926, Wu's parents introduced him to a woman his age from the county seat by the name of Shen Shuyuan.[57] The daughter of a county military official named Shen Hanpu, Shuyuan had a high school education and was interested in primary school teaching. Wu Zuxiang and Shen Shuyuan exchanged letters for several months before he returned to Maolin in April 1927 to marry her in the village ancestral temple.

Their marriage was modern or "civilized" [*wenming*] in the sense that bride and groom were not still strangers by their wedding date, as was typical in the traditional arranged marriage system, but had long since gotten acquainted with one another.[58] Yet in other ways their marriage had a traditional rural flavor. They were quite young at the time of the wedding, both still shy of their twentieth birthdays. Unlike most middle-to-upper-class couples in the modern industrial city, they would soon bear a large number of children in rapid succession, beginning with a daughter named Jiu in 1928. Furthermore, like a typical pre-modern merchant or many a popular urban writer of the 1920s, Wu would often live apart from his wife, who stayed more regularly with her mother-in-law than at her husband's side for the first few years of their married life.[59] Not only throughout his Shanghai schooling, but also during Wu's half decade at Beijing's Qinghua university—where he roomed in bachelors' quarters most of the time—he could rarely find both the time and means to invite his new family to reside with him.

No long separation between husband and wife occurred during the very first year of their marriage, however. Instead of returning to Shanghai for the 1927–1928 academic year, Wu worked as an elementary school instructor in Maolin.[60]

Because of a July 1928 upsurge in warlord strife and bandit raids near Maolin, Wu Zuxiang accompanied his wife, parents, and sister-in-law on a short trek to Wuhu, where they waited out the unrest for several weeks. By the end of that summer, after peace had returned to the area around Maolin, Wu returned to Shanghai for the fall semester of the 1928–1929 academic year. His family, including the baby girl Jiu, subsequently journeyed back to Maolin without him. On the way home from Wuhu, his father became seriously ill, and died in December 1928 shortly after reaching Maolin. Just after becoming a father himself, Wu Zuxiang thus lost his own father in turn.

He did not return home to pay his last respects at his father's deathbed, however, for he was busily preparing for the highly competitive entrance exams to Qinghua University. The funeral for Wu Qingyu was carried out by Zuxiang's elder brother, Zuguang, who as the eldest surviving son bore the major responsibility for coordinating such rites.[61] Wu Zuxiang's absence from the funeral cannot be interpreted as a result of indifference or hostility on his part; in fact, for decades to come he would recurrently have a dream, apparently of wish-fulfillment, in which his father had returned to the living. [62]

One such dream of wish-fulfillment is recorded in Wu's diary under the entry for 4 July 1942, nearly fifteen years after his father's death.[63] Zuxiang dreamed that while strolling along the streets of Shanghai one day, he overheard passersby mention that British cigarettes were available for the rock-bottom price of four packs per dollar. His pleasure increased all the more when he spotted his favorite brand with its familiar logo of a boat on the wrapper. After purchasing the cigarettes, Wu boarded a riverboat. He suddenly noticed that his father was sprawled diagonally across a sofa that had been left on the riverbank, and from the sofa was making some sort of announcement over a loudspeaker; at that point the dream faded from Wu's recollection.

This dream follows the wish-fulfillment pattern first analyzed by Freud at the turn of the century.[64] By 1942, Wu had indeed been missing the material comforts that everyone had taken for granted prior to the War of Resistance against Japan. His living conditions in Chongqing had been difficult, for his work had rarely been steady enough to provide financial security amidst the shaky wartime economy with its high inflation. Imported goods like cigarettes, abundant in Shanghai during the 1920s, were neither plentiful nor reasonably priced during the war years in Chongqing.[65] The ease with which Wu as dreamer bought these goods in Shanghai contrasts sharply with the anxiety he felt about the all but unaffordable prices he was paying for mediocre tobacco in Chongqing.

The alacrity with which Wu boards the riverboat also suggests wish-fulfillment, particularly since dreams of departing on a conveyance usually symbolize an ability to progress in life, while missing a boat or train represents a frustration of progress.[66] As Wu spots his late father speaking in his direction while sprawled on a sofa onshore, he achieves a type of communication with his father that does not hinder the boat's advance. Not only can Zuxiang continue to advance through life along the rivercourse, but he can briefly re-establish contact with a stern and yet respected late authority figure confined to immobility onshore, whose death-like confinement he need not share.

An authority figure to rely on in the family can at times relieve the insecurities of a younger family member who feels inadequate in exercising his own authority. Wu Zuxiang's familial responsibilities underwent a major change in 1928, when only a few months after becoming a new father, his own father died in turn. Wu had difficulty coping with this new and heavy burden of authority; in an autobiographical essay published in 1935, he is especially frank in admitting his shortage of the kind of paternal concern that true familial authority demands:

> I've never particularly cherished my own children. At the very least, I feel that my children have rarely received fatherly affection from me. I generally don't pay much attention to them. Sometimes while glancing at one of those silly little faces that more or less resembles my own, my interest will perk up; yet I wind up doing nothing more than leading the child over to my side, tousling the hair on his little head, and then making him scoot with a light shove. At times I can't even derive pleasure from all this unless I bully my children a bit. For instance, I often make ghastly faces at them, keeping on with it until they suspect I really might be the bogeyman, and start wailing in fear. Even I don't quite comprehend this sort of immature behavior on my part; I'm afraid it's due to my age, to simply not having had the time to develop the emotions proper for a father.[67]

During his early fatherhood, Wu Zuxiang proved himself responsible in materially providing for his children, even as he felt emotionally unequal to the task of actively concerning himself with their joys and sorrows. Just as he unconsciously longed to recover a lost authority figure in the family when dreaming of his late father in 1942, his mock gestures of rejection toward his children in 1935 expressed his deep-seated unpreparedness for filling the role of head of household.

Wu's anxieties about the father-son relationship in general led him to avoid its depiction in his fiction, where it is extremely rare in comparison to the relationships between mother and daughter, husband and wife, or sibling and sibling. Even in the semi-autobiographical story set in Wu's childhood, "The Woodcutter," his mother is described at length while his father is merely referred to once as being present, but never described or even mentioned again throughout the story.[68] Only in the last of Wu's 1920s stories, "He Sings of Ramona" [*Ge Leimengna zhe*], published in 1929, does Wu say anything at all substantive about his father:[69] "The starlet of *Ramona* had drifted into an unfamiliar region in much the same way I had. Her family also consisted of a lonely mother, an elder brother burdened with cares, and a father who had recently died."[70]

Nothing Wu published after 1929 would again broach the subject of his original father-son relationship with such specificity. Yet the story reveals more than the gradual submerging into the unconscious of anxieties over a lost authority figure. The self-pity in the quote above also indicates that Wu had hardly begun to outgrow his youthful tendency of maudlin sentimentalism by the time of his first schoolyear (1929–1930) at Qinghua University. The shallowness of the story gives some indication of how far Wu would have to progress in intellectual development before he could write a story as unsentimental and perceptive as "On the Eve of Leaving Home" in 1931; and the fact that Wu could sustain the high quality of his writing by the relatively early date of 1931 indicates how congenial an environment the Qinghua Chinese Department proved to be in fostering the development of his literary imagination.

### Getting Started at Qinghua University in Beijing

During the sweltering midsummer of 1929 in Shanghai, Wu had passed the grueling three-day college entrance examinations with aplomb, ranking twenty-third among the 150 passing students selected from an overall field of several thousand aspirants. The section of the exam that gave Wu the most trouble was mathematics.[71] Nevertheless, he followed in the footsteps of his brother Zuguang and initially majored in economics at Qinghua. In light of the fact that he began to publish literary pieces almost from the moment he arrived in Beijing in 1929, it is little wonder that his fondness and aptitude for literature as opposed to economics would lead him to abandon the math-related major in favor of something less practical but more stimulating. At the beginning of his sophomore year in the fall of 1930, Wu formally left the Economics Department for the Chinese Department. An essay he wrote in 1948 puts this important event in whimsical terms:

> In those days we students had the strange idea that in the pursuit of learning, you should take one subject of study as your wife, and another subject as your mistress. I took literature as my mistress, for I had enjoyed it ever since my early youth; nevertheless, the department I entered was Economics. . . . By my sophomore year, my fellow student Yu Guanying encouraged

me to settle down to marrying my "mistress," and I formally transferred to the Chinese Department.[72]

Because Wu published nothing as a sophomore major in Chinese during the 1930–31 academic year, his trials at fiction in Qinghua University are limited to his freshman work, "He Sings of Ramona." This story has more in common with his early sentimental works than with his later serious writings; one cannot expect much in the way of serious realism or naturalism from a story that is partly a recapitulation of a maudlin 1928 American movie classified as a "romance" even by the standards of Hollywood.[73] Nevertheless, a brief examination of the story reveals some significant improvements as compared with "Soaring Hawks and Plunging Fish."

The narrator and his friend, both young men in their early twenties, are humming their way through the theme song from the movie *Ramona*. The friend recounts the story line of the movie to the narrator: the Amerindian heroine of the film suffers the deaths of her husband and child before all ends happily by means of her eventual pastoral reunion with her old everloyal lover. The narrator's friend goes on to contrast all this with the sad fate of his own girlfriend: her foreign stepmother sold her as a concubine to a rapacious old merchant, who has been making her life miserable ever since.

The logic of disillusionment present in "Soaring Hawks and Plunging Fish" also operates in this story. In the previous story, an auspicious motto proves to be hollow in the milieu where it is displayed; in "He Sings of Ramona," a song about exuberant passion and fulfillment through love, as found in the movie *Ramona*, contrasts vividly with the painful and intractable isolation of the young Chinese lovers.

"He Sings of Ramona" is just as brief and sketchy as Wu's earlier stories, again in the range of 1500 words. Yet the story does reveal that a process of artistic maturation has gotten well underway. The author's new restraint in the use of exclamations decreases the stridency of tone; the narrator himself voices a mere three exclamations, as compared to over ten in each of the previous stories. Moreover, the dialogue is much more sustained and carefully wrought than in previous stories, and suggests something of the colorful repartee that would mark many of Wu's later works.

### The 1920s: Prelude to a Decade of Achievement

If Wu Zuxiang had not vastly improved on his 1920s writings beginning from his third year at Qinghua, he would be forgotten today as just another ephemeral poetaster. In fact, prior to the 1980s, Wu never mentioned his 1920s writings; most pre-1980 articles about him follow his autobiographical preface to the 1954 anthology, *An Anthology of Fiction and Prose by Wu Zuxiang* [*Wu Zuxiang xiaoshuo sanwen ji*]. There he inaccurately states that he began writing about 1930, and mistakenly dates his first fictional work of merit, "On the Eve of Leaving Home," as January 1930 instead of the correct date of July 1931.[74] Yet in a heuristic sense Wu's dating was sensible, for his career as a serious writer began in the 1930s, and from that decade down to at least the mid-1980s, Wu had never deemed any of his 1920s works as worthy of anthologizing.

At the same time, Wu's decision in the 1980s to mention and discuss his stories from the 1920s tacitly acknowledges their relevance to his evolution as a writer. For example, beginning with "Soaring Hawks and Plunging Fish," the vast majority of his works would take the region of his home village for their setting, where the focus would remain on the harsh and backward aspects of life in the "semi-feudal" rural social order. The same story also initiates an ethic of populism that was to run through most of his later works; power and benevolence are opposed to one another as two poles of a dichotomy, in that a character leaning toward one pole automatically leans away from the other. Moreover, "Soaring Hawks and Plunging Fish" and "He Sings of Ramona" both give dialogue a key role in furthering the plot and delineating major characters, which is a pattern common to nearly all of Wu's later works. Finally, and most important in the context of the author's entire corpus, all three of the early stories portray a growing isolation of the main characters and a sense of breakdown and fragmentation in their social surroundings. This sense of isolation or alienation from the social milieu also holds sway in Wu's corpus through the early part of the 1930s. It is only around the mid-1930s that his fiction shifts to a vision of growing social cohesion and re-integration of main characters into their social milieu.

With regard to Wu's shift from a childhood in rural residence to an adulthood largely in an urban environment, he found himself preferring life in the city at the same time that he wrote determinedly about little else but the countryside. In this respect he resembled Shen Congwen: both writers had moved away from the countryside to the city by their early twenties, and yet nearly all of their most distinguished fiction is set in backward and remote rural regions, even more so with Wu than with the astonishingly versatile Shen. Urban educational and publishing opportunities were not only attractive but necessary for an up-and-coming writer; the alternative was to languish in anonymity back in the provinces.

If modern literature owes much of its characteristic restlessness and *angst* to the writer's alienation from his civilization, as Trilling argues,[75] the very backwardness and decay of the modern Chinese countryside lent it a great potential for alienating urban-educated countrymen like Wu Zuxiang and Shen Congwen.[76] Intimate with the complexities of rural society in ways that only a native can be, Wu Zuxiang found himself further and further removed from it in spirit each time he revisited his old home during a break from studies or work. The increasing alienation he felt toward his home village milieu would not subside until he stopped his visits there in 1934—at which time the possibilities for the recovery of cohesion in rural society surface in his fiction in an unprecedented way. The next chapter will examine the first phase of his career as a bona fide writer, when his stories explore the widening gulf in values and quality of life between the city, on the one hand, and the countryside, on the other.

# 2

## A Vision of Contrasts:
## Rural Versus Urban, 1931–1932

During Wu Zuxiang's half decade at Qinghua University, he annually migrated from Beijing back to Maolin, where he would pass the summer before returning north to his studies. The abruptness of these seasonal changes of abode between a metropolitan cultural center and an uplands village backwater heightened his sensitivity to the stark contrasts between the two realms. In five out of the six stories Wu completed during 1931 and 1932, he embodied his personal experiences of these contrasts in fictional encounters between various facets of urban and rural ways of life. Instead of examining a rural social unit from an internal and isolated standpoint, as in "Soaring Hawks and Plunging Fish," he would bring in the perspective of an "outsider" character to throw local rural customs, perceptions, and values in high relief.

Throughout the early 1930s, Wu found Qinghua a congenial place to pursue his literary interests in the urban/rural dichotomy. Rather than putting all students within a given discipline through a rigidly uniform mill of course requirements—as has so often been the case on Chinese campuses in recent decades—Qinghua's academic advisers usually tailored the individual student's program of study to fit the student's personal interests as closely as possible. Wu's professors in the Chinese Department saw to it that he was not overloaded with departmental course requirements, for they encouraged him to take electives in related fields like French literature. He recalls having had abundant leisure to browse through the university's open library stacks; in contrast, Chinese college students over the past few decades have had to contend with closed-stack libraries and other restrictions on extending their breadth of cultural awareness. Furthermore, the Chairman of the Chinese Department at that time, Zhu Ziqing, was himself a writer and poet on the side; he strongly encouraged students with literary talent to become active in editing circles

Members of the Chinese Literature Association at Qinghua University in the early 1930s. Wu is standing second from right; Liu Wendian is seated second from right; Zheng Zhenduo is seated third from right. (*Photo by the author*)

and publish their best efforts at fiction, poetry, or literary criticism. As a result, Wu's imaginative and expressive powers developed rapidly at Qinghua, making his half decade there the most productive and distinguished of his entire writing career. [1]

### Urban Career Ambitions Versus Rural Family Duties

Wu's first story of enduring worth, "On the Eve of Leaving Home" [*Li jia de qianye*/1931], is one of his shorter works, even though its 3500 words make it bulk to well over twice the length of any of his previous stories.[2] The story's autobiographical narrator and his wife, Die (pronounced "dyeh"), decide to leave their teething baby with a wet nurse in the husband's village in order to return to their schools in the city. The baby, Jiu, at first cannot bear her mother's temporary withdrawal from the scene, and howls her refusal to feed at the wet nurse's breast. Die's uneasiness over all this is intensified by her conservative mother-in-law's reproaches about the duties of a "proper" mother. Though little Jiu finally begins to accommodate herself to the wet nurse, in the end Die cannot bring herself to leave the baby alone in the village, and decides to give up school for the time being.

The core conflict in the story lies between Die's desire for an independent life at her urban school and the emotional attachment she feels—and realizes that she "ought" to feel—for her baby in the village. Naturally, her rural mother-in-law loudly disapproves of a young mother even temporarily putting her own child under a wet nurse's care for the sake of studies: "These days women live in a different world, all right; they've got to study. After marrying, they've still got to study; and after having children, they've *still* got to study!"[3]

Nevertheless, the mother of the narrator makes these testy comments only while her daughter-in-law is within earshot but out of sight; she lacks the gall to scold Die to her face.[4] Moreover, her attitude shifts to one of guarded support for Die towards the latter part of the story, by which time the baby has begun to get used to feeding at the wet nurse's breast. Before Die goes to the home of the wet nurse to check on her child, her now conciliatory mother-in-law urges her to have a square meal before going, and even offers to accompany her.[5] It would thus seem that Die and her mother-in-law are not actually the key foci of conflict in the story.[6] The conflict is largely within Die herself: during the climax in which the baby recognizes her voice and calls out for her as she is standing just outside the wet nurse's house, she impulsively rushes indoors to embrace her baby, whose acclimatization to the nanny is thus dealt a serious setback.[7] Rather than begin anew the long and painful process of acclimatization to the wet nurse, Die finally elects to stay on and continue breast-feeding the child herself.

At the same time that the conflict in values between urban career and rural domestic concerns is internalized within Die, other characters manage to exert some influence on the conflict's resolution. Die's two peers in their early twenties, her husband and the wet nurse, see nothing at all wrong in temporarily leaving the baby behind in order that Die be able to further her studies. As a representative of the urbanized and Western-influenced intelligentsia, the narrator not surprisingly approves of his wife's desire for learning and a vocation. The young village wet nurse takes a somewhat different approach, justifying Die's quest for a more challenging future as supporting rather than violating the traditional ethic of filiality. In the early part of the story when the old woman is complaining about Die, the wet nurse cheerfully attempts to comfort her: "After your daughter-in-law graduates, she'll earn enough as a lady instructor to help look after you in your later years!"[8]

While Die is never in danger of losing respect in the eyes of her husband or the wet nurse, her mother-in-law repeatedly articulates the potentiality for losing face in the eyes of the older and more conservative villagers like herself. Even after the baby gets acclimatized to the wet nurse and the mother-in-law restrains her impulse to criticize Die, Die's level of anxiety about her maternal role remains high; she is too nervous to eat anything when packing up for an early departure from the village the next morning.[9]

Die's decision to remain in the countryside has its genesis in much more than the maternal love which Wu has not only considered to be the story's dominating force, but over which his narrator waxes lyrical toward the end of the story: "Though young and with childish airs, Die was also imbued with very intense maternal love."[10] The critic Shen Zhenyu incisively notes that maternal love in itself does not adequately explain the motivation behind Die's final decision; he implicates rural "feudal" social values as the real stumbling block to her independence, but stops short of explaining how these values were articulated.[11] Perhaps the main reason Die could not go through with her plan to part with the toddler is due to the fear of losing face among the more patriarchal and hidebound locals, who would stigmatize her independent striving after a career in the city as the neglect of basic familial duties in favor of overweening ambitions. Without denying the role of maternal love in Die's decision to stay with her child, one must nevertheless acknowledge that the mother-in-law appeals not to maternal love so much as the sense of shame connected with violating the elder villagers' expectations as to how a mother should behave. The immediate impetus for Die to rush into the wet nurse's house and embrace her baby may have been a surge of maternal love; but this emotion was merely the catalyst for the long-standing uneasiness over violating "feudal" village norms of family behavior as articulated by her mother-in-law.

Wu Zuxiang considers this story to be mostly autobiographical, with the proviso that his wife, Shuyuan, actually faced this sort of conflict on two successive occasions. In the first instance, she left her young child behind with her mother-in-law in order to resume her studies at an urban teacher's college, while on the next occasion she set aside her schooling and career in favor of maternal duties tying her to the village.[12]

The narrator's unwillingness to defend his wife from his mother's verbal thrusts is very much in line with the way Wu Zuxiang and many other modern Chinese writers who were considered more or less revolutionary in spirit could be extremely deferential as sons or daughters. Here is the exchange between husband and wife just after the mother-in-law has loudly and indignantly complained about Die:

> At a loss for what to do, I softly chuckled.
> "And there you go laughing!" It was clear that the quaver in Die's voice bespoke tears.[13]

The embarrassed chuckle of the narrator tacitly expresses not only his disagreement with his provincial mother, but more importantly, his inability to articulate that disagreement and thereby violate the social taboo against confounding the wishes of one's parents. As William Lyell has pointed out, even a social critic as outspoken and full of vitriol as Lu Xun could hold devastatingly critical views on the traditional Chinese family system "without actually putting them into practice. "[14] Not only did Lu Xun obey his mother with regard to going through with an arranged marriage that he deplored on both personal and philosophical grounds, but also during subsequent controversies within his Peking household of the early 1920s, Lu Xun "would always defer to her wishes, showing his displeasure only through silence. "[15] As Randall Chang has mentioned in a similar vein, the boldest Chinese writer of confessional fiction in the early 1920s, Yu Dafu, "refused to challenge his mother's authority" when she prodded him into an arranged marriage that he likewise opposed in principle.[16] In the case of Wu Zuxiang, one of the impressions of family life in the West that disturbed him the most during his 1946–47 visit to America was the apparent lack of filial piety among the children of some Chinese-Americans he met.[17] Evidently, many modern Chinese writers who have publicly made a passionate and self-conscious break both with various pre-modern cultural traditions and with the contemporary status quo have remained staunchly observant of time-worn, even anachronistic norms of filial piety in their private lives. Lucian Pye has indicated how it is possible for docile sons and daughters to derive satisfaction from rebelling against surrogate forms of authority outside the family: "Since the possibility of catharsis from the expression against surrogate forms of authority made it easier for sons to remain filial within the family context, attacks on political authority were consistent with remarkably docile acceptance of traditional parental authority."[18] In short, the deep-seated filiality that prevents the citified narrator of the story from taking issue with his provincial mother is to a large degree a mark of Wu himself, along with many of his contemporaries similarly partisan to radical social change in China.

A technical development in "On the Eve of Leaving Home" that would gain momentum through Wu's works of the 1930s is the preponderance of aural, or auditory, description over visual description. James Guetti has characterized this type of fiction as "voiced narrative" that the reader "does not so much see as hear."[19] Aurally evocative dialogue markedly outweighs straight narration (*récit*) in this work, and is also the vehicle for the climax of this story as well as many others to come. Furthermore, aside from one paragraph of visual description of the wet-nurse, there is practically no visually evocative prose in the story; instead of describing the frowning visage of the crying baby, Wu tends to render her wails and sobs via an unusually rich variety of onomatopoeic interjections.[20] And even when the narrator turns to a visual description of the wet-nurse, he seems to do so as a result of a lull in the conversation and the momentary lack of aural stimuli, prefacing his visual description with the note that "everyone grew silent."[21] Rather than paint with words, Wu used them to dramatize—and then resonate audibly through his tightly compressed scenes.

## Foregrounding Hardships of the Lower Classes

Wu's first treatment of class-based social injustice appears in the only other work he published in 1931, "Two Young Sparrows" [*Liang zhi xiao maque*], which appeared on December 15 in the Qinghua University *Literary Monthly*.[22] "Two Young Sparrows" features the same setting and central core of characters as "On the Eve of Leaving Home": a young man and his wife are spending their vacation from an urban college in their relatives' genteel village household, where the man's mother has been taking care of their young son with hired help. Yet the servant-class characters in this story find it much more difficult to make ends meet than in "On the Eve": the hard-pressed husband and undernourished son of the maid visibly suffer from socio-economic pressures on the rural underclass. The rural poor whom the reader repeatedly encounters in Wu's major works throughout the 1930s thus make their first appearance in "Two Young Sparrows."

The citified wife narrates the story of how the former wet nurse of her five-year-old son, Xiao Huaizi, arrives on a visit from her riverside village of Hekou.[23] During a conversation about the merits of various kinds of pets, Xiao Huaizi grows entranced over sparrows and stubbornly insists on acquiring one to raise at home. The former wet nurse cheerfully volunteers to catch some wild sparrows for him. Just after she catches two young sparrows from a nest, her husband and their undernourished young son, Ah Bao, drop by. Upon recounting the hardships that have befallen the peasant family due to marauding rural bandits and burdensome militia levies, Ah Bao's father returns alone to his village, leaving his son under his wife's care for a few days.

Xiao Huaizi soon wearies of playing with the sparrows, especially when he has such lively playmates as Ah Bao and the young housemaid Jade to keep him company. Abandoned in a lonely side courtyard, the two young sparrows chirp until their mother swoops down to peck open their bamboo cage; but only the smaller of the two sparrows manages to squeeze out of the hole in the cage to freedom, while the larger hatchling eventually dies in the cage.

Xiao Huaizi suddenly regains his former infatuation for birds when he catches sight of Jade throwing away the tiny corpse of the fledgling sparrow. Deaf to the narrator's motherly remonstrances to leave wild creatures alone and find something else to play with, the boy continues to whine his demand for more sparrows until the wet nurse arrives on the scene, promising to catch him some waterfowl. The narrator at first imagines that this promise is merely a ploy to soothe her volatile little boy, but the wet nurse does in fact go back alone to her riverside village, planning to return with some new pet birds for Xiao Huaizi.

Soon thereafter, heavy rains cause scattered flooding, and the narrator's family suddenly receives the shocking news that the wet nurse was swept away by the torrential flood waters before her husband and mother-in-law could pull her into their skiff. The narrator reacts to the news with particular intensity, first suffering an attack of nausea and later having a series of nightmares in which she envisions encounters with demonic apparitions and the wet nurse's ghost. At the story's finale, the narrator assumes personal responsibility for the wet nurse's death, remorsefully interpreting the situation to the sobbing Ah Bao: "It was our Xiao Huaizi that was the death of your mother."[24]

Most of the suffering in this story appears highly coincidental in nature. For example, rural bandits [*tufei*] just happen to injure the wet nurse's husband in a way that renders him unfit to farm but still capable of fishing for a living.[25] More importantly, the wet nurse goes off in search of riverfowl at the very moment that heavy rains and flooding are on the way. When the narrator blames herself and Xiao Huaizi for the wet nurse's drowning, she implies that they were somehow responsible for the environmental hazards encountered by a former employee on a self-appointed errand. However emotionally distressing such accidents may be to the friends and loved ones of the deceased, nothing of true moral significance is involved.

If the narrator and her in-laws were not directly responsible for the troubles befalling Ah Bao's mother and father, as part of the local elite they nonetheless take advantage of their social status to stand aloof from the sufferings of the menial classes. They offer scant comfort to Ah Bao's newly disabled father, with his fears about how to continue supporting his family; and the shock of his wife's drowning wears off quickly among all of the gentry characters except for the narrator. In their shortage of compassion for the working classes, these privileged characters treat rural menials not wholly unlike caged birds—sources of convenience or companionship that need to be fed and otherwise provided for, but not necessarily commiserated with. For example, just as the narrator's husband, Jia, is adamant in his approval of caging wild birds, he is likewise short on compassion for Ah Bao's parents: he does not share his wife's concern over the fate of Ah Bao's mother, and makes a half-hearted and futile attempt to comfort Ah Bao's father with some optimistic but vague political slogans he has garnered at the faraway university. [26] The lack of compas-

sion the local elite extends to the menials of this story thus finds its figurative expression in the lopsided relationship between man and caged bird.

The mood of horror and grief at the climax and finale contrasts vividly
with the light-hearted sentiments predominating throughout most of the
rest of the story. One type of jocular comment of which Jia is particularly
fond is the rejoinder to his wife's exhortations to treat wild animals hu-
manely. She has just claimed that the two young sparrows abducted from
the mother sparrow ought to be returned to their nest:

> "You've not only abducted another person's child to help keep your own
> child amused—you've also abducted another person's mother to help you
> take care of your child!" said Jia. "What should you do first—work for the
> equality of mankind or struggle to free sparrows from mankind?"
>
> Chuckling, the wet nurse said, "I wasn't abducted from anywhere. It was
> my own choice to come here."
>
> "Every time you open your mouth, it's 'freedom' this and 'equality' that!"
> I said, laughing at Jia. "Let me tell you, *I'm* not one for that revolutionary
> spirit you're forever spouting."[27]

The author also draws on punning for humorous effect. Jia's uneducated rural mother is not at all conversant with imported socio-political
terms that her urban-educated son enjoys using, such as *shehui* ["social"].
On one occasion, she disparagingly substitutes the homonymous nonsense phrase *she hui* ["snake organization"] for this odd urban-sounding
term.[28]

For a story that ends on such a grim note, "Two Young Sparrows" is a
humorous and piquant work. Though humor is totally absent from Wu's
1920s works and even a few of his later works, one cannot agree with
Masuda Wataru's contention that humor is generally lacking in Wu's fiction.[29] It is true that somber moods prevail over wit and humor in Wu's
canon as a whole; and perhaps one of the reasons "Two Young Sparrows"
seems unable to achieve a convincingly somber tone at its climactic conclusion is that such a mood goes against the grain of the story's overall
lighthearted tone.

The abrupt and disconnected shift of mood at the story's climax exudes
an almost dreamlike atmosphere, as does the narrator's somewhat irrational confession of her complicity in the drowning of the wet nurse. As
Freud has said, "Dreams are disconnected, they accept the most violent
contradictions without the least objection, they admit impossibilities, they
disregard knowledge which carries great weight with us in the daytime,
and they reveal us as ethical and moral imbeciles."[30] The final section of
the story includes a vivid description of a horrible dream by the narrator,
further underlining the nightmarish twist in a story that had begun on

such a casual, buoyant note. News of the wet nurse's drowning has just reached the narrator:

> After vomiting for a spell, I went back to my bedroom in an attempt to sleep off my anguish. Vaguely in the distance I saw a band of robbers break into the house; but on closer inspection they turned out not to be robbers, but ghouls with green faces and scarlet teeth. I tried to run away, but seemed all but rooted to the spot, as if I were wearing unwieldy platform clogs. Suddenly, one of the ghouls caught up with me and grabbed me round the throat.... I screamed, and with eyes agog, saw that the wet nurse was sitting next to me on the bed and restraining my thrashing head with her hand. "Didn't you drown already? " I shouted, my voice rasping hoarsely.
>
> "What's that you're saying? It's *me* here! It's me!" The reply was in fact from Jia.[31]

This is the first nightmare of the score or so that would eventually appear either directly in Wu's works as recounted dreams, or else indirectly as the shape of a plot marked by an irrational or abruptly catastrophic turn of events. Among dreams about the dead who return to life, there is a special type described by Freud in which the dreamer takes wary note of the fact that the dead person does not seem to realize that he is actually dead. According to Freud, this dream makes sense only if we insert "in consequence of the dreamer's wish" after the words, "that he is actually dead."[32] This does not mean that the dreamer had ever consciously wished death on the deceased, but that the infantile components of any person's unconscious, ignorant of the irreversibility of death, are capable of angrily wishing death on even treasured loved ones.[33]

The narrator may have never harbored conscious enmity toward the wet nurse, but she may well have unconsciously resented her intrusion as not only a strong influence on Xiao Huaizi, but also as a rival for the young boy's affections. Vaguely aware of having wronged the wet nurse in her dream by both associating the peasant woman with ghouls and expressing shock instead of joy at her return to the living, the narrator ends up remorsefully implicating herself in the drowning by telling Ah Bao that her own genteel family is to blame for the fatal accident. The fact that the story could conclude on such an irrational note would seem to imply that the author was well acquainted with the inverted logic of dreams and nightmares. Since Wu drew on nightmares so often in his fiction, and even wrote an essay entitled "On My Dreams" in 1935, it would appear that by the early 1930s he had already cultivated a sensitivity to unconscious impulses that imparted to many of his characters a complexity of motivational conflicts not commonly encountered during that decade of Chinese fiction.

Aside from Wu's vivid insights into the irrational side of human psychology, another indication of the acumen with which he observed human behavior was his unprettified portrayal of the thoroughgoing egoism characteristic of small children. Of course, a child of Xiao Huaizi's age cannot develop a sense of altruism without moral guidance from his elders, and in this regard they are at best inexperienced. By traditional Chinese standards, Jia and his wife are perhaps too ready and willing to give in to their son's whims. As Li Shangyin (813–858) claimed in his manual of etiquette, *Miscellanea of Yishan* [*Yishan lizuan*], one type of "want of judgment" was "to allow a son to cage animals."[34]

As it turns out, the couple's largest failed opportunity to offer guidance to the uneducated occurs during the visit from Ah Bao's father early in the story. Partially disabled from a raid by rural bandits and squeezed hard by the local militia levies,[35] the care-worn peasant man asks the couple about his superstitious fears much in the manner of Xianglin Sao from Lu Xun's "The New Year's Sacrifice" [*Zhu fu*]:[36]

"Sir, you've been out to see the world, and would surely know—there's something I've been thinking about asking you." With a serious expression on his face, Ah Bao's father went on: "I've heard that the Daoist high priest in Jiangxi Province has been telling everyone that the reign of the Republic will last only forty years. What's more, in this new reign we've had both an old-fashioned lunar calendar and a new-fangled Western calendar, so there are two New Year's Days to celebrate each year. Some folks say that with a rule of forty years, after twenty years the Republic's mandate will be all used up. Isn't this very year the twentieth year of the Republic?"

Even before he had finished, I couldn't keep myself from erupting in laughter. Ah Bao's father immediately blushed bright red, and shamefacedly went on: "I don't really put much stock in that story, either. It's just that everybody's talking about it these days, so I reckoned I'd see what you thought."

Having managed to restrain himself from laughing, Jia replied in all seriousness, "You mustn't believe in that priest, that Zhang fellow; what he has to say is nothing but a hoax. What you *should* believe in is your own strength. You villagers are the masters of our nation, the backbone elements of our society—"

Jia thought for a moment, but instead of finding anything else to say, all he could manage was a frustrated glance in my direction. He probably felt the exasperation of wanting to say so much that he hadn't an inkling of where he ought to begin. He might have talked on all day, but not in such a way as to make the whys and wherefores comprehensible to Ah Bao's puzzled father. I felt embarrassed for Jia, but was even less capable of speaking out than he.

"With that bunged-up hand of his, he can't farm the land any more," said Mother. "What's left of his 'own strength,' or whatever it is you just called it?!"

. . . With no reliable answer in the offing, Ah Bao's father rose to leave for the return trip home. He said that he'd hired a couple of farm hands to hoe weeds for him.

"Ma'am," he said to Mother, as they walked together to the front gate, "What a strange world it's become lately! I've got to pay them three *jiao* each for a day's work, not counting what they eat and carry off now and then.[37] If I don't keep an eye on them while they work, they slip away to a patch of shade somewhere and take a nap. I tell you, I'm gonna call it quits next year with farming that lousy cropland. I've decided to return my tenant's deed to the landlord, and see if I can't make a living as a fisherman next year instead." He quietly walked out the front gate.[38]

In Lu Xun's "The New Year's Sacrifice," the narrator compromises his disbelief in the supernatural by telling an inquisitive old maidservant what he imagines she would like to hear about the afterlife. After she presses him to be specific about the hereafter, which he has suggested might exist, he retreats to a non-committal position that leaves her even more dissatisfied and baffled than she had been at the outset.

Jia of "Two Young Sparrows" fares little better in his strategy of forthrightly stating his skepticism of superstition and concomitant belief in the ordinary citizen's ability to control his own destiny. Jia simply preaches at the peasant man, utterly bungling an opportunity to establish a genuine rapport with him. Jia's vagueness is matched by his inability to sound out and deal with the peasant's concrete fears. His evangelistic political rhetoric rings hollow in the context of the peasant's quandary, as his mother tellingly points out. She, at least, understands the serious consequences arising from the hand injury of the peasant, who dissapointedly turns away from the urbanized young couple to share a few words with her before departing. Clearly, alienation in "Two Young Sparrows" is not a one-sided affair; the peasant feels just as alienated from the urbanized couple as they feel cut off from him—and rural life in general.

### Economic Dislocations and Fractured Families

The combination of Wu's gentry background and his tendency to stick to semi-autobiographical narrators when writing first-person stories prevented him from ever choosing a first-person (or "participant") narrator from the menial classes. Without exception in Wu's canon, stories featuring the middling-to-poor are narrated in the third person, while those set in a genteel household or among well-educated protagonists are rendered in the first-person.[39] This class-based relationship between author and narrator makes its presence felt in Wu's first story of 1932, "Xiao Hua's Birthday" [*Xiao Hua de shengri*].[40] At this juncture, Wu alters his rural fictional setting from the spacious village residence of the local elite to a cramped cottage of the middling-to-poor, and for the first time in nearly a decade adopts the more "objective" third-person point of view. Along with this downward shift in class emphasis is Wu's new departure of foregrounding economic problems as the major cause of the growing social anomie in the troubled 1930s.

The protagonist, Meirong, is a thirtyish working-class village mother struggling to support her two young sons and husband, a lanky store clerk laid off due to severe economic depression. Her meager earnings from clothes washing and sewing can barely keep her family fed. The genteel matron to whom Meirong confides her woes, San Taitai (lit., "Madam of the Third Eldest"), hits upon the idea of Meirong hosting a mahjongg gathering on the occasion of her infant son Xiao Hua's first birthday. On such an occasion, the mahjongg players, all from the village local elite, customarily donate a generous portion of the cardtable wagers to the hostess; and since it is the birthday of her youngest son, they also feel obliged to donate some spare clothes to Meirong's shabbily clad children.

One of San Taitai's three matronly companions in mahjongg cannot attend, so Meirong calls on various residences throughout the village to find a substitute fourth player. Since no other woman from the local elite is available that day, Meirong decides to accept the offer of a wealthy young man from the neighborhood to fill in as the fourth player. The round of games has nearly concluded when the concupiscent young squire wanders into the kitchen and makes a pass at Meirong, stuffing a gift handkerchief into her bodice after she refuses to accept it as a present. Just as she is frantically pushing him away, her husband strides into the kitchen from the back entranceway, startling the wealthy young rascal into breathless flight through the sitting room and out the front door.

Already frustrated by yet another failed attempt to find work, the husband rashly blames his wife for the rascal's impudence and begins to assault her verbally and physically. After striking Meirong several blows, he stomps into the sitting room and roars out insults to the three remaining mahjongg players. The stunned ladies subsequently leave in a huff, vowing to break off relations once and for all with a family given to such violent outbursts. A moment later, Meirong manages to scramble away from her husband's second round of vicious kicks and blows. She snatches up young Xiao Hua in her arms and lurches through the pouring rain toward the main road leading out of the village.

Among the core group of characters from the previous two stories—kindly but conservative rural matron, urban-educated son and daughter-in-law, and maid—only the matron remains in "Xiao Hua's Birthday." It is no coincidence that her name in this story, San Taitai, is but a slight variation from the common term of address for Wu Zuxiang's own mother, Si

Taitai (lit., "Madam of the Fourth Eldest"), who in real life was also a mahjongg enthusiast.[41]

The sincerely felt noblesse oblige of San Taitai is roughly rejected by Meirong's volatile husband, who is violently impatient with his dismal plight during this period of acute economic stagnation. One senses that economic-related frustrations have intensified to the point where even the voluntary sharing of resources during lean times by the "economically moral" portion of the local elite would not necessarily lessen class tensions.[42] Owing to the role of class tensions in the story, distinctions between haves and have-nots count for more than gradations within family hierarchies. The wealthy young rascal is not a close relative of any of the genteel ladies at the mahjongg table, and the husband's furious accusation of them as accessories in a plot to cuckold him derives from the guests' hierarchical similarity of class, not of family:

> "You let that scoundrel who just slipped in here get away, did you? *Now* I get it! While I was away from home you ladies 'of good family' came up with a scheme to tempt a fellow's own wife!"
>
> Her hair wildly tousled and blood oozing out of her nostrils and various facial wounds, Meirong lurched into the room, shrieking a rebuke to him between sobs: "If only that devilish mug of yours was taken straight to the chopping block! When a pumpkin's too thick skinned for you to cut open, you cut into a squash instead! You run into a brick wall looking for pull with that imposing uncle of yours, and when you come home it's me you take it out on! Even when cursing or beating someone in anger, you ought to have the sense to tell white from black! Haven't you noticed who those people sitting in front of you *are*?"
>
> "Oh, so *that's* it! Seems your husband is the only one left around here who's not afraid of people with a bit of money and influence!" Snarling like a wolf, he lunged into the mahjongg table, upending it with a crash.[43]

This class animosity reaches its apogee of intensity in the midst of extended dialogue, the typical medium for the climax in Wu's fiction. The overall effect is highly dramatic, and reminiscent of the passionate climaxes Jaroslav Průšek noted in two of the most important playwrights of the modern period, Tian Han and Cao Yu: "Their plays try to give expression to one single climax, where all the contradictions culminate and clash in a tragic, sometimes frightening, conflict."[44]

"Xiao Hua's Birthday" draws to some extent on what Peter Brooks has called the "melodramatic imagination," particularly through the intense emotionalism with which it portrays unrestrained villainy directed against protagonists of apparently sterling character.[45] Melodrama tends to thrive during ages like the most recent two centuries, during which traditional norms of truth and ethics have been violently undermined and yet the social motivation to search for alternatives remains strong. Melodrama as well as more serious and restrained world literature from recent times has tended to give vent to what Henry James called "the imagination of disaster," a force one senses at work in the nightmarish finale of "Xiao Hua's Birthday."[46]

The intense conflict in the story imparts a level of harshness to the main characters that makes this Wu's first work of naturalism, a mode of fiction writing that appeared in China as early as the late Ming.[47] Graphic harshness amidst "human animals" appears not only in the wealthy rascal's perfidious rapacity and the husband's ferocious bent for vengeance, but also erupts in the otherwise positive characters, Meirong and San Taitai. Meirong commonly takes out her frustrations on her eight-year-old son Da Hua, whom she often criticizes as incapable of anything more constructive than eating and sleeping, thus indirectly rebuking a husband who can no longer provide for his family:

> Da Hua . . . was squatting alone in front of the stove, on the door of which he had propped one of his bare feet still purplish from cold. He greedily gobbled down noodles from the large bowl in his hands, hardly waiting to finish chewing one mouthful before slurping up another mouthful. Two glistening trails of mucus stretched from his nostrils to his upper lip.
>
> "Just look at yourself, you greedy little pig!" complained Meirong. "From morning till night, you can't do anything but eat and sleep! But when it comes to chores, you can't handle a single thing right! Hurry up and finish eating so you can go see if any of our guests need a cup of tea or a smoke."[48]

San Taitai also betrays a bit of callousness, in this case toward Meirong, after the young husband has rashly accused the genteel matrons of having tempted Meirong into unfaithfulness:

> "I won't forgive you for lording it over everyone with these malicious slanders! Out of pity for your Xiao Hua, who doesn't have any heavy winter clothes, I gathered a few ladies together for some mahjongg. I haven't the slightest idea of what these filthy goings-on around your wife are all about!" As she spoke, she led the other two ladies toward the front door. "This family is as good as finished—there's no way to talk sense with them. Ladies, let's get out of here!"[49]

In a story noted for its dramatic power rather than narrative technique, the one narrative feature that signals an advance in Wu's style is his abundant use of foreshadowing. The crow, a traditional omen of ill tidings, appears at the beginning and midway through the story, and caws shrilly on both occasions.[50] Even more ominous is a dialogue early in the story in which San Taitai tries to console Meirong about her husband's increasingly bad temper over being unemployed. San Taitai points out that he is far better behaved than many of the unemployed sons of her gentry friends, who have often gotten mixed up with smoking opium, gambling away jewelry filched from their own wives or mothers, or installing sleek concubines in their households. The casual nature of Meirong's reply conceals its seriousness as a foreshadowing of catastrophe:

> Meirong murmured her agreement, smiling before she spoke up: "You've flattered him with comparisons to people above his station. Those men you mentioned are all young squires; it doesn't really matter much if they pull off some shenanigans. But what sort of family do *we* amount to, anyway? We can't even afford three meals of gruel a day—how could he come up with the money to go mucking about like them?"[51]

The wealthy young rascal who catalyzes the latent brutality of Meirong's husband is one of the more or less disreputable unemployed young squires to whom San Taitai compares the husband. The husband's capacity for causing a disturbance turns out to be far greater than the squires, however, since his passions and frustrations have grown so intense that they now override his pragmatic concern for maintaining his reputation in the village community.

The husband is a victim of both the long-standing labor surplus in China and the deepening bankruptcy of the rural economy as a result of the worldwide Great Depression.[52] He thus slips into criminal behavior from the route of socio-economic crisis rather than from idleness or incompetence in his profession, and is the first in a long line of Wu Zuxiang characters to do so.[53] Because society has played a major role in causing a character like the husband to turn to criminal violence, the author's apparent indictment of him as a villain functions more importantly as an indictment of society itself. In this way, "Xiao Hua's Birthday" stands as Wu Zuxiang's first story that is overwhelmingly meliorist in spirit.

Despite the story's significance in the evolution of Wu's meliorist fiction, it was not anthologized in any of his collections appearing from the 1930s to the mid-1980s. No doubt a major factor in Wu's reluctance to reprint the story lies in its mixing of strongly incompatible prose styles. Amidst a mainstream of down-to-earth naturalistic narration and dialogue, one occasionally runs across such jarringly lyrical conceits as "A bunch of large red roses bloomed in Meirong's heart" and "Her aching head throbbed, as though a ping pong ball were being volleyed back and forth inside her skull."[54] More suitable in poetry than in realist or naturalist fiction, these clichéd and strained conceits would soon be discarded, just as the overabundant narratorial exclamations that marred Wu's 1920s works had been jettisoned.

### Migrant in Limbo

What might have happened if an unemployed rustic shopkeeper like the one in "Xiao Hua's Birthday" had left the destitute village to seek after the broader field of job opportunities in the city? "The Flowering Gardenia" [*Zhizi hua*], published less than a month after the previous story, supplies precisely this scenario.[55] Again, the constellation of rural characters shifts a great deal; the conservative matron disappears from the scene, as do all children. Nor is the wife of the shopkeeper much of a personality, for nearly all of what little we see of her is through the eyes of her husband.

Resurfacing in this story is the urban-educated young local, accompanied not with his wife but now with his elder brother; both of them reside in faraway Beijing, where the elder works in commerce and the younger attends a university. Like Wu's two stories from 1931, "The Flowering Gardenia" is partly autobiographical; the elder brother in this story bears a close resemblance to Wu Zuguang, who worked at commerce in Beijing during much of the period that his brother Zuxiang was studying at Qinghua University.[56]

The shopkeeper protagonist, Xiangfa, respectfully hails the two brothers as "Elder Uncle" [*da tang shu*] and "Younger Uncle" [*er tang shu*], even though in terms of age he is not their inferior. Desperate over the lack of jobs in the village, Xiangfa pleads long and hard with the vacationing brothers to help find him a job in Beijing. Elder Uncle eventually manages to reserve Xiangfa a copyist's position at a Beijing government bureau. Like many civil servants at that time, Xiangfa receives his meager wages on an irregular basis; far from saving money, as he had counted on, he barely manages to cover his monthly room and board. Moreover, he cannot break through the surface impersonality of urban life, and in the midst of this friendless existence finds himself missing his wife and home all the more. Finally, the bureau lays off all of its copyists as the result of an austerity measure, and neither Xiangfa nor Elder Uncle can find another opening. Xiangfa is left with no alternative but to borrow travel expenses from Elder Uncle and return to the poverty-stricken village and its consolations of wife and hearth. Upon arriving home, however, he is aghast to discover that there is no trace of his wife to be found inside his house, which is now silent except for the furtive scurrying of rats. As he rushes into the courtyard, he sees the broken-down and pitiful remnants of the very flowering gardenia bush which he has long associated with domestic security and pleasure, and blacks out from acute anxiety as the story concludes.

The climax once again occurs at the very end of the story, and as in many other stories by Wu, the main character meets with a calamity of nightmarish, even apocalyptic, proportions. [57] The narrator underlines the role of the unconscious in Xiangfa's reactions to his dilapidated home, whose uncanny and nightmarish atmosphere is intensified by the scurrying of rats that have replaced humans as dwellers:

> Arriving at the front doorstep, he pushed open the dilapidated, unhinged door. The house was chilly. The door to his wife's room was unlatched, and he stepped inside. Not a soul was there, only total stillness. A layer of dust an inch thick had collected on the stools and tables, and an overpowering odor of mildew permeated the room. Glancing at her bed, he noticed that it was littered with stuffing from the straw mattress, and that both the bed curtains and quilt were missing. Stricken with panic, he felt as though somebody had doused him with a bucket of cold water.
>
> He unconsciously called out for his wife a few times. He heard a series of frantic rustlings from rats scuttling along the floor, and listened in vain for a reply from his wife. His wits only half about him, he found his way to the side courtyard. Saturated with the gloomy drizzle of the rainy season, the courtyard was infused with a miasma of desolation. Not a trace of his wife was present, only ash piles of burnt mattress stuffing and spirit money.
>
> The old lopsided section of wall on the west side had apparently failed to withstand the ravages of the elements, for it had already caved in. Its bricks and scattered rubble had all but buried the gardenia bush, which had nevertheless managed to put forth two or three sprays of withered and tattered white blossoms through crevices in the debris. Unable to bear it any longer, Xiangfa felt everything go black in front of his eyes, and collapsed onto the muddy ground. [58]

Aside from the general dilapidation of the premises, a clear expression of decay and death, the paper spirit money commonly used for sacrifices to the dead and the references to ashes and dust both intensify the ominous mood. The wretched state of the gardenia bush reinforces the loss of what has been dearest to Xiangfa, for he had earlier remarked that the two things he would miss most while away from the village were his wife and the gardenia bush. [59] Like the hawk in "Soaring Hawks and Plunging Fish" and the dying sparrow in "Two Young Sparrows," the battered gardenia imagistically expresses the plight of a calamity-stricken character. In his collapse to the ground, Xiangfa himself parallels the physical deterioration of his home environment, including house and courtyard; moreover, he resembles the typical dreamer of a nightmare, who, in a state Freud defines as "motor paralysis" during sleep, often imagines himself to be powerless or rooted to the spot during a discomfiting dream episode. [60]

Xiangfa's concluding isolation from his home village milieu depends largely on events beyond his control, such as the mysterious disappearance of his wife before his return home. Yet from the very beginning Xiangfa and his wife are both hopeful of leaving the village permanently to establish themselves in Beijing. Instead of urging Xiangfa to return home soon, she asks him to save enough money for her travel expenses to Beijing so that they might start up a household together there.[61] Xiangfa, for his part, reacts to his visiting uncles' discussions about urban life with a catalogue of the features he finds disagreeable in village life:

> His native place was dull in the extreme: dilapidated old houses, crumbling courtyard walls, winding rocky roads, opium dens, gambling stalls, and shabby-looking men and women, all of whose faces bore anxious and gloomy expressions, their conversations never straying far from the fluctuations of grain prices or the depredations of bandits and soldiers.[62]

Xiangfa seems unencumbered with the traditional Chinese villager's reluctance to venture into the unknown, a tendency that Chiang Yee and William Mallory have discussed.[63] As Mallory reminds us, Chinese proverbs tend to emphasize "the desirability of a quiet life at home and compare such security and serenity with the perils and discomfort to be met in traveling abroad."[64]

Xiangfa does indeed cut an impetuous figure in his desire to leave the village, but his rusticity and traditionalism resurface in other ways. Totally lacking the *savoir faire* of his young uncles, he constantly gawks at city folk and their unfamiliar ways, and is too self-conscious to approach strangers for conversation. Moreover, he is intensely superstitious, and resents Second Uncle from beginning to end for having set the original date of departure simply to harmonize with the train schedule instead of with the local almanac's prognosticative advice on lucky and unlucky traveling days. The citified uncles are well acquainted with the superstitious ways of many a rural simpleton, but even they are taken aback by the weight Xiangfa places on destiny and omens when he encounters job troubles in Beijing:

> "Egads, this luck of mine!" sighed Xiangfa.
> "You're not the only one down on his luck," said Elder Uncle. "Everybody's in a fix these days. Even I've had to pawn things lately just to get by."
> "When I was about to set off from home, I already knew that this trip couldn't turn out well. Younger Uncle wouldn't budge from setting the date of departure for the eighteenth."
> "The eighteenth? So what?" asked Elder Uncle in surprise.
> "The eighteenth was an unlucky day."
> Elder Uncle laughed in exasperation. "Don't tell me, my good sir, that you've got the time to worry over such trifles when everybody else nowadays is stuck in the same sort of mess!"[65]

The Great Depression may have indeed hit rural China longer and harder than urban China, but the common notion that the city was an unshakable haven of prosperity proved to be little more than a figment in the imagination of uneducated rural folk. Nevertheless, droves of villagers like Xiangfa had to learn this the painful way, returning to the countryside poorer and more frustrated than they had been before leaving it in the first place.

Social problems such as acute unemployment need not only be illustrated through the vicissitudes of a particular character, of course. Group conversations about general ideas, or "symposia" as some critics call them, may render these issues in more directly discursive terms. Incidents of symposia within Wu's canon appeared earlier with discussions on banditry and dynastic succession in "Two Young Sparrows." The symposium in "The Flowering Gardenia," with its display of terms associated with tough-talking meliorist rhetoric like "imperialism" and "dialectics," marks a trend toward self-conscious intellectual respectability in comparison with the downright whimsical symposia of earlier stories. This symposium, dominated by two university-educated young men instead of a village matron or a peasant, is nevertheless still colored by Wu's piquant wit:

> "Unless a thoroughgoing revolution takes place in China, there just won't be any hope for this country!" Elder Uncle heaved a passionate sigh before completing the point he was making to Second Uncle. "The economy has been completely trampled underfoot by the imperialists [*diguozhuyizhe*]; politics is more chaotic now than ever; feudal society in the nation's interior is collapsing at a breakneck pace; and the unemployed can't find refuge even in our cities. Everybody's on a dead-end path. Unless a fellow goes off and turns bandit, there's nothing for him to do but sit at home, slowly eating up his past gains. All in all, people like Xiangfa are the most fortunate [*xingyun*]."
>
> "There's an old saying that a shift in the world's fortunes [*shiyun*] takes place every sixty years," blurted Xiangfa, in a state of semi-comprehension.[66] "I believe that a monarch [*dizhu*] with a true Mandate will appear before long, and he'll put a stop to all this mess!"[67]
>
> Second Uncle broke out with laughter.
>
> "Now, don't you laugh at him," bantered Elder Uncle. "This hypothesis of his actually bears some resemblance to the dialectical theory of social development!"[68]

According to Frank O'Connor, such conversations about general ideas often enhance the general significance or typicality of fictional characters.[69] Far from being "of no necessary relation to the overall development of the story line, " as one critic has claimed, the above symposium not only enhances the general significance of Elder Uncle and Xiangfa as characters, but also individualizes them by allowing them to speak at length in their own special voices, or "idiolects."[70]

Although the beginning and concluding portions of "The Flowering Gardenia" are set in the countryside, the long middle portion takes place in the city of Beijing. In his next story, Wu Zuxiang would go on to make the setting urban from beginning to end, before finally returning to rural backdrops for practically all his works thereafter.

### Two Fiancées: Urban Versus Rural

Wu's first and only work set entirely in an urban milieu, "Miss Jin and the Xue Girl" [*Jin Xiaojie yu Xue Guniang*], was published in February 1932.[71] The narrator, a recent college graduate, is teaching high school in Beijing. He has stopped corresponding with his old high-school girlfriend, Xue, for her reputation has been ruined due to numerous entanglements in premarital sex. He nevertheless does not scorn her, as do his callous peers; and when he happens to run into her at a movie theatre one day, he accepts her invitation to dinner in spite of his increasingly serious involvement with a homely and old-fashioned but scrupulously dutiful young woman surnamed Jin.

Xue informs him at dinner that she must get an abortion before her impending betrothal as the second wife of an old rural county magistrate, though she hints that she would prefer marrying the narrator instead. As he continues to see Xue now and then, he procrastinates over the quandary of whether or not to take a chance on getting married to her. Meanwhile, Jin finds out about his renewed liaison with Xue and consequently moves back to her home in the rural interior. From there she sends him a letter formally breaking off their relationship, and in a tone of cold politeness wishes him well in his old romance with Xue.

Though full of remorse for having kept Jin in the dark, the indecisive young man is grateful for having someone else solve his love-triangle problem, even if merely through the process of elimination. Yet he soon makes the terrifying discovery that Xue has interpreted his procrastination as a rejection of her, and in desperation has undergone a dangerous, and ultimately fatal, back-alley abortion. He faints at the sight of her waxen and blood-stained corpse, and the story ends as he regains consciousness in a hospital ward.

Although the story is autobiographical in form, its subject matter strays further from Wu's world of personal experience than most of what he had hitherto written. Nothing could contrast more with the kind of early and orderly arranged marriage that Wu made in 1927 than the suspenseful, drawn-out triangular love affair portrayed in "Jin and Xue." Moreover, the rural figures dominating Wu's canon were never susceptible to such vacillations over the issue of romantic love. The problems of simply eking out a living and getting along with one's neighbors were of absorbing interest in the countryside, and the traditional system of formal introduction and marriage brokering had not unravelled there to the extent it had in the cities.

The continuities of theme and milieu between "Jin and Xue" and other works in Wu's canon are thus remarkably few. The story it resembles most is "He Sings of Ramona," another work in which dark forces in society serve to frustrate a quest for love and marriage. Yet the 1929 story clears the unfortunate young woman of any possible taint of personal responsibility for her fallen state; she is sold against her will into concubinage by her avaricious foreign guardian. In contrast, the fallen young woman of "Jin and Xue" assumes some personal responsibility for her degradation by having voluntarily taken up the somewhat disreputable activities of taxi dancing and non-marital cohabitation with a lover. As Zhao Yuan has mentioned, Xue can be considered the first of a long line of Wu's characters who commit a societal transgression of small proportions and yet suffer retribution of serious or even devastating magnitude.[72] Aside from the motifs of lopsided retribution and the rural/urban dichotomy, however, this work is something of an anomaly among Wu's 1930s stories.

The portrayals of the two young women as embodiments of fast city living versus musty but solid rural values make for a stark contrast. Here is the countrified Miss Jin on the occasion in which friends of the narrator, Ling Ziyan, first introduce her to him:

> Miss Jin stole several furtive glances in my direction. As soon as I tried to meet her gaze, she averted her blushing face to examine the furnishings in my flat. . . . She appeared to be already looking on me as her future spouse, and was making an investigation of sorts to determine how worthy a spouse this fellow might turn out to be, just as a young lady of days gone by would steal a glance at the boy whom her parents had selected as her life-long mate. Aside from sending furtive looks of solicitude my way, she occupied herself with nothing more than attending to the general drift of my friends' conversation with a forlorn smile. Unless you made a point of singling her out with a query, she was not apt to say anything at all.[73]

Jin's inner disposition of demure solicitude finds its outer expression in her daily concern for her new boyfriend's domestic life:

> Miss Jin did in fact understand what was involved in loving a husband. In any given week, she would bring over four or five tasty things to eat, and would iron the wrinkles out of my rumpled ties, which somehow increased in number from half a dozen to nearly twenty. By the time I'd known her only two weeks, she had already given one of the maintenance men the worn old pair of pillows I'd slept on for several years, replacing them with a new pair she'd personally embroidered with a design of owls singing in a

white poplar under the crescent moon. . . . As far as my toiletries and small articles of daily use were concerned, she had long since replaced all the old with the new. . . . And thanks to her, the room of mine which had once re-sembled a pig sty had now been tidied and dolled up to where it would have qualified to grace the pages of a home pictorial magazine.[74]

By contrast, the citified Xue proves to be as impetuous and immoderate as Jin is shy and mild. Xue and Ling Ziyan have a reunion so tempestuous that both shed tears of pain before parting. Even in one of the lower-key moments of the meeting at her apartment, her lack of moderation dismays Ling:

> "I invited you here for a chat. Don't just sit there without making a sound! Tell me, who was that person watching the movie with you—your wife or your lover?"
> "Not my wife, and not my lover, either" I said, forcing a smile. "She's a new girlfriend I met only recently."
> "Your girlfriend? Isn't that the same thing as saying she's your lover?" laughed Xue.[75]

Xue's lack of inner restraint is externally reflected in the disorder of her room:

> Her things were scattered helter skelter in the messy room: clothes, socks, and towels were piled in a jumble all over her box-spring bed next to the wall; of the two or three suitcases lying on the floor in disarray, one had been left open—inside were clothes of red and other bright hues, boxes, and pic-torial magazines; an old wooden table top was crowded not only with books like *Fate in Tears and Laughter*[76] and *A Guidebook to Beijing*, but also with con-tainers, some capped and other left open, including bottles of perfume, soap dishes, face-powder compacts, and cigarette boxes.[77]

The author underlines the contrasts between the two young women by cataloguing the effects they have on the rooms imbued with their person-alities. Jin enhances the order and renovates the objects in one room, while Xue lives amidst a cluttered breakdown of order in another. Ling obvi-ously prefers the state of order that Jin maintains, but he is unable to feel romantic passion for her, as he does for Xue. Instead, he can "only feel pity and gratitude" for Jin.[78] In contrast, Xue had been Ling's first steady girlfriend in their high school days, and his long-dormant romantic pas-sion for her is easily rekindled.

Somewhat like Daiyu of the 18th-century masterpiece *Dream of the Red Chamber*, Xue "acts upon impulse and feeling," while Jin is self-controlled and restrained like Baochai of the same novel.[79] Yet the author attributes the differences between Jin and Xue not to a premodern concept of "essential nature," but to the social environments that have molded them, namely the rural "feudal" order versus the urban capitalist order: "Jin had been laid low by the feudal tradition's poison in our society, while Xue had been trampled in the filth by the capitalist order within our society."[80]

The crowded and fast-paced atmosphere characteristic of urban life is missing in both "Jin and Xue" and "Gardenia." Wu Zuxiang simply chooses not to describe the sights and sounds of an urban landscape. Due to the sparseness of dialogue between the urban locals, it is not surprising that the reader hardly detects any clues that he is in Beijing, as opposed to somewhere else; unlike Lao She's novels, there is no dialectal flavor of the North in this work. In fact, the one and only sort of region-specific vocabulary to be found in the story consists of expressions from the Shanghai and Suzhou dialects uttered by Xue and her maid.[81] These dialectal expressions apparently function to remind the reader that the two women have come under the influence of Shanghai, the freewheeling but injustice-laden treaty port which our meliorist author condemned in 1931 as "the central point of infection of the disease affecting all China."[82] In other words, dialect in this story reflects a Shanghai milieu that fails to resonate with the actual setting of Beijing.

Wu would portray the ill effects of China's urban "central infection point" in one more story before returning permanently to the rural interior and the fragmentation of its premodern social framework.

### Rural Tonics for Urban Ailments

"Little Lord Guanguan's Tonic" [*Guanguan de bupin*], the last story Wu Zuxiang published in 1932, was his first work to be critiqued in print.[83] Well-deserving of its reputation as Wu's finest and most complex early work, the story adopts a mode of pungently ironic narratorial presentation whose prominence in Swift and Maupassant contrasts with its rarity in Chinese fiction.[84]

Guanguan, the smug and thrill-seeking son of a wealthy landlord, serves as the narrator of his adventures in Shanghai and the southeastern Anhui countryside. After a near-fatal auto accident in the metropolis, the young squire gets a blood transfusion from a poverty-stricken hometown peasant tenant named Baldy, who has been looking in vain for work in Shanghai. Each day during Guanguan's subsequent convalescence in the countryside, he follows the superstitious recuperative regimen of drinking a pint of human milk, supplied by none other than the wife of the blood donor, Baldy. She is forced into the demeaning task of milking herself due to her husband's inability to make a steady living either in the village or in Shanghai, both of which are in the throes of economic depression.

Several months go by, and the desperate husband, now back in the countryside, wards off starvation by carrying messages for bandit gangs until the local gentry's militia catches him in the act and arrests him. Guanguan's uncle, who serves as the militia chief, summarily sentences Baldy to death by decapitation. After a village crowd gathers to gape at the gory spectacle of beheading, the story concludes with the anguished protests of Baldy's widow and the landlord family headmaid's aggressive rebuttal in defense of the execution.

This is Wu Zuxiang's harshest work of fiction, in its inclusion of a graphically described execution, gallows humor over a fatal car accident, and a callous scorn toward indigents, whom the narrator views as little better than beasts of burden. The author manages to distance himself a bit from the harsh subject matter by submerging it in the personality of his youthful narrator, the "unlovable rogue" Guanguan.[85] A distancing strategy of this sort proves useful "whenever a theme is too crude or harsh for direct impact," as O'Faolain has mentioned with regard to Maupassant.[86] And as another study of fiction has pointed out, this narrative device bestows the reader with "a special burden of enjoyable ratiocination, as he seeks to understand what the character telling the story cannot himself comprehend."[87]

Like Jia of "Two Young Sparrows," Guanguan takes pleasure in making off-color jokes at the expense of the rural poor.[88] In a notable passage highlighted by C. T. Hsia, Guanguan facetiously remarks that even though all peasants bear a strong resemblance to oxen in their weather-beaten and toil-worn features, Baldy's wife must be smarter than a cow, since she has bargained her way into receiving cash payments for her breast milk.[89] Other metaphors that slight disadvantaged peasants as less than fully human include the headmaid Tie Bajiao Saozi's fondness for referring to Baldy's infant son as "turtle spawn." Within earshot of Baldy's wife, the family headmaid also mockingly urges the infant to steer clear of the footloose ways of his father, and instead grow up to work like an ox in the rice paddies so as to support his mother in her old age.[90]

Guanguan, his mother, and the headmaid Tie Bajiao Saozi all coldly ignore the most basic sensitivities of Baldy's wife when they first hire her to sell her milk to them. The peasant woman is visibly embarrassed when ordered to unbutton her blouse and squeeze out a sample of her "tonic" milk in front of all three of them. An affront to human dignity anywhere, this would be particularly degrading in the context of China's long-standing prudential mores that once forbade even a doctor from viewing an unclothed female patient; traditionally, the male doctor would hand a female patient a doll, and ask her to point at the body region of the doll corresponding to where she felt pain in her own body. In contrast, one can sense Guanguan's amused lack of discretion during this episode through his meticulous description of the milking process, particularly its visual dimensions, as well as the swooshing sound of milk spurting into a bowl.[91]

If Guanguan can inspire readers to contempt or embarrassment while actually trying to amuse, he can also unintentionally amuse us when attempting to narrate in a "straight" manner. In one of Wu Zuxiang's most effective uses of black humor, Guanguan recounts how he and a taxi dancer got involved in a serious automobile accident:

> Lu Rouji and I were sitting in the back seat. I urged the driver to speed up so that a cooling gust of air would blow all over us. Rouji pressed her face against my chest, and the wind blew her richly perfumed hair into my face, where it lightly brushed against my cheeks. Before I knew it, I felt drunk with joy, and came on to her with one of those vows that all the writers in vogue go for:
> "I'd like to die at this very moment by your side. Ah, if only our taxi was like the cars in the news that crashed into light poles or flipped into the river! Arm in arm and with smiles on our faces, we'd suddenly die without even realizing what had been happening. Could there be any better way to go?!"
> I didn't realize that these words spoken in fun would turn out to be a prophecy; whether the driver was drunk or simply tired I don't know, but he missed a corner and overturned the car into a ditch at the side of the road. . . . Lu Rouji had already died by the time they got us to the hospital.[92]

The sort of writer to whom Wu sardonically refers was the popular urban novelist who purveyed romantic love and other more or less politically disengaged themes. Meliorist writers like Wu Zuxiang tended to view such novelists as irresponsible exploiters who catered to the lowest common denominator of the urban marketplace, distracting readers from the serious problem-oriented fiction that ought to be read.[93] To be sure, the romantic sentiments such a writer would spin out often proved to be self-deceiving flights of fancy; far from allowing the couple a transport of bliss through death, the car accident results in suffering and chaos for both the victims and their families.

Wu Zuxiang had extremely negative impressions of the treaty port of Shanghai, as noted in the previous section. He expresses the glaring contrast between wealth and poverty in Shanghai by shifting his purview from the glitter of dancehalls and limousines to a shiftless rabble of eager blood donors crowding outside the immaculate sickrooms of the foreign-run hospital where Guanguan is recovering from his injuries. The European doctor in charge of Guanguan chuckles at the naîveté of the young squire, who had been totally unaware of how blood for his upcoming transfusion could be easily bought:

"You're a pure and innocent young squire, all right!" said the foreign doctor, with a pat on my shoulder. "One thing this world's got in spades is the down-and-out. They don't have the skills required to earn a living, but their stomachs won't let them off the hook, they've got to eat just the same. If they don't sell their blood, they simply go hungry. Got it? When you get to feeling a little better, just go over to the doorway and take a look. Every day a bunch of ragged and filthy derelicts line up on those benches on both sides of the door, all of them waiting there to sell their blood."[94]

Guanguan's uncle remembers having bumped into Baldy at the train station, and realizes that his ex-tenant's blood would be far less likely to be diseased than would be the case with the ragged group of unemployed urban donors on the benches outside. He summons Baldy, and haggles with him to get the lowest possible price for the blood, which is in fact pure of any taint from the urban epidemics of venereal diseases. Not long after the "tonic" transfusion, Guanguan recovers enough to make the journey back to his village home, but neither he nor the rest of his family feel any gratitude to their ex-tenant for the disease-free blood transfusion. Instead, Guanguan's uncle decides to make an example of Baldy immediately upon the hapless peasant's subsequent arrest as a bandit messenger: instead of "merely" having Baldy shot, the uncle orders his summary decapitation, and refuses his request to see his family one last time:

With one kick, the executioner knocked Baldy onto the rock-strewn bank. Now, this Baldy fellow was crafty down to his dying breath, and did all he could to make his head stay put on top of a huge rock. Try as anyone might, they couldn't budge him from that spot. So the executioner just let well enough alone and raised his saber in both hands, hacking away at Baldy with three or four angular strokes, much as if chopping firewood.

A pall of silence descended on the crowd of onlookers, aside from a few stray urchins who clapped.

By the time Baldy had been struck a few hard whacks, his blood was spattered all over the nearby rocks. Since he was already sprawled out and motionless, the militiamen went over to lead the executioner off. Suddenly, what we all thought was a corpse lurched upright, and raising both of his hands high in the air, let out a string of shrill wails, one after the other, like some kind of demon. Everybody was so scared that we all ran off as far as we could, shouting and stumbling along the way. A few of the braver peasants grouped together to pick up some heavy rocks and hurl them at that stiff's head, much as if they were killing a snake. The ground was soon spattered with splotches of red and white.[95]

The explicit violence portrayed in this scene owes something to naturalism and *grand guignol* melodrama alike, but that does not begin to exhaust its significance. Execution scenes held a special place in the imagination of early 20th-century Chinese writers, both those like Lu Xun who are known for meliorist attitudes, as well as the less ideological and more evocative writers like Shen Congwen. The apparent catalyst for Lu Xun's decision to devote himself to meliorist literature was his moral indignation over a newsreel in which a crowd of Chinese apathetically looked on as one of their own countrymen was executed at the hands of a foreigner.[96] Prušek notes how this image reappeared in Lu Xun's fiction: "The circle of eyes watching a tortured victim with apathetic interest which constantly reappears in Lu Xun's stories is an expression of the feelings that haunted every intellectual."[97]

Shen Congwen was also "haunted" by this image to a certain extent, but as an evocative writer less inclined to moral pronouncements than an avowedly meliorist writer could be, Shen was able to approach the relativist mode of observation that most modern anthropologists cultivate. Thus Shen felt more "dazed" than indignant at the spectacle of a public decapitation he witnessed in 1930. Instead of simply standing apart from the dull crowd of onlookers and criticizing its gross foibles, Shen "acknowledged and returned their smiles" to appear as if he were "one of them."[98] As it turns out, Shen's descriptions also substantiate the typicality of certain features Wu Zuxiang attributes to the execution, such as the summary nature of the interrogation prior to sentencing, as well as the preference for riverbanks as execution sites. Yet as to whether Wu's execution scene leans more to meliorism or evocativeness in mood, he does in fact resemble Lu Xun more closely than Shen Congwen.

By focusing on the injustice of the execution, Wu enriches his readers' meliorist sentiments. For one thing, the militiamen prove themselves heartless by refusing Baldy a last chance to see his family. Wu Zuxiang would seem to have believed that even criminal types often maintain a respect for filiality, since his diaries mention a dream from November 1942 in which he implores a gunman in hot pursuit to let him off out of mercy so that he can fulfill his pressing duty to look after his aged mother.[99]

The executioner also tips us off to the injustice of his task by drinking in order to summon up the courage to go through with it. Had the executioner been certain that Baldy actually was a vicious desperado for whom such drastic punishment would be entirely appropriate, he would have felt no need for liquor to stiffen his resolve.

The most pointed expression of injustice is the panic that ensues upon Baldy's final howls of defiance. The militiamen and even their leaders scatter wildly in all directions, leaving only a few of the braver peasants to finish the grim job that the militia had started; the implication is that the armed militia's resoluteness in action pales before that of unarmed peasants. Moreover, Chinese anecdotes about panic breaking out immediately after an execution have typically implied that the sentence was a travesty of justice. A Chinese historian once remarked that directly after the noted literary critic Jin Shengtan had been wrongfully executed in the late 17th-century by the Manchu authorities, "armed soldiers ran in all directions, and the officials dispersed in fear." According to John Wang, the panic of the soldiers and officials "is presumably the historian's shorthand way of indicating the unjustness of the case."[100]

If the panicked atmosphere surrounding Jin Shengtan's execution resonates with that of Baldy, are there any literary antecedents to Baldy's miraculous final act of defiance? A 19th-century English poem by Ebenezer Elliot entitled "The Splendid Village" also uses the image of the wronged dead among the peasantry arising to take vengeance on their oppressors:

> ... Vampires quit your prey!
> Or vainly tremble, when the dead arise,
> Clarion'd to vengeance by shriek-shaken skies. ... [101]

The violence and cruelty of "Little Lord Guanguan's Tonic" is more comprehensible, and thus less shocking, when viewed in the context of the socio-economic crises rippling through most of rural China through the 1930s. A vast array of thorny problems faced the would-be rural social reformer, including a lack of serious attention to rural problems by the Nationalist Government; local effects of the worldwide Depression; the breakup of large sectors within rural handicrafts production; the depredations of bandit gangs, warlord armies, and gentry militias; and the proliferation of ruthless local political kingpins who were filling the power vacuum created by the retreat of better educated and more idealistic persons to the cities.[102] Discussions of these problems sometimes concluded in speculations over what one key factor lay behind the bulk of China's difficulties. The symposium in "Little Lord Guanguan's Tonic," longer and more serious in tone than that of any previous story, contrasts two possible answers to this sweeping question. An old militiaman representative of his generation argues that the cycle of Fate is in a downturn, not only in China but even worldwide, as evidenced by the terrible effects of the Great Depression even in industrially advanced countries like America and Japan. A young businessman vacationing at home from his firm in Shanghai argues instead that the incursion of foreigners and their economic interests are at the bottom of China's crisis.[103] He catalogues the various kinds of articles that the Chinese formerly manufactured on a small-scale for their own consumption like homespun cloth, tobacco & pipes, and bean oil for lamps, showing how in each case foreign manufacturers eventually drained profits out of China by capturing the market with products like factory-made textiles, machine-rolled cigarettes, and refinery kerosene.[104] In this symposium, the author's many-sided grasp of a number of important issues in modern socio-economic history is telling proof that the occasionally nightmarish and apocalyptic quality one detects in his fiction is not the overheated product of a merely melodramatic imagination.

## A Defamiliarized Rural Landscape

Over the course of many years' schooling away from his home village, Wu Zuxiang developed an urbanized perspective that shows up in his fiction of 1931–32. The traditional way of life in his village had come to seem strange and foreign to him, and he wished to portray the yawning gulf between the rural and urban realms to a readership that rarely had more than a vague knowledge of what was really going on in China's vast rural interior.

Wu's urbanized perspective, often embodied in semi-autobiographical characters, finds itself at odds with the narrow rural view of women as mere child-bearing homemakers ("On the Eve of Leaving Home" and "Miss Jin and the Xue Girl"); is confronted with entrenched superstitions that prevent villagers from thinking through problems logically ("Two Young Sparrows" and "The Flowering Gardenia"); and observes with mingled fascination and horror gentry figures who are callous to the suffering of the toiling peasants ("Two Young Sparrows" and "Little Lord Guanguan's Tonic").[105] These varieties of theme-based "defamiliarization" are complemented by the defamiliarizing technique of the nightmare (or irrational, nightmare-like scene) used to structure the climax of each of the 1931–32 stories except for "On the Eve of Leaving Home."[106] Wu invariably defeats our expectations of encountering a tidy denouement at the conclusion of any of these stories, tinged as they are with the irrational aspects of human consciousness; instead, he breaks off the action at its very peak of intensity. In doing so, he forces his readers to form their own conclusions, thereby increasing the aesthetic act's "difficulty and span of perception"—a key feature of enduring art, in Shklovsky's view.[107]

# 3

## Contrasts Within the Village: Past Equilibrium Versus Present Decline, 1933–1934

Wu's stories of 1931 and 1932 could be characterized as synchronic in thrust, for within a sharply constricted temporal setting each story focuses on the gulf in worldview and way of life between the village and the city. The contrasts between the rural and urban realms appear as frozen within a narrow time frame instead of portrayed as merely the latest development of a protracted process of historical development. Though characters from this period such as Ah Bao's father ("Two Young Sparrows") and Xiangfa ("The Flowering Gardenia") may briefly compare their present dire straits with the relative normalcy of times past, the author seems to be emphasizing the present-day lack of mutual understanding between these villagers and the educated urban-based characters whom they encounter.

Wu's fiction of 1933 and 1934 takes the urban/rural gap as a sort of "given," and turns abruptly away from the city to focus exclusively on the countryside. The key contrast which emerges at this juncture lies between the fragmented and declining rural social order of the present-day (1930s) versus the sound and thriving village social structure of the recent past. The new emphasis on temporality and historical change in these stories suggests that the author has tacitly shifted from a synchronic to a diachronic approach. A dearth of background material with which to enrich the historical setting of a story had infused Wu's works of 1931–32 with a sketchy quality, which he overcame in his works of the subsequent two years by providing a sense of historical depth.

### Apparitions Unveiled

Wu's first piece of fiction in the diachronic mode, "The Verdant Bamboo Hermitage" [*Luzhu shanfang*], appeared in January 1933. It was the final story Wu published before going on to graduate school at Qinghua, and marks a further development of his interest in the irrational side of the human psyche.[1]

"The Verdant Bamboo Hermitage" contrasts the grimly eccentric existence of an old gentry widow with the wistful tales of her amorous passions as a vivacious young woman over twenty years previously. The semi-autobiographical young married couple, consisting of the narrator and his wife Ah Yuan, have been visiting his Elder Aunt [*Da Boniang*] in the countryside during the summer.[2] The combination of sultry heat in the foothills village and the colorful life story of the narrator's Second Aunt [*Er Gugu*], who resides in a cool hillside bamboo grove, make the aunt's invitation to the couple for a visit seem doubly attractive. They ascend through a lush landscape to the secluded abode of the middle-aged and diffident Second Aunt and her similarly taciturn maid. The drawn visage of Second Aunt saddens the couple with intimations of mutability, for they both know the story of how she once had an illicit affair with a young gallant who finally became her husband only via a posthumous ceremony following his accidental drowning. The narrator either ignores or indulgently smiles at the eccentric behavior of the older women, such as their repetitive references to the late husband as if he were still alive, but Ah Yuan grows increasingly apprehensive. The narrator finally shares her growing anxiety when they overhear ghostly rustlings outside their bedroom door late at night. Leaping up to the door in a few bounds, the narrator brings the story to a close by discovering the "ghosts" to be none other than the two older women peeping in at the married couple.

The cast of characters reverts to something like the assortment from Wu's semi-autobiographical stories of 1931, "On the Eve of Leaving Home" and "Two Young Sparrows." The partly autobiographical characterization of the young couple back in the countryside from the city is underlined by the fact that the name "Ah Yuan" is a variation on the name of Mrs. Wu herself.[3] The new development within the characterization of this story consists of focusing on the two aunts of the narrator instead of his mother, who had represented the older generation of the local elite in many previous stories.

One of the highlights of "The Verdant Bamboo Hermitage" is the antithetical relationship between the personalities of the two middle-aged rural women, Elder Aunt and Second Aunt. Elder Aunt lives near the narrator's mother in the village located in the foothills region.[4] For a woman well into middle age, her enthusiasm upon meeting the newlywed couple is remarkable. Elder Aunt not only bids Ah Yuan sit on her lap and vivaciously pats the young woman, but titillatingly urges Ah Yuan to kiss the narrator for her right there and then. Ah Yuan blushes beet red at this cajolery, and when at last alone with her husband again, she tells him that she has had her fill of visits with his aunts. He attempts to dissuade her from this reluctance by emphasizing Second Aunt's curious background, recounting how the family of her drowned boyfriend had arranged a post-humous marriage between her and the dead boy in order to provide him with a partner in the ancestral graveyard.[5] On a note of ironic foreshadowing, the narrator consoles Ah Yuan that Second Aunt "could never come on as strong" to her as Elder Aunt just had.[6] Second Aunt soon proves herself to be soft-spoken to the point of inscrutability, but the aura of mystery and eeriness pervading her behavior and surroundings eventually proves to upset Ah Yuan far more than Elder Aunt's antics ever had.

The couple's encounter with Second Aunt vividly evokes the frightening and uncanny mood of a horror story. The author creates a Gothic atmosphere charged with suspense through the interaction of three forces: the enigmatic ways of Second Aunt and her maid Orchid [*Lanhua*], the growingly alarmed reactions of their young guests, and the mysterious setting of the secluded dwelling and its lushly forested environs.

The old women behave eccentrically from the very start. The first thing Second Aunt tells the young couple is that she had a mysterious premonition that they were coming. Appealing to superstitions connected to both numerology and animism, she explains the grounds for her premonition: "The lamp wick got charred in three places last night, and a magpie came by to chirp three times today."[7] Second Aunt also refers to her husband as if he were still alive, and matter-of-factly mentions the presence of bats and other animals as if they were human:

> We sweep these rooms out each year around the time that my husband comes home. . . . Grandfather Bat and Papa Lizard will stay out of your way while you're here.[8]

Orchid mirrors the behavior of her mistress, and also vouches for it:

> Her husband appears in her dreams every few days or so. I've often seen him, too. From time to time he paces through the courtyard wearing a scholar's cap and a sapphire-blue robe. [9]

The physical description of Second Aunt as "pale, withered, and expressionless" intensifies the Gothic mood by portraying her as almost cadaverous in appearance.[10] Indeed, one of the dreams Wu Zuxiang felt as having left the greatest impression on him in the early 1930s dramatized his encounter with a deceased middle-aged female relative who had the same sort of gloomy demeanor as Second Aunt. [11] Her associations with death are compounded by the fact that the maid who preceded Orchid in her service had died at the hermitage. Both older women strike the reader as morbidly remote from the ordinary world in appearance and behavior—so remote that they call to mind various Western Gothic stories featuring cadaverous characters.[12]

The narrator and Ah Yuan react to the strangeness they observe with a crescendo of intensity that is relieved only at the finale. There, what had seemed uncanny is revealed as merely an outbreak of suppressed libido reminiscent of numerous fanciful satires of all-too-human monks and nuns in pre-modern Chinese fiction and drama.[13]

When the narrator and Ah Yuan meet Second Aunt for the first time, the couple exchange knowing smiles at the strange deportment of their hostesses. Later, Ah Yuan pulls at the hem of the narrator's tunic in alarm over references to "Grandpa Bat" and "Papa Lizard."[14] When this sort of talk continues, Ah Yuan reaches the stage of openly staring in alarm at Orchid. The narrator begins to find the hostesses more intimidating than amusing at this point, and finally stiffens with fright when he hears the rustling of footsteps outside the guest bedroom at night. Ah Yuan has become paralyzed from terror by that point, and even the narrator is unsure how he "got up the courage to push aside Ah Yuan, dash to the door in three bounds, and pull it open."[15] The eerie behavior of Second Aunt and Orchid and the increasingly fearful reactions of the married couple thus function as a kind of drama of suspense.

On the other hand, the mood of suspense in the story is created in large part by the setting. Darkness often evokes a mood of eeriness, and the dense canopy of tall bamboos and trees near Second Aunt's house throws the footpaths into heavy shade. Moreover, the plashing and gurgling sounds from nearby hill creeks impart an animation to the natural environment conducive to ghostly imaginings. The "imposing and gloomy" house of Second Aunt is tainted with signs of reclusion and even death, for it is spotted with moss on the outside and is moldy and mildewed indoors.[16] As soon as they are opened, rooms normally left closed such as the guestroom reveal an unsettling assortment of bats and lizards amidst cobwebs and thick dust. Associations with the supernatural in the guestroom include its prominent painting of the mythic protector against evil spirits, Zhong Kui, an apparition which occasionally appeared in Wu Zuxiang's dreams as well.[17] Finally, the guestroom seems all the more mysterious and forlorn during a nighttime rainshower when the only light in the room comes from the dim and wavering flame of an old bean-oil lamp.

Eerie features of the house and its environs are related to the superstitious and gloomy personality type of Second Aunt and Orchid not only by indirect association, but also through explicit comparison. As the narrator puts it, "The imposing and gloomy quality of the house harmonized with Second Aunt's personality make-up."[18]

Wu Zuxiang also calls attention to the role of fiction writing per se in the story through the use of a large number of terms and names related specifically to fiction, such as "story, " "legend," "scholar-meets-beauty romance, " *chuanqi* (a complex literary term first used in the Tang dynasty), the author and playwright Li Yu, and the story collection *Liaozhai zhi yi*.[19] Wu is thus placing fiction writing itself in the foreground of his story, and in doing so he resembles a large number of writers worldwide who self-consciously interrupt the verisimilitude of presentation with reminders that they are intruding into their works of art, and thus cannot be passively "mirroring reality."[20]

Stories of the uncanny like "The Verdant Bamboo Hermitage" are seldom noted for their profundity of thought or meliorist sentiments, but are perhaps more adequately judged by their power to grip the reader into an emotional identification with the narrator or main character, as Tsvetan Todorov has maintained.[21] A highly dramatized narrator of the sort found in this story may well be especially effective at bringing off such an identification, according to Todorov, for the most successful fantastic stories by Maupassant and Poe adopt precisely this narrative standpoint. Prior to the 20th century, however, Chinese vernacular fiction had not utilized dramatized first-person narrators, as Milena Doleželová-Velingerová mentions in connection with the difference between *qi* [the strange] in most pre-modern Chinese fiction *vis-à-vis* a 20th-century novel by Wu Woyao: "Unlike the 'strange' [*qi*] of traditional fiction as designating something which everybody could see but no one could explain, the strange or abnormal in Wu Woyao's novel is an invisible, imperceptible property of 'normal' things, events, and characters and is unveiled as such by an 'alien' narrator."[22] The narrator of "The Verdant Bamboo Hermitage" is precisely this type of figure who is alien to the setting, and thereby demystifies its bizarre goings-on by happening upon mundane and commonplace factors that explain what had originally seemed inscrutable.

Readers can distinguish a Gothic horror story that takes itself seriously from one that is relatively agnostic according to whether its mood comes to rest in mystification or demystification. Cheng Peikai suggests that Wu's story takes itself seriously, for he likens it to Poe's "The Fall of the House of Usher" and Hawthorne's "Rappaccini's Daughter," a pair of works in which mystification holds sway.[23] "The Verdant Bamboo Hermitage" admittedly resembles those stories in its portrayal of a household where bizarre goings-on surprise visitors from the world of more normal passions. However, Wu's story does not inflate the aberrations of its bizarre characters to such lengths that their demise seems to be most appropriate way of bringing their story to closure, as is the case with Poe's Roderick Usher and Hawthorne's Beatrice Rappaccini. Instead, the Chinese story re-integrates the bizarre characters with the world of normal passions that their behavior had seemed to negate. Moreover, the somber tone of the above two American stories implies that Gothic intimations of a supernatural presence are to be taken seriously, while the ironic tone of the narrator throughout much of Wu's story undercuts the mystery in the suspenseful moments leading up to the climax. In light of the demystifying motives of "The Verdant Bamboo Hermitage," it might be more aptly compared to a Western work like Jane Austen's *Northanger Abbey*, in which a rationalist heroine indulges in fearful and fantasy-ridden imaginings in a Gothic setting before re-integrating herself with society via mundane social and romantic attachments in the novel's comic resolution.[24]

The re-integration of Second Aunt into society is hardly this successful, however, for she can only fulfill her repressed desires for a romantic attachment vicariously by peeping at others. In this way, she may be likened to the protagonist in Shi Zhecun's "Injurious Courses" [*Modao*], who flounders in suffering due to having confused the two realms of ordinary social intercourse and romantic attachment.[25] Even in Wu's comic resolution of the story, the sufferings of a reclusive widowhood for Second Aunt come to the fore with special intensity. As soon as her perplexing behavior is recognized as warped emanations of repressed desires for a normal adult existence more integrated with society, she invokes our sympathy instead of our apprehension. Therefore, few critics have agreed with Yuan Liangjun's disparagement of the story as so "gloomy and ghoulish" that it is "anachronistic in the twentieth century."[26] According to Zhao Yuan, for instance, the narrator achieves a modern psychological insight into the causes of irrational behavior, and imparts a sense of liberation from mystery and free-floating anxiety in the process. Yet whatever humor exists within this concluding insight is wry at best, for it is colored by an "astringent aftertaste" of pity for Second Aunt.[27]

An evocative piquancy runs through the story, but a concluding sense of restrained pity for Second Aunt implies that meliorist sentiments are not wholly absent. Left-leaning writers sometimes reserve their sympathies for the financially strapped, but Wu proves himself able to extend his compassion to the more affluent sufferers from harsh patriarchal traditions like China's long-standing forced chastity for widows. Perhaps this ability came rather naturally to him, for his own elder sister Wu Runbao was widowed in her mid-teens, and yet felt compelled by social pressures to maintain a chaste widowhood over the several remaining decades of her life.[28] Whatever the case may be, the subtle meliorist undercurrents in "The Verdant Bamboo Hermitage" would gather force in his next several stories: his subsequent work, "Twilight," would address a larger range of social problems at the expense of quite such a meticulously evocative style.

## An Evening Cantata of Rural Anomie

In "Twilight" [*Huanghun*], another story at least partly autobiographical, the young married couple who have appeared in so many stories by
Wu Zuxiang are back in the village residence of the husband's family.[29]
The only other member of the household present during dusk on the midsummer night when the story takes place is the housemaid named Jade,
who made her first appearance in "Two Young Sparrows. " Yet the focus is
not on any of these three characters who are enjoying the cool evening
breeze in the courtyard by the front gate, but instead on a half dozen villagers who voice their various sufferings within earshot of the three.

The narrator and his wife are chagrined at the effects of the rural economic depression, which has deprived many of the villagers not only of a
decent livelihood, but of their spiritual equilibrium as well. Some residents have sunk into petty thievery to help support themselves, as in the
case of the landlord's son who has been reduced to itinerant fishmonger-
ing as his sole formal calling. Other villagers evince obsessions, as in the
case of a woman who has nothing to say but angry accusations of suspects
in the theft of her brood of chickens. Still others have succumbed to fits of
full-blown insanity, as in the case of an unemployed shopkeeper whose
sudden outbursts of demented laughter have become notorious through
the village. The narrator concludes with a laconic sigh of incredulity: "So
*this* is what my village has come to?"[30]

A pair of compositional strands run throughout "Twilight" to unify the
work. First, the strand of social decline appears not only in the metaphorically significant title, but also in the accounts of woe regarding the many
local figures whose fortunes have lately taken a sharp turn for the worse.
In addition, each of the unfortunate villagers' oral accounts is introduced
by a repetitive utterance or sound that aptly represents his or her plight.
For instance, an opium-addicted fishmonger hawks his wares in a listless
tone of voice, since his extreme penury prevents him from buying a fix
that would alleviate his acute withdrawal symptoms; an old widow recently bereaved of her bankrupt son and daughter-in-law mournfully
chants a shamanist ritual hymn on behalf of her incurably ill grandson;
and a string of intimidating curses introduces the furious housewife who
storms through the village alleyways in search of her stolen brood of
chickens.[31]

Far from referring merely to the temporal setting of the story, the title
"Twilight" suggests socio-political decay. With reference to pre-Tang poetry, James Hightower has noted that "the declining sun is always suspect
as a dynastic symbol. "[32] The sense of *fin de siècle* is further underlined by
the narrator's wife; she explicitly compares her village to the ones described in Oliver Goldsmith's "The Deserted Village," a long poem which

laments the sharp decline of English rural society during the early stages of the Industrial Revolution:

> "The past six months in the village have been especially dreary in the day-time. When I hear these old walls creak and crack, or see some creepy-crawly slug drag itself along the edge of a moss-covered stair, it's all I can do to keep from dozing off in sheer boredom. But as soon as twilight arrives it's not the least bit lonely here. On all sides voices emerge from the neighboring houses, courtyards, and alleyways. You recall the stories of these people's lives when you hear their voices, just as if you were reading a poem like Goldsmith's "Deserted Village"; you can't help but realize how—"
>
> "Fish for sale! How about buying some fish, today, Ma'am?" A skinny, bare-chested fellow hoisting a pair of baskets on his carrying pole appeared at the gateway to the courtyard.[33]

The motif of twilight and darkness, introduced at some length, recurs sporadically in various brief sections throughout the rest of the story.[34] By the end of the above passage, however, the focus on the metaphor of twilight shifts from its vehicle to its tenor, from twilight to decline. Each figure who appears from this point on has recently undergone some sort of decline in status or wealth.

The fishmonger, named Jiaqing and nicknamed "Fix" because of his opium addiction, is a grandson of an official who once held an exalted post in the Central Secretariat at the Qing court. Yet by his thirtieth birthday, Jiaqing has squandered what little part of the estate that his own father had not frittered away over a lifetime of profligacy. He literally supports himself by hook or crook, on the one hand vending whatever freshwater fish he can catch, and on the other furtively selling fowl and livestock that he has pilfered. Though his voice grates with the spiritless-ness of an addict going through the early pangs of withdrawal, he is so persistent in peddling his wares that the housemaid impatiently takes him to task for dealing in stolen ducks:

> "So they're *yours*, are they?" said Jade with a grimace. "If they're yours, why've you got them hidden inside that burlap umbrella bag?"
>
> "D-Don't y-you get on my case, young Miss. I-I'm . . . I'm . . . ." He hemmed and hawed for what seemed ages, but unable to spit anything out that made sense, he finally just rubbed away the beads of sweat that had formed around his mouth.[35]

Persistence finally pays off, and "Fix" sells the narrator a small fish before shuffling off to resume his cries of "Fish for sale!" "Fix" thus achieves a small measure of success that no other villager in the story manages to equal, even though he is the least deserving of all the story's characters due to his weaknesses for opium, thievery, and profligate ways in general. He is what Goldsmith would describe as a squire whose prosperity or impoverishment has little direct bearing on a given village's level of well-being, compared with the all-important peasantry:

> Ill fares the land, to hastening ills a prey,
> Where wealth accumulates, and men decay;
> Princes and lords may flourish or may fade,
> A breath can make them, as a breath has made:
> But a bold peasantry, their country's pride,
> When once destroyed, can never be supplied.[36]

Far more unfortunate than "Fix" is the grandmother of her only surviving descendant, Fu Baozi, who is dying of a terminal disease. She believes Fu Baozi's illness has struck because his soul had been frightened away from his physical body. Therefore, she follows the ancient southern Chinese shamanist custom that the *Chu ci* [Songs of Chu] describes as "summoning the soul" on his behalf:[37]

> "Fu Baozi, going to or fro between home and school, on a lane wide or narrow, you suffered a fright—come back home to your grandmother! . . . Fu Baozi, in the dark or in the light, you met with a fright—come back to the ever-shining light at your grandmother's, and take your place as master of the house!"[38]

The father of Fu Baozi had been a prosperous village merchant before the rural Depression. Eventually bankrupt and sorely pressed by creditors, he and his wife committed suicide together.

Another bankrupt village shopkeeper named Songshou has also lost the ability to cope with the misery of being unable to provide for his family. Instead of committing suicide, he sinks into dementia, breaking out with an unearthly cackle whenever his weeping wife takes him to task for their descent into poverty. The combined sounds of Songshou's eerie cackling and the sobbing of his wife are among the most unnerving things heard all evening. [39]

The three central characters subsequently hear a few snatches of a popular song played with flute and two-stringed Chinese fiddle, but a gong approaches nearer and nearer until it drowns out all other sounds. Lao Bage, the first and only true peasant in the story, is banging the gong in order to assemble a group of peasants to repair the dikes and levies in the vicinity. Lao Bage suffers from a racking cough, and seems worn down from worry over fluctuations in the price of rice. He and the young couple hold a brief discussion on current events similar to the symposia mentioned above:

"You won't be coming up short on the harvest this year, will you?" I asked.

"That all depends on the mercy of Heaven Above—" He tried to stifle his cough, but couldn't manage to hold it in. After hacking for a spell, he went on: "I heard the price for rice back north is a dollar and a half. That so? And is there really peace up there, or not?"

"No, up north the Japanese army is still on the march!" I replied.

"Didn't the government recently borrow fifty million dollars' worth of wheat and cotton from America?" asked my wife, as if a dormant memory had suddenly surfaced in her mind. "It's true, isn't it?"

"I suppose that's not off base," I said. "They say it's supposed to help revive the farming villages."

"If they do borrow all that, won't the price for rice here fall even lower? With things come to that state, what'd be the use of pulling in a good harvest?" Lao Bage began coughing so hard that he bent far forward at the waist.[40]

Unlike many previous stories in which village rustics are ignorant butts of humor, the peasant Lao Bage in "Twilight" proves himself both articulate and even better versed than the well-educated narrator on certain issues such as the local market impact of imported foodstuffs. This shift in the direction of populism also accents the motives of meliorism in the story: an unprecedentedly enlightened peasantry is able to see through an ineffectual governmental policy, and could very well imagine what sorts of measures a sounder body of authority might adopt.

The last voice to appear in the story is that of an enraged woman, Cassia, who is stomping through the entire village while cursing the undiscovered thief of her eight chickens. Ordinarily a self-respecting and level-headed woman, Cassia shocks the narrator and his companions with her intemperate rage. Barring the front gate before retiring for the night, the travel-worn narrator sighs out of seeming hopelessness—a reaction that would eventually irritate the prominent left-wing literary critic Mao Dun.[41]

In 1934, Mao Dun criticized the narrator's attitude of apparent resignation as a typical example of Wu Zuxiang's "purely objective" attitude to writing, which was manifested by his alleged unwillingness to express an opinion or judgment about the suffering he has beheld.[42] In recent years, Wu has voiced strong disagreement with Mao Dun's judgment on this point. Incisively claiming that Mao Dun was in effect urging writers to preach, Wu argues that his works are infused by both *ganqing* [emotion] and a progressive socio-political tendency [*qingxiang*].[43] Shen Zhenyu defends Wu on this point, citing the author's conscious adherence to the long-established aesthetic principle of avoiding superfluous explanation in a literary work.[44] Yuan Liangjun also refutes the charge that Wu wrote in a "purely objective" manner, blaming "the influence of 'leftist' proletarian literary theory" for clouding Mao Dun's judgment of Wu.[45] Although everyone agrees that Wu has never been a preachy writer of the type who avoids all ambiguity of expression in favor of an explicitly didactic style, there has been a growing trend among Chinese critics in recent years to approve of the very subtleties and indirections of his style that earlier critics had once tendentiously frowned upon.

Recent trends away from a one-sided didacticism in contemporary Chinese literary criticism have allowed the imaginative side of writing to receive more attention. Yuan Liangjun and Zhao Yuan have both commented on the aural quality of "Twilight." Yuan calls the story "stereophonic" and "symphonic" by turn.[46] Zhao Yuan notes that the aural side of the work outweighs its visual side in importance; it would be better likened to a symphony than portraiture.[47] Without a doubt, "Twilight" is even more strongly aural than "On the Eve of Leaving Home," and achieves a special piquant quality on that account; many of the personages in "Twilight" never actually come into view, but are introduced and fleshed out via the words and sounds they make. Indeed, the vividness and ubiquity of dialogue in the story starkly contrast with the small amount of visual description present.[48] "Twilight" thus presents the reader with an aural rendition of a rural society in decline.

### Recovering the Past in the Unbearable Present

"Splay-petaled Honeysuckle" [Wanzi jinyinhua] was Wu's last story of 1933, but his earliest work to be individually reviewed by a major critic.[49] The story has also held a high place in Wu's own estimation; in his diaries from the early 1940s, Wu mentions having read his college students this story out loud, along with "The Verdant Bamboo Hermitage," when teaching survey courses in modern Chinese literature.[50]

As the story begins, the narrator is back in his southern Chinese home village visiting his wife and mother during summer holiday from the university. Just outside the village he stumbles upon an abandoned shed where a lone young widow about his own age is caught in the final throes of an illicitly conceived pregnancy. Over a decade earlier, the two of them had gotten a crush on one another while at the brink of adolescence. Of late, however, she has been branded a family outcast by her cruelly self-righteous uncle. She recognizes the narrator first, and calls forth his memories of her by mentioning the splay-petaled honeysuckle blossoms they had once discussed together. The narrator becomes nauseous from grief, and hurries home to ask for help in the matter from his elder relatives, whom he believes might have some pull with the young widow's relatives. Before the narrator can do anything else of assistance, he succumbs to an attack of Dostoevskian brain fever, from which he does not awaken until a week later. He then learns that the widow's uncle would not listen to any appeals on her behalf, and that she had subsequently died during unattended childbirth. But the story does not end on a note of total despair, for the narrator's wife is preparing to make an offering to the grave of the deceased with the same variety of honeysuckle as that with which he had expressed his pre-adolescent affections over a decade previously.

Like Lu Xun's "My Old Home," "Splay-petaled Honeysuckle" reveals the painful side of a narrator's childhood memories. Both narrators feel burdened by the pressures of the adult world, and return to their provincial homes with expectations of enjoying an interlude amidst surroundings that call up wistful memories of childhood. Instead, the narrator of "My Old Home" finds that the locals either resent him as a stingy city slicker or else treat him with a fulsome respect that rules out the kind of heartfelt rapport he had shared with many of them during his youth. Similarly, Wu Zuxiang's narrator discovers that harsh and backward local mores have stigmatized a decent young widow, who is allowed to die unattended in childbirth on account of the illegitimacy of her pregnancy. Both stories thus begin on a note of nostalgia for childhood in the provinces, but conclude with a painful recognition of the human degradation accompanying hidebound folkways. The stories' two narrators share an urbanized outlook on provincial life, alternating between nostalgia when viewing the provinces superficially or at a distance, and disillusion, the result of a close encounter with provincial ways.

Yet for all these similarities, the reader encounters a more authentic rendition of the inner life with the narrator of "Splay-petaled Honeysuckle" than with his counterpart in "My Old Home." The nostalgic reveries of Lu Xun's narrator for his home provincial town draw almost exclusively from his vivid recollections of a peasant boy named Runtu, even though the narrator had been acquainted with Runtu for no longer than a month at a point some twenty years prior to the fictional present. Moreover, the mere mention of the name "Runtu" by the narrator's mother is sufficient to call forth the "miraculous picture" in the narrator's mind of the peasant boy scrambling after a varmint in an moonlit seaside melon patch.[51] Significantly, the narrator had never observed this moonlit scene firsthand, but had instead imaginatively constructed it from fragments of stories Runtu had told him twenty years previously. In effect, these detailed and sensuous recollections from childhood are indexed under the name "Runtu" in the memory of the narrator; he recalls the concrete via the abstract label of a name. This method of recollection blends well enough into the story's overall structure of nostalgia and disillusion, but does it really show much insight into the psychological mechanisms involved in the recovery of dormant childhood memories? In light of the powerful forces that restrict access to dormant memories, including the sheer weight of two decades as well as what Freud calls the "amnesia of childhood," could such forces be effortlessly overcome in an instant by the mere mention of a long-lost acquaintance's name?[52]

Aside from fitting into an overall structure of nostalgia and disillusion, "Splay-petaled Honeysuckle" vividly and compellingly portrays the recovery of dormant memories through a concrete object seemingly trivial in itself. Freud has maintained that detailed and emotionally significant memories from childhood tend to be represented in the memory not by abstractions, labels, or names, but by some palpable object of "apparently trivial" nature.[53] Along somewhat similar lines, Marcel Proust has illustrated that long-dormant memories can almost never be recovered in their fullness by a sheer act of will (e.g., searching for memories indexed under a certain name); instead, the adult must duplicate a certain action which, during childhood, was drenched with associations to a wide range of childhood activities. In this way, re-enactments of seemingly trivial childhood actions, such as eating a cookie dipped in tea or tottering on an uneven flagstone, serve to bring tracts of dormant memory flooding back into conscious awareness.[54]

In the fictional design of Wu Zuxiang, the apparently trivial object that calls forth the narrator's childhood memories is nothing other than the honeysuckle flowers of the story title. When the young widow explains her recognition of the young man by referring to the splay-petaled honeysuckle in his courtyard, he notices that her facial features indeed resemble those of the lost pre-adolescent girl to whom his family gave temporary shelter over a decade previously. This is the point at which the long flashback begins—a flashback that bulks to over one-third of the entire story, dominating the story's technical framework of reverie and self-discovery.[55]

In the flashback, the narrator is once again a boy of eleven, just on the brink of adolescence. He has been trying to distract the girl from her apprehension and loneliness at having gotten separated from her relatives after a night at the theater. She takes a momentary interest in his cigarette label collection, and folds him some paper hats as part of their show-and-tell communication. Yet she continues to revert to sobbing in longing for her relatives until the narrator finally piques her interest with a kind of flower of which she has never heard:

> "I'll bet you like flowers. There's some splay-petaled honeysuckle in our courtyard here." I was afraid she would start weeping again, and after having mulled things over for awhile, finally came up with this suggestion.
> "Splay-petaled honeysuckle? What's that?" she listlessly asked.
> "You haven't heard of it? It's quite a pretty flower. Each blossom looks like the character *wan*, the swastika that you see on Buddhist temples. These

flowers bloom once in spring, again in June, and one final time in September. Right now they're in full bloom, and it makes for a pretty sight."

"You mean that even flowers can write characters? That's amazing!" Her
face, long pinched with anxiety, now brightened with joy, bringing her pair
of deeply creased dimples back into view.

I lit a torch at once, and was on the verge of leading her outside to the
courtyard when I heard the sound of gongs in the lane. Someone was shouting: "Lost a young girl dressed in boy's clothing! Eleven years old!"[56]

The narrator's family hails the strangers with the good news that a lost
girl matching their description is sitting indoors. She recognizes her uncle's voice, and gleefully dashes outdoors to greet him. Yet as she looks
back at the boy now distractedly gazing at her with a lit torch in his hand,
she remembers the delicate rapport they had just established.

> "There's some splay-petaled honeysuckle in the courtyard here at his
> house. I'll pick some before we leave." The girl looked over at me as she said
> this to her uncle.
> Her uncle broke out in laughter, and shaking his head, said: "Back at
> home your grandmother is so worried she could faint! You can come back
> tomorrow and get the flowers. Troublesome creature, how did you manage
> to vanish as soon as things got crowded at the final curtain of the play?"
> "I'm not sure—but I want some splay-petaled honeysuckle now. . . ."
> Her uncle led her off, alternately admonishing and humoring her along
> the way.[57]

As it turns out, the uncle does not allow her to visit the narrator on the
next day and pick up the honeysuckle. The narrator learns this the hard
way when he carries a bunch of the honeysuckle blossoms to her grandmother's home on the day after meeting the girl. The grandmother chuckles, and wistfully remarks that the girl had kept on and on about that honeysuckle even as she was being escorted back to her home in another
village.

The narrator feels so chagrined over this frustration of youthful affection by insensitive elders that he spends the rest of the day absorbed in
vain yearnings for her companionship. But without any opportunity of
seeing her again for over a decade, his memory of their affection gradually
becomes as remote from his conscious life as the dreams of her that he occasionally has thereafter. "I couldn't even recall her name," he admits, but
she has left a deep enough impression on his unconscious for her image to
have surfaced repeatedly in his nocturnal dreams.

The concluding section of the story portrays a dream-like reminiscence
by the narrator as an adult of his relationship to the young woman. Instead of having a normal nocturnal dream, however, the narrator

undergoes a series of fevered visions lasting several days, so intense is his shock at seeing the woman in such a wretched state. Because Wu Zuxiang himself once suffered from long spells of delusion-inducing fever as a result of serious attacks of childhood malaria, his portrayal of the narrator's clouded mode of awareness has a particularly authentic ring to it:[58]

> Before my eyes swayed the image of a lovely young schoolgirl, while my ears resounded with the moans of the woman shuddering in that shed. . . .
> By the time I reached home, I was no longer playing with a full deck. I came down with a very high fever. During the five or six days this illness lasted, I never awoke from a state of semi-consciousness, but instead wildly thrashed about and groaned, my ravings never straying far from the words, "splay-petaled honeysuckle." I hadn't the slightest inkling that my wife and mother were shedding tears day and night over the state I was in.[59]

This dreamlike state of semi-consciousness underlines the symbolic function of the honeysuckle as a bond joining him and the young woman. He senses that social forces beyond his control have doomed the young woman to an untimely death, thus breaking the bond of affection shared between the two of them. His feverish repetition of the words "splay-petaled honeysuckle" is a desperate incantatory plea that the bond somehow withstand the attack from hostile social forces represented by the woman's heartlessly self-righteous uncle.

With the death of the young woman in unattended childbirth, the bond of affection symbolized by the honeysuckle is in one sense sundered, at least as a mutual interaction between two people. Yet in another sense the bond lives on with the narrator and his wife, whose respectful offering of honeysuckle at the young widow's gravesite affirms that affection still excites the heartbeat of the living partner of the bond. Therefore, aside from functioning as a key to unlock long-dormant memories of childhood, the honeysuckle also symbolizes a bond of affection between two people that outlasts the death of one of the pair.

The delicate artistry in this reflective and elegiac work makes it one of Wu's most evocative stories. Nevertheless, the lurking specter of destructive patriarchal mores ensures that meliorist sentiments are also at work.

## The Gradual Starvation of Self-respect and Piety

Nineteen thirty-four could be considered the year that was both the peak and the turning point of Wu Zuxiang's career as a writer. The three works for which he is best known, each straddling the borderline between the short story and novelette in length, were published that year.[60] The longest and most famous in China, "1800 Bushels" [*Yiqianbabai dan*], was Wu's first story to highlight social cohesion rather than disorder and decline, as will be discussed in the following chapter. But most of Wu's stories from this year continued to maintain his previous emphasis on the coming apart of the social fabric, as the following synopsis of "The World At Peace" [*Tianxia taiping*] indicates.[61]

A diligent and capable village shopkeeper named Wang Xiaofu loses his job during the Depression, and fails at every type of sideline occupation that he attempts, from peak-season agricultural labor to peddling. He is reduced to sitting morosely at home in a near-catatonic stupor; his wife is the breadwinner due to her work as a seamstress and part-time wetnurse. Finally, even those kinds of financial support disappear, and the desperate couple begin to tear their house down in the daft hope of finding a long-forgotten ancestral treasure hoard walled up or buried on the premises. They and their children are not only starving but now cold and damp to boot, and the husband is finally caught at stealing food and blankets from a neighbor. Shamed before the entire village by a public flogging, Wang Xiaofu quietly resolves to steal the sacred vase from the top of the village temple in order to get travel expenses to Shanghai and its factory jobs. Yet just as he wrenches the vase loose from its moorings on the high temple roof, he falls to his death with the vase in his fatigued clutches.

The story drives home the point that even if especially secluded areas within the Chinese rural interior managed to escape the ravages of marauding armies and pillaging bandit gangs ubiquitous in the 1930s, these areas would eventually fall victim to the Great Depression. Severe economic privation eventually leads to moral and spiritual decay, as the life cycle of Wang Xiaofu testifies. When employed in his chosen profession of shopkeeping, and head of one of the most well-to-do households in the village, "he lacked for none" of the virtues common among his fellow Fengyuan villagers: "loyalty, obedience, diligence, and frugality."[62] Like Wang Mian, the exemplary fourteenth-century character in the Qing novel *Rulin waishi* who scrimps and saves every bit of his meager allowance from his boss in order to help support his ageing mother, Wang Xiaofu scrupulously cuts down on trips to the barber in order to funnel the savings to his mother. Another sign of his virtue is that over long years of diligent shopkeeping, he becomes the top subordinate of the boss, and is the only clerk still employed at the ailing shop when bankruptcy finally forces its closure. The shop closure is the commencement of his long descent into poverty, despair, crime, and a wretched death.

"The World At Peace" is a cyclical biography of Wang's rise and fall, culminating in his ignoble death during an anarchic act of robbery. His fall into misfortune begins with the bankruptcy of his shop, for there are no other shopkeeping openings due to the Depression, and he is unprepared to compete with the pool of husky part-time farm laborers for the scanty seasonal openings as field hands or porters. Nimble at bookkeeping and the abacus but physically weaker and clumsier than these farm laborers, Wang Xiaofu always gets turned down for manual labor openings. Frustrated over the situation in which the rest of his family must labor long hours to supplement what little he can earn from cutting firewood or digging roots, he finally resorts to unfair tactics in an attempt to land a job. Indignant upon seeing a drifter from outside the village secure a job clearing mulberry trees from a field, Xiaofu thrusts himself forward as willing to do the same job at a bargain rate:

> "Sir—" He hesitated for a long spell before finally asking, "What kind of wages are you paying that roughneck from north o' the River?"[63]
>
> "Twenty cents a day, along with board," said the owner with a smile, trimming the ashes from a paper spill.[64]
>
> This man looked to be an agreeable fellow. A hope emerged in Wang Xiaofu's mind; he sidled up to the owner, and began to speak in a hushed tone. "If you hire me, I'll charge only fifteen cents; that's fifteen cents—"
>
> Wang Xiaofu peered at the owner in anticipation of a favorable reply. A loud and jolting blow from a carrying pole swung from behind caught him unawares. Visibly startled, the owner dragged Wang Xiaofu over to one side. As Wang Xiaofu finally peered behind him, he saw that the roughneck worker had raised his carrying pole in savage fury and was about to swing it down again. . . .
>
> "You're acting like a crud!" cried the owner, restraining the fearsome roughneck. "Since I've already hired you, naturally I'll let you finish the job. What's the idea of going around beating up other people? Hurry on back to your digging. Hurry up and get on with it!"[65]

The protagonist stoops to further lengths of dishonesty and foolhardiness as his troubles intensify. After his wife loses her job as a wet-nurse, he joins her in the folly of knocking down the walls of their house in search of a fabled ancestral treasure trove. All they finally discover is how bone-chilling it feels to sleep exposed to the cold night wind. Since the village usurer has already confiscated all of their blankets to make up for their unpaid debts, they have no alternative but to "burrow into the straw like hedgehogs" for warmth at night. In desperation, Wang Xiaofu subsequently resorts to stealing a blanket and some grain from a poverty-stricken neighbor not quite so badly off as himself. When his crime is discovered, the townsfolk string him up and give him a severe lashing. As he fitfully nestles his welt-covered body into the straw pile that evening, his wife agonizes over how the family can possibly avoid starvation after having sunk so low in the eyes of the community. As soon as exhaustion weighs heavily upon his eyelids, the only sound that emerges is Wang Xiaofu's incantatory soliloquy: "To the cities downriver—to the cities downriver! Travelling expenses—travelling expenses!"[66]

Remembering that a wealthy outsider has recently paid a hefty sum for an antique vase, he is gripped by an obsession to steal the temple vase for travelling expenses. He is punished for this final transgression just at the triumphant moment he wrenches the vase free from its moorings high on the roof. The shocking finale in which both he and the vase fall to their destruction mocks the sacred power of the temple vase to protect the village from harm, thus revealing the bankruptcy of the villagers' passive faith in Destiny.

The punishment of yet another of Wu's fictional characters seems overly harsh in light of the relatively minor transgression committed. Yet the severe price Xiaofu pays for his final act of defiance and desperation brings into vivid relief the intolerably harsh socio-economic forces of the day, just as do the bitter fates accruing to other breakers of social taboos in "Little Lord Guanguan's Tonic," "The Verdant Bamboo Hermitage," and "Splay-petaled Honeysuckle."[67]

Unlike the violators of social taboos from Wu's stories prior to 1934, Xiaofu and a few other characters created in 1934 occasionally commit their transgressions in a manner infused with iconoclastic overtones. During that year, Wu rendered the shattering of faith in the old social order through such iconoclastic images as the looting of a clan ancestral hall, the vandalism of the sacral vase on a village temple, and the use of religious paraphernalia like sacrificial candlesticks and Buddhist incense burners as murder weapons.[68] In Mao Dun's disparaging review of Wu's first fiction anthology, *West Willow*, he notices the pointed iconoclasm in Wang Xiaofu's theft of the temple vase even while dismissing the theft as "unrepresentative" of village life:

> Wang Xiaofu dares to steal the ancient vase—a sacred object—yet he does this for the sake of coming up with travelling expenses to the cities downriver! This idea he comes up with cannot be said to represent the major social trends of farming villages. . . . The satire that ought to be levelled at a man like Wang Xiaofu . . . thereby loses its impetus.[69]

The extremity of outlook to which Wang Xiaofu is driven does actually function as an object of subtle satire. As his mother lies on her deathbed in the grip of disease, he foolishly contracts debts by consulting a quack herbalist and a temple soothsayer on her behalf. Unable to find a paying job, he eventually joins his wife in the demented task of tearing down two walls of his house in search of valuables supposedly buried inside. Finally, he forgets to maintain a handgrip on the temple roof while prying the vase loose from its moorings; when the vase suddenly breaks free, the momentum of his tugging causes him to spring off the roof with the vase in his grasp. In each of these three situations, the overwrought emotional state and unsound thinking of Wang Xiaofu are held up to satire, albeit a satire more Juvenalian than Horatian in its severity of mood. The satirical approach Wu adopts in this story resembles that of the Ming writer Ling Mengchu, whom Patrick Hanan characterized as "greatly concerned with objective judgment, a characteristic of the satirist; he regularly notes occasions in which the emotions distort objective thinking."[70]

Wu Zuxiang knew well how the mind can play tricks on its faculty of objective judgment, for he wrote in 1935 that nearly every night he suffered from absurd and bizarre dreams.[71] It is thus little wonder that he can adroitly capture the mood of somnolent compulsiveness behind Wang Xiaofu's ill-starred quest for the rooftop vase. One of Wu's recurrent dreams described in the essay of 1935 indeed closely resembles the lengthy, almost slow-motion description of Wang Xiaofu's fall from the roof. Wu's dream and the story finale are identical in describing the feeling of bodily suspension in "mid-air" [*kong*], followed by a precipitous plunge into "pitch-darkness" [*heidong*].[72] It is not surprising that Mao Dun, Wang Hanzhuo, and two other quite literal-minded critics have found the dream-like finale of "The World At Peace" a misguided departure from the conventions of literary realism.[73] Yet Wu's interest in the irrational side of human psychology has recently drawn a more mature and appreciative response from critics like Zhao Yuan, who provided the first theoretically sophisticated interpretation of the controversial finale of this story.[74]

Facets of Wu's personal experience unrelated to his dream life also had an impact on the setting and characterization of "The World At Peace." He modeled the story's temple on the shrine to the god of war, Guan Di, in a hamlet near Maolin called Pan Village.[75] This type of temple was very widespread in traditional rural China, indeed second in ubiquity only to the temples to the local earth gods.[76] In terms of characterization, Wu, like Shen Congwen, drew on his acquaintances with a large number of village shopkeepers and traders, many of whom were relatives.[77] One of these relatives committed suicide soon after the Depression drove him into bankruptcy, and Wu Zuxiang embodies this sort of malaise in his portraits of such unemployed shopkeepers as Wang Xiaofu, Xiangfa ("The Flowering Gardenia"), and the brutalized husband in "Xiao Hua's Birthday."[78]

Yet perhaps none of these biographical factors left so singular a mark on "The World At Peace" as the personal motivations that led Wu to alter his typical dramatic style so rich in characterization via dialogue. The reason that Cheng Peikai and others have noticed a preponderance of straight narrative at the expense of dialogue in the story is that Wu had grown impatient with literary reviewers who claimed his dramatic style amounted to something less than "genuine" fiction.[79] Here is how Wu viewed the problem in retrospect during an interview in 1983:

In my fiction, I'm not content merely to inform; I aim to evoke an atmosphere. Due to the fact that my stories tend to use a great deal of dialogue and evoke a wide variety of sensory impressions, reviewers have often referred to my works as "sketches" [*suxie*]. . . . Back in the 1930s, the reviewers often labeled me a "sketch writer." They kept claiming I could not write "genuine" fiction. I'd finally had enough of their twaddle, and sat down to write "The World At Peace," which was not at all like a "sketch," but rather a story narrated at a dilatory pace from beginning to end.[80]

As a result of Wu's decision to avoid "sketchy" dramatic scenes in "The World At Peace," the story gains in straight narrative or summary [*récit*] at the expense of dialogue and vividly realized scenes. Since dialogue is perhaps Wu's main forte, it comes as little surprise that the prose style of "The World At Peace" is not generally ranked among the story's strong points. In a series of critiques of "The World At Peace" from the journal *Wenxue*, Dong Meng finds the narrative "sluggish" at the sentence level, while Wang Jiayu describes the story's diction as "labored and dull."[81] Ruo Ying adds that "The World At Peace" lacks "the narrative compression of many previous works by Wu Zuxiang."[82] All in all, Wu's attempt at trimming dialogue to a bare minimum and relying almost wholly on *récit* resulted in a diction much less distinguished than his norm.

It is a tribute to Wu Zuxiang that he consequently pulled back from a prose style that made scant use of his gift for rendering the spoken word. Wu's subsequent story, "Fan Hamlet," maintains the iconoclastic vision of rural social fragmentation found in "The World At Peace," while returning to a dramatic style in which the role of voice again asserts itself. The result is a work that many view as the apogee of Wu's career.

### An Oedipal Tragedy Infused with Iconoclasm

Though "Fan Hamlet" [*Fan jia pu*] and "The World At Peace" were both published on 1 April 1934, Wu actually completed the story of Wang Xiaofu some two months before "Fan Hamlet," which did not appear in anthologized form until 1935.[83] The story may well be the high point in Wu's canon, as Mao Dun and C. T. Hsia have both opined.[84] It is almost certainly his story richest in universal appeal: its matricide does not merely symbolize a great historical crisis in social authority, but more importantly embodies the quintessential situation of classical tragedy, in which, according to Aristotle, "suffering is inflicted upon each other by people whose relationship implies affection, as when a brother kills, or intends to kill, his brother, a son his father, a mother her son, a son his mother, or some other such action takes place."[85]

Xianzi, a young rural woman who operates a roadside tea stall, must find the financial means with which to bail her impoverished husband out of the yamen jail, where he has been thrown as an accomplice to the robbery and killing of a usurious Buddhist nun. Though Xianzi's mother has just received a sizable sum in a lottery, the woman keeps it a secret from Xianzi and even callously tells Xianzi's friends that her son-in-law is a good-for-nothing for whom death would be good riddance.

Xianzi has already heard about all this by the time her mother decides to spend the night at her cottage. After Xianzi awakens from a vivid nightmare about her beloved husband's gory death from jailhouse torture, she angrily decides to steal her mother's lottery prize. The mother discovers Xianzi in the act, and begins shrieking and clutching at Xianzi with all her might. The grappling between mother and daughter culminates with Xianzi's fatal braining of the old woman with a sacrificial candlestick. Xianzi sets the cottage afire to hide the evidence of her deed, and is frenetically dashing away on a by-path when she runs into her husband, who has just been freed from jail by yamen-storming bandits. Xianzi faints—partly from joy over her husband's prison escape, but even more from remorse over having violated to no avail the universal taboo on parricide.[86]

The plot of "Fan Hamlet" is one of the most carefully structured in Wu's entire corpus, as Cheng Peikai has briefly mentioned.[87] For one thing, the story is framed at the beginning and end with a short visual description of the majestic flowering cassia tree next to Xianzi's cottage. More importantly, there is a structural patterning of doubling or recurrence in two of the story's key turning points: the murders of Sister Lian and Xianzi's mother. Xianzi's poverty-stricken husband, Gouzi, does not turn to robbery until a fellow laborer his age named Chen persuades him to serve as an accomplice in the robbing of a Buddhist nunnery. One of the nuns there, Sister Lian, is a good friend of Xianzi's mother, and not only catches Gouzi in the act of theft, but angrily cries out his name. To keep her quiet once and for all, Chen bashes in her head with a Buddhist incense burner before making his escape with Gouzi. Chen is later caught with some of the booty from the robbery and thrown into the yamen jail, where he confesses under torture that Gouzi had been his accomplice. The authorities subsequently seize Gouzi and incarcerate him.

The thematic pattern in which a destitute young person murders a tight-fisted elder with a sacred object recurs near the finale when Xianzi fatally brains her mother with a sacrificial candlestick, an iconoclastic action reminiscent of Sister Lian's demise through blows with the incense burner. Xianzi, like Chen, does not originally intend to kill her robbery victim, only doing so when the victim offers strong resistance. Referring to this sort of recurrence within the structure of relations between characters as "the double," Todorov remarks how in Maupassant, "the double incarnates dangers: it is the harbinger of threat and terror."[88] In the similarly ominous design of Wu Zuxiang, Chen and Xianzi function as doubles, as do Sister Lian and Xianzi's mother.

Two major features of dramatic structure that Aristotle associates with tragedy are reversal [*peripeteia*] and recognition [*anagnorisis*].[89] The first major reversal in "Fan Hamlet" involves a friend of Gouzi named Qiye, a bailiff at the yamen where Chen and Gouzi have been jailed. Qiye tells Xianzi the terrifying news that Gouzi is in jail as a suspected accomplice to a murder. Although he tries to reassure her with the hope that he might be able to bribe Gouzi's way out of jail, his visit only serves to alarm her; she has nowhere but her miserly mother to turn for a sum as large as what Qiye has suggested for the bribe. The emotion of dread for her husband that wells up in Xianzi gradually finds an outlet in the growing anger she feels for her callous and tight-fisted mother; the reversal of Gouzi's imprisonment thus sets the stage for the climactic struggle between daughter and mother.

Near the end of the story is a key scene of recognition, which Aristotle defines as "a change from ignorance to knowledge of a bond of love or hate between persons who are destined for good fortune or the reverse."[90] Xianzi discovers that her husband is alive and well instead of dying from torture in jail, as she had earlier imagined during a terrifying nightmare. She thereby recognizes her great good fortune of being reunited with her husband, while with a remorseful cry of "Mother," Xianzi simultaneously laments that the love-hate relationship with her mother had reached such a disastrous conclusion. With her final pangs of remorse, Xianzi tacitly recognizes that love, or at least familial solidarity, had co-existed alongside hate in her relationship with her mother.

According to Suzanne Langer, tragedy involves a concentration of passion into a single aim that meets with a defeat.[91] Murray Krieger refers to this aim as the tragic figure's "exclusive identification with a single moral claim, a claim which, however just within its own sphere," is an overstressed particular "from the view of total morality."[92] Unable to raise the sum required to bribe Gouzi's way out of jail and its tortures, Xianzi grows so desperate for money that like Gouzi himself, she violates the moral code forbidding robbery— not to mention the plundering of a close relative. Having neglected to plan what to do in the eventuality that the robbery victim were to offer vigorous resistance, she impulsively murders her mother in the course of the ensuing struggle. Therefore, the noble aim of saving her husband from torture and probable death results in the ignoble murder of her parent, a cruel act whose ultimate futility becomes clear when Gouzi returns safe and sound from the newly unlocked yamen jail in the bandit-occupied county seat.

However callously her mother had viewed Gouzi's plight, the old woman's genuine love for Xianzi's brother reveals at least a narrow capacity for humaneness. Midway through the story, the brother himself worriedly informs Xianzi that Gouzi has "gotten into trouble," and in doing so indicates that at least some kind of fellow-feeling or mutual concern exists within their family.[93] Xianzi's act of matricide thus shatters the broad ethical imperative for a sort of basic familial cohesion, and she becomes aware of this as soon as her alarm over the fate of Gouzi is dispelled by his safe return. It is at this moment that Xianzi cries out for her mother and faints; and because the protagonists in several other stories by Wu Zuxiang faint or collapse to the ground only upon learning of the death of a loved one, Xianzi's underlying affection for her admittedly flawed mother is thus all the more apparent.[94] Far from having saved Gouzi with the stolen money, on its behalf Xianzi has killed the very person who tried to comfort her worries about Gouzi just prior to the fatal struggle:

> "If the bandits do take the county seat after all, Xianzi," said her mother, "you won't have anything to worry about. Whenever they take a county seat, they never fail to break open the jails before doing anything else. Our Gouzi will have his savior then!"
> Xianzi snorted in contempt.[95]

Xianzi seethes with fury at her mother on their last night together largely due to what one of her fellow tea-stall owners has just told her about the old woman's peevish grumblings over Gouzi. Xianzi's mother blames Gouzi as a blot on the family reputation, and has openly speculated that Xianzi is still young and attractive enough to abandon Gouzi and attempt a second marriage with a more reputable man. This willingness of the older generation to abandon any children or surrogate children (e.g., a son-in-law) who portend danger is reminiscent of King Laius' abandonment of Prince Oedipus in that archetypal family tragedy. Indeed, some philosophers and Adlerian psychologists have argued that Freud's postulate of the Oedipus complex "is only part within a larger frame" that they term the "Laius complex."[96] Since King Laius conspired with Queen Jocasta to abandon the ill-fated Oedipus in the wilderness, it was they who initiated the hostilities that later resulted in their doom; Oedipus simply reacted to the violence of these circumstances with violence of his own, further entangling himself in the family's web of suffering.

The most obvious difference between Sophocles and Wu Zuxiang is that the Chinese writer bifurcates the unitary Oedipal figure into a victimized persona, Gouzi, and a vengeful persona, Xianzi. In both tragedies, however, the child kills the parent of the same sex who has previously abandoned either the said child or its surrogate—Gouzi, in the case of "Fan Hamlet." Of course, a significant period of time must elapse before the grim ramifications of Oedipal revenge become clear to the Oedipal figure. Xianzi does not cry out in remorse or faint until she sees that Gouzi, the victimized half of the Oedipal whole the two of them form, is safe and sound. Only then does she realize that her murderous revenge was excessive; her temporary loss of consciousness through fainting is a gesture not only of shock, but also of atonement through figurative sterility and death.[97]

Neither Mao Dun nor C. T. Hsia specifically mentions the Oedipal undercurrents in the story, but both of them note that the enmity between mother and daughter involves far more than a heated quarrel over mere money.[98] Mao Dun recalls having read only one other Chinese story published prior to 1935 featuring a parricide, Wang Tongzhao's "Father and Son" [*Fu zi*].[99] He convincingly characterizes the central conflict in Wang Tongzhao's story as wholly determined by economic relations, and in Wu's story as largely psychological in expression—"great changes in people's hearts" [*ren xin da bian*], as the author recurrently puts it in "Fan Hamlet."[100] The story thus stands out in modern Chinese literature for its unusual and insightful portrayal of a murderously tragic conflict between a parent and child of the same sex.

The "great changes in people's hearts" are exacerbated by the acute socio-economic dislocation that forms the backdrop of the story. The army, normally a force that preserves order within the nation, makes for a ragtag bunch as it appears in an "awkward, unnatural formation" that marches out of step and heralds its approach with "off-key bugle notes."[101] Seeking little more than a *modus vivendi* in the region, the army timorously avoids clashes with large bandit gangs, which have so successfully intimidated the county officials by story's end that the county magistrate flees into exile.[102]

Unrest also spurs many Christian missionaries and converts to abandon their rural parishioners. One scene portrays how a group of travelling Christian converts and their servants fearfully cuts short its rest stop at Fan Hamlet upon hearing of Sister Lian's murder. The leader of the group, Sister Yu, pulls out a small American flag which she had carried for emergencies and mounts it on the front of her sedan chair. One of her colleagues cries, "Take the lead, Sister Yu—we'll be following right behind you!"[103] Confidence in the power and authority of the Chinese government had thus grown so weak in many rural areas that even Chinese nationals would readily seek protection under a foreign flag if truly hardpressed.

Dire economic conditions complement the crisis in political authority. Normally, a self-respecting peasant like Gouzi would hardly turn to robbery if he could earn a fair return from his rice farming, but to make things worse in a grain market already depressed, grain speculators have fixed prices to enrich themselves at the expense of the ordinary farmer. Hardest hit of all are the famine refugees who drift in and out of Fan Hamlet; no other story by Wu Zuxiang goes so far in revealing the indignities of dire poverty and gradual starvation:

> Several small groups of revoltingly shabby beggars sat or lay on the scattered straw matting spread under the wayside kiosk. They were famine refugees from a distant region. Unclothed above the waist, the women sat picking through large piles of filthy rags by their feet. . . . Many of the men were modeling crude-looking human figurines out of mud. . . . Some of the children were raucously bawling, their filthy faces contorted in ugly grimaces; others were crawling at random over the damp ground; now and then one of these would pick up a few cassia petals that had fallen to the ground, and stuff petal after petal into a mouth smeared with caked mud.[104]

The social dislocation portrayed in this story finds its major vehicle of metaphorical expression in the cassia tree, whose branches spread over Xianzi's cottage and tea stall. The story begins on a note reminiscent of Goldsmith's "The Deserted Village," which contrasts the present decline of the village with the integrated rural order of the past: the fragrance of autumn-blooming cassia reminds Xianzi of previous years of plenty at harvest time when her roadside tea stall would carry on a brisk business with busy coolies and prosperous merchants. Nowadays, even the peak of the harvest season brings very little traffic to the road, and the tea stand may go for days without receiving a single customer. Instead, the cassia tree now stands over roving packs of filthy and unruly famine refugees, who have congregated to squat under the awnings meant for tea-stall customers. In the story's conclusion, the cassia tree that burns during the aftermath of the murder effectively functions as a symbol of collapse within the old social order, for the cassia has traditional associations with immortality—China's Sisyphus, Wu Gang, is condemned to the endless task of cutting down an indestructable cassia tree.[105] The properties that this myth ascribes to cassia also explain the presence of the two cassia trees which are still growing today in the Wu ancestral temple in Maolin; the trees symbolize the continuity and indestructability of the clan.

Yet how does fire fit into these associations? As Derk Bodde has mentioned, fire can function in Chinese symbolism as either a destructive force or else a beneficent foe of the "powers of darkness."[106] At the same time that the burning cassia presides over a horrible scene of chaos and murder, there is also a touch of fire's function of moral purification in Gouzi's well-deserved release from prison to rejoin his wife. The cassia therefore heralds a new beginning in the life of the protagonists even as it symbolizes a rapidly fading familial and social order and disintegrates along with that order.

An awning overhangs a roadside shop in Maolin, reminiscent of the tea house described in "Fan Hamlet." (*Photo by the author*)

Since cassia is rich in associations with immortality and clan ancestral temples, we may count the burning cassia tree as one of the trio of iconoclastic symbols in "Fan Hamlet." The two others are the murder weapons used to kill Sister Lian and Xianzi's mother. Since Sister Lian is a Buddhist nun, the author's choice of a Buddhist incense burner as the murder weapon is appropriately iconoclastic. Similarly, the candleholder used for ancestral sacrifices is a blasphemous choice of weapon for the murder of Xianzi's mother, who has not only taken part in ancestral worship but also expressed a strong concern for maintaining the family line through her son. In all three cases of iconoclastic symbolism, the author manipulates the symbolic object in such a way that it boomerangs on the very pieties that it would normally reinforce.[107] "Fan Hamlet" surely marks the peak of the iconoclastic spirit running through Wu's writing.[108]

As is the case with many other stories by Wu, biographical factors have contributed significantly to the genesis of "Fan Hamlet." The road to the county seat that runs in front of Xianzi's cottage was probably based on the actual road between Jingxian and Maolin.[109] Moreover, the story's scenario of the well-to-do fleeing the county for the safety of a city downriver actually happened to Wu and his in-laws in 1928. Bandit gangs were surrounding the county seat of Jingxian, so Wu escorted a number of his in-laws to the relatively safe riverport of Wuhu. Finally, the story's climactic episode in which a daughter kills her mother is based on a piece of local news that Wu heard during the summer of 1933.[110] All in all, there is enough factual basis to the story to provide a solid point of departure for one of his career's most remarkable flights of imagination.

## In the Shadows of Prosperity: The Migrant Laborer

"Fan Hamlet" was the last of the three long works of 1934 that firmly established Wu's reputation as a major writer. He did not sustain the same breadth of social engagement and gripping drama in his works of the latter half of 1934, when his concerns took a more private and reflective turn. In the summer, he wrote a light-hearted autobiographical travel story and a few lyrics on the bittersweet qualities of village life back in childhood. He would not return to fiction illustrative of social dislocation until December 1934 with "The Woodcutter" [*Chai*], a semi-autobiographical story about a young boy's friendship with an old migrant woodcutter.[111] This story evokes an intimate mood far removed from the clamor of voices encountered in a work like "Fan Hamlet." Yet like nearly all of Wu's works from the 1933–34 period, it contrasts the present state of decline in the village with the more integrated rural order of the past. The story thus stands apart from the visions of rural recovery found in Wu's post-1934 works.[112]

In this story set during Wu's childhood, the boyish narrator listens to many of the old woodcutter's tales about his troubled past. The migrant woodcutter had formerly doubled as a sedan chair carrier; once while carrying a wealthy and influential passenger, he slipped down from a rickety bridge and took a hard fall along with his passenger. The indignant passenger had him thrown into jail for negligence, and by the time he was released several months later, his wife had already made off with all his possessions and eloped with another man.

The woodcutter has since remained single, for he can ill afford the great expense of taking another wife. Instead of raising a family he has put all his spare time into perfecting his skills in martial arts; having learned a bitter lesson about the lower classes' difficulty in gaining just treatment from their social betters, he now practices boxing religiously. The boyish narrator feels mingled fascination and sympathy for the harsh struggle that has been the woodcutter's lot. Perhaps nowhere outside the pages of *Water Margin* and other novels featuring rugged social outcasts and knight-errants had the bookish gentry boy encountered such a person.

The narrator preludes the story of the woodcutter with a retrospective autobiographical section describing how his own well-to-do family seasonally purchased firewood during his boyhood. Noting that this colorful time of stocking up for the winter "piqued my interest to the full," he recalls the sensations of joyous anticipation he felt when his mother would awaken him with the news that woodcutters had arrived to sell their wares.[113] The occasion was very much a family affair, both among buyers and sellers. Most of the narrator's family would assemble to inspect the wood and decide which kinds to purchase, while the woodcutters usually arrived as a family spanning at least three generations.

Stockpiling wood also had its harsher side. Each local family of means would hire a migrant to chop and split the newly purchased logs into pieces small enough to fit in the kitchen stove:

> Most of the men who split wood were migrants, for in this grueling line of work, one had to toil from sunrise to sunset with hardly a moment's rest aside from three meals with tea and a brief smoke. No one but the migrants could stand that. They were accustomed to suffering, simply unruffled by it. In our village we called them "Old North-o'-the-River," for they all came from north of the Yangzi. Their home villages were typically so plagued by drought, crisscrossing armies, and onerous land rents that they couldn't make ends meet, no matter how diligent and thrifty they might have been. Consequently, they would flee to the South, crossing the Yangzi. Arriving empty-handed, they would hire themselves out as farm laborers on the short term or by the year, and during the winter slack season would split wood. Many of them would return to their home villages with money to support their families. There were also many who arrived during their teens, and would save up enough money over the course of two or three decades to take a wife and start up a family where they worked, never to return to their old village homes back North.[114]

The narrator recalls how he gradually overcame his childish fear of the brawny Northern migrant who regularly split wood for his family. A friendship developed in which the migrant took the boy into his confidence, conversing with him about matters the elder felt uncomfortable mentioning to other people: "Sometimes when in the presence of a third party, he snuck a glance at me and smiled, implying that he would have a word with me as soon as the other person left."[115]

Over the months and years of their friendship, the migrant told the boy of one hardship after another that he had lived through. He had been orphaned when his father was strangled as a convict in the kind of medieval torture box called a *zhanlong* [lit., "stand-up cage"]. Later hired on as a year-round farm laborer, he was eventually beaten up and fired by his employer for a minor infraction. As he scoured the countryside in search of another job, a group of off-duty soldiers robbed him of his meager but hard-earned savings. He finally learned to protect himself by practicing boxing, and by the age of forty had saved up the bride-price for a young maid employed in a wealthy household.

The climax of the story occurs when the migrant uses the broken syntax of intense passion to complain of how his unfaithful spouse had eloped with a younger rival:

> "Let me tell you," he snorted in disgust, "there's one kind you shouldn't marry—a maid who's been working for a wealthy family." After another loud snort, he continued, "Yeah, the one underhanded sort of woman you shouldn't marry no matter what—not an ounce of goodness—"[116]

This passage is highly aural in appeal, containing a rhythm of speech rather than prose per se. Northrop Frye refers to this sort of speech rhythm as an "associative rhythm," since "in pursuit of its main theme it follows the paths of private association, which gives it a somewhat meandering course. . . . It is much more repetitive than prose, as it is in the process of working out an idea."[117]

The migrant enlarges upon the dissolution of his family before the denouement shifts the frame of reference back to twenty years after the narrator's encounter with the woodcutter. Because the narrator's home village has recently fallen into the grip of severe poverty, even the well-to-do can no longer afford to buy good firewood, not to mention hire migrants to split wood. This situation has brought even more hardship to the lot of the woodcutters; the question is no longer whether a migrant can manage to set up and raise a family after years of scrimping and saving, but whether he can continue to ward off hunger and cold in the face of an ever-dwindling pool of job opportunities. The migrants who lost out in the competition for scarce jobs had little choice but to join one of the armies, bandit gangs, or famine refugee bands that were crisscrossing the Anhui countryside in the early 1930s.

## Visions of Social Upheaval
## from a Contemplative Academic Setting

The past two chapters have shown how Wu Zuxiang explored the urban/rural gap in his stories of 1931–32, and subsequently examined rural social problems within the context of historical development through his fiction of 1933–34. Both types of approaches share a common emphasis on the harsh and anachronistic features of rural life, and the resultant suffering endured by various major characters. The dislocation of the rural economic and tax structures seemed to be intensifying hand in hand with the unraveling of the rural social fabric itself.

Yet from what standpoint was Wu recounting this onslaught of social disorganization, in which a well-integrated, relatively homogeneous rural milieu was undergoing a transformation into a "heterogeneous and disintegrated type" of society?[118] Not only did the half decade at Qinghua witness Wu's development from a mediocre poetaster into a prominent writer, it was also the most anxiety-free and settled period of his life as an active writer: he felt at home on the Qinghua campus at Beijing in a way he never had while going to school in Shanghai during the 1920s, and the years following his departure from Qinghua in 1934 were filled with dislocations involving a plethora of new job responsibilities and several years of wartime exile in the remote Southwest.

While at Qinghua, Wu lacked for nothing that a writer might hope for: leisure to write, access to excellent open-stack libraries, freedom from economic pressures, encouragement from talented literary mentors such as Zhu Ziqing, and journal and book publishers interested in his work. The brisk tenor of Wu's life during the Qinghua years thus stands in an inverse relationship to the dark view of rural Anhui society one perceives from his fiction from those years. It is as if the wrenching conflicts in a disintegrating fictional world were functioning in a vicarious manner as a substitute for the elements of struggle and conflict missing in Wu's halcyon days as a Qinghua student. Although this compensatory relationship between the author's life and literary works would persist throughout the rest of his career, the necessity of his departure from Qinghua and shouldering of multiple new job responsibilities would quickly sow the seeds for a literary portrayal of society quite different from anything he had attempted prior to 1934.

# 4

## Portraits of Rural Recovery at the Grassroots Level, 1934–1936

In Wu's stories up to 1934, the downtrodden sink into grim or even dire straits, no matter how hard they struggle to better their circumstances.[1] Society as a whole comes across as a callous entity that offers no succor to the typical provincial citizen down on his or her luck. At the top rungs of society, the sense of *noblesse oblige* often aspired to by the upper classes under the *ancien régime* shows every sign of having eroded severely by the early 1930s. In the lower levels of the social hierarchy, a vacuum of viable support networks leaves the downtrodden characters in Wu's pre-1934 fiction with nowhere to turn for efficacious assistance.

Nineteen thirty-four marks a turning point in Wu's vision of rural Chinese society, for it is at that point that his fiction begins to portray a coalescence of networks at the grassroots level that allows his lower-class characters to emerge with a modicum of strength and hope. From 1935 until the end of Wu's career as an imaginative writer in 1942, Wu's characters of humble origin would never again fall helpless before the sort of victimization typically visited upon them during the early 1930s. One factor behind this change in Wu's vision was the common duty felt by many Chinese writers of the day to emphasize the strength and resilience of the broad masses in the face of the growing threat and final actuality of a massive military invasion by Japan.

A more personal motivation for Wu's shift lay in his 1934 departure from the sheltered environment of Qinghua, which had provided him with such a conducive writing atmosphere for half a decade. An inverse relationship tended to hold sway between the circumstances of Wu's personal life and the typical circumstances of his major literary characters: when the conditions for writing were most positive for Wu during the early 1930s, his victimized characters would meet with defeat in the face of one calamity or another, and yet when he forced himself to muddle through drudgerous secretarial duties in the mid-1930s and dismal wartime exile starting in 1937, his now resilient grassroots characters evinced a remarkable vigor and capacity to prevail in the end. Up to 1934, Wu's creative imagination compensated for the rather dull security of his personal existence as a student by emphasizing the alarmingly disruptive effects of rural poverty, cultural backwardness, and social inequity. From the middle of that decade onward, Wu's growing loss of control over his day-to-day life due to occupational and military factors contributed to his portrayal of a resurgence of coalescence and self-determination among the citizenry at large; this psychological mechanism allowed him to take a vicarious pleasure in the victorious resilience of his grassroots fictional characters.

## A Peasant Uprising Confounds the Local Elite

The first work whereby Wu Zuxiang projected his intense hopes for a grassroots resurgence in rural China was "Yiqianbabai dan" [1800 Bushels], a story of novelette length which was published on 1 January 1934 in the newly founded and highly prestigious Beijing literary journal, *Wenxue jikan* [The Literature Quarterly].[2] The story portrays an organized takeover of the clan temple by pariah farmers, a group that never managed to assert its collective will in previous works by Wu. It is Wu's most renowned work within China, and the second lengthiest product of his writing career. Stylistically, "1800 Bushels" is Wu's most dramatic work, consisting of little else but dialogue and portraying a broad range of middleclass and upper middleclass opinion and internecine struggle.

The members of a rural southern Anhui clan hold a meeting to determine what to do with the 1800 bushels of rice they have stored in their dilapidated ancestral temple since the last harvest. Suggestions include selling it to undertake irrigation projects, repay old outstanding loans, reopen the bankrupt village school, beef up the local militia, and help a clan member handle some funeral expenses; some clansmen simply insist on immediately divvying up the grain among all clan members. The clan's procrastinating business manager, Botang, tacitly shirks his duty to act as arbiter, instead pleading that no decision about the rice can be reached until a certain absent clan elder shows up. In fact, the manager secretly hopes to use the grain as collateral for some of his slick investment gambits, and the clan members who are aware of this stratagem try to pressure him into putting the issue before the assembled members for a formal joint decision. A horde of hungry peasants breaks the stalemate by suddenly storming the clan temple and pillaging all the rice, thus symbolically shattering the authority of the most important institution of traditional Chinese village-level governance. At the same time, a coalescent network among the masses makes its presence felt in the organized and energetic manner in which the peasants rush on the clan temple and subsequently pillory Manager Botang.

"1800 Bushels" describes two major complementary social develop-ments in Wu's locale. While the family and the clan were growing weaker as social units, other forms of authority stepped in to take up the slack, in-cluding secret societies, peasant associations, and a modern local elite quite different in composition from the defunct pre-modern gentry it had replaced.[3] The clan in "1800 Bushels" is plagued by irresolution; far from striving towards a consensus over how to use the grain revenues, nearly all of the members at the meeting betray an uncompromising and short-sighted self-interest in their proposals for disposing of the grain. Zishou, the head of the regional chamber of commerce, wants the grain made available for loans to merchants like himself; a pettifogger named Ziyu views the communal clan property as not different from an ordinary pri-vate estate, and scoffing at the centuries-old tradition of keeping the col-lective property intact, he casually proposes dividing it equally among the various clan members; a septuagenarian named Xinqiao wants part of the clan revenues to go for old-age pensions; Shaoxuan, the head of the dis-trict militia, demands that the local armed guard get a greater share of the revenues; and Hanzhi, the principal of the local village elementary school, insists that his school will soon founder unless it receives a sharp increase in clan financial support. This jostle of conflicting narrow interests cannot unite to break Manager Botang's visegrip on the grain revenues.

Finally, the ineffectual squabbles during the clan meeting are abruptly terminated by a food riot in which the drought-ravaged tenant farmers co-ercively insure their subsistence. The shocked clan members frantically at-tempt to shut the heavy door at the front gate, but the peasant tenants have struck too swiftly, and surge through the gate in a powerful wave. Most of the tenants immediately begin to fill their baskets with grain from the storehouse, but a large contingent concerns itself instead with carry-ing out a sort of "rebel justice" by seizing Botang and the militia head Shaoxuan, the two leading clan authority figures in their midst. These ac-tivist tenants drag the two clan leaders onto a stage originally set up for sacrifices to the rain god, and prepare to punish the duo for ignoring the plight of their starving village brethren. A budding grassroots organiza-tion has thus managed to chastise wrongdoers within the fragmented clan power structure.

The story does not directly describe how the tenants have organized their onslaught of the clan temple, instead focusing on how the clan meet-ing reaches a stalemate due to an intractable conflict of private interests. C. T. Hsia has reacted to this feature of the plot by repudiating the con-cluding food riot as a "cheap trick" that "sidesteps" any enlargement on the internecine clan conflict, thus betraying the author's temporary capit-ulation to proletarian formulism.[4] Other critics have interpreted the food riot scene as a carefully foreshadowed and integral part of the plot structure, noting that far from being a mere stroke of poetic justice, the riot scene represents a likely culmination of social tensions widespread during the 1930s Depression. Cheng Peikai quotes a wide range of articles and statistical studies on the fragmenting Chinese rural economy, which created the conditions for the numerous and amply documented peasant uprisings at that time. Cheng also dissects the plot into a direct or "revealed" strand set in the ancestral temple, and an indirect or "obscure" strand that portrays the plight and response of the impoverished tenants. Shen Zhenyu restates Cheng's two-strand plot theory in the visual terms of "light and shadow" [*ming'an*], claiming that the clan meeting gets the spotlight while the peasant uprising remains in the shadows until the two strands unite at the rousing finale.[5]

The obscure or shadowy plot strand of peasant unrest appears several times in the early stages of the work, first in the interior monologue of Botang during the first section, and later in a dialogue dominated by the merchant Zishou:

> If we were to increase the land rent, our tenants would all make a big fuss, turn in their tenancy deeds en masse, and hightail it as famine refugees. Hmmm, that obviously won't do.[6]

> "In this year of drought," said Zishou, "we landowners won't have any harvest coming. What about the tenants, then? Could the heavens somehow open up and rain rice down on them? Nowadays they want to turn in their tenancy deeds and leave as famine refugees. But they can't just sprout wings and soar off, and even if they could, where would they fly off to? 'A cornered dog will leap over the wall'; they simply haven't got anything to eat here. Wouldn't be hard for all of them to turn into Daoist Immortals, would it? Wouldn't be hard for one and all to become Boddhisattvas either, would it? . . . We mustn't allow Botang to keep on pulling off stunts to fill up his own pockets; and we mustn't wait around for our tenants to come and rob us of our grain! Wouldn't you say that there's some likelihood of that happening?"

> "There sure is . . ." Mulling this over, Ziyu stroked his beard with a grass stem as he spoke.[7]

These two passages from the beginning and middle portions of the work indicate that several prominent figures in the clan have all along been aware of the tenants' desperate straits. An unemployed shopkeeper named Jingyuan even nervously warns that the tenants are holding their annual secret society festivities that very day: "'Today's the midpoint of J-J-July, and the t-t-tenant farmers are holding their yearly meeting of the Elder Brother Society. We've got to be on our g-g-g-guard.'"[8]

Because secret societies were a major vehicle of grassroots rural organization, it is likely that the invasion of the clan hall by the tenants in "1800

Bushels" was not so much a spontaneous mob action as a premeditated and well-organized act of righteous rebellion. Indeed, the original journal version of the work contains a curious paragraph (later cut out of *West Willow* and subsequent story collections) in which a youthful revolutionary from a privileged family background emerges as one of the leaders of the tenant uprising:

> A young man wearing a soiled shirt broke away from the milling crowd and leapt onto the stage set up for the rain sacrifice. Like a young military hero onstage at the theatre, he began vigorously shouting things like "Down with feudal landlords! " and "Toil-worn tenants, fling away your land deeds! "[9]

As Wu Zuxiang views his motives in retrospect for deleting this paragraph, he disapproves of the passage's implication that the peasants needed assistance from the educated elite in order to organize themselves.[10] However, Wu has never deleted another passage which describes how a burly peasant at the forefront of the surging tenants leads them to seize the clan business manager and militia head. Both passages suggest that leadership, organization, and a sense of moral indignation are important ingredients of this type of food riot.

Neither Wu Zuxiang nor his hometown relatives have heard of any food riots that took place in the vicinity of the Maolin clan temple, which was the model for the clan hall in "1800 Bushels."[11] Yet the clan-based social order in the countryside was weakened so much by political chaos and economic depression that a fertile imagination could well conceive of such an event occurring in Maolin. The cash-poor clan elite in "1800 Bushels" have seen much of their farmland go fallow, as peasant tenants discover that farming is unprofitable due to the contribution of high interest rates, a burdensome array of official and unofficial taxes, and low commodity prices. Commercial investments have also tended to go sour, as in the case of Zishou, the head of the local chamber of commerce who is less intent on coordinating community-wide commercial activity than on siphoning away clan funds to bail himself out of failed investments. Because even the better-off clansmen at center stage struggle hard for a piece of the clan property, it stands to reason that the tenant farmers in the story's "shadow" would eventually enter the fray to demand a basic level of subsistence for all the villagers, wealthy and poor. As James Scott has demonstrated, peasants often react coercively to an authority whom they suspect of compromising the "safety-first" peasant principle of maintaining subsistence for all.[12] Therefore, even though in actuality no food riots occurred in or near the Maolin clan hall, such uprisings were numerous throughout China at the time, especially in years of bad harvest when no authorities intervened to maintain subsistence for the needy.[13]

The clansmen who attempt to exert their authority on the issue of managing the clan assets could be considered "upperclass" only within the context of their rural locale; the truly wealthy upperclass at this time tended to migrate to the cities, where as urban rentiers they relied upon local agents to handle their rural landholdings and investments. None of the clansmen at the meeting belongs to this class; most of them do not even derive the greater part of their income from land rents. Some of the clansmen own no land at all, relying totally upon shopkeeping: Buqing, for example, is an old man in the lowly trade of beancurd shop proprietor.[14] Indeed, a wide variety of rural occupations is represented at the meeting, including merchant, legal notary, shopowner, shop clerk, herbalist-medic, high school teacher, elementary school principal, and two local officials. C. T. Hsia's description of these characters as middleclass is thus more accurate than the three left-leaning critics who carelessly lump them all into the "landlord class."[15]

The venality so ubiquitous in "1800 Bushels" was characteristic of imperial China's lowest ring of the gentry, the *shengyuan* or "government student," yet the clansmen at the meeting are actually associated with a local elite that is more transitional than traditional in nature.[16] For example, chambers of commerce like Zishou's that were independent of direct governmental control were not introduced into China until 1902.[17] Furthermore, the modern-style experience of university study is one of the important background influences on some of the prominent younger clansmen.

The few characters who feel a strong loyalty to the clan as an institution are either old or else, ironically, at the bottom of the clan hierarchy. The lowly beancurd proprietor Buqing is the only one present who argues from the standpoint of tradition with the clansmen determined to divvy up the common estate. Similarly, the only character who expresses sorrow over the desecration of the clan temple by rioting peasants is Shuangxi, the temple caretaker from an impoverished *déclassé* family: he plaintively cries out in despair to the deceased clan ancestors at the sight of looting and irreverent disorder within the ancient hall. A contrasting view of the clan system and temple ceremonies at their ritual height comes from the greybeard Xinqiao, who midway through the story reflects back on the long-faded age of clan prosperity and self-assuredness:

> "In times past, whenever a son of our Song clan made his way into society, he would be smart and proper in appearance and decorum. In the ancestral temple there were three minor sacrifices per month and two major sacrifices each year. As the clan members entered the temple, they would array themselves in a seated or standing position appropriate to their years. They observed the ranking of high and low, and the hierarchy of young and old. When the elders fell silent, who among the younger clansmen would dare make a sound? But what's it all like these days? A cattle market, no less!"[18]

A skylight and pool inside the Wu clan ancestral hall in Maolin.
(*Photo by the author*)

Swan songs for an elite social order gone defunct are not uncommon throughout world literature, and this passage closely resembles the proud old Russian butler's chagrin over the decline of his manor in Chekhov's *The Cherry Orchard*: "In the old days it was generals, barons, and admirals who were dancing at our balls, and now we have to send for the post office clerk and stationmaster, and even they aren't too glad to come."[19]

In contrast to these elders who repeatedly shake their heads over the modern-day decline of the local elite, Wu Zuxiang hails from a generation more sensitive to the clan organization's systemic injustices present during its florescence as well as its decline. A diary entry from February 1945 indicates how uncomfortable Wu Zuxiang felt about clan hierarchies as expressed during ceremonies in the ancestral hall. He writes of dreaming that he and his wife Shuyuan were participating in a clan ceremony held at the Maolin ancestral hall. Wu kowtowed to his elders with remarkable equanimity, but he soon grew uncomfortable with the proceedings due to two incidents: first, a certain clansman suddenly struck his wife and then strode out the temple; and later, Shuyuan was standing in an area reserved for those of a hierachical position in the clan inferior to his own.[20] He urged her to sit down beside him in a position of equality, but she refused. When he continued to insist that Shuyuan move to his side, she suddenly disappeared into thin air. Clearly, the impressive ceremonial decorum in the clan temple that fired Wu's imagination was debased by both undercurrents of violence and gender-based inequities.

The personal importance that the rural clan social order held for Wu Zuxiang appears not only in his dreams but also in the many associations between his own background and that of "1800 Bushels." Wu had once attended grade school at Maolin's Yuying ["Instruct the Valorous"] Elementary School, the name of which resembles that of Peiying ["Foster the Valorous"] Elementary School, which was administered by Principal Hanzhi of "1800 Bushels." Moreover, just as Hanzhi is one of the work's few admirable clansmen to make an appearance, Wu Zuxiang maintained an admiring correspondence with a local teacher named Pan Xiaosong long after leaving his home village for Beijing.[21] The spacious and lofty Maolin clan temple, too, remains basically the same today as it was described in "1800 Bushels"—it actually still serves as a grain warehouse nowadays— even though its paraphernalia of ancestor worship such as votive tablets have long since been scattered and lost.[22] The two finely sculpted lions that seem to be laughing with derision over the clan's economic misfortunes during the opening and closing paragraphs have been moved from outside the temple gate to atop a bridge in the county seat of Jingxian, some thirty miles distant.

The sole semi-autobiographical character in "1800 Bushels" is Shuhong, a young college-educated middle school teacher whose job is similar to that held by Wu Zuxiang from 1927 to 1928. Shuhong belongs to one of the few village families still capable of producing sons that cut a respectable figure in the world, just as Wu's family was unusual for having produced two sons as successful as both Zuguang and Zuxiang had been. Moreover, Shuhong finds it very difficult to convert his family's ailing long-term investments in land and shops back into cash, a knotty problem for Wu Zuxiang in the 1930s as well. Everyone is so short on cash during the Depression that Shuhong's debtors try in vain to repay him with land, which, as more a liability than an asset at that time, he refuses to accept in

One of the original stone lions that once stood outside the gate of the Wu clan ancestral hall in Maolin, as mentioned in "1800 Bushels." (*Photo by the author*)

lieu of cash repayments.[23] Yet perhaps the most strongly autobiographical feature of Shuhong is his intense interest in rural economic reform, as expressed during a symposium late in the work:

> "In farmland as hilly as ours, we're not like the lowlanders with their fear of floods, but worried instead about drought. . . . I've thought of a way to handle part of my acreage: I'll have my tenants dig out ponds, each of which can irrigate a couple of acres."
>
> "Brother," sighed Botang, "you're only a scholar. When it comes to book learning, you've really got what it takes. But you'd be better off not fretting

over things like farm economics. All of what you just said is merely the speculation of a dabbler!"

"The 'speculation of a dabbler'? Why, you—"

"Now listen to me! . . . The soil in our lands stretches down no more than
three or four feet deep. Dig below that and you run into solid bedrock. Even
if you asked a flock of genies to help you out, you still couldn't make it
through all that rock. Besides, are your tenants going to toil at digging ponds
with nothing but vague promises to show for it? Didn't you just get through
saying that they have to wear themselves down to the bone with work, day
in and day out?"

At a loss for words, Shuhong sighed and scratched his head.[24]

Just after the intractability of rural socioeconomic decline frustrates
Shuhong's reformist designs, a different sort of meliorist solution erupts
from the discontent of the newly organized tenants. Famine relief was one
of the major responsibilities of the pre-modern gentry, and the common
neglect of this duty by various mean-spirited local elites of Republican
China occasionally forced peasants into food riots or other types of rebellion.[25] A sense of *ganqing* [fellow-feeling] between landlord and tenant
would incline the wealthier to reduce or even waive land rents during a
famine year, but Botang conversely begins an eleventh-hour round of discussions on a proposal to increase land rents.[26] The impracticality of
Shuhong's reformist proposal and the intensification of Botang's exploitative greed both serve to clear the way for a mass uprising and a moral
victory for the poor tenants.

The intensity of critical acclaim for "1800 Bushels" exceeded that of any
other work by Wu Zuxiang.[27] Lauding Wu as "a major writer with an un-
limited future" in February 1934, Mao Dun deemed "1800 Bushels" a masterpiece of economy that sketches over a dozen thoroughly individual-
ized character portraits in a space of just under 30,000 words.[28] A reviewer
in Tianjin who had never heard of Wu Zuxiang was so impressed by the
story that he surmised it must have been the work of an established writer
hiding behind a pen name.[29]

Dissonant voices existed alongside the Chinese literary scene's generally appreciative reactions to "1800 Bushels."[30] Lu Xun, a veritable pillar
on the literary scene, dissented with Mao Dun's selection of "1800 Bushels" for Harold Isaacs' forthcoming anthology of contemporary Chinese
fiction, *Straw Sandals*. The elder writer penned a letter to Isaacs in May
1934 precisely on this subject. Lu Xun specifically urged Isaacs not to
translate "1800 Bushels" for the anthology, promising that he would locate a shorter story by Wu to substitute for it. As it turned out, Lu Xun
never submitted any such substitute. On the one hand, Lu Xun hardly
blinked at the grave conceptual and artistic flaws in Ding Ling's "Shui"
[Flood] that Yi-tsi Feuerwerker has astutely analyzed, and took it upon

himself to abridge and patch up the original draft of this diffuse and un-abashedly tendentious story so as to make it more palatable to Isaacs.[31] On the other hand, he summarily urged the discarding of "1800 Bushels," a novella only slightly longer than Ding Ling's avowedly ideological left-wing novelette, and certainly more distinguished in narrative quality.[32]

Lu Xun did not elaborate on why he thought so little of "1800 Bushels." Wendy Larson's analysis of Lu Xun's autobiography suggests that by the mid-1920s he had already grown "cynically critical" of literature as a seri-ous calling in China, at least when a given literary work struck him as having fallen short in awakening readers to the necessity of making a rev-olutionary overhaul of Chinese society.[33] Moreover, we know that Lu Xun greatly preferred "progressive" writers of leftist and organizational bent associated with Shanghai political organizations like the League of Left-wing Writers, which he had helped found.[34] He tended to distance himself from politically unaffiliated writers who were active in Beijing academic and publishing circles, such as Wu Zuxiang, Lao She, and Shen Congwen, none of whom Lu Xun deemed worthy of inclusion in *Straw Sandals*.[35] The rapidity with which the veteran writer took umbrage over a few remarks Wu Zuxiang had made in a letter to Masadu Wataru early in 1935 suggests that he was impatient with *engagé* writers who chose organizational non-alignment, particularly those writers who had more connections with the Beijing academic literary scene than with Shanghai's more politicized lit-erary leagues. Here are Lu Xun's jaundiced concluding comments on Wu Zuxiang from the May 1934 letter to Masuda Wataru:

> In light of the tenets he holds to in that letter of reply, I believe that this is a person of no consequence. . . . If he is as complacent as he appears to be, he'll stay stuck in the position of a petty bourgeois writer. . . . As I see it, your cor-respondence with him couldn't come to anything worthwhile.[36]

If politico-organizational nonalignment freed Wu from the distractions of the slogan-ridden sectarian literary debates in the 1930s, it also cut him off from the support of various champions on the literary scene who viewed "correct" political alignment as a categorical imperative for full-fledged progressive writers. Sadly for Wu and so many other modern Chi-nese writers, these sporadic charges of "petty bourgeois" heterodoxy dur-ing the 1930s were merely a prelude to the chorus of denunciation cam-paigns that were to rock the Chinese intelligentsia during the 1950s and 1960s.

Regardless of the fact that Wu Zuxiang was hardly a political activist, "1800 Bushels" is strongly meliorist in conception—perhaps more so than any other of his works. The local clan elite fails to carry out the relief proj-ects traditionally expected of the rural gentry during famine years, thus forcing the lower-class tenants to fill the vacuum of social responsibility with a coercive assertion of the right to subsistence for all.

The piquant humorous touches most often associated with poorly educated and impoverished characters in Wu's fiction of the early 1930s now emanate mostly from the local elite. Many of the clansmen are given to some curious foible or other, the most colorful of which is the foppish young squire Songling's obsessive weakness for servant girls, especially the ones with tiny bound feet. In contrast, the author generates comparatively little piquancy in his portrayal of the impoverished tenants' uprising, even though its concluding uproar of gongs, drums, and shouts from the crowd adds a colorful ritualistic dimension to what is otherwise a chaotic and often grim clash between local interests.[37]

As several critics have pointed out, it is Wu's mastery of what Zhao Yuan calls "the art of dialogue" that goes furthest toward making "1800 Bushels" such a memorable work.[38] Wu's bent for a discourse based on direct speech finds its penultimate expression in "1800 Bushels," and may reflect influence from the dramatic style of fiction in certain Western writers like Maupassant and Hemingway.[39] Moreover, the emphasis on dialogue in "1800 Bushels" is remarkably resonant with the strong tilt toward direct speech in early Chinese narrative. Zhu Ziqing has argued that "records of speech" [*ji yan*] preceded "records of events" [*ji shi*] in early Chinese historical narratives, and Burton Watson has noted that the more historically recent Chinese narratives have often been influenced by the style of early texts like the *Shu jing* [The Classic of History] and the *Zuo zhuan* [The Zuo Commentary], which are composed largely of direct speech.[40] In "1800 Bushels," the function of straight narrative [*récit*], as opposed to dramatized dialogic discourse, is hardly different from Watson's characterization of it in the *Zuo zhuan* as the vehicle which "sets the stage for a dialogue or a discussion."[41] Perhaps this predilection for speech-based narrative is one of the concrete bases for Pu Liangpei's rather sweeping comment that Wu's style owes a great deal to traditional Chinese narrative.[42] Whatever the case may be, "1800 Bushels" is a milestone of highly dramatic fiction that illustrates how coalescence among the masses can emerge from severe social fragmentation.

### Leaving Qinghua for the World of the Hired Pen

Several factors contributed to Wu Zuxiang's decision to withdraw from Qinghua University during the summer of 1934. By this time, he and Shuyuan had two children, and another was on the way. Precisely at the juncture when the growing family needed more funds, the economic situation back in Maolin had deteriorated to the point where his family's modest investments in land and property were barely yielding enough to support Wu's ageing mother; Wu could no longer dip into family funds when in a financial pinch, as he had done now and then during the 1920s and early 1930s. In a place as conspicuous as the preface to *West Willow*, Wu mentions the decline in his family's economic viability and consequent need for publishing royalties as a motivation for collecting his stories into an anthology.[43]

Wu's rapid rise to nationwide distinction as a prominent young writer also seems to have engendered a less scrupulous attitude toward the relatively mundane matter of daily coursework. Some of the courses required for graduate students in Chinese literature struck Wu as irrelevant to his interests and thus a waste of time. Instead of keeping his frustrations to himself or sharing them discreetly with trusted confidantes, as was standard practice among his more cautious peers, he would occasionally voice his complaints in public to a professor as if challenging the latter's scholarly authority. While some of the modern-thinking faculty members viewed this approach as a stimulus to class discussion, old-school academics accustomed to the student's traditional deference to the revered teacher found Wu's behavior disrespectful, even impudent. During his final year as a Qinghua graduate student in 1933–34, Wu tactlessly dismissed the subject matter of Prof. Liu Wendian's course in Six Dynasties poetry as "a literature of mere stimulation and allure." Liu refused to give Wu a passing grade for the course unless the young writer admitted to having gone a bit far with that statement, but headstrong pride made Wu loathe to retract his harsh evaluation, in spite of his friend Yu Guanying's advice to retreat a step and give Liu a bit of "face."[44] Wu stuck by his original opinion, got a lower grade in the course than the acceptable minimum for graduate students, and thereby lost any chance of applying for a government fellowship stipend for the following year. Without a continuance of the stipend which Wu enjoyed during the 1933–34 academic year, he simply would not have been in a financial position to carry on with graduate study past the summer of 1934.

Although Wu's departure from Qinghua meant the loss of a fine environment for writing and the exchange of ideas, it did not have a noticeably negative effect on his career as a literature scholar. Extensive graduate study was not a prerequisite for the college teaching posts that he would accept in Chongqing, Nanjing, and Beijing during the 1940s and the decades thereafter. Wu never felt the need to undertake further graduate study after 1934.

The author would not find a settled academic post for some eight years after leaving Qinghua, however. During this period he first supported his family as an administrative secretary at the Central Research Institute in Nanjing, where a letter of introduction from Zhu Ziqing helped Wu fill a post during the latter half of 1934. Subsequently, he took a job as a private tutor and personal secretary of General Feng Yuxiang, a once-powerful

warlord who had accepted a post of marginal importance under his former political rival, Generalissimo Chiang Kai-shek. Wu worked full-time
for Feng from 1935 to 1942, and sporadically from that point until the middle of 1947, when the General dismissed him from his entourage in the
U.S.

The job under Feng involved a great deal of business travel, separating
Wu from both family and writing desk for long stretches. This new lifestyle was a major cause of the steep falling off of Wu's writing output—
and the often sketchy nature of what little he did manage to write from
1935 to 1942.[45] In the May 1935 elegy "In Memory of Lu'er," Wu notes that
his children have seen so little of him that they sometimes shyly shrink
from him, as if from a stranger. Yet his remuneration for a job from which
he "seldom returned home at night" amounted to little more than enough
to keep all the bills paid.[46] Therefore, he and Shuyuan made a fateful decision against sending their ailing youngest son to the local hospital in
Nanjing which had severely overcharged them in the past; the boy unexpectedly died soon afterwards. Wu's frustration over neglecting family
and literature alike just to maintain a barely middleclass standard of living
comes across in the preface to his second anthology:

> The title of this book, *An After-hours Anthology,* refers to a small surplus
> left over from working to fill the larder. I use that phrase because I wrote all
> these pieces during time off from working to fill the larder.[47]

One symptom of Wu Zuxiang's insecurity and dissatisfaction with his
new job situation beginning in 1934 was an unprecedented turn to memories of childhood in his writings of that year. Contemporaneity of
narratorial presentation had been a feature dominating Wu's works from
1925 to 1933; even stories devoting considerable length to flashbacks of
childhood experience like "The Splay-petaled Honeysuckle" still begin
and conclude in a contemporaneous setting. A work from the autumn of
1934 like "The Woodcutter" turns out to be quite different, however, for it
consists almost entirely of the narrator's childhood memories of an old
woodcutter, only briefly mentioning in the short concluding paragraph
that the narrator has lost touch with the woodcutter over the dozen years
since their last meeting.

A series of poems Wu wrote a few months prior to "The Woodcutter"
during the summer of 1934 provide the earliest evidence of this nostalgic
turn to childhood reflections. Three poems in this bittersweet series entitled "Memories of My Childhood Days" [*Nen huang zhi yi*] recall the joys
of his village boyhood.[48] The speaker in "Recuperating from an Illness"
[*Bingyu*] reflects on the maternal solicitude he receives during a childhood
illness:

Courtyard flowering plants–so suddenly grown tall,
While a housefly keeps ramming into the window.
Snow-pear peelings lie scattered on the floor,
As steam roils upward from winter-melon soup.
Though my legs are still weak,
My blue heart dissolves in Mother's smile
And soars through the azure sky.[49]

Here the speaker is comforted while in a position of weakness, confined to his sickbed. Supine like the pear peelings on the floor, on his own he is no more able to leave his confinement than a housefly which is trying in vain to escape through a windowpane. A final transcendence of his helpless condition is rendered through images of uplift associated with his caring mother.

Another poem in the series even more childlike in mood is "On the Grass Heap" [*Cao dun shang*]. In this first fabular literary work by Wu in over a decade, a snake living in a grass heap scolds a trespassing sheep for nibbling away at its abode, and the sheep grimaces and bleats in belated reply.[50]

A rural idyll in the series entitled "The Vegetable Garden" [*Caiyuan*] portrays a lower-class servant woman totally content with her lot, a situation very rarely encountered in Wu's fiction. Like a number of Shen Congwen's characters, she is something of a pastoral figure, singing her way through garden chores while the wind "embroiders" her simple hairdo with pomegranate flowers.[51]

Much in contrast to the suffering-laden fiction of social decline, these poems are childhood recollections of joy in the family, in nature, and in the milder aspects of mankind's stewardship of nature. Wu had reached a crossroads in life between schooling and career when he published these poems in mid-1934, and a fresh interest in re-examining the past was a natural response to the necessity of coping with an uncertain future. By accentuating the mild and comforting sides of his childhood existence, Wu may have been mentally preparing himself to meet the future with a confidence and equanimity that his alter-ego fictional characters had rarely mustered from within their more fragmented and harsh social milieux.

Nineteen thirty-four was notable too for its mixture of triumphal achievements and bitter disappointments. "1800 Bushels" was the best received work that Wu ever wrote, and continuing critical appreciation of the "The World At Peace" and "The Fan Family Hamlet" encouraged him to publish his first anthology (*West Willow*) that August. A very favorable review of *West Willow* appeared in Beijing that October, but it was followed the next month by the Shanghai bombshell from Mao Dun so totally different in tone from the elder writer's previously positive evaluations of

Wu's fiction.[52] Even the politically cautious critic Yuan Liangjun has recently backed up Wu Zuxiang's repeated insistence on the dogmatic and ill-informed nature of Mao Dun's scathing evaluation of Wu as an "out-and-out objectivist" with "limited experience in life," whose works are generally "failures."[53]

Whatever Mao Dun's intentions may have been, his unexpectedly rancorous critique of *West Willow* helped stifle critical inquiry into Wu Zuxiang's best fiction; after 1934, historians of literature and reviewers would now and then briefly describe a work or two by Wu, but no analytical articles on his corpus as a whole would appear again until the 1970s.

Unless Lu Xun's cavalier rejection of Wu Zuxiang's "1800 Bushels" somehow catalyzed Mao Dun's sudden hardening in attitude toward Wu Zuxiang, the impact of Lu Xun's private disapproval could not be compared with the influence of Mao Dun's caustic critique.[54] The prominent P.R.C. historian of modern Chinese literature, Wang Yao, was obediently following Mao Dun and not Lu Xun when characterizing Wu's fiction as "excessively objective."[55]

Mao Dun's 1934 review of *West Willow* was a heavy blow that Wu Zuxiang remembered vividly even as late as the 1980s. Fortunately, a more supportive and reliable leading figure in Shanghai literary circles, Ba Jin, encouraged Wu to publish his second anthology in the following year. "Had it not been for Ba Jin's wholehearted enthusiasm," states Wu in his preface to *After-hours*, "I would not have had the courage to anthologize these works."[56]

The other major disappointment for Wu beginning in mid-1934 was the array of burdensome job responsibilities that left him little leisure for writing. It hardly comes as a surprise that most of the works in the appropriately titled *After-hours* are shorter and sketchier than their equivalents in the first anthology. Nevertheless, Wu opened the new year of 1935 by displaying his competence in a shorter and denser fictional form than he had previously attempted during the 1930s—the "mini-story" of under 2,000 characters in length.

### The Poor as a Model for the Wealthy

Wu published *Nüren* [The Woman], his shortest mature story, in the journal *Tai bai* during January 1935.[57] Like many of his finest previous efforts, the heavy use of dialogue within a narrowly circumscribed time frame and setting imparts a highly dramatic flavor to the story. An unprecedented economy is achieved by limiting the number of dramatis personae to only two.

A recently married upper-class Nanjing woman discovers that her maid of about the same age has left an abusively domineering husband and mother-in-law to live in exile from her rural homeland. As it turns out, the wealthy wife has also been treated highhandedly by her callous and uncommunicative husband. At first, the urban woman vents her frustrations over an unsatisfying marriage by laughing up her sleeve at the maid's ungainly appearance and awkward speech mannerisms. Yet the rural woman's dignified resolve not to stand for slighting treatment, even that which is condoned by the norms of traditional Chinese society, gradually wins the respect of the urban woman. The story concludes with the urbanite's newly emboldened reflections on what she might do in turn about her own domestic troubles.

"The Woman" is Wu's only story set in Nanjing, the city where he had been living for the half year previous to the story's publication. To help with housework and child care, Wu and his wife had hired a maid from Jiangbei (the impoverished northern parts of Jiangsu and Anhui), the region with which the maid in "The Woman" identifies herself through characteristic dialectal expressions like *dao meizi*.[58] At that time, Jiangbei women were widely known among Chinese from farther south for their stocky physiques, assertive dispositions, and preference for walking about barefoot, all features of the maid in "The Woman."[59]

The narrator not only tacitly treats the story as an extended comparison between the wealthy urban wife and the poor rustic maid, but goes on to state outright that placed side by side, "the two women made for an intriguing contrast."[60] To be sure, mistress and servant have some key features in common. Both are in their early twenties. Both feel keenly dissatisfied with their marital lives, and faced with an uncompromising, even intransigent husband, have come to the realization that their relationship will probably not improve unless they forsake the traditional forbearance expected of Chinese women and show some initiative.

On the other hand, the women differ to a startling degree in areas such as appearance: "One was coarse and ungainly, like a 2,000-year-old earthenware artifact that had been recently unearthed— . . . a rough-hewn human figurine neither polished nor waxed; the other was sleek and graceful like a resplendent, gleaming fiberglass gewgaw."[61] Their general demeanors also stand in sharp contrast, for the wealthy wife tends to maintain a genteel and occasionally sneering bearing in front of the maid, who alternately expresses a nervous humility and an indignation punctuated with expletives. Finally, the two differ in the mistreatment they suffer through their marriages. The urban woman has grown very frustrated with her husband due to the neglect he has shown her; he often goes out by himself to a restaurant without so much as a word to her in advance about dinner plans. The maid, on the other hand, is furious over the scoldings and beatings she has received at the hands of her husband and mother-in-law, whom she showers with invectives, mostly scatological in nature. The final contrast between the two women also explains why the poor often precede the well-to-do in rebellion against social injustices like the wide-spread subjection of women: lacking the pretensions to urbanity or cosmopolitanism found among the middle-to-upper classes in Nanjing, the care-worn rural poor feel little constraint in venting their day-to-day frustrations on a young newcomer to the household like the bride. With little to lose from rebelling against such socially sanctioned injustices, a small citizen at the bottom end of even this lowly pecking order may react with startling boldness and intransigence.

The story's emphasis on the contrast between the two women does not imply that their features are set in the static contours of a sketch, however. The dramatic impetus of the plot forces each of them to reveal something of herself that is not at all evident at the beginning of their encounter. Initially timid, dull, and awkward in expressing herself, the maid eventually musters a sort of rough-hewn eloquence while revealing her underlying courage and resourcefulness that led her to flee her brutal in-laws to find employment in town:

> Madam barely managed to stifle her impulse to laugh, exclaiming instead with an air of amazement, "Whew! They beat you? They ran roughshod over you? What business did they have doing that? Tell me about it—take your time, there's no hurry."
>
> "Those scoundrels! All I ever got out of their family was three bowlfuls a day. Three bowlfuls of scorched rice! . . . Whenever I think about it I get mad as the dickens! . . . Over at old Red-plumed Rooster's silversmith shop, I cashed in the jewelled hairpin that my mother'd given me. Red-plumed Rooster's an old fellow in the silver business; yeah, pretty old, all right. I left town with him, even though he didn't want to take me along. I'd known he was about to head to Shanghai, and kept begging him to let me go along with him. Once we took off, we kept on travelling straight through to Nanjing. By then I'd spent a string and a third of cash.[62] And then I went to the shop that hires out house servants. There were four people from my village there in the shop. None of them farms anymore. They all make a living through that shop now."[63]

A shift in attitude on the part of Madam also occurs during this dialogue. In the beginning of the conversation, she is either haughtily polite or else sneering towards the maid. Yet the arduous nature of the maid's struggle for dignity and independence gradually comes to impress the wealthy urbanite: "'Then you're not going to concern yourself anymore with your very own child back in the village—Xiao Tanzi?' Madam asked with solicitude and in earnest, rather touched by what she'd just heard and yet unaware of precisely when this feeling had emerged."[64]

As the story concludes, a flash of shame and frustration erupts in Madam as she happens to glance at her pillow, which is yet again moist from her tears of marital frustration:

She would no longer find this woman "amusing." She respected the woman, even envied her. Yet as far as her own situation was concerned, she didn't know what course she ought to follow. She was thinking it over.[65]

As the author adds the crowning details to a pair of character portraits which had first appeared in general outline, Madam has overcome her vain and futile self-assuredness and opens the door to learning from the maid's resourcefulness and courage. The maid has discarded her clumsy meekness before social betters like Madam, speaking boldly about her past and making unabashed requests for assistance by story's end.

As in many stories by Wu Zuxiang, characterization through dialogue is the technical mainstay of "The Woman." The other prominent technical feature in the story is the copious repetition of certain descriptive expressions, some visual, other aural, and still others metonymic in nature. The primarily visual referent *cu* [coarse] is used nearly ten times to point up the rusticity of the maid's manners and appearance, while *bian* [flat] also recurs repeatedly in unflattering reference to her lips and nose: an implicit contrast between her unassuming appearance and inner dynamism thus gradually takes shape in the reader's mind. Turning to phraseology of a more aural appeal, repetitiousness as a speech mannerism tends to express the maid's anxiety: "Madam, I'd like—I'd like—I'd like . . ."[66] Repetitious phraseology on the part of Madam points instead to a certain inflexibility of attitude: the wealthy woman's common refrain in describing the maid as "amusing" serves to highlight the former's change in attitude as she realizes the inadequacy of this patronizing term by the close of the story.

Even more illustrative of the characters' mental states are a pair of recurring metonymic expressions that express the whole through the part. The maid repeatedly wrings her hands or wriggles her bare toes when in a quandary, such as during her stammering request for Madam's assistance quoted above; the author expresses the maid's general mental state by focusing on a small part of her body, rather in the manner of a filmmaker including a sudden close-up of an actress's eyebrow. The recurring metonymic expression of Madam's marital frustration is her tear-soaked pillow, the repeated reference to which implies that she ineffectually vents her indignation in the privacy of her boudoir, where she is safe from the embarrassment of public exposure of her anguish, and yet isolated from companions who could conceivably assist her in doing something constructive about her plight. The maid, after all, has managed to extricate herself from an unbearable household situation by enlisting the aid of a sympathetic travelling silversmith.

The maid's resourceful cooperation with the silversmith and various fellow emigrés from the village now working in Nanjing marks a cohesion among the masses that provides an informal network for forward-looking laborers impatient with calcified patriarchal social customs. She appears to be little more than a foolish rustic at first glance, but Madam soon discovers that the maid's outer coarseness does not at all negate the inner presence of dignity, resolve, and a sense of justice. In spite of her total lack of formal education, the maid manages to wrest her independence, and even an apologetic letter, from her abusive village in-laws. She, an uncultured "bumpkin, " goes much further than her genteel mistress toward achieving the modern aspirations of individual initiative and brotherhood among equals.

### Travel Fiction Amidst Shifts of Abode

After five rooted years in Beijing dating from 1929, Wu moved twice in rapid succession: first to Nanjing in July 1934 and then to Mount Tai, Shandong in January 1935. These changes of abode roughly coincide with the publication of two works belonging to a genre new to Wu Zuxiang, the fictionalized travel essay. Unlike some of his straightforwardly topical non-fiction essays, each of these prose works contains a story line that narrates the complete cycle of a journey, from beginning to concluding impressions, and allows a number of characters the dramatic function of speaking at some length.

If travel accounts in general have as many affinities with fiction as Percy Adams claims they do in *Travel Literature and the Evolution of the Novel*, Wu's two efforts in this genre in 1934–35 are even more fictional, with their unitary plot structure and characterization through dialogue.[67] As Pu Liangpei has suggested, just as writers of lyrical bent such as Xiao Hong tend to lyricize non-poetic forms like the novel and the familiar essay, writers of fictional propensity like Wu Zuxiang tend to fictionalize forms such as the essay and the lyric.[68] Therefore, even though the following two works are in some respects essays, as Chinese scholars and editors have heretofore loosely classified them, they are also at least partly fictional in style.

"Yangzhou Jottings" [*Yangzhou zaji*] describes a traveler's mixed impressions of an ancient canal port and cultural center approximately a hundred kilometers northeast of Nanjing.[69] "Sights at Mount Tai" [*Taishan fengguang*] portrays a variety of popular religious festivities and entertainments from the vantage point of a skeptical traveler.[70] Though neither work refrains from satirizing certain aspects of the social milieu portrayed, the two milieux are each far more integrated and stable than the typical harsh and chaotic social setting of Wu's earlier works. These two essays present very little new evidence for the central concerns in Wu's fiction of the early 1930s, such as the inhumanity of patriarchal folkways or the breakdown in political and economic structures in provincial society.

"Yangzhou Jottings" is a strongly autobiographical account of the author's first visit to the canal city which had once been the nation's most thriving inland port, and yet had maintained an air of cultural refinement and gracious manners in spite of its sharply diminished position in the modern scheme of things. Unlike the typical visitor to Yangzhou, Wu feels little inclination to wander about the city's famous gardens or the natural landscapes on the outskirts of town; he makes the self-effacing but partly accurate claim of being "incapable of appreciating natural scenery."[71] Throughout Wu's career, he would show little interest in describing nature, architecture, or anything else that might distract him from focusing on social phenomena and individual personalities. In this piece, he seeks to observe and get a feel for the literate and leisured ambiance of a faded old entrepot hardly ruffled by the noisy and blustering incursion of twentieth-century civilization.[72]

Wu approaches the city by boat, the traditional mode of conveyance in a locale where even today no railway line has yet penetrated. He notices onshore a group of sixtyish Yangzhou men conversing with conviviality and a rich bounty of clever puns and quotes from classical verse. Wu marvels at how robust they appear in body and spirit at such an advanced age, and notes how he can now begin to understand why the city has such a reputation for a cultured and gracious lifestyle.[73]

The author spends a few days at the home of a classmate who had invited him to the canal port. There he meets his friend's family, with whom he spends the evening playing cards and exchanging yarns about the colorful Lower Yangzi region. He is impressed by the general prosperity of the local inhabitants, and compares the dense foliage of the city's willows to the modestly plump contours of the city residents, especially the local women he espies at the waterside washing clothes. In his concluding impression of Yangzhou, he views it as a place exuding an air of vigor and prosperity, making him temporarily "forget the troubles of the world," at least his world of rural China in which the century's upheavals were more sorely felt.[74]

A note of satire contrasts with the author's overwhelming approval of what he sees in Yangzhou. When Wu calls at the home of some friends who have just stepped out, their gatekeeper impatiently informs him that they have gone out to pay a social call, abruptly shutting the front gate in Wu's face when he lingers to ask directions to their destination.

> As I wiped the sweat off my brow, I reflected on how that fellow was out of synchrony with this ancient city and its cobblestone lanes. Ill at ease, I felt as if I had heard an off-key note in the middle of a sonorous symphony.[75]

Wu's aural metaphor for a minor discomfort during an overall pleasurable experience suggests that life in Yangzhou seemed not merely endurable but even enjoyable in most aspects at that time. In the author's portrayal of the townsfolk, not a single pauper is encountered, nor are there any extravagantly wealthy persons of the sort living in proximity to the dirt poor, as would be the case in a city of stark contrasts like Shanghai. Instead, Yangzhou apparently enjoys a moderate level of affluence shared by the many rather than the few, and rests in coalescent state of social equilibrium.

"Sights at Mount Tai" also portrays a milieu untainted by the pauperism and harsh victimization prevalent in Wu's early 1930s works. However, Wu's admiration for the general way of life among the Yangzhou residents he observed gives way here to a noticeable disdain for the gullibility of common folk worshipping at Mount Tai. The carnival atmosphere, infused as it is with the avarice of religious charlatans and astute panhandlers living off the superstitious and simple-minded rural worshippers, nevertheless suggests that the teeming crowds of pilgrims are at least affluent enough to afford a vacation from their home villages. Their money may indeed be ill-spent, but its very presence indicates that the economic-related social decline Wu had described around his home village was not necessarily at a similarly advanced stage in various other regions within the country.

Wu Zuxiang would have never written "Sights at Mount Tai" if his job as private secretary and tutor to Feng Yuxiang had not caused him to move to China's holiest of Holy Mountains in January 1935. Feng, the colorful "Christian General" whose international fame had far outgrown his actual political clout, first moved to Mount Tai during the summer of 1932.[76] There he lived what James Sheridan has called "a life of study" as a latter-day hermit [*yinshi*], for he had grown disillusioned with his "rubber-stamp" governmental post in Nanjing.[77] In order to staff his "research office" [*yanjiu shi*] at Mount Tai, Feng hired a number of prominent literati, including Li Da, Deng Chumin, Dong Zhicheng, Lai Yali, and Wu Zuxiang.[78] During the spring of 1934, the General first heard about Wu Zuxiang from newspaper reviews of "1800 Bushels," and had little difficulty in persuading the author to leave his drudgerous administrative post in Nanjing.[79] Wu's new job title was "Instructor of Chinese" [*guowen jiaoyuan*], though he also handled a large amount of secretarial and editorial work for Feng.[80]

At the beginning of 1935, Wu and his family lived with Feng and various other scholar-officials and their families in a Daoist temple perched alongside a trail to the summit of Mount Tai. Not until October that year did he and his family move back to Nanjing, where they remained until the Japanese invasion of China spread to the Lower Yangzi region in August 1937.

Wu has stated in retrospect that "Sights at Mount Tai" is about 80 percent autobiographical. The major non-autobiographical aspect of the work is the portrayal of the autobiographical narrator as an outsider briefly visiting his friend in the Daoist temple: "Actually, I was living in the temple at that time, not merely a visitor as the narrator was, " Wu has said.[81] In point of fact, the work can be plausibly viewed as almost entirely autobiographical by taking not the naïve narrator but his sardonic friend and guide as the autobiographical figure. Here is an exchange in which the naïve outsider asks his worldly-wise guide about a soapbox orator who is preaching from a book entitled *Wealth Comes to the Benevolent*:

> Squirming my way out of the pressing crowd of listeners, I asked my friend: "What's he up to here? I don't reckon I've ever seen such a thing."
>
> "What's he up to? He's up to something very simple," my friend replied in a self-assured tone. "Some wealthy old gentry and their wives and concubines have noticed that the world's no longer quite what it used to be; and that when people are stuck with living in hunger and cold, they sink into banditry and brigandage. The kindness in the hearts of the wealthy pours forth at this point: they come up with some kind of screwball religious troupe to spread the Way of the Ancients to ardent hearts, hiring fellows to trot about singing praises for benevolence and its rewards, lest the common people stray from their proper station in life and bring sins down upon their heads."[82]

This relationship between astonished outsider and sardonic guide is reflected in the interaction between two minor characters living in the temple: the melancholic and naïve Laorui (i.e., "Laurel"), and the boisterous and sardonic Hadai (i.e., "Hardy").

> "Gad, these fellows here from the countryside—what a pitiful lot!" sighed Laorui. "If they can't manage to eat their fill, no matter to them! If they can't manage to wear enough to keep warm, no matter to them! They're dead set on placing their faith in the Bodhisattva, come what may. It's disastrous— just look at their hare-brained zeal! I get depressed whenever I see them. These folk are supposed to be the 'masters of the nation,' and yet they're so benighted! 'Enlighten the people'—yes, if there's one watchword we need, it's 'enlighten the people.'"
>
> "'Enlighten the people,' indeed! Who's going to 'enlighten the people' for you?" laughed Hadai in rebuke. "Do you know what the only terrifying prospect I've heard of is? The dawning of the day when the people no longer believe in the Bodhisattva! Hasn't anyone ever told you that religion takes up the slack in areas that the law can't handle? Things have to be this way in order for the social order and whatnot to be maintained. If the day ever

comes when the people no longer believe in the Bodhisattva, would they still have the patience to toil bitterly at farming for you? Under such circumstances, would you, for instance, be able to go on living the plush life of a wingèd Immortal in a fine place like this?"

Laorui didn't manage to down a single sip of tea before angrily snapping, "So *I* live the plush life of a wingèd Immortal? How about *you*, pal?!"[83]

The narrator and his guide friend do not indulge in exchanges of this sort of half-jocular personal barbs, but as a duo they similarly represent a dichotomy of vision: naïve vs. cynical, astonished vs. complacently jaded, and inclined to melioristic idealism vs. delighting in the piquant incongruities of the religious festivities at Mount Tai.

The narrator finds it particularly astonishing to learn that a family of beggars has prospered at Mount Tai ever since the Qianlong Emperor (reigned 1736–1795) officially installed them there in the eighteenth century.

> I couldn't help but find it bizarre that during these economically depressed times, the family was still able to maintain a large enough income through this line of work to amass considerable land holdings. I mentioned this to my friend.
>
> "That story's not off in the slightest," he said. "They're bona fide beggars, that is, 'beggar-officials.' In a short while you'll understand just why I call them 'beggar-officials.'"[84]

The guide nudges the narrator, pointing at a stylishly dressed man in his twenties who is returning to a large house amidst immaculately manicured grounds. The narrator assumes that this young fellow is a gentryman or the manager of a business concern:

> "No, he's none other than a member of that family of beggars I just now mentioned—the one officially appointed here by the Qianlong Emperor. Take a close look at that fancy house of theirs. Does it look like the home of a ragged beggar troupe? Not quite, does it? Yet from the time of their ancestors two centuries ago all the way up to the present day, there hasn't been a single line of work that any of them have followed aside from begging. During all that time they've made a comfortable and secure living off of dupes here on pilgrimages."[85]

The sardonic guide subsequently introduces the narrator to several members of the beggar family, who in dress and demeanor seem little different from the typical family of considerable affluence. Later that night, however, he observes them at work: shabbily dressed and with soiled faces, they aggressively tug at the sleeves of passing pilgrims and plaintively beg for money. Milling about in the crowd, the narrator shrugs off one or two come-ons from these beggars before encountering a particularly stubborn one:

> Suddenly a person grabbed hold of me. According to my previous experience that evening, as long as I shrugged a bit I would be able to break loose. This time it didn't work. Caught unawares, I was wrenched away from the crowd. As I fixed my gaze on this person with a delicate complexion but a coarsely braided pigtail and clad in a tattered overcoat, I discovered that she was none other than the seventeen-year-old girl of stylish dress and well-scrubbed appearance whom I had seen that very afternoon. In my alarmed and disarrayed state, I heard Mr. Hadai roar with laughter.
>
> A man standing near a gate far in the distance was shouting, "That's no worshipper! That's one of the gentlemen from the temple up the trail!" I could tell that I'd seen that man before, too. He was that twentyish fellow whom I'd noticed walking along the road earlier that day.
>
> Before I knew what had happened, the girl awoke to her gaffe and shame-facedly gave me a rough push to one side. She then scurried off into the darkness like a startled rabbit.
>
> After this brush with danger, I wouldn't countenance any more mucking around with these crowds of worshippers, lest I blindly meet up with another calamity. I was the butt of Hadai's jests all the way back to the temple.[86]

Hadai's piquant quips and hearty laughter represent one type of response to this vulgar but basically harmless side of Chinese popular culture. At the other extreme, Laorui, if present, would have probably responded by coming forth with a melioristic plea for some kind of effort to "enlighten the people." Along the middle of the spectrum in between these two polarized reactions are the relatively moderate responses of the narrator, whose sense of restraint allows him to observe the scene with an objective keenness that accounts for Wu's recent characterization of the work as social investigation.[87]

"Sights at Mount Tai" is far more than a straightforward piece of social investigation, however. In characterization, the work deftly plays the ingénu against the sardonic guide. In plot, the piece explores the relationship between the lower-class worshippers and the disreputable "beggar-officials" who live off their gullibility, climaxing with the narrator's unnerving encounter with the beggar girl.

The passive, herd-like quality of the lower-class pilgrims to Mount Tai makes for a telling contrast with the initiative and moral fiber demonstrated by the peasant maid in "The Woman." A glimmer of hope nonetheless resides in the total lack of harsh victimization of the sort that pervades Wu Zuxiang's fiction through 1934. Even the herd-like propensity of the peasant pilgrims on the mountain could conceivably be deflected in a positive direction if channeled toward something more meaningful than the popular religious rituals described. However ignorant and supersti-tious the peasant worshippers may seem, they inspire far less fear or con-cern for the future of Chinese society than the pitiful doomed rural figures from Wu's earlier works.

### Peasant Resistance to Parasites from Above

Wu's fictional output steadily dwindled following his departure from Qinghua in 1934. He published only two new fictional pieces in 1935, one in 1936, and none at all in 1937. Fortunately, the one story he did manage to write in Nanjing during 1936 ranks among his half dozen finest. "A Certain Day" [*Mouri*] is also Wu's only important work of fiction to have been anthologized without having first appeared in a periodical.[88] More-over, the story embodies Wu's most optimistic vision of grassroots social coalescence in the countryside—a type of cohesion that needs no stimulus from an alien force, such as the Japanese invasion that forces villagers to unite in Wu's wartime novel.

A sixtyish squire in bad financial straits tries to make a scandalous scene at his peasant son-in-law's home by feigning ignorance of his daughter's death during her second childbirth. The son-in-law, Da Mao, naturally grows indignant, for his father-in-law had hardly ever bothered to concern himself with the couple's affairs in times past. Furthermore, the older man's ill-tempered and self-indulgent daughter had been a bad in-fluence on Da Mao's son, having set an example for the boy to scorn his own father as low-born. Instead of successfully intimidating Da Mao, the scheming old man is accosted by a small group of Dao Mao's neighbors, who insistently argue that Da Mao is innocent of negligence or any other wrongdoing in connection with the death of his late wife; some of the neighbors even vow that they will resort to coercion if the father-in-law persists in his underhanded accusatory tactics. The presumptuous old fel-low can only retreat in the face of this grass-roots peasant solidarity.

The solidarity among Da Mao's peasant neighbors is not at all formu-laic or monotonous in tone, even if they do so much of the talking that he says very little of substance himself. His aunt takes care to be extremely tactful and gracious in the face of the father-in-law's outrageous insinua-tions of foul play, while a peasant man only slightly younger than Da Mao, nicknamed "Splay-toes" [*Meihua jiao*], ventures to criticize the father-in-law while defending Da Mao. Most outspoken of all is Huang Xiaodou, a peasant who bluntly accuses the father-in-law of scheming to fleece Da Mao, thereby forcing the elder to back down.

As the story begins, the old interloper from the local elite is the one who first throws down the gauntlet with an overheated and rhetorical la-ment addressed to the soul of his dead daughter:

"Ill-fated one, your soul cannot be far away! What brought you to your death? Tell your dear father! The caps of high office worn by eleven of your ancestors will protect you! Their ancestral tablets enshrining lofty examination degrees will protect you! Ill-fated one, your father will stand up to denounce and avenge this insult!"[89]

Da Mao's shocked aunt is the first to reply, trying her utmost to be conciliatory: "Oh! What a thing to say!"[90] She subsequently cajoles Huang Xiaodou to leave the cottage when he abruptly accuses the father-in-law of trying to put the squeeze on Da Mao. Next, she attempts to explain the specific circumstances which led to the young woman's death:

". . . All in all, your esteemed family favored our humble peasant family from the very start, willing as you were to give us your daughter in marriage. . . . Her pregnancy had come to term by July. You yourself know how she was always a tad casual in her ways—not that there's anything wrong with that, of course. At any rate, Dragon King operas were playing at the local market town in June.[91] She went to the theater seven nights running, even though the path there was long, and the chill evening dews were heavy.

"Though a delicate person of high birth, she gorged herself with food. That's how she caught a cold and wound up with swellings all over her body. What's more, she was a little reckless in what sorts of things she ate; she was always snacking on peanuts, deep-fried fermented bean curd, and all sorts of raw foods; she couldn't do without eating some watermelon before retiring at night. When it came to sleeping, she used a bamboo bed by the draughty front door, and wouldn't take the trouble to quilt her thin bedspread with heavy cotton wadding. As the time for childbirth drew near, her hands and feet were so swollen that they glistened, and her face was as puffed out as a big red festival lantern. We asked Mr. Jubao from the oil-press shop to have a look at her, but she refused to take any of the medicine he offered."[92]

The aunt takes care to reiterate her fulsome respect for the father-in-law's social status as she explains how his daughter had dug her own grave through careless and irresponsible neglect of her health. Domineering and gluttonous like another important late-1930s fictional character who dies in childbirth, Huniu of Lao She's *Luotuo Xiangzi* [Camel Xiangzi], the ill-tempered wife of Da Mao has none of the redeeming warmth and vitality of Huniu.[93]

Throughout the gentle remonstrance by Da Mao's diplomatic aunt, she refrains from criticizing the abrasive old squire. However, the young male peasant friends of Da Mao do not care to show such restraint. The young peasant man nicknamed "Splay-toes" categorizes the father along with his daughter as persons inclined to harsh conduct:

"Just how many heads does Da Mao have on his shoulders? The very idea of him plotting to kill your daughter! How could you say such a thing? What sort of a person was your daughter, anyway? Everybody from around here knows how Da Mao always had to bend his head to her will—who'd dream of getting angry at her in public? Even someone as far along in her years as Da Mao's aunt had to play up to that half-blind deformed girl of yours! . . . And did Da Mao ever get to cut the figure of a real husband at her side? She serenaded him, all right—'You no-good headless ghost!' or 'You foreign-devil cannon fodder!' As soon as trouble began to brew between them, she'd grab him by the hair for all she was worth, yelling: 'You grubber in the dirt, go on disobeying your superiors and your family will wind up like ants on a hot stove–headed straight for the chain gang!'"[94]

Another young peasant man, Huang Xiaodou, is even more outspoken than "Splay-toes":

Xiaodou strode up to Da Mao, restraining him with a tug on his shirt. His broad mouth was twisted in a grimace as he spoke with anger. "He's come here to cheat you! His story doesn't hold water."

"Just who are *you*, anyway?!" The father-in-law craned his neck in a display of imposing grandeur, but the muted nasal quality of his voice smacked of feebleness. In reality, he was sorely fatigued.

"My name's Huang Xiaodou. See if you don't recognize me," he said, pointing at the bridge of his own nose. "Last year you asked me to buy your lottery ticket—don't you remember? What have you got up your sleeve for me now? I've got a notion to cheat *you* for a change!"[95]

The confrontation with the father-in-law concludes with victory for the peasants, among whom Huang Xiaodou stands out as the most defiant, even going so far as to shout threats at the retreating old bully. This victory for grassroots social cohesion is foreshadowed by Da Mao's effective disciplining of his disobedient son early in the story. The young boy had picked up his mother's habit of scorning Da Mao as low-born, and has the temerity to reply with an obscenity to his father's request to stop tearing up their sacrificial paraphernalia.[96] When Da Mao drags his son into his cottage for a spanking, the reactions of his fellow peasants again diverge along generational lines. Da Mao's aunt presses her nephew to be gentle, reminding him of the boy's tender years and recent maternal bereavement. "Splay-toes" counters that Da Mao must assert his paternal authority in order to break the hold of the late mother's despicable anti-peasant prejudices over the child. As it turns out, the young boy throws no more tantrums over the rest of the story, and behaves obediently and unobtrusively during the final troublesome scene that his interloping grandfather stirs up. In effect, the harmful influence of corrupt elements from the local elite is first purged from Da Mao's son before it is finally driven off in the person of the father-in-law.

Since the overall plot structure consists of the victorious and thus comic outcome of the two struggles between grass-roots virtue and elite corruption, it is not surprising that the setting also suggests the triumph of cohesion among the masses. High in the crisp autumn skies, "fish scales" of cirrus clouds appear as an envelope at the opening and closing scenes.[97] Somewhat scattered at first, the clouds finally assemble in a manner that strongly suggests the cohesion of what they overhang: "The clouds, as white as fish scales, had begun to gather in the sky, where, suffused with a diaphanous and crystalline glow, they shone on field and cottage with unusual clarity and charm."[98] Furthermore, the vegetation in the story is so lush and fruitful that Da Mao is extremely busy with harvesting clumps of an oilseed fruit from a tree called the *wujiu*.[99] In contrast, foregrounded vegetation in Wu's gloomier fiction up to 1934 tends either to droop ("Soaring Hawks and Plunging Fish," "Two Young Sparrows," and "The Flowering Gardenia") or else to burst aflame ("The Fan Family Hamlet"). Finally, the story concludes with a particularly striking image of what Cheng Peikai calls "the new order that had already arisen in the rural villages," the triumphant crowing of a rooster at dusk:[100] "A rooster stood atop a dunghill, and while flapping its wings began to raise its self-assured voice to a high-pitched crow."[101]

Cheng's "new order" of communality and mutual aid among peasants actually had its roots in traditional rural society, for as C. K. Yang points out, poor and middle peasants often had to pool their resources in labor and draught animals to exploit farmland efficiently during the peak seasons of planting and harvesting.[102] James C. Scott also argues that the traditional rural social order involved an "inverse relationship of reliability and resources"; that is, the more wealthy an individual or governmental body was, the less accessible it tended to be to the individual destitute peasant, who depended most on help from his fellow common folk that were, in material if not moral terms, the least equipped to provide help.[103] In "A Certain Day," moral support is indeed of great importance to Da Mao, whose financial position as a middle peasant appears quite sound. During peak seasons, Da Mao has more work to do on his farm than he can handle alone, and thus he temporarily hires Huang Xiaodou and other villagers who must make up for their paucity of land by working stints as hired hands. Since Da Mao treats them fairly and considerately, they fulfill their moral obligation to stand up for him when his in-law from the local elite makes an intrusion of ill will. Therefore, the story points to the existence of a self-generating and informal system of mutual aid in the village, but there is no reason to characterize this system as "new" rather than traditional. What truly periodizes "A Certain Day" is neither grassroots solidarity nor the instance of a rural squire "reduced" to marrying his defective offspring into the peasantry, a type of incident that is also described in a famous pre-Tang prose collection.[104] Instead, the story manifests a revulsion for a modern local elite that is a mere husk of the more socially responsible gentry under the *ancien régime*. As Da Mao's aunt describes the father-in-law, "He's the descendant of a provincial-level degree holder [*juren*]; the bean curd has fallen to the ground, but the curd frame is still intact."[105]

"A Certain Day" was Wu's final work of village-based fiction in the 1930s. In a way, it is the culmination of his vision of grassroots coalescence in the countryside. The strength of grassroots moral fiber may have triumphed over the lassitude and indecision of the upperclass elite in "1800 Bushels" and "The Woman," but the characters of humble origin in these works are still dependent on grain or wages distributed by that same local elite. In "A Certain Day," the characters of humble origin support themselves independently from the local elite, a representative of whom attempts to parasitize his social "inferiors." The outside threat causes the peasants to draw together and force the invading parasite out of their territory, thereby maintaining the prosperity and security of their village. While piquant touches appear only in the ill-conceived and scandalous bluff tactics of the slippery father-in-law, the author's meliorist vision surfaces in the impressive show of village solidarity via the decisive defusement of a threat from the corrupt figure of the local elite.

Without a doubt, Wu's last work before the War portrays the rural masses in a more coalescent state than ever before in his career. This victorious coalescence expressed through Wu's imaginative vision served partly as a psychological compensation for the frustrating turn of events in Wu's personal life beginning in the mid-1930s. Once the rumblings of war with Japan were to break out into the storm of all-out invasion in 1937, the resulting dislocations in Wu's life, along with his sense of duty to highlight the strengths of the Chinese masses during a time of national crisis, would accentuate the trend towards optimistic portrayals of grassroots solidarity. The thoroughgoing pessimism of Wu's meliorist vision during the early 1930s had withered by the middle of the decade, and would be totally eclipsed by a spirit of somewhat forced optimism during the War years.

# 5

## Wartime Visions of
## Infectious Nationalism, 1937–1943

*Shan hong*, Wu's novel of 1943, eventually insured that the final half-decade of his writing career would stand out as one of his most productive periods. Yet during the late 1930s, it appeared for a while as if he had already abandoned fiction. Between "A Certain Day" (1936) and the first journal installments of Wu's wartime novel (1941), he published but a single short story, "The Requisitioned Boat" [*Chai chuan*] (1938).[1]

During this long hiatus in his imaginative life, Wu conversely stepped up his involvement in socio-political commentary and debate. A polemical essay he wrote for the *Xinhua ribao* in the spring of 1938 seems to have set the tone for his works of wartime fiction. In "A Few Personal Views on the National United Front of Literary Circles, " Wu's former hesitancy to align himself closely with political programs or manifestos disappears amidst the flames of patriotic fervor.[2] The sense of nationwide alarm over the massive Japanese invasion of the previous summer tended to cause even the most phlegmatic of writers to think increasingly in terms of categorical imperatives. Thus, in a brave new tone of voice, Wu stridently proclaims that Chinese writers must abandon their aim to achieve artistic excellence; otherwise, it would be impossible to bridge the vast gulf between writers and the reading public at large. In order to meet the threat to the very survival of the nation, responsible "literary workers" would have to write pieces that "cater to the taste of the masses" and "encourage our race's spirit of resistance to aggression."[3] For Wu Zuxiang and most other meliorist writers of the war period, popularization and increasingly hortatory discourse would henceforth take precedence over artistic excellence and unflinching revelations of the dark side of the Chinese cultural inheritance.

Wu's world of the imagination grew strikingly militarized after 1937. Prior to the Japanese invasion, soldiers never functioned as prominent characters in Wu's fiction, and on the few occasions in which they did make an appearance, such as in "Fan Hamlet," they came across as a ragtag, feckless lot. Yet following the invasion, military figures played a dominant and often exemplary role in each of Wu's works, while women receded from the center-stage position they had occupied in so many of Wu's earlier stories.[4] Apparently, the war effort required women to serve as colorless and practically anonymous appendages to men and the masculine cause of national resistance. Without a doubt, Wu's position within General Feng's entourage during the late 1930s encouraged the writer to highlight the impact of militarization on Chinese society, while de-emphasizing economic and familial issues unrelated to war.

### Journey Westward to Exile in the Upper Yangzi

By the late 1930s, Wu Zuxiang's elderly mother was too frail to undergo a long voyage into exile, and it appeared highly unlikely that the invading Japanese army would bother to lay siege to remote hill villages like Maolin. Therefore, Wu made arrangements to leave his young son Baizi in Maolin to keep his mother company, and towards the end of 1937 departed for Wuhan, the Middle Yangzi riverport which was to be the Chinese provisional capital from then until the following autumn.[5] Not until May 1939 would Wu finally manage to settle down in a place that afforded some semblance of long-term stability: Chongqing, the Upper Yangzi riverport which would serve as the provisional capital throughout the rest of the War. Only after settling down in Chongqing did Wu send for Shuyuan and the remaining children (sans Baizi) to come and join him in exile.

None of Wu's wartime fiction is actually set in his places of exile, whether it be Wuhan in 1937–1938 or Chongqing in 1939–1945. Just as the fiction he wrote while a student in Beijing was hardly ever set in Beijing itself, his wartime fiction had its genesis in his memories of distant places. The first of these was Anqing, a large Yangzi riverport and provincial capital of Anhui (until 1949). As Japanese military units drove further westward along the Yangzi Valley during the autumn of 1937, Wu had to stay ahead of them as he made his way to the temporary capital at Wuhan. The combination of crowds of desperate refugees and a shortage of river steamers along the Yangzi resulted in the unavailability of through tickets to Wuhan. Wu could only manage to make the trip by a series of short hops, one of which landed him at Anqing. He still had several hundred kilometers to go before reaching Wuhan. Though he would finally reach that Middle Yangzi metropolis, his trip was distressingly time-consuming and expensive, and during parts of the journey he was appalled by the grossly irresponsible conduct of certain Nationalist military officers he encountered. By the spring of 1938, Wu had published "The Requisitioned Boat," a work of semi-autobiographical fiction articulating his troubled impressions from that journey westward.

As the story opens, the extreme dearth of passenger-carrying river-boats forces the narrator of the story to make an informal arrangement with the skipper of a small craft requisitioned by the army to carry wounded soldiers to a hospital in Wuhan. The skipper promises the narrator that the voyage from Anqing to Wuhan will take no more than a couple of days, and demands to be paid the inflated passenger fare in advance. Only after the narrator pays does he discover that the boat has been making wretchedly slow time on account of the requisitioning officer's insistence on docking at every sizable riverport on his way west. At each port the officer puts the squeeze on local officials, demanding bribes in return for not shifting the financial responsibility of treating his boatload of wounded soldiers on those same officials. With the proceeds, he leisurely tours the taverns, gambling dens, and bawdy houses in every major port, never spending a cent on medicine or fresh bandages for the wounded soldiers; in fact, his disreputable escort in merry-making is none other than the attractive young head nurse in charge of caring for the wounded soldiers. The flustered narrator immediately demands a refund from first the skipper and subsequently the army officer, but the two of them merely bicker between themselves before abruptly putting the narrator back ashore with only half his original fare. He thus winds up in the same situation as he had been at the story's outset, only with less time, money, and respect for the military authorities than before.

A countervailing motif to the prominent element of exposé in the story is the laudatory portrayal of the wounded soldiers on board. They seem extremely patient and uncomplaining for having gone over ten days without a change of bandaging for their wounds. Low in terms of official status, the wounded soldiers so stoic in their patience are elevated in the story's moral universe: "The soldiers were jammed into the narrow and squat boat cabin. Some of them were playing the harmonica; some were humming battle tunes; some were sleeping soundly; others were lost in sober thought; still others were moaning."[6]

More vocal than the quietly suffering soldiers are the two squad leaders of low official rank dispatched to accompany the wounded. Both of them are dully staring at the riverbank in exasperation, and start to complain about the boat's snail-like progress when the skipper approaches within earshot. The skipper replies that his boat will proceed upstream from Anqing as soon as the commanding officer and head nurse return from onshore. The squad leaders parry with indignant protests:

"For every day we cruise, we dock for three. It's already been two days since we tied up here at Anqing. How come they're dilly-dallying onshore? Blast it! The soldiers haven't had fresh bandages for over ten days!"

"If those blackguards don't come back tonight, we'll just set off with the boat on our own!" thundered the other squad leader.[7]

The commanding officer and head nurse finally return that night laden with snack foods and phonograph records of snappy dance tunes. Their serene indifference to the plight of the wounded under their charge contrasts vividly with the same officer's blusteringly nitpicking enforcement of regulations forbidding the collection of passenger fares on requisitioned boats. Yet the central tension in the story is between the corrupt and flippant duo of officer and nurse, on the one hand, and the worthy and serious-minded folk of lower social status, on the other. Aside from the patient wounded soldiers and dutiful squad leaders, formations of drilling footsoldiers onshore and bands of raggedly clad children heartily imitating them nearby inspire the narrator with the thought that the salt of the earth make up the most worthy bloc in the war effort:

> Onshore, troops marched by, unit after unit, singing heroic martial airs. A large number of shabbily clad children had gathered on a rubbish heap to the side of a thatched-roof house. Their hands gripping a splint of bamboo or a club of wood, the children pantomimed going through a military drill, raising their childish voices in shrill shouts of "Down with Japanese imperialism!" and "Long live the Chinese people!" As these various sounds blended together, I felt as if a bubbling stream of boiling water were gushing over my anguished heart.[8]

The patriotic sentiments of the common footsoldiers and ragged children onshore increase the narrator's anguish by heightening the contrast between the masses' dedication to defending China and the official elite's apparent subversion of the war effort. Lofty rank ideally corresponds with a person's heightened dedication to the commonweal, but the narrator despondently discovers that the situation in his midst is precisely the opposite. As in much of Wu's fiction, the elite are portrayed as morally unfit to govern their upright subjects, in this case the rank-and-file soldiers and shabby children. In effect, a literary inversion of the socio-military hierarchy has taken place.

Although the corrupt military officer and nurse who represent the elite both seem beyond redemption, hope for the future is conveyed through populist references to the untarnished virtue of the ragged children and all the enlisted men, whether on board or ashore. It is true that critics like Lin Huanping have commended the story for its daring exposé of the seamy side of a war effort which most Chinese writers had been falsifying through boastful glorification.[9] Yet Wu's exposé of unmitigated corruption at the top is balanced by a corresponding portrayal of unswerving dedication among the masses. None of the wounded infantrymen expresses the slightest bit of envy of the smugly self-indulgent officer, or suggests any inclination to pull off the same sort of shenanigans if he were in the officer's shoes. Their brethren of equally humble status marching onshore exude an infectious high-spiritedness that appeals to the local lower-class children. Therefore, the virtue present among the marchers seems to be more influential than vice, which is localized merely among the officer and the head nurse.

While the benevolent grassroots characters are definitely ill-served by their profligate leaders, they nonetheless appear to be untainted by these higher-ups. Only a society with a considerable amount of coalescence among the masses and corresponding meliorist potential could exhibit this sort of resistance to corruption trickling down from the top. From this perspective, the prominent note of exposé in "The Requisitioned Boat" does in no way drown out the author's overarching spirit of optimism about widespread grassroots dedication to the war effort.

### Instruction Through Example: From Rogue to Martyr

The final short story of Wu's career appeared four years after "The Requisitioned Boat," and yet continued to probe the problem of grassroots resistance to corrupting influences from the official elite. Around the time that "Tie menzi" [Stuffy Ironsides] was published in the autumn of 1942, Wu was making the transition from an almost total economic reliance on Feng Yuxiang to a new position as a lecturer in literature at Central University [*Zhongyang daxue*] in Chongqing.[10]

"Stuffy Ironsides" depicts the turning over of a new leaf by an AWOL soldier who had long preyed on the common people in a most merciless manner. The vehicle for his moral regeneration is the switch in his martial models to emulate: at the outset, rapacious officers in the regional warlord army; later on, upright and dedicated officers and civilians connected to Central Staff Headquarters.

As the story opens, the three editors of a War of Resistance propaganda newspaper in Shandong province are retreating via freight train from the 1937 invasion of the Japanese military. The narrator, who is one of the three, grows disillusioned when he discovers that the newspaper which he has taken great pains to edit has been distributed to the target army readership in a most slipshod manner: piles of the neatly bundled newspapers have been perfunctorily dumped in a railway distribution depot, where they have been gathering dust instead of spreading news to soldiers at the front line. The story's main focus, however, is an AWOL enlisted man whom military staff officers interrogate in the editors' *tie menzi*, a windowless freight car ("stuffy ironsides"). The enlisted man at first feigns a rustic-mannered innocence of the charges against him of robbery, rape, and murder. Yet a sort of salt-of-the-earth guilelessness eventually brings about his full admission of guilt when the staff officer questions him about the colorful lingerie and jewelry found on his person. The shocked editors blame society and the corrupt, womanizing regional military leadership for his crimes, and soon persuade the staff officers to unfetter the soldier and allow him to chat with them. Soon thereafter, the soldier rewards their forgiveness and trust during an air raid by daring to sacrifice his life while disengaging the burning caboose from the rest of the ammunition-laden train. Yet accompanying the reader's admiration for his selfless bravery are the conflicting emotions generated by the unsettling, darkly humorous image of a stout soldier wearing dainty lingerie under his partially unbuttoned and newly bloodstained uniform. Even in the solemn and elegiac concluding paragraph, where the author finally discloses this patriotic lumpenproletarian's eleventh-hour decision to reenlist in the army, a disturbing piece of news surfaces: the deceased also turns out to be under investigation for two pre-enlistment murders back in his hometown of Xuzhou.

"Stuffy Ironsides" differs from most of Wu's other fiction in the way its finale recapitulates the mood present at the story's outset. In general, Wu's earlier stories illustrating social decline begin on a note of hope and conclude with despair, while his post-1934 fiction of social regeneration tends to trace the progress from despair to hope. This story, however, initially establishes a mood of buoyant optimism about the war effort and the newspaper, then plunges into despair over the AWOL soldier's heinous crimes and the newspaper distribution fiasco, and rises again in the conclusion with the soldier's heroic sacrifice of himself for the benefit of the group. The overall emotional structure of the story shapes up as A-B-A, or sonata form; the initial mood of the editors' valorous dedication to the war effort is recapitulated by the concluding heroic self-sacrifice of the AWOL soldier who had absorbed their resolute nationalistic spirit.[11]

Since Wu Zuxiang's first-person narrators generally avoid giving full rein to emotional display, the reader may arrive at a keener perception of the story's changes in mood from characters more apt to express their feelings with directness. Such a character may be found in the editors' teenage military orderly, Liu Dakai. He musters a truly exemplary dedication to helping the three editors put together their propagandist newspaper in Ji'nan, Shandong during the fall of 1937. The editorial trio seem indefatigable enough, working from early morning till late at night, but Liu Dakai toils so unceasingly that his bedroll sometimes remains untouched for days on end. Here is how the narrator introduces the young orderly:

> I prefer not to use terms like "faithful" or "diligent" as an assessment of
> his personality and character, for to do so would be very hollow and inadequate. As far as what I had observed and perceived of Liu Dakai ever since

he had been assigned to us, his consciousness seemed to have no room for anyone in this world except the three of us, not even room for his own existence. . . .

He was an enthusiast to a degree rarely encountered. If he heard anyone make some kind of remark about our side's weakness or the superiority of the enemy forces, Liu would invariably grow furious: "What do *you* know about it? Our three teachers [i.e., editors] have never talked like that! If you're so smart, why hasn't anyone asked *you* to run our newspaper? How much money have the Japanese devils given you, anyway?!"[12]

A touch of piquancy is present in the vehemently single-minded dedication of Liu Dakai, but the zeal he exudes is still matched in kind, if not in degree, by the other main characters at the story's beginning. However, disillusion begins to creep in with the orders for retreat, which include a terse stipulation to dissolve the newspaper rather than relocate it. This panicked situation occurs precisely at the time when the editors have begun planning to expand their entire journalistic operation. One of the editors consoles his crestfallen colleagues with the thought that the paper's positive effect on army morale will outlive the paper itself by far. This reasonable justification for their exertions proves to be hollow, nonetheless, when towards the middle of the story the editors discover piled-up bundles of their undelivered newspapers in the Ji'nan railway depot.

"Look at these! Just look at them!" Carrying several bundles in his arms, Liu Dakai broken-heartedly complained in between sobs, quite like a child returning to his family elders after having been mistreated by strangers. . . .

"Hmmph! That's just grand!" I exclaimed with a sneer. "The original shipping seals on them haven't even been touched!"[13]

Compounding the disillusion of the main characters during the middle section is the uncovering of the AWOL soldier's violent crimes: "'So this is what's been going on at the front! What else could General Staff Headquarters do but retreat in the face of it all?' Questions like this must have been running through the mind of each and every one of us."[14]

The recapitulation of the original mood of optimism and commitment occurs in the wake of the Japanese bombing attack on the train at the story's finale. Liu Dakai dashes over to the officers gathered by the part of the train detached from the burning caboose. Still unaware of the AWOL soldier's whereabouts, not to mention the latter's self-sacrificial act of detaching the caboose, Liu Dakai indignantly sputters that the soldier had disobediently fled from his overseers in the train during the confusion of the bombing run. "When our account of the situation made him realize with what heroism the deceased had comported himself, . . . Liu Dakai was struck dumb for a moment. Suddenly, dropping to his knees to embrace the corpse, he broke into sobs."[15]

The fruit of the editors' struggle to improve army morale finally materializes with this heroic martyrdom of a criminal rehabilitated more as a result of their deeds than their words. Their written words in the newspapers were muffled by shoddy distribution, and even their ordinary conversations about recent vicissitudes on the Chinese side seemed opaque to the comprehension of the rustic AWOL soldier. For example, the soldier makes no comments on the editor Lao Yi's lecture about the need to unite against Japan, and replies absent-mindedly to Lao Yi's simple question as to whether or not the soldier had ever read the shortlived newspaper: "The soldier nodded in surprise, after which he shook his head and said, 'No, officer, we've never read that newspaper.'"[16] What really impresses the soldier is how the officers and editors trustingly unshackle him and refrain from excluding him from their midst as a deviant. Silent in his admiration for the serious and concerned demeanor with which they discuss the newspaper, he proves his loyalty to them by never attempting to flee captivity, instead performing helpful tasks such as carrying bundles of newspapers from the Ji'nan depot to the freight car.

The editors and Central staff officers in the "stuffy ironsides" car literally infect the AWOL soldier with a sense of mission. They do not achieve this through organizational protocol, which they realize would call for the soldier's summary execution, given the magnitude of his depredations among local civilians. Instead, they follow the ancient precept of *yi shen zuo ze*, "making oneself a model for emulation," an idea whose power may be discerned in the debased form it has often taken among contemporary Communist Party leaders: in an attempt to instill the masses with respect for manual labor and civic tidiness, they have often disingenuously brandished a broom or shovel in front of media photographers.[17] Inspiration through personal example looms all the more important when organizational routine proves its ultimate unreliability, as the editors realize when they discover dusty piles of their undelivered newspapers; in the end, the editors have influenced army morale little more than the extent to which they have set a shining personal example to a lone but grateful AWOL soldier.

Volunteering to help carry bundles of propaganda newspapers serves as a sort of transition between the soldier's criminal past and his heroic final endeavor. Without a doubt, the reader may justifiably feel skeptical about such a sudden about-face in the soldier, who is literally transformed overnight from an unconscionable, rampaging predator to a selfless hero unafraid of death. However, Chinese national crises such as the War of Resistance and the May Fourth student protests of 1919 did at times inspire sympathy from the lumpenproletariat and social outcasts in general. Chow Tse-tsung has argued that during the Shanghai strikes in support of the 1919 Beijing student protests, "a sense of unity prevailed so deeply among all social forces that even the hobos, robbers, and underworld gangs and societies, such as members of the Qinghong gang [Green-Red Gang], expressed their loyalty to the movement, and helped maintain peace and order. . . . The movement had such a thorough influence on the grass roots of society," adds Chow, "that even the beggars, thieves, prostitutes, and singsong girls went on strike."[18] Similarly, representatives from all walks of life participated in the Beijing pro-democracy demonstrations of Spring 1989; even a local ring of pickpockets proclaimed in May 1989 that they were renouncing their anti-social ways, in keeping with the unusually public-spirited atmosphere of those times.[19] The AWOL soldier's metamorphosis from predatory rogue to patriotic martyr, though quite out of the ordinary, is thus not as inconceivable as it might appear at first glance.

The critic Zhao Yuan includes the AWOL soldier within the group of sympathetic characters from Wu's corpus whose transgressions involve not merely personal wrongdoing, but a strong dimension of societal injustice as well.[20] One of the Central Staff officers describes a notorious company commander in the regional warlord army whose tent housed four concubines, "three of the up-to-date variety, and one with bound feet in the classical mold." The narrator thereupon infers how rife the practice must be: "If a measly company commander could pull off something like that, there's hardly any need to mention what an officer a bit higher in rank would be capable of arranging."[21] One of the editors concludes that such exploitative regional officers were an important component of the AWOL soldier's social environment, within which they set an example of exploiting the peasantry to satisfy their instinctual needs.

The editors and Central Staff officers measure the AWOL soldier with more than a moral yardstick, however. They cannot help but titter at the grotesquely amusing sight of the stout soldier's collection of jewelry and brightly colored feminine undergarments—some of which he is wearing underneath his uniform in order to achieve an abnormal type of gratification, according to a recent interview with the author.[22] This particular image of the soldier is grotesque, at least in terms of Philip Thomson's definition of that concept as the simultaneity of the conflicting responses of attraction and repulsion, the comic and the horrible.[23] To be sure, there is something irrepressibly ludicrous about a stout soldier wearing women's underwear, particularly when appearing in juxtaposition to his coarse army uniform unbuttoned to facilitate frisking. At the same time, the onlookers are aware of the horrible fact that many of the undergarments were stolen from ill-fated rural women whom he raped and possibly murdered as well. This simultaneous attraction and repulsion accounts for the way in which the personnel present at his frisking alternately burst out in "raucous laughter" and "angry rebukes" at the soldier's clumsy offer to

give everyone there a share of his booty in return for his release.[24] The onlookers derive some emotional well-being from this grotesque spectacle,
partly from sheer catharsis, and partly from the function of the grotesque
"to bring the horrifying and disgusting aspects of existence to the surface,
there to be rendered less harmful by the introduction of a comic perspective. "[25]

Even the heroic finale of the story is slightly tinged with the grotesque,
not in the uniformly solemn reactions of the onlookers, but rather in the
narrator's significantly obtrusive reminder that portions of brightly colored undergarments remain visible underneath the rumpled, shrapnel-
torn, and bloodstained uniform of the now motionless AWOL soldier. The
concluding aside that the dead soldier has been implicated in two murders in his hometown of Xuzhou underlines the fact that he had wantonly
spilled the blood of many innocents before finally shedding his own in a
righteous cause. This dénouement leaves the reader feeling both attracted
and repulsed by the soldier, even during the immediate afterglow of his
self-sacrifice. Wu himself was fascinated by this kind of ambivalence, for
in a diary entry dated 8 December 1942, he wrote that only characters em-
bodying both vice and virtue interested him; a monopoly on either one or
the other would make a character too implausible and formulized for serious aesthetic appreciation.[26]

Wu's heavy personal involvement in the historical background of the
story makes it undoubtedly semi-autobiographical. The unsentimental
and occasionally sardonic narrator is modeled on Wu himself, and his two
editorial colleagues, Lao Yi and Lao Zhu, represent Lai Yali and Yang
Bojun. Wu, Lai, and Yang were appointed by Feng Yuxiang in the fall of
1937 to operate the newspaper *Kangri zao bao* [The Resist-Japan Morning
Post] in Ji'nan. Instead of being distributed in a normal and efficient fashion, their newspapers were somehow held up in storage at the Ji'nan railway depot. Liu Dequan, the dedicated orderly on whom Liu Dakai is
modeled, had become particularly outraged upon the discovery of the
newspaper delivery fiasco.[27] Finally, while the heroic about-face of the
AWOL soldier is more a product of the imagination than of history, Wu
has reported firsthand observation of Chinese soldiers at that time who
had brazenly seized booty exactly of the sort carried and worn by the
AWOL soldier.[28] Each of these personal experiences and observations
played a significant role in the genesis of "Stuffy Ironsides."

"Stuffy Ironsides" draws heavily on a pair of important ideas from the
modern Chinese literary scene which often stood in opposition to one another: the optimistic view of the extensive malleability of the human personality, and the pastoral vision of provincial man's basic benevolence. On
the one hand, the rapid transformation of the soldier from rapacious
rogue to heroic martyr implies an optimistic belief in the supreme mallea-

bility of human character. As Cheng Peikai has mentioned, one of the fore-runners of "Stuffy Ironsides" which adopted this optimistic stance toward human perfectability was Yao Xueyin's "Cha ban che maijie" [Off By a Cartload of Wheatstraw].[29] It is the story of a selfish and irresponsible simpleton who eventually turns over a new leaf by martyring himself during a raid he himself had organized against the Japanese occupation forces. On the other hand, both Wu Zuxiang and Yao Xueyin seem to be following the pastoral approach of Shen Congwen by pausing to take delight in the rusticity they portray as a sort of benign ignorance. The two protagonists in their formative benightedness are described with considerable piquancy, and even come across as laughingstocks among the relatively urbane shortly before undergoing the change of heart which leads to their martyrdom on the nation's behalf. In short, both protagonists function partly as backward but unpretentious pastoral figures, and partly as heroic personages willing to risk all to benefit their compatriots. Perhaps in no other work by Wu Zuxiang do the countervailing tendencies of meliorism and piquancy appear in such sharp relief.

A final feature of "Stuffy Ironsides" that compares favorably with Wu's previous stories is the metaphorical richness of its very title. Yuan Liangjun argues that the stuffy freight car is a pun which refers not only to part of the concrete story setting, but also to "the political atmosphere at that time" and its "stifling effect on the Chinese people's enthusiasm for the War of Resistance."[30] Though perceptive of the title's figurative dimension, Yuan's interpretation neglects significant factors outside the political arena. A key passage in "Stuffy Ironsides" connects the freight-car image of a restive but stifling insularity to the problem of social backwardness in the Chinese rural interior. The regional army officers were almost totally independent of the central government and its "political atmosphere," and thus were free to intimidate villagers into complying with their unjust demands for material goods and concubines:

> The Central Staff officer remarked that this kind of exploitation of the common folk was a tradition dating back a good many years, and was not actually a phenomenon that had just arisen since the outbreak of the War of Resistance. The common folk had long been too trusting; whenever greeting a small-time powerholder with the hail of "our upright master," it had been as if the folk were shut tight inside their own "stuffy ironsides," without a ray of light and hardly a breath of fresh air for the taking.[31]

The plight of rural society's vulnerability to predators like the regional army officers involves far more than the "political atmosphere" among either the Nationalist or Communist ruling elites, since at that period of history neither side had a truly overriding political influence over the bulk of the nation's interior. Instead, the shortage of socio-political coherence throughout most of rural China allowed a variety of predators to exploit those commoners who were too cowed or apathetic to fight back through vigilante secret societies or other means. To be sure, the defeatist resignation with which a large portion responded to elite exploitation was not merely an imaginative flight of writers like Lu Xun, who also portrayed China as lethargically suffocating within the "iron house" of its anachronistic and often inhumane cultural traditions.[32] Even though several ecologically harsh regions in China were prone to grassroots rebellion, many other regions experienced very little in the way of uprisings even during periods of great social stress; as previously noted, there is no record of any peasant rebellion in Wu Zuxiang's own village of Maolin.[33] Most Western anthropological literature on peasant societies indeed backs up Marx's view that peasants are usually a conservative force in social development, exhibiting considerable deference in dealings with authority;[34] peasant rebellions have made such a heavy worldwide impact on modern revolutionary politics partly due to historical factors unique to the modern world, such as the unprecedented rapidity of socio-economic change, plus far-flung military adventures affecting heretofore isolated rural areas. The relative ease with which the regional military strongmen exert their heavy-handed control over timid countrymen in "Stuffy Ironsides" indicates that meliorist initiatives aimed at overhauling an authoritarian rural social order face strong obstacles at the local level. It would seem necessary to receive strong guidance and support at the national level if rural reformers were to succeed in leading their more timid brethren to pierce the iron walls of a suffocatingly repressive social order.

### A Rising Torrent of National Sentiment
### Among the Peasantry

Each of Wu's trio of works from the last five years of his writing career portrays the intensification of nationalistic attitudes at the grassroots level of Chinese society. Among educated urban Chinese, nationalism had already made major inroads on the traditional mindset of "culturalism" (to borrow Joseph Levenson's term) by the early part of this century.[35] Yet as Chalmers Johnson has shown, nationalism made comparatively little headway among the rural masses in the interior until the War of Resistance provided a common enemy against which to organize.[36] In "Stuffy Ironsides," the AWOL soldier abruptly awakens to the need for concerted national resistance to the invader. In contrast, Wu's novel *Shan hong* [Mountain Torrent] portrays the incremental process of the peasants' gradual shift from clannish insularity to a nationalist fervor for large-scale organization against the invaders.[37]

*Mountain Torrent* first appeared in two journal installments during early 1941, but was not published as a novel in its entirety until March 1943, some four months later than "Stuffy Ironsides."[38] By far Wu's largest work in scope, it bulks to five times the length of his most ambitious previous effort, "1800 Bushels."

The twentyish Anhui peasant protagonist, Zhang Sanguan, does all he can at the outbreak of the War of Resistance to avoid military conscription. This behavior dovetails very smoothly with the old peasant saw, "You don't make nails out of good iron, and you don't make a soldier out of a good man." Yet before long, Zhang is not only shocked by oral accounts of the invaders' brutality to Chinese civilians, but also favorably impressed by the Chinese army and guerilla units that he encounters: they almost never carry out the sort of depredations that have routinely led Chinese peasants to view soldiers and bandits as all but indistinguishable. Dismissing objections from his wife and mother over his porterage of army supplies and military documents for the Resistance forces, Zhang eventually takes up the post of chief liaison for guerilla activities in his village. Yet his change of attitude does not occur with the suddenness and finality of the AWOL soldier's in "Stuffy Ironsides," for even toward the end of the novel he occasionally draws back from involvement in military affairs when he realizes how these activities may put both him and his family in danger. Zhang's will to resist the Japanese invaders seems stronger than ever at the novel's conclusion, but he and most of the other characters in the novel never completely transcend their regional and particularistic loyalties in order to become exemplary patriots or nationalists.

Like "A Certain Day," *Mountain Torrent* focuses more on grassroots organizational networks among peasants than on problems related to economic depression or anachronistic social traditions. One of the major developments in Wu's fictional canon after 1934 is the total disappearance of severely destitute characters, and *Mountain Torrent* adheres to this pattern. Wu's village society is portrayed as having coalesced to the point where economic subsistence no longer seems to count as an issue. What Wu's villagers fear in "A Certain Day" and *Mountain Torrent* are bullying intruders, whether in the form of an intimidating relative from the local elite or maurauding soldiers.

The peasants in *Mountain Torrent* cannot initially discern whether the approaching Chinese soldiers are friends or foes. Even the protagonist of the novel, Zhang Sanguan, who since his school days has always held that China should stand firm in the face of foreign invaders, dreads being impressed into the infantry. As many able-bodied peasants have done through the ages, he flees to the hills when military recruiting officers make their rounds in the village. The shrewd Anhui peasants are almost instinctively wary of the kind of rapacious warlord armies Wu alluded to in "Stuffy Ironsides." "As far as the civilian population is concerned," William Mallory once wrote in connection with this issue, "the soldiers are not much better than the bandits. They live off the country in which they are billeted."[39] A leading authority on the Anti-Japanese War, Hsi-sheng Ch'i, has similarly vouched that such peasants typically "feared the Chinese armies just a shade less than they feared the Japanese."[40] This reaction resonates with an age-old distrust of soldiers by Chinese peasants, as can be seen from a ninth-century Tang poem by Li Shangyin, who complains of soldierly perfidity from the vantage point of his peasant persona:

> The government soldiers carry bows at their waists,
> Claiming they are on official patrol;
> But we fear, when they come to a desolate place,
> These men will shoot at the common people![41]

As the villagers in *Mountain Torrent* hide from the Chinese army nearby, one of them recently arrived from the valley relates a rumor which she picked up along the way: "Haven't you heard? They say that people are hiding in the hills, and that the army is going to head on up and nab them!"[42]

Nothing of the sort takes place. Instead, the frightened peasants soon learn that the soldiers had been conducting themselves in an orderly and civil manner all along. A lone simple-minded old man who had stayed behind in the village and served the soldiers tea, Dong Laodie, remarks that the only sore point in dealing with the soldiers was their indignant complaint about fighting on behalf of a citizenry that distrusted them.

Another factor that breaks down the peasants' knee-jerk reaction of fear of all soldiers is the sharp contrast between rumors about the defending Chinese armies on the one hand, and the invading Japanese forces on the other. The local grapevine has passed along very few tales of violence and plunder associated with Chinese guerilla armies as compared with the invading Japanese army.[43] Moreover, the villagers realize that the Chinese army from which they have hidden is retreating westward; the villagers thus might not be able to expect any government military support if the Japanese were to invade the village from the east. Before long, the villagers even begin to regret the retreat of the Chinese army. By the time that Chinese guerilla army units march from the west into the village later in the novel, Zhang Sanguan and his fellow villagers no longer hide from the troops.

The increasingly trusting and patriotic attitudes of the villagers appear in their willingness to join many of the local associations set up by the visiting guerilla officers. Associations of shoulder-pole carriers and boatmen are established to help move supplies for the guerillas.[44] Other associations aim at improving the morale of the locals by mobilizing sectors of the populace that had generally been ignored in traditional political life.

For example, the Women's Association and Children's Association described in *Mountain Torrent* resemble the groups of similar designation in Communist-occupied territory at that time as portrayed by Wang Ruowang.[45]

At any rate, Zhang Sanguan works at both talking up the war effort at home and shouldering a carrying pole to transport supplies afar. Though he cuts quite a stalwart figure in both undertakings, reversals in fortune occasionally set him to wondering whether or not his committment to the cause has exacted too heavy a price. During one long and arduous porterage, he hears Japanese warplanes approach overhead. Lunging to the ground in panic, Zhang accidentally shatters the ammunition box hanging from his bamboo pole. The furious commanding officer of the guerilla unit lashes him two strokes with a whip in punishment. By this point, Zhang's fellow volunteers from the village are afraid that they might be pressed into conscription and forced to the battlefront by the enraged officer. Zhang himself is "so anguished . . . that he began to feel homesick," a rare emotion for him amid the enlivening bustle of work for the militia.[46]

Nevertheless, these setbacks do not hamper Zhang's patriotic enthusiasm for long. By the end of the novel, he has been promoted to the top position of responsibility in the village militia.[47] Reminiscent of the Stakhanovite devotees to political organization in the old Soviet lore of socialist realism, Zhang becomes fond of shrugging off suggestions to return home in the evening for dinner. At dinnertime one evening shortly after his promotion in the militia, Zhang's nephew arrives at the militia office with a message from Zhang's elderly mother to return home and handle some family affairs.

> Without so much as glancing up, Zhang replied with a cold and gravelly voice, "I can't get involved with this family stuff. Have my older brother take care of it."
>
> "But your wife wants you to go home for dinner," added his nephew.
>
> "I'm not eating tonight. If I was, I'd have you bring my dinner over here."[48]

However steadfastly solemn Zhang Sanguan may appear at such times, he is also capable of behaving extremely foolishly during comic interludes in the novel. One of his simple-minded peasant friends argues that the village oxen could be pressed into military service by tying daggers onto their horns and then stampeding them towards the Japanese army. "A serious expression spread over Sanguan's face; he felt that this suggestion was worth pondering."[49] Nor does Zhang Sanguan scoff at the same peasant's next "strategy" of dispatching Chinese air force bombers to blind the Japanese invaders by dumping limestone dust all over their

encampments. Even by the time Zhang has gained considerable experience in the village militia, he regularly panics whenever he hears an approaching Japanese warplane; it never occurs to him that the Japanese
military has far more important targets to hit than his remote village. On
one such occasion, he dashes into his house to load his antiquated
handcrafted musket, but the plane is almost out of sight by the time he
rushes back outdoors with the gun loaded and cocked:

> Zhang was frustrated; he hated himself for appearing to have lost his cool.
> Some of the men might have thought he had dashed home in fear of the en-
> emy plane, but in reality he had hurried there to pick up his old musket.
> Though still others might have thought that he had fetched the old musket
> due to vain hopes of shooting down the enemy plane, he hadn't fetched it on
> that account, but merely because he felt he ought to have a weapon in his
> grip during such a tense situation. Regardless of whether the others thought
> he was cowardly or ignorant, the prominence that he had recently achieved
> would not brook the cramping of his lofty aspirations.
>     "If you want to shoot down an airplane with that old musket," drawled
> the ward chief, "I'm afraid you'll be out of luck."[50]

The humor in this passage is vitiated by what the distinguished critic Li
Changzhi saw as a major shortcoming of *Mountain Torrent*: an intense vein
of self-consciousness highly unlikely for a poorly educated peasant protagonist.[51] While it is plausible that an unusually introspective peasant
might silently guess at possible reasons for the disapproval he encounters,
it is farfetched indeed that in his harried state of mind he could come up
with the neat arrangement of two alternate interpretations, each accompanied by a rebuttal. The self-absorbed musings of Zhang Sanguan are probably more elaborate than those of any other character in Wu's fiction, intellectuals no less than peasants and country squires.

Wu's increasing estrangement from rural ways accounts for a large
measure of his novel's common inability to convey the more direct and
less convoluted patterns of genuine peasant thinking. By the time he
wrote *Mountain Torrent* in 1941, he had already been cut off from his rural
homeland for seven years running, as compared with only two years in
the case of his next to last rural work, "A Certain Day. " A desultory correspondence with a relative back in Maolin kept him informed on news in
the locale, but hardly sufficed to refresh his faded recollections of patterns
of peasant thinking. The better part of decade had passed since Wu had
last enjoyed an extended visit with the distaff relatives on whom he based
many of the novel's characters.[52]

At the same time, several novelists in wartime Chongqing found themselves increasingly wedded to an intricate Europeanized lexicon when
representing the emotional and psychological states of even their most

rustic characters. As Edward Gunn has shown, this period witnessed the advent of the basically untutored peasant character with a keen, self-conscious awareness of his "subconscious" or "unconscious" mental states; the pre-war distinction between the psychological acuity of the narrator and the relatively unreflective consciousness of the poorly educated peasant character broke down, with the narrator projecting all kinds of intricate Western-based neologisms onto the mental universe of the highly provincial peasant.[53]

Aside from a bent toward full-blown self-consciousness in the protagonist, two other features peculiar to *Mountain Torrent* are its abundant descriptions of panoramic landscapes and the abstract, *gainianhua* [conceptualized] quality of many of the narrator's statements and protagonist's musings.[54] The two features are both evident in a key passage portraying Zhang Sanguan's change of heart as he views the retreating Chinese troops from the villagers' mountain hideout:

> Amid indistinct clumps of trees and bushes far away in the mountain pass, those greyish columns on the march were still partly visible. Faintly in the distance, Zhang heard the hubbub of crowded men, the clatter of metal gear, and the rumble of random footsteps, all of which blended into a nondescript hum; from still further away rose the echoes of rhythmical and vigorous strains of song, like the soughing of pines in a strong wind, or the roaring of a river during spring floods.
>
> Sanguan had never before witnessed such a magnificent and moving spectacle. He suddenly felt his chest suffused with a burning sensation, which rose to enlarge the lump now swelling in his throat. His heart stepped up its beat, and felt as if something incomparably gigantic were pressing down upon it.
>
> Standing there ramrod straight, he forgot his fears, forgot his worries, forgot about his mother and cousin, and even forgot about his own existence. It was as if he had finally come to a concrete recognition of the tangible entity known as "China," the source of truths that his village schoolmaster, Mr. Wang, had once explained to him. As he gazed at the vast and mighty greyish stream grandly surge ahead, slowly but without hesitation, through the mountains stretching to the west, he felt disappointment and sorrow of a sort that he had never previously experienced.
>
> Did China no longer want his own region? Did it no longer want his village, his family, even him? Was there no longer any hope that all this could be saved?[55]

Commentators like Ye Yiqun and Marston Anderson have acclaimed the novel for the evocative power of its expansive landscape settings and its invitation to identification with a benevolent crowd.[56] The lushness and grandeur of the landscape certainly contribute to the mood of uplift in which momentous changes for the better seem to be in the offing. The

stirring martial songs resounding from the distant grey-clad troops remind Zhang of his past enthusiasm for stiff resistance to foreign invaders
like Japan; it is only at this epiphanic moment in the novel that he finally
gives up the idea of fleeing westward with his cousin into exile.

Zhang's mother and wife have favored exile over the alternative of
staying at home within easy striking distance of the advancing Japanese
army, but Zhang's determination to stay put finally hardens, even though
over the latter half of the novel he often vacillates over just how deeply he
dares to get involved in the War of Resistance. Enthusiasm for the impressive scale of the Chinese war effort spurs Zhang to forego exile, carry military supplies for the guerillas, and join the village militia. However, infantry duty on the front lines is always a chilling prospect that he and his
fellow villagers either recoil from in fear, or else simply taboo from their
conversations.

The panoramic setting of *Mountain Torrent* provides the backdrop for
not only the pouring forth of nationalist and collectivist feeling among the
peasants, but also the proliferation of vague and overblown abstractions
quite unlike anything else in Wu's corpus. Volker Klöpsch has thus wryly
characterized Zhang Sanguan's impassioned musings quoted above as
"something like a fit of enlightenment."[57] No other fictional character created by Wu claims in such a stiffly oratorical fashion to have forgotten so
many things, much less something so abstract as "his own existence."
Moreover, while many characters in Wu's previous works display their
serious concern for China through dialogue or symposia, none of them refers to China with the self-consciously reverential tone of Zhang Sanguan,
nor do any of them silently ruminate about "China" itself in so many
words. Zhang's rhetorical question, "Did China no longer want his region?" represents an abstract and speculative tenor of thought very unlikely for a peasant impressed by the idea of bombing Japanese encampments in China with bags of limestone powder. As Li Changzhi astutely
notes in his review of *Mountain Torrent*, peasants are hardly ever as "con-
ceptual-minded, introspective, emotionally fragile, . . . or susceptible to
melancholy" as Zhang Sanguan appears to be.[58]

If young Sanguan represents a somewhat contrived portrait of the
modern Chinese peasant who is not quite heroic but nevertheless increasingly nationalistic in temper, the traditional peasant's uppermost loyalty
to clan ties comes across through the eminently authentic character of
Dong Laodie. Dong Laodie is the first local villager to take the risk of
greeting the newly arrived Chinese army, and no villager works harder at
carrying supplies or water for the Resistance forces than he. But when his
young relative Si Gouzi is arrested by the guerillas as a suspected stool pi-
geon for having gone on unauthorized sojourns through enemy-occupied
territory, Dong Laodie puts aside his porterage duties in order to plead

strenuously on Si Gouzi's behalf. Most of his fellow villagers, particularly the younger and more nationalistic ones like Zhang Sanguan, chide him for pitying an avaricious, unpatriotic clansman like Si Gouzi. Dong Laodie counters with the rustic proverb celebrating familial cohesion, "Falling leaves return to the roots," and insists on trying to save a fellow clansman in trouble. Wu Zuxiang's sensitivity to ambivalence in character psychology helped produce this cogent illustration of how even peasants at the forefront of the village-level struggle for national salvation may have overriding particularistic loyalties.

Although *Mountain Torrent* was one of Wu's major creative achievements, his disappointment over aspects of the novel appeared both during the genesis of the work and after its mixed reception by reviewers. Wu's previous works had emerged almost spontaneously from his pen after weeks or months of the subject matter's incubation in his mind, but he encountered something akin to writer's block during the composition of *Mountain Torrent*. He found himself unable to keep writing the novel at an even pace, and went so far as to put it aside unfinished for a year. A spell of poor health during the early months of 1942 turned out to be a blessing in disguise, since Wu finally finished *Mountain Torrent* under the same circumstances of the Japanese writer Nagai Kafū, who completed his long-neglected novel manuscript *Dwarf Bamboo* during the tedium of a long illness.[59]

The noticeably tepid critical reaction to *Mountain Torrent* did not measure up to Wu Zuxiang's expectations. While each of the novel's reviewers remarked on the skillful use of dialogue in the novel, all of them except Yu Guanying added that the abstract, vague, and implausible portions of *Mountain Torrent* weakened its total impact.[60] Lao She went so far as to suggest in June 1943 that the novel had probably not yet been completed, and he looked forward to seeing the "flaccid" ending revised in the near future![61] This was not to come to pass, even though Wu Zuxiang had ample opportunity to make revisions before the second edition of *Mountain Torrent* came out in 1946.

A diary passage from February 1944 expresses Wu Zuxiang's intense disappointment over the reception of *Mountain Torrent*. He writes that his novel and Sha Ting's *Tao jin ji* [A Tale of Gold Prospecting] amount to two of the finest works that have appeared in recent years, and yet had received very little recognition in literary circles.[62] According to Wu, both of these novels treat universal themes whose appeal is not limited to a particular time or place; similarly, the enduring value of the novels of Zola and Goncharov was not recognized until these works gained a steady following among later generations and in countries outside of the authors' abode. By way of contrast, certain novels which had garnered effusive praise from Chongqing college students at that time like Yao Xueyin's *Xin miao* [New Sprouts] struck Wu as superficial, contrived, and ephemeral.[63]

During wartime, serious authors were in a bind—they wanted to write fiction of enduring value, but their creative strategies were limited by the widely observed imperative to write within a limited range of patriotic themes and for a localized and growingly war-weary readership.[64] The reading public's "scanty interest" in *Mountain Torrent*, as Wu frankly put it, intensified his frustration over the low evaluations given the novel by colleagues in literature at Central University like Zhang Huasuo and Liu Jiahua.[65] If a work so strongly didactic in conception appealed to so few readers, the very justification for its existence appeared to be thrown into doubt. It is little wonder that Wu "lacked the verve" to revise anything more than the title when a Shanghai publisher reprinted his novel in 1946.[66] Readers in the wartime capital of Chongqing itself had exhibited little appreciation for his patriotic novel; could he expect greater enthusiasm from Shanghai readers eager to put the war behind them and return to a state of civilian normalcy?

Wu nevertheless has maintained that the enduring historical value of *Mountain Torrent* will become more apparent as it is evaluated by a broader readership, for he mentions in the 1982 edition's afterword that his major motive for republishing the novel was to satisfy an "objective need" felt by teachers and researchers of modern Chinese literature both at home and abroad.[67] And if the contemporary reader cannot rank *Mountain Torrent* among the top three or four works by Wu, it still stands as one of the finest peasant novels to have emerged from the troubled War period.

### The End of the Line for Wu as a Writer

The output of most prominent Chinese writers fell dramatically for a time due to dislocations resulting from the massive 1937 invasion by the Japanese army. Like Wu, his friends Zhang Tianyi and Ba Jin could not sustain the creative momentum they had built up during the early 1930s. Yet Wu labored under a handicap that few of his fellow raconteurs shared: as the tutor and private secretary of a famous KMT official heavily involved in wartime consultations and propagandizing, Wu found comparatively little time or energy to devote to fiction. He only managed to complete his novel during the enforced leisure of a long bout of illness, and would sometimes daydream aloud in his diaries about writing full-time as a professional after the war. It might seem unfair that a writer who approached his craft with the meticulous standards of the professional would be stuck in the position of an amateur, finding time for writing only in moments left over from his onerous job responsibilities. However, Wu's amateur status would eventually seem a veritable boon in comparison to the restricted literary horizons enforced by the new government after 1949: his 1930s fiction of lucid, freewheeling social criticism within a contemporaneous setting would no longer be welcome—or even safe to practice—under Mao's rigid Stalinist literary controls.

The forced optimism toward one's own society and political culture which Stalinist-Maoist literary policy mandates was not unilaterally imposed on Chinese writers, however. Wu Zuxiang's polemical essay of 1938 and his novel of 1943 both aim to invigorate the reader with patriotic ardor and buoyant optimism at the expense of telling the whole truth about the Chinese cultural inheritance, including its dark side. Like so many of his doubtlessly well-intentioned colleagues on the literary scene, Wu willingly forsook the May Fourth legacy of trenchant and deflating socio-cultural criticism for the sake of short-term nationalistic objectives. If he later entertained hopes of reverting back to his pre-War ways of bold, contemporaneous social criticism, the new Maoist government had already sealed off the road back to the May Fourth literary ethos: Mao's Yan'an Talks, soon to be the law of the land, decreed in no uncertain terms that the sort of no-holds-barred social criticism represented by Lu Xun's satiric prose would no longer be an appropriate model to emulate under the glorious rule of the ideologically "correct" Communist Party.[68] The War presented Wu with the opportunity to stray away from the critical May Fourth spirit, but he would not get a chance to rediscover it until the post-Mao decade of 1979–1989, by which time he had gotten too far along in years to relearn the craft of writing fiction. Wu Zuxiang's literary career thus ended in the 1940s with neither a bang nor a whimper, but a salute and a forced smile of hope.

### PART TWO

# Technical Proclivities

# 6

## Dramatization and Typicality in Characterization

If one reviews Wu's oeuvre as a totality, an image likely to come to mind is a theatrical stage thronged with voices, each distinguishable from the other. His flair for both dialogue and the revealing dramatic incident makes for characters who are representative of a certain societal nîche at the same time that they stand clearly apart from one another as unique individuals.

This knack for the delineation of character functions as a constant in his fiction largely on account of the keen sensitivity he cultivated for literary portraiture. Two of Wu's critical essays from 1941 note that characterization has all along played a dominant role in both the composition of his own narratives and his appreciation of other novelists' works.[1] By comparison, plot structure is a matter of secondary importance, as is setting and any other type of descriptive prose. One of the essays adds that the "inner being" of a character reveals itself most clearly and convincingly through his oral speech; by comparison, the character's outward appearance, including gesture and facial expression, is relatively superficial.[2] Wu thus tends to relegate the sort of descriptive prose used for setting and background to a very minor position, while dramatization through spoken dialogue and interior monologue dominates his stories.

The opening two paragraphs of "Twilight," a story consisting almost entirely of mixed dialogue and monologue, indicate how rapidly Wu can make the transition from setting to dramatic dialogue:

> I arrived back home at five o'clock in the afternoon. By the time I'd taken a bath and eaten dinner, it was almost twilight. The sense of intimacy I felt at the sight of my ancient home village, from which I had been absent for some time, seemed exactly as if I were seeing my aged mother again after a long parting. Wanting to catch up on the local goings-on, I asked my wife about them in rather sweeping terms: "So how have things been in our village these days?"

On the verge of replying, my wife suddenly seemed at a loss for words. After pondering the matter for a moment, a nimble-witted smile formed on her lips, and she ordered Jade to move a bamboo settee out into the courtyard. "How about just going out to the courtyard for a spell in the cool night breeze?"[3]

The scenario at the beginning of "Twilight," in which the woman declines to sum up the bleak situation but instead bids the man to observe and judge for himself, serves as an apt metaphor for Wu's basic approach to composing fiction. A novel or story may embody general truths, but a skillful writer is less likely to conceptualize them in baldly general terms than to render them obliquely through a series of concrete illustrations. While cooling down for awhile in the night breeze as his wife has suggested, the narrator overhears various conversations and harangues from houses in the vicinity, and thereby receives a series of vivid impressions of the increasingly bitter struggle for economic survival facing most of the villagers. His wife and the maidservant, Jade, both familiar with the latest local news, are only then willing to join him in discussing some quandaries faced by the local residents whose troubled voices interrupt the evening stillness. Apparently, abstract generalizations cannot hold much significance for the author unless preceded by careful listening and painstaking observation. Only after the narrator learns the detailed accounts of several residents' bitter circumstances does he allow himself a tentative generalization as to the sorry state of his village. Moreover, he points out that his wife refrains from adding anything or even replying to his generalization, as if signifying the inferiority of discursive generalizations to observations of social life in its densely detailed concreteness.[4]

Critics since the 1960s have mostly approved of Wu's restraint in discursive commentary and preference for letting his characters speak for themselves.[5] After all, world literature over the past century has tended to move in the direction of suggestiveness, placing a greater burden of interpretation on the actively engaged reader than on the heavy-handedly instructive author. Yet as influential a critic as Mao Dun vehemently berated Wu in 1934 for the alleged impersonal aloofness of the younger writer's dramatized style of narration:

Most recent fiction portraying life in the countryside has sought to reveal the actuality of rural bankruptcy. . . . Its authors have "brought the village to us," as if to point directly at us and exclaim, "Just look! These are the sorts of things now taking place out there!"

. . . Wu Zuxiang's style in *West Willow* is precisely the opposite. He "takes us to the village." Like a conscientious guide who must not divulge any of his private reactions, his eyes flit over our faces as if to say: "Gentle reader, this is the village of the present day; it is all here before you, so please examine it for yourselves. Please examine it and judge for yourselves how good or bad it is. . . ."

Wu Zuxiang does not put forward any of his own personal opinions. Wu's writing attitude is extremely objective, and excessively objective. . . . We definitely must demand that such purely objective writers progress further in outlook.[6]

During the 1950s, the literary historian Wang Yao agreed with Mao Dun's interpretation and dutifully reiterated the charge that Wu erred through "excessive objectivity" of perspective.[7] Not too long after Mao Dun's death, however, Wang Yao admitted in a 1983 interview that the late literatus "was a leftist critic who expected younger writers to follow his lead"; in particular, Mao Dun had little insight into how the mechanisms of literary response may cause a narrative of almost clinical objectivity to exert a more powerful emotional impact on the reader than would a discursive or sentimental didactic work.[8] The reader who actively pieces together an interpretation after reading a relatively objective narrative is not only more intellectually involved than the reader who passively gulps down a predigested interpretation from a pointedly didactic author, but also tends to be more emotionally engaged as well.[9]

Wu defends his distaste for excessive discursiveness by citing a classic aesthetic principle first formulated in the Song Buddhist critic Yan Yu's *Canglang shi hua* [Canlang's Remarks on Poetry]:[10]

> There is a tradition in Chinese art of "leaving no trace of superfluous explanations" [*bu luo yan quan*]. That is, the artist avoids putting things too directly, too obviously. He ought not view the reader as some kind of fool who needs to be told outright, "This is a good person over here! That's a bad one over there!" . . . Only someone short on common sense could claim that my fiction lacks a social standpoint. I don't accept the label of "pure objectivism," for a vigorous social inclination may be found in my fiction.[11]

Anton Chekhov once faced the same kind of challenge from tendentious critics, and his reply also suggests how a serious aesthetic commitment to a subtly and objectively dramatized mode of characterization can rarely be appreciated by persons accustomed to thinking in blunt, dogmatic terms:

> You scold me for my objectivity, calling it indifference to good and evil, lack of ideal and ideas, and so on. When I describe horse thieves, you would always have me say, "Stealing horses is evil."[12]

Chekhov and Wu belong to the class of writers bent on illustrating various social tendencies of their age, but wary of sinking into the morass of

tendentiousness. Although both were occasionally censured for this by
critics with political axes to grind, the numerous reprints and wide critical
appreciation of their fiction suggest that their objective and dramatic
mode of characterizaion has weathered the test of time, at least from a present-day perspective. It is instead the type of heavy-handed advocate of
ideological conformity and mechanical obedience to powerful apparatchiks who has increasingly met with derision among modern literati as a
self-deceived purveyor of "vulgar Marxism."[13]

In light of the intensely dramatized quality in Wu's fiction, it may seem
surprising that he did not share Chekhov's keen interest in modern
drama. In 1940, he wrote: "As far as modern playscripts are concerned,
there are only a handful that I have ever read, and nary a one have I ever
seen performed onstage."[14] Wu even recalls having chided Lao She for devoting so much time to the writing of playscripts instead of novels.[15] Perhaps Wu's low regard for the stage stemmed from his correspondingly
high estimation of vernacular fiction as an instrument for disseminating
modern ideas on political renovation and scientific enlightenment throughout his society. He seems to have regarded the theatre as a mere public entertainment of little social significance, while perceiving an almost unlim-
ited meliorist potential in the novel and short story, much as Liang Qichao
had championed the novel during the late Qing as a guide to social progress.[16] Unfortunately, Wu may have passed up a double opportunity
when he gave the theatre a wide berth: his skills in dramatization might
have resulted in not only a number of fine plays, but also an opportunity
to sample the lifestyle of the professional writer. As it turned out, when
Wu's dreams of writing fiction professionally were dashed by the sharply
narrowed latitude allowed Chinese fiction writers beginning in the late
1940s, he apparently returned to academia without giving the theatre so
much as a second thought as a possible career alternative. Perhaps Wu
showed wise instincts in refraining from embarking on a transition from
fiction to drama, which was somewhat less rigorously controlled than
non-performative literature. After all, it was the theatre that kept Lao She
at the forefront of the Maoist literary scene, thus making him a fatally
prominent target for rampaging Red Guards in 1966.

### Typicality in Characterization Through Symposia

A variety of dramatized scene which Wu uses to particularly good effect is the multi-character conversation about current societal problems.
Social-minded realists have often asserted their commitment to a meliorist
standpoint by lacing their fiction with multi-character conversations, or
symposia, about current social questions. As pointed out in Chapter 2,
such weighty discussions about issues of the day tend to generalize and
broaden the significance of a particular character.[17] These symposia, in

turn, fall under the larger rubric of what many Marxist critics refer to as typicality, in which a character manages to express a certain tendency or pattern in social history—and yet without losing his or her individuality in the process.[18]

Of the nineteenth-century European realists well-known among modern Chinese intellectuals, and to Wu in particular, Ivan Turgenev was especially fond of buttressing the typicality of his characters through symposia on controversial social questions.[19] As in Wu's fiction, characters in Turgenev's *Hunting Sketches* often functioned as vocal advocates on various issues facing a largely agricultural society in the midst of major socioeconomic change.

In the story from the *Hunting Sketches* entitled "Ovsianikov, the Freeholder," the seventy-year-old rich peasant Luka Petrovich Ovsianokov discusses transformations in the rural social order with his pettifogging nephew Mitya and the Westernized gentry narrator, both of the younger generation:

> "So how does Squire Alexander Vladimirych manage his estate?" I asked Ovsianikov.
>
> "He's introducing new ways all the time. The muzhiks aren't singing his praises, but then it's no use listening to them. Alexander Vladimirych is doing the right thing."
>
> "But how is that, Luka Petrovich? I thought you were an adherent to the old order of things."
>
> "It's different with me. For I'm no nobleman and no landed proprietor. What does my estate amount to, really? . . . The young gentry have no liking for the old ways; I praise them for that. It's time we came to our senses. The only trouble is that the young gentry are far too clever. They treat the muzhik like a moppet; they'll twist him and turn him, wear him out, and then cast him aside. And then the clerk, who is himself a serf, or an estate manager who is German by birth, will get the peasant into his paws again. . . . The old has died out, but the new has yet to be born."[20]

The problems illustrated in this passage resonate closely with the conversation about pond-digging excerpted in the earlier section on "1800 Bushels" between the young and idealistic squire, Shuhong, and the avaricious clan estate manager, Botang. Shuhong proposes organizing his own tenants to dig ponds, so that losses during future droughts will decrease. Botang glibly dismisses this proposal, noting that the tenants have to work from dawn to dusk just to eke out their subsistence, and have no extra time or energy to invest in high-sounding experiments of doubtful workability. Since Botang also urges raising tenancy rents further, it is clear that he sees nothing wrong in exploiting tenants to the point where they must struggle terribly hard merely to keep body and soul together, and have no energy to spare for sideline irrigation projects of long-term benefit to the community. Botang's short-sighted avarice nevertheless holds sway over the poorly conceived reformist schemes of modern-thinking squires like Shuhong, whose laudable populist intentions are not sufficient in and of themselves to have much impact on the rigid but crumbling social order at hand. Like Alexander Vladimirych, Shuhong represents the high-minded and well-educated young squire who seeks in vain to reform the decaying traditional rural order.

Less idealistic squires of the younger generation may speak volubly of egalitarian fairness and other modern ethical principles while actually acting out of motives of mere personal enrichment. Two such figures are the pettifoggers Ziyu of "1800 Bushels" and Mitya of "Ovsianikov, Freeholder":[21]

> Mitya said, ". . . The Shutolomov muzhiks are paying quitrent, mind you; their landowner has gone abroad. Who's to intercede for them? Judge for yourself. And the land is theirs, beyond any dispute, the deeds for it going back to times out of mind. Well, then, they came to me and said, 'Write a petition for us.' And write it I did. . . ."
>
> ". . . I know exactly what you're going to say to me," interrupted Ovsianikov. "Right: a man must live in accordance with what is right and is obliged to help his fellow man. . . . But then, are your actions always of that nature? Do people take you to some tavern, or don't they? 'Dmitrii Alexeich, our father, help us, now, and as for our gratitude, be sure we'll show it'— and a ruble note, or even greater, passes from under the skirt of some coat and into your hand. Eh? Isn't that what happens? Tell me, isn't it?"
>
> "I am guilty of that, true enough," Mitya answered, his eyes cast down. "But I don't take anything from the poor; and I don't pervert my soul!" "You may not be taking anything now, but if you should find yourself in a tight spot you will. You don't pervert your soul? Oh, you! I guess it's only saints you're always sticking up for!"[22]

Like Turgenev's Mitya, Ziyu of "1800 Bushels" seeks to profit from the crumbling of the old rural order in the name of a populist ethic. Ziyu views the clan land holdings that have remained intact for dozens of generations as no more than an ordinary piece of property ripe for subdividing among the present clan members. Ziyu's seemingly enlightened principle of "an equal share for all" thus masks a petty and short-sighted self-interest, just as Mitya deceives himself into thinking that his lucrative wheeling and dealing in and out of court is a noble defense of peasant rights.

While the younger generation of squires, out of motives of idealism or personal profit, often seeks to change the traditional rural order, many older squires strongly oppose any modification whatsoever of the status quo. Such oldsters abide by the antediluvian viewpoint that rural society, having apparently changed for the worse under the impact of the modern industrialized world, would be better off returning at once to a full embrace of the old traditional ways. This view is representative of many elder figures of the local elite like Xinqiao of "1800 Bushels," who sees a sign of the modern breakdown of traditional hierarchies in the way a marketplace-like clamor now echoes through the stately aisles and formerly hushed confines of the sacred ancestral temple.[23] Xinqiao's fellow aging clansman, Minzhai, expresses his fear of changing values in starker and even violent terms. Insisting that his ancestors would expect him to punish younger clan members who have seriously violated long-standing local precepts, he indignantly threatens to kill his university-educated son, Zhutang, for having colluded in rebellion with local Communists:

> "If it's true that Zhutang has turned Communist, there could be no atonement for his crimes, even if his corpse were sliced into a thousand shreds. I wouldn't be the only one to get a feeling of satisfaction from putting an end to his mucking about; the ancestors would also see it as a riddance of harm. If the government doesn't kill him, *I'm* not about to let him off the hook."[24]

Rural elders of more passive bent balk at adopting a stance of either reform or reaction, withdrawing instead into an attitude of religious fatalism. From this standpoint, individual efforts at either recovering the supposed glories of the traditional order, or else hastening the advent of a presumably progressive future are equally futile; history will simply keep on moving along in accord with the dictates of Heavenly Fate. Some characters like the beancurd shopowner Buqing of "1800 Bushels" personify fate by conceiving of it in ethical terms:

> "There certainly have been a lot of droughts over the past twenty years," sighed the petty official [Shitang]. . . . "We've had good harvests only two years out of the nearly ten since I've been at home. I just can't figure out what's behind all this."
> . . . Buqing spoke up. "So you can't figure out what's behind all this, Shitang? Two lines are all I need to get the point across:
> 'Heaven's Law cannot condone
> The hearts of men to evil drawn.'
> Turning his head around to address the geomancer Weisheng, Buqing said, "What do you think of that, Weisheng?"
> "It's a question of fate all right, a question of fate."
> "Naturally it's a question of fate!"[25]

Instead of ascribing a moral character to the workings of fate, other rural characters view destiny as a remote, impersonal force beyond good and evil, something closer to a mechanism of foreordination than a karmic wheel of recompense and retribution. Chapter 2 relates how an impoverished peasant in "Two Young Sparrows" is fascinated by a numerological, non-ethical Daoist prophecy of the immanent loss of the Nationalist Mandate of Heaven. An old rural militiaman in "Little Lord Guanguan's Tonic" similarly views fate as an impersonal force unfettered by ethical imperatives. After a young citified clansman makes a blanket condemnation of Western imperialism as the malefactor behind all of China's economic woes, the old man cannily replies:

> "No matter if you keep jawing from here to the horizon yonder, fate'll always be there to reckon with," rejoined the old man. "If not, why is it that foreigners didn't used to be able to make off with our Chinese money, but only just lately came to cheat us? What else could this add up to but fate?"
>
> Boy, has that cousin of mine ever got a knack for wrangling: "We Chinese used to seal off our borders and keep to ourselves," he said. "Foreigners simply weren't permitted to come to our country. But ever since we started losing wars to the foreigners, they've been pouring in non-stop; wouldn't you agree that from that time on China's been getting poorer each day?"
>
> "I've heard that the foreigners themselves are at sixes and sevens, too! Didn't the newspapers say a few days back that there are several million unemployed workers in America, and millions of the unemployed in Japan to boot? Doesn't this really show that whether it's China or a foreign country, there's no escape from fate? As I see it, whenever you get down to the root of the problem, fate'll be there!"[26]

The opposite end of the spectrum from a resigned complacency is the rebel's hope for overturning the existing rural social order. This attitude is expressed with the least directness and frequency of all, for Wu's rebellious characters rarely state their views in general terms within the context of a settled discussion. Instead, his rebels tend to blurt out things of a rather direct and non-speculative nature while actively storming a granary, fleeing the authorities, or some related action. One exception to this pattern is the impoverished peasant Gouzi of "Fan Hamlet," who sullenly enters into a discussion between Xianzi's mother and Sister Lian on the topic of rural economic decline. Gouzi has just been paid an outrageously low price for the rice he has arduously harvested, and he castigates the grain brokers involved as "cannibals," a term of abuse which had gained wide circulation among the rebellious of spirit since Lu Xun popularized it in 1918.[27] Gouzi's fury is so intense that he blurts out what amounts to murderous designs against his exploiters, thus openly expressing his insurrectionist inclinations. Although the succinct and concrete manner in which Gouzi expresses his views falls somewhat short of the loquacity normal for symposia, he represents an important current of opinion in the countryside at that time.

The participants in Wu's symposia argue from various generalized standpoints on the traditional rural order, whether idealistically engaging in reform, cannily using the rhetoric of reform to mask motives of pure self-interest, anachronistically hoping to restore the ways of the settled past, withdrawing from rationalist judgment into fatalism, or voicing the need for rebellion. The older-generation provincials tend to be fatalistic or else intent upon restoring the ways of the settled past. By way of contrast, younger-generation provincials of peasant stock like Gouzi tend to be rebellious "angry young man" types. Well-educated young upperclass characters such as Shuhong usually argue in vain for a vigorous program of social reform, while provincials slightly lower in status and education often rationalize their headlong scramble for personal gain with populist pronouncements in the egalitarian mold. Each of these viewpoints is representative of a particular force or vested interest in society, which is the very kernel of typicality as conceived by many Marxist critics.[28]

### Exploring Irrational Character Psychology

If the above symposia illustrate the meliorist bent of Wu's literary sensibility, the piquant dark depths of many a character come across through his fascination with the irrational side of human consciousness. Although subordinate to typicality, the unpredictable quirks of the human psyche play an important role in his overall approach to characterization. The irrational proclivities of many of his characters stem at least in part from his view that each and every person bears at least some extraordinary feature, as long as the observer searches carefully enough.[29]

Two of the uncanniest characters conjured forth by any meliorist's pen in the 1930s surface in "The Verdant Bamboo Hermitage." The narrator's aunt and her maid are strikingly reticent and soft-spoken, and walk about at a lugubriously slow pace. What little they do say is larded with matter-of-fact references to supernatural phenomena, such as talking animals and the return of the aunt's late husband to the living. But the duo's intense curiosity about the marital relations of the young couple leads to a surprising negation of nearly twenty years of Buddhist austerities, as they cannot resist a nocturnal bout of voyeurism outside the boudoir of the young visitors. The couple's visit, originally planned as a pleasant hillside respite from the hot lowland weather, turns out to be an intensely embarrassing experience for all. At the very least, the old hillside hermits can no longer maintain their self-image of abstemious purity, which had brought some solace to an existence tormented by loneliness and deprivation.

"The Verdant Bamboo Hermitage" bears a remarkable affinity with one of Turgenev's mysterious tales, "Faust: A Story in Nine Letters."[30] The forbidden fruit in the European story is not the normal sexual life denied to chaste widows, but instead the normal imaginative life denied a young rural woman named Vera. Vera's parents sternly forbid her the pleasures of reading literature, instilling within her the notion that calamities befall people who cultivate their imagination. The fortyish narrator, who had once gotten a crush on Vera as a teenager, has come back to the countryside to visit her and her husband. Vera's long-standing resistance to literature of any sort breaks down in the face of the narrator's eloquence on the joys of reading *Faust*. Strange and uncontrollable passions begin to well up within her, culminating in an amatory attraction to the narrator, which he reciprocates. Before they take the final step of an illicit tryst, however, her terror of the possible consequences of adultery causes Vera to take to her sickbed, where she dies of consumption within a fortnight.

Both stories illustrate how purity cultivated in bucolic isolation may be uncannily fragile. Such purity may readily shatter as a result of a casual encounter with facets of everyday life in the outside world. Like the eccentric aunt in Wu's story, Vera is of extremely quiet and unhurried demeanor: "Vera was not like ordinary Russian young ladies. She seemed marked in some special way. I was struck from the very first by the remarkably placid way she moved and spoke. She never seemed to fuss or become disturbed about anything." Yet this very mildness of disposition is perhaps all the more vulnerable to what Turgenev calls "the secret forces life rests on, which only occasionally, but without warning, break through to the surface."[31]

The breaking through of these dark forces of the psyche is carefully foreshadowed in both the Russian and Chinese stories. In Turgenev's story, Vera was "protected" by her elders from the passions lurking in literature, precisely because passion had been the undoing of so many of her ill-fated relatives. In "The Verdant Bamboo Hermitage," the aunt was severely chastised for slipping into a teenage pre-marital dalliance, and managed to repress the passionate side of her nature for some twenty years between that girlhood incident and the young couple's visit. It is not so much passion itself that surprises the characters and readers of the two stories, but the rapidity and intensity with which passion inflames the heretofore icily mild-mannered heroines. This uncanny volatility of personality make-up necessarily precludes a strong role for typicality in characterization within "The Verdant Bamboo Hermitage."

Wu Zuxiang also shares Turgenev's unfailing curiosity for dreams and the uncanny "darker recesses of the human mind" in general.[32] The importance of dreams and nightmares in Wu's imaginative life appears in numerous diary entries and especially his essay from 1934, "On My Dreams." Most of the dreams he recounts from both sources are extremely unsettling nightmares with a disturbing frequency of occurrence, at least weekly and sometimes even nightly.[33]

Many vivid and significant nightmares are filtered through the consciousnesses of Wu's characters. The first of many fictional nightmares appears when the guilt-ridden narrator of "Two Young Sparrows" dreams that her drowned maid has returned from the dead to seek her out. Similarly, the aunt in "The Verdant Bamboo Hermitage" often dreams that her late husband has returned home. Vivid, memorable dreams of the dead who return to life are also found in Wu's diaries; in 1942, he dreamed of the resurrection of both his late father (July) and late mother (December).[34]

Wu's characters sometimes have disturbing and influential dreams of the murder of a loved one. Xianzi, of "Fan Hamlet," dreams of her husband's bloody death by prison torture, and only at that point does she finally decide to go through with her violent and fateful urge to pilfer her mother's lottery prize. Wu himself occasionally suffered from nightmares of this sort: a diary entry of 29 October 1942 records a particularly wrenching dream in which a cousin named Weisheng has been bloodily murdered under mysterious circumstances. Though Wu's mother assures him and his wife of their total innocence in the matter, the married couple are both aghast at their bloody hands, which like the Macbeths', seem resistant to being washed clean. Both dreams of murder involve the dreamer's sense of complicity in the death; this very sense of guilt for her husband's impending murder by yamen underlings spurs Xianzi to steal the lottery prize as the sum with which to bribe the prison guards holding her husband. Had it not been for the irrational explosiveness of Xianzi's nightmare, her subsequent acts of desperate brigandage would have seemed incompatible with her earlier restraint in behavior.

If dreams can allow the dead a brief return to the living, they can also preside over the coming to life of purely inanimate objects. Sister Lian of "Fan Hamlet" dreams of a large Boddhisattva statue which stirs to life, angrily brandishing a whip in a northwesterly direction.[35] This dream bears a remarkable resemblance to one which Wu reported having dreamt himself in 1934: a sculptured Boddhisattva figure in a temple suddenly comes to life and moves about before freezing back into solid and inanimate statuary once again.[36] According to Hadfield, dreams of inanimate objects coming to life suggest latent potentialities within the dreamer that were dormant until awakened by some chance stimulus.[37] The menacing grimaces on the faces of the normally serene bodhisattva statues in both of these dreams might well reflect a self-awareness of growing angst, or perhaps hostile defensiveness, on the part of the dreamer.

Another important dream-based pattern of characterization in Wu's fiction is the nightmarish physical collapse of the protagonist at the close of many stories. Characters who fall into unconsciousness at the finale include Xiangfa of "The Flowering Gardenia," Ling Ziyan of "Miss Jin and the Xue Girl," and Xianzi of "Fan Hamlet." While each of the above three characters collapses in a faint upon the discovery that a person close to them has died, Wang Xiaofu of "The World At Peace" is both tumbler and victim in one, falling to his death from a temple roof.

Wu has personally reported many vivid dreams of falling from which he would awaken with a start.[38] Though some dreams of falling are caused in part by physiological factors like the drop in blood pressure of a sleeping person, the act of falling itself is of metaphorical significance as well.[39] To some extent, a dream of falling embodies what George Lakoff and Mark Johnson term an "orientational metaphor." Positions along a longitudinal axis are often used as metaphors with which to evaluate the current condition of one's existence, such as "up" for a sense of well-being, and "down" for a condition of stress or emotional pain.[40] In terms of longitudinal orientational metaphors, one could conclude that the above four characters *under* great stress have *fallen* into despondency due to some sort of *decline* in their situations.

Freud believed that most dreams of falling are expressions of anxiety, while Hadfield went on to specify the connection between this type of dream and fears of moral lapse and occupational failure.[41] A major factor behind the final "fall" of Xiangfa and Wang Xiaofu is their common inability to succeed in any occupation once the Depression forces them out of their chosen trade of shopkeeping. Even more important is the sense of moral lapse tormenting these characters: Xiangfa does not return home from Beijing soon enough to rescue his wife from sickness and death; Wang Xiaofu has been shamefully flogged in front of the whole village for having stolen food and blankets for his shivering, hungry family; Ling Ziyan's indecisiveness over whom to marry indirectly results in the death of the Xue girl at the hands of a back-alley abortionist; and Xianzi finally discovers that bandits have released her husband from prison, thus nullifying the benefit from braining her mother in quest of a jail bribe. All of these four characters have both literally and metaphorically fallen down in their responsibilities to loved ones, though the larger socio-economic milieu in which they move is at least partly to blame for their failings.

### Balancing the Typical with the Extraordinary

The fascination shared by Wu Zuxiang and Ivan Turgenev for the changing social relations within an overridingly agricultural society impelled them to create a set of characters that would typify the various forces at work as provinciality collided with the modern world. Stories like "1800 Bushels" and "Ovsianikov, the Freeholder" capture the clash of economic interests and diversity of moral values within a rural society in transition.

On the other hand, Wu and Turgenev occasionally turned from an outer focus on the realities of provincial society to an inward-looking exploration of the dark and irrational side of individual human consciousness. "The Verdant Bamboo Hermitage" and "Faust: A Story in Nine Letters" portray the aberrations of personality that can result when a character is forced to remain a societal nîche that represses her most intense subconscious yearnings. Wu's almost nightly encounters with disturbing dream vignettes contributed to his interest in the irrational side of character psychology. Like Cao Xueqin, he utilized dreams and dreamlike motifs to uncover the fears and obsessions that characters normally repressed or masked during their waking hours. As a result, the reader enjoys a certain depth in Wu's characters which is often lacking in the meliorist writings of his contemporaries.

# 7

# Variegated Narrative Voice and Minimalist Plot Structure

Wu's reflections on craftsmanship in fiction emphasize characterization at the expense of narrative voice, plot, and other elements of prose style.[1] His almost instinctual aversion to highly embellished and far-fetched plot structures led him to adopt a minimalist approach, drawing on the most basic plot elements so as to avoid overshadowing the detailed portraits of key characters.[2] Nearly all his works make do with a single or unitary plot line, and contain little or no variance from a chronological order of presentation. Since Wu preferred writing shorter fictional forms over the novel, his spartan adherence to the single plot line did not generally restrict the flow of narrative, and often imparted a quality of rough-hewn spontaneity to it. Only in his lone novel did this approach to plot structure betray its limitations for narratives of larger scope, creating an impediment to an appropriate expansiveness of incident and perspective.

More variety and experimentation may be found in Wu's handling of narrative voice than in his structuring of plot. "Little Lord Guanguan's Tonic" stands out as a very rare and skillful Chinese example of presentational irony or "unreliable narration," in which the reader must arrive at an interpretation of the story's events far different from the one offered by the woefully inadequate narrator. His radical departure from the first-person May Fourth norm of a reliable semi-autobiographical narrator bespeaks his familiarity with Western models of ironic narrative voice such as Maupassant.[3] Moreover, his *oeuvre* reveals a curious shift from first-person to third-person narrative in the later stages of his career, suggesting an increased absorption with lower-class characters at the expense of the social elite.

## The Shift to Third-Person Narration and Lower-class Protagonists

Like most of Wu's stories featuring a protagonist of elite class background, "Little Lord Guanguan's Tonic" is a first-person narrative. Except for his anomalous sophomoric fable of 1923, each of his stories prior to 1932 similarly features an elite protagonist, first-person narration, and a material setting of comfortable prosperity. But with the publication of "Xiao Hua's Birthday" and "The Flowering Gardenia" in 1932, bona fide third-person narration appears for the first time, and lower-class protagonists and settings of shabbiness and penury make their first appearance. These lower-class protagonists have suddenly risen to the status of central "focalizer," a term used by Susan Lanser and Gérard Genette for the character whose perceptions and consciousness filter most of what the narrator recounts.[4] That is, the events in such a narrative are viewed from the perspective of a single character, specifically what Henry James refers to as the "central intelligence," instead of from the viewpoint of a dramatized first-person narrator or a set of characters.[5]

In Wu's third-person fiction, which grew ever larger in bulk through the rest of his career, the character who serves as the central focalizer nearly always turns out to be an indigent lower-class figure, thereby reflecting the author's growing concern for the deteriorating economic and political conditions within local rural society. For instance, the selective omniscience of the narrator in both "Xiao Hua's Birthday" and "The Flowering Gardenia" is limited solely to the impoverished protagonists of the two stories, Meirong and Xiangfa. In each of these stories, the reader gets "beneath the skin" to the thoughts of only one character—Meirong or Xiangfa—and perceives the story's events unfold solely from the perspective of that same character. Wu did not depart from this Jamesian mode of handling third-person narrative until writing his two longest works, "1800 Bushels" and *Mountain Torrent*, which revert to a more traditional type of thoroughgoing authorial omniscience by delving at whim into the private thoughts and perceptions of several different characters.

If Wu unhesitatingly explored the inner life of lower-class characters in his third-person works, he nevertheless refrained from using any lower-class narrators in any of his first-person stories, even after 1932. This pattern should not surprise us, for the overwhelming majority of Western classics of realist and naturalist fiction which feature lower-class protagonists also utilize third-person narration.[6] However much compassion writers like Emile Zola and Hamlin Garland may have felt for the lower-class protagonists in their fiction, they never really identified themselves with that barely literate class; and the affinity naturally present between author and narrator would have had a difficult time spanning the large gap in values and background between well-heeled author and lower-class raconteur. As Lanser has suggested, the gap in values and sensibility tends to be much narrower between author and narrator than between author and character.[7] Therefore, well aware of his social standing as a scion of the local elite, Wu also found it unnatural to narrate his stories with a voice from the opposite side of the class spectrum.

Although Wu continued to pen first-person narratives through the early 1940s, his overall preference in narrative mode had already decisively shifted from first-person to third-person by 1934. His three longest works from the 1930s, "1800 Bushels," "The World At Peace," and "Fan Hamlet," are all third-person narratives from 1934. While these and his other third-person works amount to merely nine out of the total twenty-three works in his *oeuvre*, they account for some two-thirds of his total volume of fiction. The surge of literary output in the third-person mode which reached an early climax in 1934 thus not only resulted in the primacy of that mode in Wu's overall *oeuvre*, but also swelled the ranks of lower-class protagonists as compared with characters from the local elite.[8] This foregrounding of lower-class characters resonates with Wu's accentuation, beginning in 1934, of the coalescence of grassroots forces in his rural homeland.

### Experimental First-Person Narrators

In the formative years of the modern Chinese short story, the early-to-mid 1920s, a first-person narrator was almost always an alter ego of the author—at least something of a semi-autobiographical figure. Yu Dafu and Ba Jin made their autobiographical leanings in fiction explicit from the start, and invariably project much of themselves onto their first-person narrators.[9] In reference to the semi-autobiographical quality pervading much of Lu Xun's first collection of fiction, Leo Ou-fan Lee has argued that most of these early stories can be read as literary exorcisms of "those aspects of Lu Xun's past life that continued to haunt him."[10] Similarly, the first-person narrators in stories like "On the Eve of Leaving Home," "Twilight," "The Verdant Bamboo Hermitage," and "Stuffy Ironsides" bear a very strong resemblance to the contemporary figure of Wu himself. It is only in "The Woodcutter" and "Little Lord Guanguan's Tonic" in which a sizable distance between author and narrator emerges.

The boy narrator of "The Woodcutter" is also autobiographical in nature, but separated by nearly two decades from the author at the time of writing. Wu's sole story narrated from the vantage point of a child, it describes how a sensitive scion of the local elite achieves his first vivid awareness of the many-sided hardships endured by the menial classes. The author here avoids portraying himself within the standard frame of contemporaneity, but instead re-examines a key turning point in his childhood when the impact of poverty and injustice on ordinary rural laborers first stirred his sense of social responsibility. Some twenty years later, the young narrator of elite background would still be at work articulating the needs and interests of the politically underrepresented and long-neglected rural poor.

An even more unusual narrative voice among Wu's first-person efforts emerges from the narrator of "Little Lord Guanguan's Tonic." Foolhardy or cruel characters are sprinkled throughout Wu's *oeuvre*, but Guanguan is Wu's only narrative persona who combines these two disagreeable attributes. Guanguan qualitatively stands apart from Wu's other first-person narrators, all of whom come across as ethical and responsible semi-autobiographical figures. The young squire sees nothing at all wrong with his frivolous and dissolute existence in Shanghai, which is funded by his rural family's mercenary gouging of their impoverished agricultural tenants. Guanguan's unrestrained praise for such tinsel trappings of city life as dancehalls and cinemas is neatly dovetailed with his supercilious scorn for unwashed peasants, whom he facetiously likens to the cows and water buffalo that toil alongside them in the rice paddies. These attitudes on the part of Guanguan are diametrically opposed to Wu Zuxiang's populist compassion for the rural underclass and nativist scorn for nearly all aspects of life in semi-colonialist treaty ports like Shanghai. According to Wayne Booth's typology of the signposts of irony, this attitudinal discrepancy is a classic example of irony based on conflicts of belief between the narrator, on the one hand, and the author or ordinary reader, on the other.[11]

Another of Booth's signposts of ironic narrative voice clearly evident within this story is a clash in levels of style.[12] In his capacity as narrator, Guanguan often turns abruptly to colloquialisms in the midst of semi-formal, almost bookish narrative passages:

> The bandits wrote a letter to the county yamen demanding an extortion payment of $30,000; unless that sum were tendered to the very penny within one week, they would immediately launch an assault on the county seat and visit rapine and plunder upon towns and villages in the vicinity. As rumors about this began to circulate, the local militias in every village and town engaged in a flurry of joint defense preparations, stationing sentries day and night at watchposts along the roads. In the event they happened to come across anyone who looked suspicious, they would detain him for a body search and interrogation.
>
> My uncle is the Militia Commandant, and has been working full-time at the Command Post. Since staying at home is as boring as all get out, I head over there every day to get the latest news and have a chat. It's even more fun whenever they nab and question some suspicious-looking guy.[13]

The final two sentences impart an ironic flavor to the narration, for their obtrusive colloquiality clashes with the relative elegance of what precedes them. Through the chatty diction in this final pair of sentences,

Guanguan betrays his own flippant simple-mindedness and taste for the lurid. When compared with the objective phraseology and sophisticated diction at the beginning, the concluding expressions of his gaping curiosity for thrills seem all the more juvenile in tone.

Further signs of ironic narration that Booth outlines include the narrator's simple statement of an obvious falsehood, as well as an authorially designed conflict of facts within a given literary work.[14] Guanguan parades his ignorance of peasant folk remedies and herbal medicines when he falsely takes the local villagers to task for knowing nothing whatsoever about tonics: "When it comes to nourishment, these country people are only familiar with gruel and boiled rice; how could they know about anything else a body should take?"[15] A glaring example of a conflict of facts within an ironic narrative is Guanguan's subsequent claim that he has "saved" Baldy from being stuck in Shanghai without travel expenses for a return trip back home. While it is true that Guanguan has paid Baldy what amounts to one-way travel fare for the crucial blood transfusion, the young squire would have had to pay about the same to someone else if Baldy had been unavailable. Moreover, if the blood transfusion "saves" anyone, it rescues Guanguan, who does not fully recover from his car wreck injuries until after the transfusion. By way of contrast, towards the end of the story, Guanguan becomes a willing accomplice in the militia's decision to behead Baldy: he indicates his total approval of the homiletic justification for wielding harsh punishment, "Kill one to warn a hundred."[16] Instead of "saving" Baldy, a remorseless Guanguan eagerly gapes at the cruel spectacle of the hapless peasant's summary execution.

As Patrick Hanan has argued, what little irony may be found in premodern Chinese fiction tends to flow from characters instead of narrators; Chinese narratorial or presentational irony has been largely a borrowing from Western writers like Maupassant, and even so was very rare among Chinese authors during the first half of this century.[17] While Lu Xun made use of presentational irony and unreliable narrators far more than most of his contemporaries on the literary scene, his narrators in such stories as "Kong Yiji" and "The New Year's Sacrifice" tend to come across as either moral weaklings or else simply naïve; none of them forces the reader to confront a harshly inhumane narratorial perspective, as does the callous young squire Guanguan.

One of the only other modern Chinese writers who consciously exploited this kind of morally pungent presentational irony was Mu Shiying, who in 1932 published a remarkable collection of short stories entitled *Nan bei ji* [The North and South Poles].[18] Although Zhu Ziqing singled out this story collection for its unusually adroit handling of pure, non-Europeanized North Chinese vernacular, he also remarked on its convincing reflection of some unsavory aspects of treaty-port life through the eyes of bellicose, hard-boiled narrators with proletarian and under-world connections.[19] Reminiscent of Guanguan's sneeringly amoral callousness toward the plight of the poor, the first-person narrators in Mu Shiying's collection tend to reveal an amoral nonchalance about inflicting suffering on others, in this case the upper middleclass and the wealthy instead of the poor. In order to cope with this pungent unreliability of presentation, the reader must actively scrutinize such a narrator's judgments, re-interpreting the work at a deeper level that resonates with the values of the implied author instead of the narrator.[20] Wu Zuxiang thus emerges as one author among a select few in modern China who have attempted to communicate with the reader "from behind their narrators' backs," as Booth has described the task of the presentational ironist.[21]

### Spartan Plot Construction

One might wonder why a writer so sensitive to the subtleties of characterization and narrative voice would favor a simple unitary plot structure and straightforward chronological order of presentation. A major factor in Wu's preference for plain plot structure has been the influence from various Western realist writers to emphasize characterization at the expense of intricate plot structuration. This trend was especially pronounced in the latter part of the nineteenth century, the period represented by two of Wu's favorite Western authors, Maupassant and Tolstoy.[22] Various fiction critics have also argued that realist or "mimetic" characterization of the sort Wu aimed at demands a certain degree of freedom from plot: "The ultimate form of mimetic plot is the 'slice of life,' virtually an 'unplot.'"[23] The realist novelists Edith Wharton and E. M. Forster have forcefully argued that among recent practioners of realist fiction, the Aristotelian primacy traditionally bestowed upon plot has lost ground to finely wrought characterization and explorations of the inner life.[24] Herman Melville, from another perspective, makes plot a flexible adjunct to open-ended philosophical discussion in his fiction.[25] However indispensable a certain attentiveness to plot may be, it was relegated to a secondary role in composition by many leading Western writers in the late nineteenth and early twentieth centuries.[26]

The origins of the modern Chinese short story similarly reveal a decided break with the vernacular tradition and its "meticulous care in plotting" required to satisfy a popular readership's expectations for titillatingly complex yarns.[27] As V. I. Semanov has pointed out, the pioneer of the modern Chinese short story, Lu Xun, radically simplified the convoluted, multi-stranded plot structure common in traditional Chinese vernacular stories; in his premier anthology, *Outcry*, no story except "Medicine" has more than a single plot line.[28] Through this Spartan approach to narratorial structuration, Lu Xun not only focused the reader's attention on the stark interplay between society and the individual, but also avoided the common flaw of prolixity that Theodore Huters has mentioned.[29] Wu Zuxiang's own meliorist leanings and aesthetic preference for concision prompted him to follow suit with a minimalist approach to plot construction.[30]

## Chronological Order—and Variations

Wu's plots adhere very closely to the chronological order of the incidents portrayed. Many of his stories, such as "Twilight" and "A Certain Day," hold so tightly to a chronological manner of unfolding as to resemble a documentary. None of his works opens *in media res*, an approach favored by legions of writers as far removed in space and time as Homer and Wang Meng. Only one story, "The World At Peace," begins with a prefatory statement suggestive of the work's final outcome—in this case, the disastrous finale of the protagonist's long struggle to provide for his family: "Due to the occurrence of an astonishingly unusual incident, let us now turn to the story of Wang Xiaofu's household."[31] At that point, the narrative of "The World At Peace" turns to a strictly chronological progression that continues all the way to the end.

A more common—and yet similarly unobtrusive—variation from strict chronological plotting emerges from the habit of dramatized narrators to backtrack in time in order to explain how they have arrived at the situation in the story's opening scene. For example, after introducing himself as an imbiber of tonics, the notorious Guanguan recounts the story of his car accident and incomplete recuperation from it, which brought about his recourse to special health remedies. Similarly, the narrator of "The Verdant Bamboo Hermitage" introduces himself and his present state of affairs before backtracking some two decades to relate the story of his middle-aged aunt's unhappy teenage romance.

Perhaps Wu's most overt divergence from his mainstream adherence to chronological plot order occurs in the occasional flashback among his longer works. These flashbacks may be character-based, as in "Fan Hamlet," when Xianzi recalls in her mind's eye how the road by her teahouse used to be bustling with traffic back in the years when commerce was still brisk. Under other circumstances, the flashback may stem from a dramatized narrator who seems to follow a train of partially involuntary memories rather than consciously deciding to explain the present through the past. The narrator-protagonist of "Splay-petaled Honeysuckle" undergoes a flashback of this type which amounts to approximately one-third of the entire story; he identifies the supine pregnant woman only after she jogs his memory by mentioning the type of honeysuckle which he had offered her some ten years previously. Yet even though this flashback runs for a third of the story, it is continuous, involving none of the rapid cinematic "cross-cutting" back and forth between past and present of the type that has become an overused and mannered structural device in post-Mao fiction.[32] In "Splay-petaled Honeysuckle," as in the rest of Wu's fiction, the occasional divergence from a chronological order of exposition is always handled in a restrained fashion.

Just as the flashback compresses novelistic time toward the past, foreshadowing telescopes time in the direction of the future. In doing so, foreshadowing increases the coherence of plot structure by suggesting a pattern of recurrence among incidents that are widely separated in time. The first case of foreshadowing in Wu's *oeuvre* appears in "Xiao Hua's Birthday": the thirtyish protagonist brushes off an older friend's casual remark that her husband, an unemployed shop clerk, could get into the same kind of trouble endemic then among unemployed young men from wealthy families. That is, the younger woman believes that her husband's humble familial origins would aid him in enduring the hardships of unemployment with more stoicism and patience than the pampered scions of wealthy families could muster. As it turns out, however, the protagonist's opinion is an inverted prophecy, for later in the story he flies into a violent and uncontrolled rage that not only disgraces his family in the eyes of the community, but also drives his terrified wife away from him for good.

Foreshadowing functions as an inverted prophecy of embarrassment rather than doom in the early part of "The Verdant Bamboo Hermitage." The young wife of the narrator recoils from his vivacious Elder Aunt, who immodestly cuddles the young woman and cajoles her to kiss the narrator in her presence. The abashed young wife complains to her husband that she has seen more than her fill of his village relatives, but he insists that Second Aunt, a soft-spoken and reclusive woman who lives in a hillside hermitage, is a totally different sort of person. Second Aunt's introverted personality indeed turns out to be much different, but she, too, offends and embarrasses the young wife by indulging in a moment of wanton voyeurism.

On the other hand, foreshadowing may be direct and to the point rather than inverted in approach. In "The Flowering Gardenia," one of the rural protagonist's worldly-wise uncles insistently warns him of the great difficulties he will encounter in trying to adapt to city life. The protagonist brushes these warnings aside, but does in fact fail miserably in his attempt to establish a nîche for himself in the urban workforce.

A similar case of foreshadowing as direct prophecy takes place in the early stages of "1800 Bushels." The merchant Zishou and the shopkeeper Jingyuan both remark on the considerable likelihood of a food riot breaking out among the starving tenants. During the climax, they manage to escape from the pillaging mob of tenants, but the very man who scoffed the most at their earlier warnings, Botang, is pilloried by the same mob.

While Wu's plots tend to adhere closely to chronological order, his use of flashbacks and foreshadowing enhances the sense of connectedness and recurrence of fictional incident in both backward and forward directions in time. His dramatized first-person narrators are particularly apt to backtrack in time after introducing themselves at the story's outset, while his less obtrusive third-person narrators nearly always stick to a rigorously chronological order of presentation.

## The Benefits of Technical Experimentation

Wu Zuxiang's impetuous experiment with an unreliable narrator in "Little Lord Guanguan's Tonic" suddenly provided him with a high profile on the Beijing literary scene. This story was his first to be reviewed by critics, and marked the watershed between a small and local readership before its publication in 1932, and a larger and increasingly nationwide audience beginning in the following year.

By way of contrast, Wu's minimalist approach to plot construction would eventually prove a barrier to his hope of excelling in the realm of the long novel. In the food riot subplot of "1800 Bushels," the author showed signs of advancing toward double or multiple plot lines, but he reverted to a more simple approach with his novel *Mountain Torrent*. This is not to say that he took plot lightly, for the tightly knit webs of incident within his stories betray no mark of sloppy execution; nevertheless, he did not explore the intricacies of plot construction with the same attentiveness that he brought to bear on other aspects of his craft, especially characterization. Nor was Wu an anomaly among May Fourth writers in preferring a minimalist plot structure—a writer as celebrated for intricate craftsmanship as Lu Xun also favored the single plot line in his stories. In a more settled political environment with fewer impediments to unbridled literary expression, Wu might have eventually mastered the more complex varieties of plot composition that are *de rigeur* in the long novel; but lacking the opportunity to try his hand at a second novel, he never really acquired the versatility to excel in forms outside the novella and short story.

# 8

# Central Patterns
of Metaphor Usage

In an essay entitled "Fiction and the 'Analogical Matrix,'" Mark Schorer explores the major differences in conceptualization through metaphor between Jane Austen's *Persuasion*, Emily Bronte's *Wuthering Heights*, and George Eliot's *Middlemarch*.[1] *Persuasion* portrays courtship in terms suggestive of financial transactions; *Wuthering Heights* describes the inhumanly intense passions of Catherine and Heathcliff with melodramatic metaphors of tempestuous weather and menacing animals; *Middlemarch* brims with metaphors of steady and purposive progress that embody George Eliot's forward-looking views of societal evolution.[2] These writers' analogical tendencies are less distilled and rich than the brilliantly original metaphors of fine lyric poets, but they do help us form a better acquaintance with a given writer's habits of thought and basic sensibility. "We all of us," Schorer quotes George Eliot as saying, "grave or light, get our thoughts entangled in metaphors, and act fatally on the strength of them."[3]

Wu Zuxiang did not reflect on fiction's analogical matrix with the sharply analytical self-consciousness of Eliot, but his *oeuvre* reveals a number of patterns of metaphor usage crucial to our understanding of his major categories of thought and overall literary sensibility. Early in the 1930s, for example, his alarm over the lower classes' difficulty in merely eking out a bare subsistence led to his rendering of the brutalizing effects of poverty in animalistic terms. Later, as he perceived a grassroots resurgence unfolding toward the middle of the decade, the crowd suddenly becomes an important metaphor for a broadening of social cohesion and empowerment of the previously atomized lower classes. This chapter will examine these partially submerged and yet pervasive patterns of metaphor usage that run through his works and help hold them together as a total corpus.

## *Animalistic Metaphors of Subsistence in Rural Society*

Many of Wu's metaphors portray some aspect of human existence in non-human terms. Animalistic metaphors are the major variety of such non-human metaphors in his fiction. Schorer describes how animalistic metaphors work in Bronte's *Wuthering Heights*: the demoniacal Heathcliff is often sketched in terms of a wolf or some other predatory beast.[4] Wu's animals belong to a different order altogether, for they tend to be meek and powerless rather than vicious and predatory, in keeping with the early-1930s status of Wu's lower-class characters as hapless victims of socio-economic deterioration. For example, the lame father of the tenant farmer Baldy in "Little Lord Guanguan's Tonic" reminds the callous narrator of "a snail crawling along."[5] Similarly, the glum features of the depressed unemployed shopkeeper of "The World At Peace" are often likened to the melancholy mien of a forlorn monkey. During a flogging later in the same story, the protagonist "howled . . . like a wolf with a head injury," and his wife "stomped about and wailed like a wild sow" at the sight of her husband's agony under the whip.[6] In general, the only animals of potential ferocity that Wu uses metaphorically are in a weakened or wounded condition, and he is more apt to use relatively weak and submissive-looking animals to illustrate the harsh fate of his early 1930s lower-class protagonists.

Aside from martialing animalistic metaphors to emphasize the toilsome, dispirited, or undignified quality of life in an individual main character, Wu also utilizes the metaphor of parasitism to describe the relations among many of his characters. On several occasions, he directly inserts the term "parasitism" itself into "The World At Peace" to indicate how Wang Xiaofu lives off of the odd-job earnings of his wife, mother, and son: "There was no job he could find, no matter at what hour of the day, so he became completely parasitic upon his wife, his mother, and even his child."[7] For the most part, however, Wu illustrates parasitism with more subtlety and concreteness, especially in episodes portraying lower-class figures subsisting on the sale of their blood or mother's milk. Wet-nurses in particular abound in his stories; the only one in their ranks who is spared a cruel fate is the young nanny in "On the Eve of Leaving Home." In "Two Young Sparrows," the growth of the wet-nurse's children is stunted during their breast-feeding stage, due to the Young Master Xiao Huaizi's demands on their mother's limited milk supply. In "Little Lord Guanguan's Tonic," the wealthy narrator parasitizes a lower-class couple, buying a blood transfusion from the husband and human milk as a tonic from the wife. Wang Xiaofu's wife in "The World At Peace" earns enough to feed most of her family by selling her own milk to wealthy tonic-imbibing villagers. As a result, however, her own infant wastes away and finally perishes due to the lack of milk in her mother's overtaxed breasts. Parasitism can thus be viewed as operating at two distinct levels: not only do the wealthy parasitize the poor by hiring them as wet-nurses, but lower-class adults themselves parasitize their children by drastically reducing their own infants' milk intake in order to sell mother's milk and buy grain with the proceeds.

In the economics of acute scarcity which afflicted much of rural China in the early 1930s, villagers in the economically hard-hit regions like the Anhui uplands tended to be more concerned about subsistence than prosperity.[8] While Jane Austen's prosperous milieu reveals itself through metaphors of banking and accountancy (e.g., "*funds* of enjoyment"), Wu Zuxiang's earthy economic metaphors reflect a struggle for subsistence that is degrading and often dehumanizing.[9] For instance, young Mrs. Wang of "The World At Peace" occasionally reviles her hungry baby daughter as a "red-ink commodity." Even more representative of this bitter struggle for subsistence are the words of an old widow usurer who justifies her harsh and unrelenting demands for interest on a loan to Wang Xiaofu: "My money is my blood, no less."[10] Economic resources have become so scarce that they include life-sustaining fluids, like the blood and mother's milk ordinarily stored within the body itself, and are no longer viewed simply as things to be stored outside the body in bins or coffers, much less in banks or brokerages. Under such acutely depressed economic circumstances, and compounded by the gross inadequacy or total absence of relief agencies, severe privation often leads to starvation, not merely the unpleasant but survivable "belt-tightening" periodically experienced by the poor in an economically advanced welfare state. The villagers need money for subsistence no less than they need their own blood, and they must occasionally sell even that blood or human milk to ward off starvation. It is little wonder that such rural characters are prone to speak of money in the biological, somewhat animalistic terms of blood and other bodily fluids.[11]

## Metaphors for Emotions

Among the varieties of metaphor Wu utilizes to portray characters' emotions, fluidity stands out as most prominent. For instance, the narrator of "Miss Jin and the Xue Girl" expresses his shock over the apparent moral degeneracy of his childhood sweetheart: "A hot surge of indescribable discomfort was boiling up in my heart."[12] Similarly, when the hapless shopkeeper in "The World At Peace" gets scolded as a fool for having torn down part of his house, the consequent unpleasant emotion compounded of shock and shame is compared to a sudden dousing with cold water: "A bucket of cold water had been poured over Wang Xiaofu's head; his fatigued body went limp from head to toe."[13]

Relatively pleasant emotions also seem to behave like liquids on occasion. During the climax of "The Verdant Bamboo Hermitage," courage "welled up" in the narrator.[14] Feelings of romantic passion may wax so intense that they roil about in search of an outlet: "In Miss Jin's bowels and veins, the ardor which could find no opportunity to dissipate so much as a drop of itself over some ten-odd years was now like the billowing, tumultuous waters of a swollen river that had come upon a lock gate, into which they gushed in flooding torrents."[15]

On many occasions, Wu attributes qualities of brightness and temperature to emotions. He describes romantic ardor as bright and hot, like a flame spreading through dry kindling.[16] In another story involving the passions of youth, "Flames were brightly glittering in the heart" of Die, the studious and idealistic wife of the autobiographical narrator in "On the Eve of Leaving Home."[17] In contrast, the wife of the semi-autobiographical narrator of "Twilight" finds life boring and lonely in his family's *fengjian* ["feudal"] home village, which as late as June seems "chilly even in the daytime" and replete with cold-resistant organisms like moss and millipedes.[18] Her counterpart in "On the Eve of Leaving Home" attributes the cold and dark qualities of a tomb to the village family compound, declaring, "I'm a living, red-blooded person—I can't stay buried in this ancient tomb like some kind of corpse. . . ."[19] In "Verdant Bamboo Hermitage," the chilly mustiness of Second Aunt's abode resonates with the family-imposed isolation that has grievously stunted her development as an individual. For Wu Zuxiang, a cold and dark setting thus suggest primitivity, along with a sense of doom hanging over people stuck in a backward, patriarchal milieu, while heat and light are associated with modern-looking idealism and youthful passion.

Drawing back from metaphors of doom and mortality to the realm of curable maladies, Wu sometimes renders emotions in terms of medicine or illness. This type of metaphor is one of his least unusual, since it regularly occurs in classic plays and novels such as *Romance of the Western Chamber* and *Dream of the Red Chamber*, in which a young lover pines away on a sickbed with amatory longing unless a suitable tryst or marriage is arranged. Yet this metaphor eventually took on a special modern ambience, for two of the leading May Fourth literati, Lu Xun and Guo Moruo, joined the literary crusade to purge the hidebound traditions from their countrymen's souls only after abandoning medical studies undertaken to alleviate the ills in their countrymen's bodies.[20] Lu Xun's predilection for using metaphors of illness to illustrate socio-cultural problems appealed to a broad range of May Fourth writers, as can be observed in Wu Zuxiang's description of Shanghai as the city where "infection" from negative features of Western civilization is the most grave. Most of Wu's metaphors of illness are considerably less ponderous than his thunderclap pronouncement on Shanghai. Like many characters in both popular and serious fiction, the narrator of "Miss Jin and the Xue Girl" suffers from "the illness of melancholia"—but the proffered cure of romantic passion smacks of the popular tradition, as the narrator's friend self-assuredly advises him that "a woman is the only remedy."[21] In such instances, an emotion like romantic ardor is portrayed as a curative potion.

Other types of passion seem poisonous at first glance, but eventually prove to be curative in a cathartic manner. Such are the circumstances behind the narrator's emotional agony over the barbarously stigmatized pregnant widow in "Splay-petaled Honeysuckle": "I had contracted a very dangerous fever, and didn't come out of my delirium for five or six days, during which time I thrashed about and bellowed wildly, the phrase 'splay-petaled honeysuckle' never far from my lips. "[22] The narrator eventually recovers to recount his tale, but only after purging the poisonous shock of the pregnant woman's harsh fate from his system by means of a cathartic fever.

### The Metaphor of Life as a Story

Wu Zuxiang's patterns of metaphor tend to buttress the meliorist cast of his *oeuvre*, but the piquant side of his sensibility also utilizes certain types of analogies as vehicles for its expression. Chief among these is the metaphor of life as a story. Lakoff and Johnson note the importance of this metaphor to "the entire biographical and autobiographical tradition," which "is based on the assumption . . . that everyone's life is structured like a story."[23] Wu particularly favors this metaphor in his stories with a strong element of romantic love interest; it is almost as if the love motif has at its very core a storybook quality.

The most widely read works of Chinese fiction during the first half of the twentieth century were not May Fourth novels about social problems, but sentimental love stories like Zhang Henshui's best-seller of 1930, *Fate in Tears and Laughter*, as is suggested by the reading preferences of Wu's femme fatale in "Miss Jin and the Xue Girl."[24] A love-centered plot provided most of the mass appeal of Zhang Henshui's novel, and Wu seems to have self-consciously feared that to embellish his own fiction with such a plot was to risk luring readers with cheap popular entertainment at the expense of literary edification.

The strange power to enthrall an audience with a love story all but obsesses the semi-autobiographical narrator in "The Verdant Bamboo Hermitage," Wu's work richest in the metaphor of life as a story. The narrator's impressionable wife, Ah Yuan, urges him on several occasions to cut short their summertime rural vacation stay and return to the city, but he repeatedly uses the medium of storytelling to persuade her to develop an appreciation for the piquant side of bucolic life. He has very good story material to work with, namely his aunt's teenage love scandal involving a boy who eventually drowned during a riverboat accident, and whom she finally "married" in a lugubrious combination of wedding and funeral. After twenty years of lonely widowhood in a hillside hermitage, the aunt is always eager to host the occasional guest travelling through the vicinity, and she has sent an invitation down to the nearby lowland village where the narrator and Ah Yuan are staying. According to the narrator, "If it had not been for the story about Auntie's past, we wouldn't have been nearly so eager to visit her."[25]

After one of the garrulous old women in the village compound given to salacious banter unintentionally offends Ah Yuan, the narrator repeatedly assures his embarrassed wife that Auntie is a completely different sort of person who would never behave in such a boisterous way. Nevertheless, Ah Yuan does not regain her enthusiasm for making the visit until the narrator resumes recounting Auntie's life story in a captivating manner:

> I know how to cater to the tastes of a young woman, and managed to im-
> provise several touching episodes based on the original story of Auntie,
> holding forth until she was so touched that she heaved a few long sighs and
> her eyes reddened. . . . When she listened to me go on with Auntie's story,
> she found it as delightful as something one might come across in an old-
> fashioned string-bound volume. . . . Consequently, Ah Yuan shed her origi-
> nal reluctance to make the trip and grew eager to set off. [26]

Later in the story when the increasingly uneasy narrator and his fright-ened wife are preparing to spend the night in a dark, spooky part of Auntie's house, he again resorts to storytelling in the face of her restive mood. This time, however, he "spontaneously" chooses to recount ghost stories from the old collection *Liao zhai zhi yi.* Not surprisingly, the ghost stories cause Ah Yuan to grow even more spooked: "After I had held forth for awhile, she huddled even closer to me. . . . Beads of sweat began to seep out onto her forehead and nose."[27] In this instance, the narrator is again able to use storytelling in a powerfully influential way, but by mis-take he magnifies the very fear in Ah Yuan that he had earlier sought to palliate. Yet both types of stories, love romance and ghost thriller, appeal to Ah Yuan when she is in the proper frame of mind, sentimental in the earlier episode and fearful in the latter. This parallel between the heroine's state of mind and the type of story her husband chooses to tell intensifies the storybook quality of both characters' existence.

By following Schorer in his inclusion of pertinent traits of diction under the rubric of the general metaphorical quality of a fictional work, one dis-covers that the plethora of terminology about storytelling in "The Verdant Bamboo Hermitage" bolsters the work's key metaphor of life as a story. On nearly ten separate occasions, the narrator likens the strange personal history of his love-sick hermit aunt to a story.[28] "Whenever I would think back on my home village," muses the narrator at one point, "it was exactly as if I had recalled an ancient legend." Near the suspenseful climax of the story, the narrator explicitly places himself and his wife within the frame of such stories and legends: "I had the feeling that . . . even Ah Yuan and I had undergone a transformation into the characters of a ghost story."[29] Similarly, the term "episode" is mentioned in the husband's cajoling of Ah Yuan quoted above, and the narrator refers to Auntie's odd cermonial marriage to her dead boyfriend as "the climax of her sorrowful story."[30] Finally, Auntie's story reminds the narrator of the sort of traditional tales that can be found either in "old-fashioned string-bound volumes," "vernacular fiction reprints," or "talent-meets-beauty comedies."[31] The density of such references to storytelling makes "The Verdant Bamboo Hermitage" a story largely about storytelling itself, for it is narrated by a self-conscious persona "well aware of himself as a writer," as Wayne Booth has described this type of situation.[32]

"The Verdant Bamboo Hermitage" is hardly an anomalous exercise in the metaphor of life as a story, for some of Wu's other works containing a love interest also draw on this metaphor. For instance, the wife of the narrator in "Splay-petaled Honeysuckle" refers to the "story" of his adolescent crush on a young woman whom he had not seen for over a decade since.[33] In Wu's lone experiment with the theme of the love triangle, "Miss Jin and the Xue Girl," the narrator decides to initiate a romantic liaison that might enable him to put an unhappy past romance behind him once and for all. His metaphor for this determination to start afresh in his love life is "concocting a story" that will mask over old amatory disappointments. When this new romance with Miss Jin also sputters to an inglorious halt, she writes him an abrupt letter of farewell, declaring that their "strange relationship" has been "a scene out of a farce."[34] In other words, Jin concurs in the narrator's metaphorical interpretation of their romance as a literary contrivance.

A basically mimetic writer of strong regionalistic bent, Wu Zuxiang shouldered the tasks of imaginatively recreating a recognizable social milieu and capturing the ambiance and rhythms of life in a particular locale. However, his few works which draw substantially on the metaphor of life as a story seem to exist, in the words of John Fletcher and Malcolm Bradbury, "on the border between the mimetic and autotelic species of literature, between an art made by imitating things outside itself, and an art that is an internally coherent making."[35] Instead of art imitating life, in the stories just mentioned life imitates art, at least insofar as many of Wu's unquestionably life-like characters are repeatedly compared to stylized, conventional role-models such as the talented scholar and beautiful maiden of the old-style sentimental romance.

### Metaphors of Containment: Emptiness and Fullness

Lakoff and Johnson have pointed out that a very broad assortment of activities and processes, such as vision, can be conceptualized as containments of some sort (e.g., "the center of my field of vision").[36] Mao Dun's review of *West Willow*, so intolerant in its condemnation of Wu's preference for concreteness and objectivity of observation, utilizes such a containment metaphor with the tongue-in-cheek comment that Wu "has yearned to leap clear of 'the morass of abstract generalizations'" instead of wallowing within it.[37]

Schorer has detected a variety of the containment metaphor in George Eliot's *Middlemarch* which conceptualizes intellectual growth as "fullness," in the sense of ethico-spiritual nourishment.[38] Nourishment also plays an important role in Wu's fiction up to the mid-1930s, though at a fundamental level of basic economic subsistence for his many indigent characters who lack the resources and peace of mind to undertake spiritual or moral self-cultivation. For Wu, the 1930s Depression economics of acute scarcity lent a special significance to the concepts of fullness and emptiness; emptiness incrementally spread through store and household coffers, store shelves, moneypurses, and finally hands and even stomachs. A passage in "The World At Peace" vividly describes the sounds of growling and churning made by a hunger-shrunken stomach,[39] but Wu favors the image of empty hands for what must be considered his representative metaphorical expression of penury.[40] In "Little Lord Guanguan's Tonic," a nativist member of the rural local elite who blames all of China's economic ills on foreigners claims that all the wealthy residents of the Chinese countryside have fled to the cities, leaving the villages in the stewardship of "dirt-broke paupers with bare hands and empty fists."[41] Adopting a similar turn of phrase, Botang attempts to dismiss concerns over the acute poverty afflicting the clan's tenant farmers: "They're barehanded and empty-fisted; do they still count on earning big money?" Poetic justice is served later in the same story when a group of famished "barehanded" tenants angrily seizes Botang and bustles him off for a public drubbing outdoors.[42] In "The World At Peace," the laborious peddling of wares by members of the Wang family often bears the grim result of "a pair of empty fists." Wang Xiaofu's especially earnest yearning to make an honest living through peddling usually comes to naught, and he often disconsolately returns home at night with "a pair of empty hands."[43] In each of these several episodes, subsistence is not quite within reach of desperately indigent, "empty-handed" characters.[44]

Human existence in a faltering and depressed subsistence economy is often hand-to-mouth, and a connection between the two body parts might be expected among Wu's indigent characters, for they have no money in their hands, and little or no food in their mouths. To be sure, the reader rarely glimpses these characters partaking of a decent meal, and with good reason. However, Wu does not utilize the empty mouth as a metaphor for poverty in the way that he makes use of growling stomachs and empty hands. Instead, he prefers to portray the mouth in its state of fullness [*man*, in Chinese]: not full of palpable food, but rather of the far less tangible spoken word.[45] Since a largesse with words, or of speaking by the "mouthful," has never been a trademark of the ordinary lower-class villager, it should come as no surprise that the phrase "mouthful" almost always appears within descriptions of the relatively well-to-do. The affluent narrator of "Splay-petaled Honeysuckle" utters a "mouthful of nothing but 'splay-petaled honeysuckle'" during a bout of feverish delirium.[46] The only Western character in Wu's fiction, the jovial but callous European who practices medicine at a Shanghai hospital in "Little Lord Guanguan's Tonic," speaks with "a mouthful of foreign-legation Shanghainese."[47] Similarly, the extroverted lowland aunt of the narrator in "The Verdant Bamboo Hermitage" showers the narrator and his young wife with "a mouthful . . . of embarrassing praise."[48] Finally, Zhutang, a young man of elite background who has been leading farm-tenant uprisings in "1800 Bushels," declaims "a mouthful of 'Russia this, Russia that," and "a mouthful of 'equality' and 'the proletariat.'"[49]

In each of the above cases, the speaker's character type or role in society is summed up by the particular words "filling" his mouth. The speaker in the first story cannot emotionally accept the nightmarish turn of events involving the young woman with whom he once chatted about honeysuckle as a child. In "Little Lord Guanguan's Tonic," the only sort of Chinese that the European doctor in Shanghai can speak is a sort of pidgin Shanghainese, which goes far in illustrating the insular, aloof mode of existence led by most foreigners in Chinese treaty ports. Moving back to the countryside, the unrestrainedly ardent praise bestowed upon the narrator's' wife by Elder Aunt in "The Verdant Bamboo Hermitage" is a sign that she has not lost the vitality and spontaneity of her youth, unlike her psychologically twisted counterpart in the hillside hermitage. Finally, the leftist slogans shouted by the rural clansman Zhutang in "1800 Bushels" indicate that modern ideologies of rebellion have often been proselytized by political activists hailing from such bastions of conservatism as the rural clan elite.

Wu Zuxiang thus portrays the rural destitute as empty-handed and their elite social betters as spinning out words by the mouthful; as Roland Barthes has argued in *Mythologies*, the speech of the poor and oppressed is often mired in the monotonous daily round of humble activities, and can rarely rise to true eloquence. It is the relatively well-educated and wealthy portion of society that can more imaginatively discuss either their own lives or else the "lower depths," whichever they would choose.[50] Yet even the "wealthy" in such a destitute society as Wu's homeland in the early 1930s are themselves far too strapped to be rendered in metaphors of the bank or counting house, as are Jane Austen's upper-class characters. Their largesse is that of garrulity; in "1800 Bushels," for example, none of the clan elite suffer a want for words, but nearly all have practically run out of personal savings, and thus hope to find some way to tap the clan granary.

Wu's fondness for metaphors of containment can be deduced from his decided preference for *man* [lit., "full"] among the various quantitative adjectives expressing entirety or completeness. According to Yuen Ren Chao, quantitate adjectives of the "determinative" category express a relative amount of something instead of a specific or quantified amount (e.g., "loaded with medals" or "covered with medals" instead of "wearing three Iron Crosses").[51] In Wu Zuxiang's major collection of fiction, *West Willow*, *man* is by far the most prominent of among the four relatively common quantitative adjectives expressing completeness, which include *man*, *yi* ("to the whole extent of"), *quan* ("entire"), and *zheng* ("whole").[52] He is especially fond of using *man* in the sense of "all over" or "covered with," which extends the concept of replete containment to include the sense of planar coverage. For example, Wu often writes of something "covering" [*man*] the face or cheeks, such as a beard, a modest smile, a wry smile, tears, redness, sweat, or a hot flash.[53]

At other times, Wu uses *man* as a quantitative adjective in reference to other parts of the body or the body as a whole, like in the phrases "The skin over her entire body was cracked and peeling" and "His heart brimmed with excitement."[54] *Man* is also often used in reference to places instead of the body, including: "red and white blotches spattered all over the ground"; "people were crowded all over the riverbank"; "the fields covered with water";[55] "a skyful of stars";[56] "a wall grown packed with moss";[57] "crowded all around the side of the feed bin";[58] and "crowded all around the gate of the ancestral temple."[59] Clearly, Wu exhibits an unconscious bent toward the metaphor of containment in his choice among quantitative adjectives, and this in turn suggests something of the overall metaphorical density of the full-empty dichotomy.

As a writer living in an unusually prosperous and confident nation, George Eliot uses fullness as a metaphor for spiritual plenty. In Wu Zuxiang's fiction set in the impoverished Chinese countryside, fullness and emptiness illustrate the overriding problems of maintaining subsistence and slowing the trend towards social deterioration. With the hands of the poor empty, and the mouths of the wealthy full of ominous remarks about social decline, Wu's characters lack the emotional security that is an starting point of the quest for spiritual plenty that Eliot's novels so often portray.

## Crowds as Metaphors for Social Coalescence

Wu's fiction up to 1934 features an abundance of characters who are cut adrift from their peers amidst a declining rural social order. Many meet with an untimely death, such as the unemployed shopkeeper of "The World At Peace," the fallen heroine of "Miss Jin and the Xue Girl," the outcast pregnant widow of "Splay-petaled Honeysuckle," and the peasant Baldy of "Little Lord Guanguan's Tonic." Others become separated from a loved one or a cherished social group, such as classmates in "On the Eve of Leaving Home," or a spouse or family members in "Two Young Sparrows," "The Flowering Gardenia," "The Verdant Bamboo Hermitage," "Little Lord Guanguan's Tonic," and "The Woodcutter." In one way or another, main characters in his works of social decline tend to become isolated.

On the sole occasion that crowding or banding together takes place in Wu's stories from the early 1930s, an assembly of mostly poor villagers collects on a riverbank in "Little Lord Guanguan's Tonic" to gape at the lurid execution of the peasant Baldy. For the most part, the crowd remains silent immediately following the hackings of the executioner's sword; however, a small group of "footloose urchins" [*ye haizi*] has the temerity to clap in raucous approval. After Baldy's bloody head surprisingly snaps back to an upright position, a group of vigorous peasants in the crowd hurries forward to hurl rocks at his head "as if they were attacking a snake."[60] In a more formulistic work of mainstream leftist fiction, lower-class youths and peasants would hardly be portrayed as cheering and abetting the brutal execution of one of their own class. Yet this story, which belongs to Wu's early fiction reflecting social disintegration, leaves open the possibility that collective action by the rural masses might not only fail to forestall the destruction of a sympathetic peasant character, but could even hasten the lower-class character's demise.

Beginning in 1934, collective action of the rural masses was transformed into playing a positive role in Wu's fiction, which was becoming more mainstream leftist. The famished tenants of "1800 Bushels" stage a successful food riot, "grandly surging ahead" [*haohaodangdang*] to seize the grain squirrelled away in the ancestral temple by the increasingly feckless local elite.[61] The crowd of indigent tenants is led by Zhutang, the youthful revolutionary of elite background who has returned to his rural homeland from an urban center of radical political movements, most likely Shanghai:

> A large crowd of bare-chested men were pouring this way and that in the general direction of the ancestral hall. The sound of gongs and drums grew more cacophonous, along with the devilish racket generated by footloose urchins who leaped about, shouting and whistling. . . .

The large crowd of men had already grandly surged ahead to the gate of the ancestral hall. Now jumbled together with uproarious, thrill-seeking footloose urchins, the crowd of men were carrying wooden buckets, hempen sacks, winnowing baskets, rice-washing baskets, and carrying-pole baskets; they were jammed together in the threshhold.[62]

Significantly, the "footloose urchins" [*ye haizi*] who formerly applauded the beheading of a fellow indigent villager are now portrayed as comrades in the peasant food riot, cheering on the crowd of adult tenants with shouts and whistles.[63] Moreover, the grassroots crowd itself has changed from a threatening and amoral mob of gaping onlookers to a "positive" and powerful force in society. This incident was a watershed for Wu Zuxiang, for he would never again revert to an unflinchingly negative portrayal of the rural crowd throughout the rest of his writing career.

Collective action by the masses is geared to the defensive rather than the offensive for the peasant villagers in "A Certain Day." The peasants defend their fellow villager, Da Mao, from his local-elite father-in-law who has bitterly accused the young peasant man of having done away with his own wife, the old squire's late daughter. Da Mao naturally fumes with indignation over his father-in-law's slanderous charge, but refrains from forcefully confronting him, wary of the elder's network among the local elite. Yet Da Mao's peasant friends soon assemble in his defense, and reply to the old interloper's threats with warnings of their own: "You'd better scram with your tail between your legs while you still have the chance! " In the face of this firm solidarity among the masses, the greatly outnumbered old squire does in fact beat a hasty retreat: "Everybody crowded together at Da Mao's gate, staring and raucously shouting at the retreating weasel-like figure, who was slowly and unsteadily shuffling away across the grain-drying yard."[64]

With the 1938 publication of "The Requisitioned Boat," crowding signals the vital social regimentation necessary for wartime military preparedness. A number of shabbily clad children of poverty "crowd together" near the docks of Anqing to imitate a platoon of Chinese soldiers which is marching and shouting Anti-Japanese slogans.[65] This show of spontaneous organizing ability and patriotism on the part of the masses makes the narrator all the more frustrated over the neglect of the war effort by corrupt officers like the commander on board the boat. The populist message of this story comes across with clarity—the grassroots folk, including even bands of ragged children, are solidly behind the War of Resistance, but their solidarity is being abused by a number of crooked elite officers who sabotage the public weal for the sake of personal gain.

Elite abuse of privileges is no longer a major stumbling block that would compromise wartime solidarity in *Mountain Torrent*. What prevents the peasants from joining the war effort at first is their traditional fear of warlord armies, along with their suspicion that any soldier is capable of behaving like a bandit and getting away with it unpunished. In order to avoid the possibility of harassment from their own nation's guerila army, the peasants in *Mountain Torrent* at one point flee together to a hilltop fastness. At this point, the peasant Zhang Sanguan gradually begins to stare with mingled awe and disappointment at the crowded ranks of the retreating Chinese army: "As he gazed at the vast and mighty greyish stream grandly surging ahead [*haohaodangdang*], . . . he felt disappointment and sorrow of a sort that he had never previously experienced."[66]

Zhang and the other peasants in hiding finally realize that this retreating army is the only major buffer between their village and the marauding Japanese invaders. When the Chinese guerila army returns to the region later in the work, the villagers strike a compromise between hiding from the army and enlisting: they serve as supply-carriers for the army and form a village defense militia. Unlike active duty in the army, neither of these types of alternative service involves much risk of death or even prolonged absence from home. The peasants have become part of the Resistance crowd, but have managed to avoid taking the drastic step of joining the ranks at the front line.

Though *Mountain Torrent* may be a patriotic wartime novel, it does not glorify a reckless spirit of self-sacrificing bellicosity. To the contrary, the narrator at one point outright declares, "Patriotic fervor of the knight-errant's sort is flimsy and worthless."[67] A guerila leader in the novel argues instead that the grassroots citizenry must be channeled and concentrated into large units in order "to begin the necessary organization of the people" and facilitate "cooperation between civilians and the military."[68] While a knight-errant acts largely from personal initiative and often sheer bravado, an effective military defense depends on the large-scale regimentation that the author of "The Requisitioned Boat" and *Mountain Torrent* patriotically supports. Crowds and collective action thus function as a metaphor for progressive solidarity among the masses in Wu's later works; in Wu's works prior to the mid-1930s, rural crowds are either absent or else malignantly regressive, as in the execution scene of "Little Lord Guanguan's Tonic." Grassroots crowds in "1800 Bushels" and "A Certain Day" grapple successfully with the local elite, but these class antagonisms gradually wither away in Wu's wartime fiction of full-blown unity behind the national cause. Crowding thus varies greatly over the course of Wu's career, depending on whether it occurs in an early work of socio-economic fragmentation and paralysis at the grassroots level, a mid-1930s class-based work reflecting a resurgent coalescence among the masses, or a wartime novel of across-the-board unification against the foreign invader.

## A Meliorist Slant in Metaphor Usage

The meliorist thrust of key metaphors in Wu Zuxiang's fiction appears quite early in his *oeuvre*. The patriarchal mode of life in his home village is described in terms of darkness and decay, while the hard-pressed lower-class characters repeatedly reveal their hands as being utterly empty. The economically better-off characters may not find themselves in such dire straits of destitution, but they nevertheless wax eloquent with mouthfuls of sobering revelations of the severe socio-economic decline over recent years. In contrast, from the mid-1930s to the end of Wu's writing career in the 1940s, crowding serves as an optimistic metaphor of societal coalescence and grassrooots resurgence, as the themes of acute impoverishment and overt class conflict gradually recede from center stage.

Other metaphor patterns function mainly to intensify the piquancy of Wu's stories. His portrayal of emotions as liquids, along with the metaphor of life as a story, are particularly effective in providing an imaginative respite from a decidedly sober mimetic rendition of a rural society struggling to pull itself out of a cycle of decline.

### PART THREE

# Pullback from Contemporaneity

# 9

# From Dramatizing the Present
# to Reclaiming the Heritage

A contemporaneity of perspective remained a constant in Wu Zuxiang's fiction from the early days until his final efforts in the 1940s. Even on those rare occasions in which the narrative would backtrack one or two decades from the present historical moment to the recent past, as in "The Verdant Bamboo Hermitage" and "The Woodcutter," Wu would conclude by framing the story within a period close or identical to the narrative present. The past held little interest for him unless it could highlight or explain some facet of present-day society, as with the contrastive utilization of history in his stories of 1933–1934, in which bygone days of prosperity and social harmony throw the impoverishment and social disintegration of the narrative present into sharp relief.

By the mid-1950s, however, Wu's writings of a contemporary mold consisted largely of made-to-order essays about model proletarian workers and other such testaments of fealty to the new regime in Beijing. Contemporaneity as serious literary practice had simply ceased to exist for him: he had not written any fiction for over a decade, and would indeed never again come forth with another story. Except for some brief stints as manuscript editor for journals like *Renmin wenxue* [People's Literature], his serious involvement with literature rarely strayed from his post-1949 academic specialization in pre-modern Chinese fiction. It was as if Wu had taken his laboriously crafted creations on canvas and scroll, piled them in an inconspicuous corner of his studio to gather dust, and set off at once for the local museum to take up a permanent post as curator of dynastic art. His high profile in the academic field of the Ming-Qing vernacular novel gradually came to overshadow his former identity as a creative writer, so that up-and-coming generations on the Beijing literary scene came to regard his earlier achievements in fiction writing as secondary to his recent activities in Ming-Qing literary research.

At the midpoint of this century, Wu was certainly not alone in adopting the discreet strategy of leaving aside his fiction of autonomous, contemporary, and socially engaged discourse in favor of serving as an unobtrusive preserver of the nation's ancient literary heritage. Shen Congwen went so far as to abandon his public involvement in the field of literature, becoming a literal, not merely figurative, museum curator.[1] As Joseph Levenson pointed out, the vigilant new regime tended to allow a considerable amount of latitude for artistic expressions of ideology counter to Maoism, as long as these heresies were embodied in cultural artifacts from the inert imperial past rather than emanating from dynamic contemporary cultural discourse: "The communists knew they had living men to assail, non-communists just as modern and post-Confucian as themselves, not the stuffed men from a costume past (whose clothes they were stealing anyway, to display as their 'national heritage')."[2] This basic strategy of shifting one's frame of professional inquiry back in time toward the relatively innocuous museum world of past dynasties naturally involved a heavy forfeiture of literary creativity for both Wu and Shen, but it certainly paid off over the long haul in terms of survival value, as they both emerged from the Cultural Revolution in far better shape than their colleagues who had maintained a high profile on the post-1949 literary scene.[3]

Although the nationwide implementation of Mao's pervasive and intimidating political controls over literature in 1949 was a key factor in Wu's gravitation towards the cultural past, he had begun distancing himself from the contemporary literary scene at least two years in advance of the Communist civil war victory.[4] This may seem surprising in light of his decision in 1946 to take a leave of absence from his academic post in order to resume his relatively high-profile post as personal secretary to General Feng Yuxiang, the ambitious KMT military official who was cultivating his image among literati and the media alike as a contemporary populist leader of exemplary rectitude. Yet the subsequent inglorious outcome of the working relationship between the General and his right-hand secretary proved instrumental in hastening Wu's disengagement from the sort of active public role within the contemporary literary scene that he had often played in Wuhan and Chongqing during the War.

### The Trip to America in Feng Yuxiang's Entourage

Busy with teaching classes at Central University in Chongqing between 1942 and 1946, Wu naturally accepted a smaller volume of work assignments from Feng than he had prior to his Sichuan academic appointment. Nevertheless, he regularly edited manuscripts that Feng sent him, even though he often complained in his diaries about their clumsy diction and simple-minded, repetitive content.[5] In a word, these shortcomings could be overlooked in writings designed to galvanize the broad popular masses in resistance to the invader, especially the speeches and poems from the initial three years of the War when Chinese morale was still relatively high and Feng's optimism seemed spontaneous rather than forced.[6]

Feng once again began making frequent contacts with Wu at the beginning of 1946, when he formally invited the writer to accompany him on a long government assignment abroad. Wu at first hesitated, citing the difficulty of securing a leave of absence from his university.[7] Moreover, Shuyuan disapproved of the idea on financial grounds, reminding her husband that Feng had failed to reimburse him for business travel expenses on several occasions; she was surely not thrilled with the idea of being separated from him for a whole year, either.[8]

Nevertheless, the reasons in favor of a trip abroad finally proved compelling to Wu. For one thing, the university president was insisting that he add a course in rhetoric and drop his "pet" modern Chinese literature class, which had never drawn more than a few students, and was thus not at all cost-effective from the administration's perspective. Wu, in turn, was quite adamant in his unwillingness to teach a course such as rhetoric, which he felt was totally unrelated to his area of expertise.[9] Notwithstanding Wu's growing dissatisfaction with the conditions of employment at Central University, he was more and more unhappy about the increasing problem of personal safety in and around the campus itself. A rash of bandit attacks on campus early in 1946 led to the administration's cancellation of all evening classes by March of that year.[10] Last but not least among Wu's considerations was his curiosity about the overseas civilization of which he had read a great deal but never had a chance to observe from close range.

Wu set off from Chongqing with Feng and part of the General's family in July 1946, and after arriving in Shanghai completed preparations for a September ocean passage to the United States. As a high-level Nationalist official, Feng's mission was to tour and report on selected U.S. irrigation and water conservation facilities. He had previously made a successful petition to Chiang Kai-shek's inner leadership circle to be appointed to a commission investigating U.S. water conservation technology, an area in which the General had no significant knowledge or previous interest. James Sheridan has surmised that the real reason for going abroad was Feng's uncertainty over what course of action to take in the rapidly expanding struggle between the Nationalists and the Communists—by staying abroad, he could avoid being stampeded into prematurely committing himself one way or the other.[11]

This political interpretation of the General's motives is borne out not only by his exhortatory September 1946 letter to Chiang Kai-shek advocating peace and political reform, but more importantly by the fact that he showed little interest in water conservancy during the tour, instead busying himself with getting filmed and photographed, as well as dictating

Wu standing between General Feng Yuxiang (right) and one of
the General's aides; America, winter 1946–1947. (*Photo cour-
tesy of Wu Zuxiang*)

streams of letters and articles about Chinese politics.[12] U.S. Soil Conservation Service Assistant Chief Walter Lowdermilk led Feng's tour group
through about one-third of its itinerary before the General's utter lack of
interest in water conservancy persuaded Lowdermilk to take leave of the
group and cancel the rest of the itinerary.

Although Feng maintained a regular correspondence with Chiang Kai-
shek during the early stages of his American sojourn, by the time several
months had passed he came forth with a number of speeches and press re-
leases that denounced the Nationalist strongman as a warmongering dic-

tator unworthy of U.S. support. The immanent break in relations between Feng and Chiang is presaged in one of the General's speeches from the autumn of 1947:

> "An American friend asked me whether or not China needs America's assistance now that the War has come to a victorious conclusion. I can say with conviction that there is a need for American assistance. But we must not rise to the aid of a dictatorial government; we must certainly not assist the Chinese people in slaughtering one another."[13]

Defying a stern Nationalist order in December 1947 to return immediately to China, Feng stayed in the U.S. to voice strong opposition to Chiang Kai-shek for several more months. As the tide of the Civil War turned strongly in favor of the Communists during the first half of 1948, Feng prepared to go back to China "to start mending—or, perhaps, building—political fences there." But he never made it back, dying along with his daughter Feng Xiaoda from the effects of a projection-room fire aboard the Soviet ocean liner *Pobeda* in the Black Sea.[14]

Even if Feng had managed to survive the accident aboard the Soviet vessel, he would probably not have resumed his working relationship with Wu Zuxiang. According to one of the long-time members of Feng's U.S. entourage, Zhang Yuanxi, during the summer of 1947 Feng and Wu had gotten embroiled in an altercation which led to Wu's abrupt dismissal. Wu had long been complaining to Zhang in private about Feng's authoritarian and boorish ways, but what tried Wu's patience more than anything else was the task of editing and recopying Feng's long-winded diaries. Because the General tended to repeat himself regularly, Wu was often able to condense Feng's daily average of ten pages of rough draft into one or two pages of edited copy. Feng had been fuming for some time over the extent of these editorial deletions, but Wu firmly refused to alter his approach to handling the diary material, nor was he in any mood to apologize for his supposed excesses in abridgement. Finally flying into a rage when it became obvious that the anticipated words of contrition were not forthcoming, Feng immediately fired him, making Wu the second private secretary to be ousted from the General's U.S. entourage.[15]

Wu Zuxiang had already begun distancing himself from Feng and the contemporary socio-political situation several weeks before this incident broke out, for in the only report he published on his American travels, he did not so much as mention Feng Yuxiang anywhere in the essay.[16] Nor did Wu have anything to say upon the occasion of Feng's death in 1948, as he would that same year in a restrained but affectionate memorial tribute upon the passing of the distinguished scholar Zhu Ziqing.[17] The unpleasant and even humiliating conclusion of Wu's dozen years in service under

Feng seems to have firmed his resolve to stick with university teaching as a profession—never again would he enter employment as a private secretary for a political or military patron.

Wu did not touch on anything of a political nature in the few essays he published between the end of the World War and the collapse of the Nationalist regime in 1949. He seemed to be following a wisely discreet strategy of "wait and see." Publicly favoring one or the other of the two authoritarian political parties grappling for power was to risk reprisals from the opposing party. Even as early as 1945, when Wu's dreams of becoming a professional writer were still alive, a diary entry from 30 August reveals his thoroughgoing pessimism about the likelihood of democracy emerging from China's entrenched political authoritarianism and glaring lack of the concept of a loyal opposition in government.[18]

As careful as Wu had been to avoid political controversy, he could not return to his previous academic post at Central University, whose administration had already fired him. In retrospect, Wu believes his dismissal from Central, a Nationalist-run college, to be a direct result of his past association with Feng; considering the Nationalists' escalating intolerance of dissent shortly before their collapse on the mainland, the controversial nature of Wu's connection to Feng may well have been a factor in his dismissal.[19] Whatever the actual behind-the-scenes circumstances may have been, Wu still felt politically secure enough to settle down in the Nationalist capital, where in the autumn of 1947 he found a teaching post at the Nanjing Women's Academy of Arts and Sciences. Unfortunately, the Academy depended largely upon U.S. educational foundation support, which dried up with the 1949 Communist victory in the civil war. Through no real fault of his own, Wu once again found himself without a teaching post.

### The Transition to Life Under Maoism

Wu knew that Mao Zedong and his fellow party leaders had instituted strict political controls over literature and art in their wartime capital of Yan'an, and were unlikely to grow suddenly tolerant now that they had moved their capital to Beijing. Yet for Wu and most of his peers, there seemed to be no alternative but to remain in China under Communist rule. Chiang Kai-shek's reputation, fairly solid among non-aligned intellectuals like Wu as recently as 1945, had plummeted to new depths in the wake of his inept leadership in the debacle with the Communists.[20] Only a small minority of China's major writers and intellectuals fled to exile in Taiwan with what remained of Chiang's defeated regime.[21]

The new Communist government in Beijing sent out a nationwide call in the autumn of 1949 for an organizational meeting of writers and humanities academics. Wu's participation in the Beijing meeting enabled him to land a literature professorship at his old alma mater of Qinghua University. He taught there only until 1952, at which time the Maoist government transformed the formerly diversified university into a Soviet-style institute of engineering and natural sciences. Wu thereupon got transferred to Beijing University, which was now unrivalled as the capital's elite institute of higher education in the social sciences and humanities. Here Wu would remain for the rest of his career, no more than a short bicycle ride from the campus where he had written most of his stories during the 1930s.

Half a decade later, the party-orchestrated Hundred Flowers Campaign of 1956–57 stirred hopes that the government's political and organizational regimentation of the intelligentsia might be loosening up at long last, finally allowing them the freedom of inquiry and expression so necessary for the full blossoming of intellectual creativity.[22] Wu was one of the many literati swept up in the optimistic ferment that first began in 1956. This was the year in which he entered the Communist Party and accepted a salaried administrative post in the secretariat of the Chinese Writers' Association; it was around this time, too, when he joined the editorial board of the nation's most prominent journal of contemporary literature, *Renmin wenxue*. Yet the Anti-Rightist Purge of 1957–58 chilled his hopes for a rebirth of a vital, honest, and non-formulaic contemporary literature; by 1958 he had withdrawn from his salaried administrative post in the Writers' Association, and had also decided to cut down on editorial activities connected with contemporary literature. There were plenty of interesting topics to research in the area of the classic vernacular novel, and much less political interference and doctrinaire gibberish to contend with.[23]

Political storm clouds had once again gathered by the middle of the 1960s, however, and the chaotic Cultural Revolution decade of 1966–1976 brought Wu Zuxiang his share of misery. Although spared the savage Red Guard beatings that drove friends like Lao She to suicide, Wu was forced to clean campus privies regularly, and had to live apart from his family in an improvised lock-up from July to December in 1968.[24] He managed to bear up under this psychological strain with fewer ill effects than Shuyuan, whose psychological scars from a nervous breakdown of sorts during this period continued to trouble her intermittently until her death in the mid-1980s.[25]

Nearly every prominent intellectual family had their house ransacked by Red Guards during the Cultural Revolution, and the Wus were no exception: he lost a number of old manuscripts of fiction and diaries this way in 1966.[26] But the worst loss of all might have been the spiritual aridity and stifling of creativity that resulted from the harsh intimidation of intellectuals during that tumultuous decade. Never was Wu's literary career so barren as during the fourteen years between 1963 and 1977, the longest period during his adult life over which he published nothing at all.

Fortunately, Wu was able to resume his research on the classic novel soon after the the Cultural Revolution finally ground to a halt. In fact, both before and after that decade of chaos (1966–1976), his post-1949 non-fiction writings have been of no small significance. Yet if Wu was able to re-kindle his skills in composing scholarly treatises after the Cultural Revolution, why could he not manage to revive his old knack for fiction writing as well?

The roots of the problem go back to many years before Mao formulated and enforced the idea of politics being "in command" of literature. As an extremely utilitarian view of literature expanded rapidly during the 1930s and 1940s, the expectation that serious writers do their share on behalf of "national salvation" [*jiuguo*] was becoming an onerous preoccupation among Chinese literati. The moral burden of having to justify the social utility of one's literary works became more and more pervasive during the national crisis of the 1937–1945 Sino-Japanese conflict. Even before that time, various literary pressure groups and political front organizations such as the League of Left-wing Writers had been engaged in interminable debates over what sorts of things a socially responsible writer ought to communicate through his works. However, before 1937, it was not yet too difficult for many writers to look the other way as these heated factional quarrels and "battles of slogans" raged, choosing simply to write, instead of wrangling protractedly over exactly how and what one "ought" to write.

The sense of national urgency inspired by the Japanese invasion of 1937 caused even the less factional-minded of Chinese writers like Wu Zuxiang to think increasingly in terms of categorical imperatives. As mentioned in Chapter 5, Wu was hardly alone in setting aside the May Fourth spirit of no-holds-barred socio-cultural criticism to call for popularized and optimistic literature that would bolster "the race's spirit of resistance to aggression."[27] The typical result of these bold manifestos was that the works written under such premises, such as *Mountain Torrent*, neither catalyzed a growth in popularity among the mass public nor marked an advance in objective aesthetic standards.

China's rapid drift into civil war following the defeat of Japan plunged war-weary writers and readers back into a state of acute anxiety about the future. Relieved at the cessation of fighting brought about by the Communist triumph, writers like Wu were simultaneously wary of the new regime's stringent cultural policy. Appealing phrases like "New Democracy" might be sanguinely bandied about, but Mao's directives on literature and art were a far stiffer and more enforceable version of the populist and didactic imperatives of the wartime Nationalists. Henceforth, writers who did not specifically cater to an audience of "workers, peasants, and soldiers" would be petty bourgeois deviants at best, counterrevolutionary enemies of the people at worst.[28] Mao magnanimously exempted himself from this edict, writing dozens of classical-meter poems over the following decades which were hardly comprehensible to the all-important "broad masses." However, ordinary Chinese writers without such exalted political standing would not dare to enjoy the prerogative of tacitly ignoring this straitjacket on literary creativity until some two to three years after the Mao's death in 1976. By that time, practically nobody in Wu Zuxiang's generation seemed interested in writing fiction anymore; Wu's recent publication of memoirs in essay form has been typical of his generation's efforts of late.[29]

Almost every bit of the significant fiction written in China since the cultural thaw of 1978–79 has been penned by writers at middle age or even younger. There has simply not yet been a writer in 20th-century China who has continued to produce quality serious fiction for several decades on end in the manner of such U.S. notables as Willa Cather or John Steinbeck. Some P.R.C. literary critics like Yuan Liangjun may well deride C. T. Hsia's speculation over whether Wu Zuxiang "would have emerged as a truly great story writer if he had lived under a different ideological climate."[30] Yet Hsia was perceptive in his recognition of Wu's inability to succeed as the type of heavily didactic and populist writer encouraged and sponsored by China's various authoritarian regimes from 1937 to 1977. While out of the public spotlight, Wu himself tacitly admitted his inability to write well for a popular readership, noting in his diary of 1945 that "the standards of serious literature should not be lowered in order to cater to the masses' tastes, but should be maintained so that the masses' cultural level might be raised."[31] Wu's deep-seated May Fourth literati values conflict with Mao's 1942 decree that popularization be given priority over elevation in cultural policy;[32] according to Wu, the universalization of education and improvement of the masses' standard of living could contribute to the popularization of culture much more effectively than governmental experiments with the production and distribution of subliterature. To categorically circumscribe the problem of popularizing culture within the scope of a policy on literature was totally wrongheaded, in his view.[33]

The heterodoxy of Wu's private views on serious literature, when viewed in the context of Mao's anti-intellectual decrees on cultural policy, have surely played a crucial role in the unrealizability of the dream so often articulated in his wartime diaries: a post-war career as a professional writer. His inability during the War to attract a popular readership led naturally to his abandonment of imaginative writing in the face of decade after decade of saber-rattling populist P.R.C. governmental directives on literary creation. If the latitude of tolerance which the Deng leadership temporarily extended to writers in the late 1970s had somehow been instituted with viable legal safeguards three decades earlier, perhaps Wu might have indeed become a "truly great story writer" by virtue of a prolific fictional output spanning five decades instead of two.

### Writings After the Abandonment of Fiction

Beginning in the 1950s, Wu maintained a role in the world of Chinese letters as a publishing academic. Of the various types of articles he wrote after giving up fiction, his essays in literary history and criticism constitute his most signficant contribution.[34] They reflect the professional dimension of the latter half of his life: research and teaching in the field of pre-modern Chinese fiction. Workmanlike and readable if not exactly brilliant or groundbreaking, these articles tend to analyze fiction either in relation to technical features or else in terms of Marxist-oriented class theory.[35]

A more personal and spontaneous type of writing that Wu has undertaken during this period is the memoir in essay form. These anecdotal essays present vivid recollections of Wu's past and his association with peers on the 1930s literary scene like Zhu Ziqing and Zhang Tianyi. When Wu strays from personal recollections to a mode of reconstructing hazy impressions, however, his memoirs in essay form lose much of their appealing authenticity. For example, his 1982 retrospective essay on Lu Xun acknowledges that the two writers never met or corresponded, yet claims that Wu had often had vivid dreams of Lu Xun during his former days as an active writer.[36] However, when reading through Wu's voluminous wartime diaries, I found no mention at all of Lu Xun, much less any reference to the senior author as a dream apparition: it was Zhang Tianyi, Wu's close friend from his days in Nanjing before the War, who often appeared in the dreams that Wu recorded in his diaries from the early 1940s.[37] The Maoist government's apotheosis of Lu Xun to the status of an infallible cult figure is surely a factor in the less authentic ring to Wu's retrospective essay on him, as compared with the more intimate and unaffected essays on Zhang Tianyi and Zhu Ziqing.

The other type of article Wu has written from time to time since mid-century is didactic and political in tone, as well as contemporaneous in terms of subject matter. From time to time, Wu dared to join the chorus of voices opposing the creeping politicization of all aspects of life and work in the People's Republic. For example, during the short thaw of the 1956–57 Hundred Flowers period, he criticized the habit among many poorly educated party cultural apparatchiks of offhandedly rushing into condemning a work of literature *in toto* on the basis of little or no research, but rather some overblown perception of ideological heresy.[38] More daring, still, was Wu Zuxiang's signing of a petition to Deng Xiaoping early in 1989 calling for the release of all political prisoners, including the dissident Wei Jingsheng, a *bête noire* of Deng's.[39]

During the first decade of the Maoist regime, however, Wu usually deferred to the political exigencies of the time, not only through refraining from criticism of the government or its representatives, but also by actively responding to various party-led campaigns for unifying public opinion and stamping out heresy. For example, practically the entire August 1951 issue of *Xin guancha* [New Observer] was devoted to laudatory articles about the invariably exemplary behavior of the Communist armies as they marched through cities newly liberated from the retreating Nationalists; in this issue, Wu's article glowingly describes the victory march of the Liberation Army through Nanjing.[40] Though the end of the Civil War was undoubtedly welcomed by most of the war-weary populace, Wu's image of the soldiers' march as an extremely festive occasion seems drummed up and hyperbolic, particularly if compared with the sober eyewitness account by Doak Barnett, a social scientist present at similar victory marches in Beijing.[41] One can only surmise that for Wu Zuxiang in the early 1950s, a balanced and restrained factuality was secondary to making an emphatic gesture of loyalty to the wary new government. Czeslaw Milosz has aptly portrayed the accommodating frame of mind of many an intellectual under state socialism: "Obviously, I must pay for the right to practice my profession with a certain number of articles and odes in the way of tribute. Still, one's life on earth is not judged by transitory panegyrics written out of necessity."[42]

Wu Zuxiang's written gestures of fidelity to Beijing included both encomiums of Chinese exemplars and vitriolic satire of foreign interventionists. Since Washington was still sticking to an intransigent policy of nonrecognition toward Beijing, a January 1951 issue of the *New Observer* was devoted to articles condemning what were portrayed as the oddities and decadence of the "bourgeois" way of life in the U.S. For that issue, Wu contributed a sardonic article recounting the rude and shameless antics of some unemployed young U.S. war veterans whom he had encountered during his 1946–47 trip to America.[43] In a later issue of *New Observer* devoted to exemplary north Chinese industrial workers, an article by Wu dutifully extols the diligence and modesty of a model Stakhanovite steel worker in An'gang.[44]

By contributing articles on the shortcomings of certain literati who had incurred the party's wrath, Wu played an active but not inflammatory role in the campaigns of denunciation against the literary historian Yu Pingbo in 1954, as well as the writers Ding Ling and Feng Xuefeng in 1957.[45] Like most establishment intellectuals who played a visible role in these harsh campaigns of the 1950s, Wu has of late preferred not to discuss his participation in them, and would impatiently change the subject as soon as it came up in interviews.[46] To his credit, however, ever since 1959 he has avoided joining ranks with party apparatchiks in the ongoing cycle of denunciation campaigns targeted against talented writers and scholars.

Besides the Hundred Flowers polemic "A View of Mine," another highly politicized article in the literary realm about which Wu feels proud rather than regretful came out in 1978 during the early stages of the post-Mao thaw. Without actually naming any taboo names, the article "On *Water Margin*" rebuts Chairman Mao's notorious argument that the classic novel *Shui hu zhuan* [Water Margin] "preached a capitulationist line."[47] The ultra-leftist political campaign instigated by Mao in the middle of 1975 to denounce *Water Margin* had been targeted against both Zhou Enlai and Deng Xiaoping for their supposed capitulation to capitalism.[48] Wu argues in reply that the hero of the novel, the outlaw chief Song Jiang, was not the capitalist miscreant that the ultra-leftists had wrongheadedly accused him of being, but was instead sincerely trying to carry out the traditional ethical imperatives of loyalty to the emperor and filial piety toward his parents, both of which were nearly universal in China at the time the novel was written.[49] By defending the worthiness of Song Jiang's motives in a historical context, Wu made a deft gesture of support for Deng Xiaoping, who not only had been nicknamed "Song Jiang" in the early 1950s, but had also seemed as willing as Song Jiang to deal pragmatically with the powers that be in the world, instead of defensively sealing his kingdom off from extensive contact with the outside world.[50] Wu's Aesopian defense of the modern-day "capitulationist" counterparts of Song Jiang suggests that as a curator of the literary heritage, he would not limit himself to the antiquarian's protection of artifacts from the past, but would occasionally utilize the artifacts to serve present exigencies—as Mao himself had so often urged.

## A Twilight Nod to the 20th-Century Literary Heritage

Most of Wu's energies in the 1980s were spent on Ming-Qing literary research, as well as the training of a new generation of academic specialists in pre-modern Chinese fiction at Beijing University. Because recurrent anti-intellectual purges under Mao had devastated the formative period in the careers of the current middle-aged generation of P.R.C. humanities scholars, elderly scholars who had laid down a solid foundation in scholarship prior to 1949 had to play a crucial role in re-establishing and expanding academic programs that had been suppressed or deformed during the Cultural Revolution.[51] As late as 1983, Wu Zuxiang was one of but a small handful of humanities professors at Beijing University technically qualified to chair a doctoral dissertation committee; his middle-aged counterparts were still learning the ropes, and needed to consult with him regularly over matters that they would have mastered long ago under normal peacetime circumstances.

In spite of these demands on Wu's inevitably flagging energies, during the 1980s he managed to cultivate a side interest in 20th-century Chinese prose, chairing a learned society of modern essay enthusiasts, and writing an introduction to a definitive collection of the vernacular Chinese essay during the decade of 1927–37.[52] Moreover, the relatively tolerant climate of openness to foreign influences under the first decade of Deng's reign, unprecedented in the People's Republic, provided Wu with his first chance to visit the West since the late 1940s. He was a member of the Chinese delegation of writers and critics that attended an international conference on Lu Xun convened near Monterey, California in August 1981. However, to recapture a skill like fiction writing after four decades of neglect would not be quite so easy to arrange. As it turned out, though, Wu achieved a certain success in this area through new reprints of his old works: first *Mountain Torrent* in 1982, and later the much more aesthetically well-wrought "Verdant Bamboo Hermitage" in 1984.[53] The fact that the latter work was reprinted in one of the leading journals of post-Mao fiction suggests that the very works Wu did not pointedly design for a mass readership may actually endure to reach the broadest readership of all in the end.

# Conclusion

In a country where never less than three-fourths of the population has maintained a rural abode, the Chinese villager has only recently emerged from the most marginal sort of role in vernacular prose literature.[1] Intimate and many-sided evocations of the texture of village life were extremely rare in past centuries: the Chinese fiction writer, usually hailing from a town or city, would deem it sufficient to sketch his rural subject in broad strokes and with considerable poetic license. Indeed, the average traditional reader would expect little else, being yet another product of the town or city himself.[2]

By contrast, twentieth-century Chinese fiction has elevated the villager from a tiny figure in an idyllic landscape—or a bit character in a play—to a stature befitting a center-stage role.[3] Both the material conditions and the emotional and spiritual tenor of rural life have come across with more subtlety and detail over the course of this century than during any other. Within the generation of May Fourth "New Culture" activists chiefly responsible for instituting this trend, no major writer focused so singlemindedly on village life as Wu Zuxiang.

Wu's boyhood friendship with a migrant woodcutter from the poverty-stricken region to the north of the Yangzi River left him with a particularly vivid impression of how "the other half" had to struggle merely to eke out the barest sort of subsistence. At the same time, his genteel background and close acquaintance with a broad spectrum of the local elite enabled him to avoid the simplistic caricaturing of the upper and middle classes, a common foible in Ye Zi and other undistiguished leftist writers who uncritically apotheosized the Marxist-Leninist doctrine of class struggle. Even though Wu's fiction reinforces a familiar central doctrine of leftist populism, namely that a relationship of inverse proportionality often exists between wealth and benevolence, his writings also illustrate an often overlooked phenomenon: the function of horizontal ties of community and clan to ease the vertical class tensions within the countryside. For this reason, his fiction serves to counterbalance the large body of doctrinaire leftist peasant literature in the same way that Tanigawa Michio's theory of community relations in China's clan-based rural order functions as a corrective to the overemphasis on class struggle by many modern historians in China.[4]

At the same time, Wu stands apart from the highly creative but devastatingly pessimistic writers who would negate the entire pre-modern socio-political heritage at one fell swoop, for stories like "1800 Bushels" and "Fan Hamlet" include several allusions to bygone days of peace and plenty for the wealthy and working-class locals alike. His narrators do not indulge in speculations about building a road of societal development where none has existed before, as Lu Xun's autobiographical narrator fantasizes taking place at the conclusion of "My Old Home." Instead, Wu's fictional alter-egos tend to keep their hopes for the future alive by recalling how local conditions in the past were not nearly as grim as in the present day, thus opening possibilities for amelioration of a gradualist sort. The existing road of development might well be riddled with gullies, and thus require drastic repairs, but it need not be summarily abandoned in favor of a brave new swath through uncharted wilderness.[5]

As Wu vacillated during the 1940s over whether to write another novel after *Mountain Torrent*, history itself intervened with the chaotic post-war struggle between the Nationalists and the Communists. When the new Communist government was founded in 1949, the nationwide enforcement of Mao Zedong's stringent political controls on literature left Wu little choice but to abandon his mid-1940s dreams of a postwar career as a professional novelist in favor of an academic post within the comparatively secure field of the classic Chinese novel. Even though Wu's talent for writing could not escape the decades of political deep freeze intact, the spate of studies and reprints of his fiction which came out during the cultural thaw decade of 1979–89 testifies to his enduring impact on the 20th-century literary scene.

Dominated by dialogue and oral cadences, Wu Zuxiang's "voiced" narratives compel us not so much to observe the village as to listen to it. Readers with an appreciation for his mastery of dialogue resemble traditional-style drama afficianados, who usually describe what they do at the theatre as "listenening to plays" [*ting xi*] rather than mere watching. Throughout Wu's *oeuvre*, speech rhythms and patterns of diction combine to leave a stamp of distinctiveness on a character whose visual appearance is usually vague by comparison, insofar as it is less readily distinguishable from the outward aspect of other characters. Indeed, Wu hardly ever paints with words, but instead uses them to dramatize social conflicts and resonate audibly through tightly compressed scenes. Naturally, Wu pays a price for this proclivity. Except for "The Verdant Bamboo Hermitage" and *Mountain Torrent*, his two works richest in landscape description, the settings of his fiction receive a sparse, bare-bones treatment that is liable to disappoint the more visual-minded of his readers. Nowhere does this tendency make its presence felt so clearly as in his smattering of stories with urban settings, wherein the crowding, bustle, and fast tempo of city life are strangely missing. A sense that the reader is actually taking in the sights of the cityscape in old Beijing, which much of Lao She's fiction conjures forth so brilliantly, does not come across at all in a story like "Miss Jin and the Xue Girl."

Evidently, the selfsame urban environment that Wu Zuxiang found congenial as a place to live and work could somehow never provide his imaginative faculties with the proper nourishment. Instead, just as Turgenev had been intrigued by the 19th-century transformation in the relations between Russian peasants and landowners, Wu was fascinated by this century's unprecedented challenges to the traditional Chinese rural order. In the early part of his writing career, he focused on the negative effects of rural China's incorporation into the world economy, such as escalating unemployment, wild price fluctuations, shrinking demand for finished cottage handicrafts, capital shortages, and severe impoverishment, all of which were aggravating class tensions and intensifying social anomie. Beginning in the mid-1930s, Wu switched to emphasizing the positive developments that were leading to a more integrated and equitable rural social order, including the eventual awakening of a national consciousness among the peasantry—an unexpected blessing in the wake of harsh foreign invasion. But no matter whether bleak or optimistic, these portrayals of his rustic homeland join in toppling the stereotype of the Chinese village as a stagnant milieu utterly lacking in internal dynamism.

Like Shen Congwen and Zhao Shuli, Wu Zuxiang applied the great bulk of his literary energies to evoking the textures of village life in his upland home locale. While these three were not the only figures among modern China's top echelon of writers to delve into village society, their urban-minded peers would inevitably turn back to the town or city for a more familiar literary setting. As modern Chinese fiction's pre-eminent specialists in the countryside, the trio complement one another in capturing the essentials of vastly different regions and bringing a representative sample of authorial interpretations to their subjects. The self-taught son of a military official, Shen Congwen invoked the pastoral to celebrate the pre-Confucian virtues of his borderland rustics in the rugged but fertile Southwest; a true scion of the poor peasant class, Zhao Shuli adopted folk storyteller idioms of his arid northern loess region to describe the improved lot of the poor during the earliest stages of communist rule there; and Wu, the suit-clad college squire from the southern uplands of the Lower Yangzi, sounded a belated meliorist's warning of the long-neglected economic and political crises that were downgrading life even in formerly prosperous villages along market routes. No canon of masterpieces on the modern Chinese village could be complete without a major place for all three authors.

The countryside still continues to exert a powerful pull on China's novelists, as writings from the "Roots-seeking" movement of the mid-1980s testify. This literary rediscovery of China's culturally rich but materially deprived rural areas owes much to the Anhui writer who gave voice to the formerly silent villagers of Maolin. However the new crop of post-Mao writers may diverge from Wu Zuxiang in terms of technical preferences and ideological bent, they would have to agree with the credo he lived through his fiction: no thorough understanding of Chinese culture can be possible without delving into the rural milieu and putting one's imagination to work on it.

# Notes

## Notes to the Introduction

1. It is little wonder that visits to Maolin by light-haired foreigners continue to elicit the same gawks of wonder from the locals that P. T. Barnum once catered to when erecting tents in American small towns to exhibit equatorial chieftains in full regalia.

2. Three leading authorities who have rated Wu as one of the most skilled practioners of the Chinese short story during the 1930s are Bonnie S. McDougall ("Writers and Performers, Their Works, and Their Audiences in the First Three Decades," in McDougall, ed., *Popular Chinese Literature and the Performing Arts in the People's Republic of China* [Berkeley: Univ. of California Press, 1984], p. 271), C. T. Hsia (*A History of Modern Chinese Fiction* [New Haven: Yale Univ. Press, 1970], p. 281), and Su Hsüeh-lin (in Joseph Schyns et al., eds., *1500 Modern Chinese Novels and Plays* [Beijing 1948; rpt. Hong Kong: Lung Men Bookstore, 1966], pp. xxvii–xxviii).

3. Jaroslav Prušek has uncovered a process of "schematization of characters" in Mao Dun's fiction, in which the individual character tends to come across as "a mere straw" passively caught up in "storms in the history of humanity." See *The Lyrical and the Epic: Studies of Modern Chinese Literature*, ed. Leo Ou-fan Lee (Bloomington: Indiana Univ. Press, 1980), p. 93.

4. Re the issue of high morale during the early War years, see Immanuel C. Y. Hsu, *The Rise of Modern China*, 3rd ed. (New York: Oxford Univ. Press, 1983), p. 583, and John King Fairbank, *The Great Chinese Revolution, 1800–1985* (New York: Harper and Row, 1986), p. 241.

5. Jeffrey C. Kinkley, "Shen Congwen and the Uses of Regionalism in Modern Chinese Literature," *Modern Chinese Literature*, vol. 1, no. 2 (Spring 1985), p. 171.

6. T. A. Hsia, *The Gate of Darkness* (Seattle: Univ. of Washington Press, 1968), p. 71.

7. For a synopsis of Jung's theory of compensation, see J. A. Hadfield, *Dreams and Nightmares* (Baltimore: Penguin, 1954), pp. 50–51, 103.

8. H. Ernest Lewald, *The Cry of Home: Cultural Nationalism and the Modern Writer* (Knoxville: Univ. of Tennessee Press, 1972), p. 6.

9. Xu Dishan's "Yuguan" has been excised from nearly all P.R.C. collections of the author's fiction since the story appeared in the 1947 anthology, *Wei chao zhui jian* [Missives From an Imperilled Nest]; a Hong Kong reprint of this anthology (Zhaoli chubanshe, 1977, pp. 172–232) is perhaps the most accessible source. "Yuguan" has been translated by Cecile Chu-shin Sun in Joseph S. M. Lau, C. T. Hsia, and Leo Ou-fan Lee, eds., *Modern Chinese Stories and Novellas* (New York: Columbia Univ. Press, 1981), pp. 51–87.

10. See Ai Wu, "Autumn Harvest," *Ai Wu xuanji* (Hong Kong: Xianggang wen-xue yanjiushe, 1979), pp. 98–133. I have not been able to locate this work in P.R.C. editions of Ai Wu's works.

11. "Autumn Harvest," *Ai Wu xuanji*, p. 98. The gist of one such lowbrow army song is: "Too bad the woman washing clothes over there isn't my wife; if she were, I'd have her stop washing. "

12. "Autumn Harvest," *Ai Wu xuanji*, p. 99.

13. Interview with Wu Zuxiang, 7 December 1982.

14. Wu Zuxiang, "Hou jie" [The Back Street], *Kangzhan wenyi*, vol. 8, nos. 1–2 (November 1942), p. 84.

15. Wu Zuxiang, "Dui deng" [Facing My Lamp], *Shi yu chao wenyi*, vol. 2, no. 5 (June 1943), pp. 47–48.

16. Regarding Qu Qiubai's prison confession that he belonged to the same inef-fectual type of intellectual as Hu Shi and others whom he had previously criticized as "superfluous," see Paul G. Pickowicz, *Marxist Literary Thought in China: The Influ-ence of Ch'ü Ch'iu-pai* (Berkeley: Univ. of California Press, 1981), p. 216. Mau-sang Ng amplifies the Turgenevian accents in Qu Qiubai's eleventh-hour confession in *The Russian Hero in Modern Chinese Fiction* (Albany: State Univ. of New York Press, 1988), p. 67.

17. Interview with Wu Zuxiang, 7 March 1983.

18. Writing about early 20th-century literature in the West, Charles I. Glicksberg noted that it was practically "impossible not to heed the call to commitment during the 1930s." See *The Literature of Commitment* (Lewisburg: Bucknell Univ. Press, 1976), p. 96. On the presence of this trend in Southeast Asian fiction of the same period, see Jeremy H. C. S. Davidson and Helen Cordell, eds., *The Short Story in South East Asia: Aspects of a Genre* (London: School of Oriental and African Studies, 1982), pp. 13, 207.

19. Wu Zuxiang, "Tantan Qinghua de wenfeng" [A Discussion of the Literary Climate at Qinghua], *Qinghua zhoukan fukan*, vol. 36, no. 3 (November 1931), pp. 2–5.

20. Henry James, *Partial Portraits* (1888; rpt. New York: Haskell House, 1968), p. 322.

21. "Critical realism" is the term favored by C. T. Hsia for the mainstream of seri-ous writing in this period; see Hsia's use of this term in a rejoinder to a critique of his *History of Modern Chinese Fiction* by Jaroslav Prušek in *The Lyrical and the Epic: Stud-ies in Modern Chinese Literature*, p. 236.

22. See Richard Ellman and Charles J. Feidelson, Jr., *The Modern Tradition* (New York: Oxford Univ. Press, 1965), p. 229.

23. Ellman and Feidelson, *The Modern Tradition*, p. 232.

24. I will use "meliorism" to refer both to the idea of social progress and the liter-ary advocacy of social progress.

25. Bonnie McDougall points out that the *"impassibilité"* of Flaubert and the un-dercurrent of cynicism in many writings from Western critical realism had practi-cally no counterpart on the Chinese literary scene in the wake of the May Fourth New Culture Movement. See *The Introduction of Western Literary Theories Into Mod-ern China* (Tokyo: The Center for East Asian Cultural Studies, 1971), p. 260.

26. Mao Dun's charge that Wu maintained a "purely objective" standpoint will be discussed further in Chapters 4 and 6. Wu refuted this allegation in an interview on 7 March 1983. Yuan Liangjun added that Wu's "sentiments of sympathy and disapproval are expressed with clarity and intensity"; see "Bai lian gang huawei raozhi rou: Wu Zuxiang xiaoshuo yishu manbi" [Tempered Steel Pounded Into Flexible Wire: An Informal Discussion of the Fictional Artistry of Wu Zuxiang], *Beijing daxue xuebao*, no. 6 (December 1982), p. 51.

27. Bonnie McDougall, *Popular Chinese Literature*, p. 284.

28. Interview with Wu Zuxiang, 23 March 1983. In *Yuan Hung-tao and the Kung-an School* (Cambridge: Cambridge Univ. Press, 1988), Chou Chih-p'ing mentions various possible English renderings for *qu*, the late Ming precursor of the term *quwei*: "zest," "gusto," and "flair." Unfortunately, none of these terms incorporates the important component of "flavor" or *wei*, a significant critical concept itself, as noted by Timothy Wixted ("The Literary Criticism of Yuan Hao-wen," vol. 1, Diss. Oxford 1976, pp. 265–267) and Pauline Yu (*The Poetry of Wang Wei: New Translations and Commentary* [Bloomington: Indiana Univ. Press, 1980], p. 13). And even more troublesome is the way in which each of the three above renderings has been vulgarized by Madison Avenue advertisers, while David Pollard's alternative of "piquancy" has not, at least as of 1992; see *A Chinese Look at Literature: The Literary Values of Chou Tso-jen in Relation to the Tradition* (Berkeley: Univ. of California Press, 1973), p. 72.

29. In *Yuan Hung-tao and the Kung-an School*, Chou Chih-p'ing describes how Yuan, whose impact on May Fourth literati was probably unsurpassed among Ming critics, invoked the concept of *qu* [verve] as a balance to the primary attribute of *zhi* [substance] in a literary work (pp. 52–54).

30. For an unembellished rendering of Horace's classic formulation of combining pleasure with instruction in literary design, see T. S. Dorsch, trans., *Classical Literary Criticism: Aristotle, Horace, and Longinus* (Harmondsworth, U.K.: Penguin, 1965), pp. 90–91.

## Notes to Chapter 1

1. As of the mid–1980s, many of Wu's relatives were still engaged in bamboo handicrafts.

2. A similar plaque on the lintel of the house belonging to Wu's mother in nearby Fengcun reads "Residence of the Former County Magistrate" [*Sima di*].

3. Wu Shangmo was one of the comparatively few clan members to rise to fame in the Ming period. The Qing period witnessed a substantial rise in the clan's fortunes, reaching a high-water mark in the Jiaqing reign (1796–1820), according to an interview with Wu Monong, 14 May 1983. See also *Jingxian zhi* [Jingxian Gazetteer], ed. Huang Chengzu, vol. 231 (1806; rpt. Taibei: Chengwen chubanshe, 1975), no. 4, pp. 1401–1402.

4. *Jingxian zhi*, vol. 231, no. 3, pp. 1188–1189.

5. The largest group of Wu's notable Qing dynasty forbears consisted of scholars whose brief biographies are located in the "Literati Corner" [*wen yuan*] of the county gazetteer. Wu Weijun received the "presented scholar" [*jinshi*] civil service degree in 1670 and wrote poetry as well as some commentaries on the Confucian

Four Books. Wu Shiji was an eighteenth-century philosopher well known in the locale who left one volume of poetry and essays. Finally, Wu Jianzi specialized in long narrative poems on historical themes, while Wu Dashen left twenty-four volumes of lyric verse. See *Jingxian zhi*, vol. 231, no. 4, pp. 1524, 1542, 1545.

6. There are no extent genealogical records that would enlarge upon what is known about Wu's ancestors from gazetteers and interviews. The Wu clan genealogy [*zongpu*] which formerly rested in the clan ancestral temple has been lost, according to a 14 May 1983 interview with Wu Jinglin, the head of the cultural station [*wenhua zhan*] in Maolin. Information on Wu Shifan is based on an interview with Wu Zuxiang on 7 December 1982.

7. Interview with Wu Zuxiang, 7 December 1982. Great-uncle Wu Shaolie was related by marriage to Ye Mingchen (1807–1859), a famous viceroy of Guangzhou whom the British captured and incarcerated in India for the final two years of his life.

8. Interview with Wu Zuxiang, 7 December 1982. Wu Yanglie managed his far-flung commercial investments in riverports like Wuhu through clansmen whom he dispatched from his luxurious residence in Maolin.

9. During my stay at Maolin on 14–16 May 1983, many villagers referred to the Wu clan's seventh branch as an "eminent local family." Granted that the branch's wealth fluctuated, it could nevertheless afford to hire numerous servants, whose families in turn were "often menials of several generations standing" (interview with Wu Zuxiang, 7 December 1982).

10. Wu Zuxiang claimed on 7 December 1982 that Wu Jixin's family of little wealth and numerous descendants (five sons lived to early adulthood) was suspected of avaricious designs by Wu Yanglie's family of few descendants and abundant wealth. Therefore, Wu Jixin had to look elsewhere for investment capital to fuel his enterprises.

11. Investing savings in these clan ventures would usually yield around two per cent more annual interest than bank savings, according to Wu Zuxiang (7 December 1982). For a description of one of these collective clan-based investment associations in the Anhui mercantile center of Huizhou, see Mark Elvin, *The Pattern of the Chinese Past* (Oxford: Oxford Univ. Press, 1973), p. 295.

12. Interview with Wu Zuxiang, 7 December 1982. Five acres would seem to be a small parcel of land by Western standards, but in southern Chinese intensive rice culture it is considered a large enough unit size to form the borderline between the landholdings of a rich peasant and those of a landlord. See C. K. Yang, *A Chinese Village in Early Communist Transition* (Cambridge: M.I.T. Press, 1959), pp. 40–41.

13. Interview with Wu Zuxiang, 7 December 1982.

14. For example, Kang Youwei disliked the format of the civil service examinations, particularly the "eight-legged essay" requirement, yet it was through taking part in them that he came close to succeeding in reforming Chinese institutions through his pull in the bureaucracy. The Chinese defeat in the Sino-Japanese War of 1895 marked an unprecedented rise in doubts as to whether the traditional examination subject matter could actually aid in selecting officials capable of handling the challenges presented by the modern world. Wu Qingyu was already 31 by 1895; it is unlikely that he would have been quite so critical of the examination system during

the previous decade, when he was already of age to sit for the exams. With regard to changing the material on the exams, the Hundred Days Reform of 1898 held a brief and transitory turn to an increased practicality of subject matter with the abolition of the sections on poetry writing as well as eight-legged essays on the Four Books. See Chung-li Chang, *The Chinese Gentry: Studies on Their Role in Nineteenth-Century Chinese Society* (Seattle: Univ. of Washington Press, 1955), pp. 206–207.

15. See C. T. Hsia's comments on the genesis of Wu Jingzi's *Rulin waishi* [The Scholars] in *The Classic Chinese Novel* (New York: Columbia Univ. Press, 1968), pp. 206, 360n.

16. Wu Zuxiang, "Song—jingzeng Beijing Yiyuan Zhang Hong deng qiwei hushi tongzhi" [An Ode Presented to Beijing Hospital's Seven Nurses Led by Zhang Hong], *Renmin ribao*, 11 April 1980, p. 8. Wu compares his warm feelings for the nurses with the way he treasured his mother's care during boyhood illnesses. In a poem published in 1934, he describes a fond childhood memory of his mother cooking him winter-melon soup while he was sick. See "Bing yu" [Recovering from Illness], in "Nen huang zhi yi" [Memories of Childhood Days], in *Wenxue jikan*, vol. 1, no. 3 (July 1934), p. 258.

17. Wu Zuxiang, "He dajia tantan keneng ba" [Surely it's Possible to Discuss This with Everybody], *Funü zazhi* [The Women's Magazine], vol. 11, no. 11 (November 1925), pp. 1722–1724. Wu writes that in the light of the Chinese father's "traditional" severity towards his children, only the relatively tenderhearted mother plays an emotionally nurturing role: he cites the character Jia Zheng from *Dream of the Red Chamber* as an example of a father who kept his sons at a stiff distance even at times when his private thoughts about them waxed tender (p. 1722). The tradition to which Wu refers is the stern line of Confucianism bequeathed by Xun Zi, not that of Mencius, who urged that a father relegate the moral instruction of his children to a reliable friend or relative.

18. During an interview on 29 December 1982, Wu Zuxiang put it this way: "In our archaic social ways, there was a rule that the teacher or father would maintain quite a distance from his boy. Whenever the teacher or father would speak to the boy, they'd admonish him over this or that matter. So, back during my childhood when visiting relatives would leave, I'd often shed a tear or two at the prospect of having to do without their congenial company."

19. Interview with Wu Zuxiang, 24 November 1982.

20. Interview with Wu Zuxiang, 29 December 1982. Wu reckons that most, if not all, of his ten siblings who were short-lived had died of pneumonic complications from malaria.

21. Interview with Wu Zuxiang, 29 December 1982.

22. Interview with Wu Zuxiang, 22 October 1982.

23. There are no significant characters in Wu's fiction reminiscent of his father, and only three major characters modeled closely after his mother, in the stories "Li jia de qianye" [On the Eve of Leaving Home], "Xiao Hua de shengri" [Xiao Hua's Birthday], and "Chai" [The Woodcutter].

24. Interview with Wu Zuxiang, 7 December 1982.

25. Wu Zuxiang, "Kan 'Tian xian pei'" [Watching "A Match for the Beauty"], *Beijing ribao*, 1956: 3 October, p. 6 and 4 October, p. 3.

26. Wu Zuxiang's brother, Zuguang, should not be confused with the famous contemporary dramatist of the same name.

27. Interview with Wu Zuxiang, 29 December 1982.

28. Interview on 14 May 1983 with Pan Songshou, a friend of Wu's since childhood who lived in a neighboring village.

29. Interview with Wu Zuxiang, 29 December 1982. All of Wu's Qinghua roommates eventually found employment outside of China in either business or engineering.

30. Interviews with Wu Zuxiang, 24 November and 29 December 1982.

31. Interviews with Wu Zuxiang, 24 November and 29 December 1982.

32. Although the journey from Maolin to Wuhu was under 100 miles, it took "three days and three nights" in those days, according to an interview with the author on 24 November 1982. The terrain was so hilly that the traveler had to go by foot or sedan chair for much of the way. Although a paved highway now connects the stretch from Wuhu to Jingxian, the hilly stretch from Jingxian to Maolin is still quite rough and difficult to negotiate.

33. Interview with Wu Zuxiang, 24 November 1982.

34. Wu Zuxiang, "Wei Shaochang 'Hong lou meng banben xiao kao' daixu" [A Preface to Wei Shaochang's "Brief Investigations into the Editions of *Dream of the Red Chamber*"], *Hong lou meng xuekan*, no. 3 (August), 1981, pp. 23–32.

35. A member of the Chinese Department in the Teachers' College at Wuhu informed me in May 1983 that the school library's copy of *Zhe shan*, which he saw in the early 1960s, had been missing ever since the Cultural Revolution. In light of the far greater distribution of national newspapers *vis-à-vis* local school magazines, it is not surprising that the newspaper would outlast the journal in this case.

36. Wu Zuxiang, "Buxing de xiao cao," *Minguo ribao*, 7 October 1923, pp. 3–4. Wu remembers sending other snatches of writings to periodicals well before October 1923, but even if one or two of them happened to have gotten published, no one appears to have discovered them as yet.

37. In an interview with Wu Zuxiang on 29 December 1982, he mentioned that his first teacher at Maolin drilled him in parallelism and antithetical verse construction.

38. "Buxing de xiao cao," *Minguo ribao*, 7 October 1923, p. 3.

39. Ma Meng, introduction to D. C. Lai, *Chinese Couplets* (Hong Kong: Kelly and Walsh, 1969), p. x.

40. Wu Zuxiang, "Wei Shaochang 'Hong lou meng banben xiao kao' daixu," *Hong lou meng xuekan*, no. 3, 1981, p. 25.

41. The fable occupies a decidedly minor place in Chinese literary history, according to Zheng Zhenduo's *Zhongguo wenxue yanjiu* [Studies in Chinese Literature] (Beijing: Zuojia chubanshe, 1957), vol. 3, pp. 1207–1210. Zheng notes that the modern-day upsurge of interest in folk literature has encouraged scholars to record and collect folk fables that had previously survived chiefly through oral transmission.

42. Li Bangnong, ed., *Huangshan de chuanshuo* [Legends of the Yellow Mountains] (Beijing: Zhongguo minjian wenyi chubanshe, 1982).

43. "Aoyu tuo jin gui," *Legends of the Yellow Mountains*, pp. 69–71.

44. Warlord factionalism in Nanjing during 1924 played a role in the failure of such fledgling schools as the Renovate-the-People Middle School.

45. Wu's father supplied much of his youngest son's tuition and living expenses during the 1920s by selling off land in Maolin, according to an interview with Pan Songshou on 14 May 1983. Still, his father was unable to help Zuxiang with his school expenses to the degree that he had aided Zuguang, according to an interview with Wu Xiaohan on 15 May 1983.

46. Wu Zuxiang, "Yuan fei yu yue," *Funü zazhi*, vol. 2, no. 3 (March 1925), pp. 542–546. I translate *yue*, literally "leap," as "plunge" in the context of this poem.

47. James Legge, ed., *The Book of Poetry*, the Chinese Classics, vol. 4 (Hong Kong: London Missionary Society's Printing Office, 1939), pp. 444–446. The translation is mine.

48. Legge, *The Book of Poetry*, p. 444.

49. The poem mentions such ingredients of ancestor worship as a sacrificial bull, ceremonial wine, libation cups, and firewood.

50. Wu Zuxiang, "Yuan fei yu yue," pp. 542, 545.

51. *Qinghua zhoukan*, vol. 33, no. 14 (July 1930), p. 85.

52. Interview with Wu Jinglin, 14 May 1983.

53. Two informants agreed that no food riots have occurred in Maolin within at least the past century: first, Wu Zuxiang on 7 March 1983, and later Wu Monong on 14 May 1983.

54. For a succinct account of the traditional Chinese age hierarchy and its breakup in modern times, see C. K. Yang, *The Chinese Family in the Communist Revolution*, pp. 86–97.

55. See Shen Zhenyu, "Shilun Wu Zuxiang de xiaoshuo chuangzuo" [An Exploratory Essay on Wu Zuxiang's Fiction], in *Zhongguo wenxue yanjiu*, ed. Lu Yaodong, Huang Manjun, and Zhou Bo (Wuhan: Hubei sheng wenxue xuehui, 1981), pp. 335–336. Also see Yuan Liangjun, "Bai lian gang huawei rao zhi rou—Wu Zuxiang xiaoshuo manbi" [Tempered Steel Pounded into Flexible Wire—an Informal Look at Wu Zuxiang's Fictional Art], *Beijing daxue xuebao*, no. 6 (December 1982), p. 60.

56. With "Soaring Hawks and Plunging Fish" Wu basically discards the personification of animals and plants in his fiction. Wu would on rare occasion return to the use of personification when writing poetry: a snake thinks verbally in "Memories of Childhood Days," *Wenxue jikan*, vol. 1, no. 3, pp. 258–259. At the same time, a vestige of personification remains in "Soaring Hawks and Plunging Fish," for the author attaches the pluralizing suffix *-men*, which is normally limited to human referents, to words like "birds" [*niaormen*] and "weeds" [*yecaomen*] (pp. 542, 545). "Soaring Hawks" also presages the later appearance of a number of character types in Wu's fiction. One figure reappearing in 1930s stories is the kindly but ineffectual male elder who is unable to give succor to such an ill-treated young person. As far as heroines are concerned, the young uncle's wife who stands up to the domineering matron presages the appearance of several dignified and independent-minded young heroines in Wu's later stories. These 1930s stories also feature domineering old women who expect more obedience than they receive from the younger generation. A final character prototype first appearing in "Soaring Hawks and Plunging

Fish" is the nun who fulsomely justifies her cronies' harsh put-downs of independent-minded youth.

57. The original characters in Shen Shuyuan's given name meant "graceful
maiden," a phrase that smacked of anachronistic gentility to the self-consciously
modern young couple. Mrs. Wu thereupon switched to an innocuous homonym
meaning "bean field." Variants also exist in Wu Zuxiang's given name, which in its
original form meant "ancestral scroll sheath." In order to cast away the unwelcome
archaic associations of the word *zu*, meaning "ancestors," Wu adopted a homonym
meaning "organized" to result in a given name meaning "organized scroll sheath."
Since 1930, the couple have not further altered their given names.

58. Interview with Wu Baohua, 14 May 1983. Another "civilized" feature of the
wedding was the eschewing of the traditional ceremonial kowtow.

59. Popular urban writers of the 1910s and 1920s in Shanghai, generally from
rather affluent families, would often "leave wives and children at home in the provinces." See Perry Link, *Mandarin Ducks and Butterflies: Popular Fiction in Early Twentieth-Century Chinese Cities* (Berkeley: Univ. of California Press, 1981), p. 156.

60. Wu worked in two elementary schools, the Yang zheng xiaoxue [The Instill-
Rectitude Primary School] and the Fu qun xiaoxue [The Benefit-the-Multitude Primary School]. He taught English, Chinese, mathematics, music, and physical education. Many elderly locals in Maolin still clearly remember Wu's stint as an elementary school instructor, since it was the final instance he stayed in the village for more
than a couple of months at a time.

61. Interview with Wu Monong, 14 May 1983.

62. Wu Zuxiang mentioned the repetitiveness of his dreams about his father's return to life during an interview on 24 November 1982.

63. In keeping with Wu Zuxiang's requests, whenever possible I have para-
phrased his diary entries rather than quoting them verbatim. Re the wish-fulfillment dream in which a dead parent comes back to life, Wu recorded a dream about
his mother on 7 December 1942. She had already died in her bed at Maolin when
Zuxiang and Zuguang arrived in Maolin, so the dream went, but her eyes opened
and she sighed upon hearing their voices.

64. Freud argues how dreams function as wish fulfillments in the fourth chapter
of *The Interpretation of Dreams*, tr. James Strachey (New York: Avon Books, 1965), pp.
167–195.

65. Wu complains about the high price and poor quality of wartime tobacco in an
essay entitled "Yan" [Tobacco], *Shi yu chao wenyi*, vol. 4, no. 3 (November 1944), pp.
13–16.

66. J. A. Hadfield, *Dreams and Nightmares* (Harmondsworth, U.K.: Penguin,
1954), p. 171.

67. Wu Zuxiang, "Dao Lu'er" [In Memory of Lu'er], *Fan yu ji* ["An After-hours
Anthology," hereafter abbreviated as "After-hours"] (Shanghai: Shenghuo shudian, 1935), pp. 116–117.

68. Wu Zuxiang, "Chai" [The Woodcutter], *After-hours*, p. 90.

69. Wu Zuxiang, "Ge Leimengna zhe" [He Sings of Ramona], *Qinghua zhoukan*,
vol. 32, no. 8 (December 1929), pp. 63–66.

70. Wu Zuxiang, "He Sings of Ramona," p. 63.

71. Interview with Wu Zuxiang, 23 March 1983. Theodore Huters has noted that Qian Zhongshu, undoubtedly Wu's most talented classmate in literature at Qinghua, also found mathematics the most difficult portion of the entrance exam; see *Qian Zhongshu* (Boston: Twayne Publishers, 1982), p. 3.

72. Wu Zuxiang, "Jingdao Peixian Xiansheng" [In Memory of Zhu Ziqing], *Wen xun yuekan*, vol. 9, no. 3 (1948), pp. 132–133.

73. The classification of *Ramona* as romance comes from John Stewart, *The Flaming Years, 1920–1929*, Filmarama, vol. II (Metuchen, N.J.: Scarecrow Press, 1977), p. 124. For a short description of the 1928 film, see DeWitt Bodeen, "Delores Del Rio Was the First Mexican Of Family to Act in Hollywood," *Films in Review*, vol. 17, no. 5 (May 1967), pp. 268–269. The film was based on the novel of the same title by Helen Hunt Jackson (Boston: Little, Brown, and Co., 1884).

74. See Wu Zuxiang, *Wu Zuxiang xiaoshuo sanwen ji* ["An Anthology of Wu Zuxiang's Fiction and Prose," hereafter abbreviated as "Fiction and Prose"] (Beijing: Renmin wenxue chubanshe, 1954), pp. 1, 9. Instead of dating from January 1930, Wu's first story in this anthology was published in *Funü zazhi*, vol. 17, no. 7, pp. 119–123.

75. See Lionel Trilling, "On the Teaching of Modern Literature," *Beyond Culture: Essays on Literature and Learning* (New York: Viking Press, 1965), pp. 3–30.

76. Fei Xiaotong has pinpointed the factor of Westernization (or modernization, as the case might be) as having created much of the huge gap between urban and rural life in China: "The modern Chinese city is a product of the contact between East and West. Those individuals who, through contact with Western culture, have changed their way of life and thinking, will not find themselves able to live in the countryside any longer." See *China's Gentry* (Chicago: Univ. of Chicago Press, 1953), p. 138.

## Notes to Chapter 2

1. Information on the atmosphere of learning at Qinghua University during the early 1930s is based on interviews of Wu Zuxiang by the author on 29 November 1982 and by Perry Link in August 1981.

2. "On the Eve of Leaving Home" (July 1931) was first anthologized in Wu's *Xi liu ji* ["West Willow Anthology," hereafter abbreviated as "West Willow"] (Shanghai, 1934), pp. 1–18. As with other stories appearing in Wu's mid-1930s anthologies, *West Willow* and *After-hours*, I take the anthologized 1930s version of "On the Eve of Leaving Home" as my basic text; the version of this story in Wu's 1954 anthology, *Wu Zuxiang xiaoshuo sanwen ji* [Fiction and Prose], was edited in an unrestrained and intrusive manner that could occasionally be characterized as bowdlerization (to get an inside view of how editorial heavy-handedness has dogged Chinese writers since the 1950s, see the playwright Wu Zuguang's eulogy in memorium to Ye Shengtao in *Wenyi bao*, 27 February 1988, p. 4). Unless a scrupulously edited and unexpurgated anthology of Wu Zuxiang's works appears, the reader would keep closer to the author's original conception of his stories by adopting the 1930s anthologies as the definitive texts for his other stories as well. Although the two 1930s anthologies were out of print for some time, the Shanghai Shudian reprinted a paper-

back facsimile edition of *West Willow* in 1987, and *After-hours* may eventually appear in similar format. Translations of "On the Eve of Leaving Home" include: S. R. Munro, in *Genesis of a Revolution: An Anthology of Short Stories* (Singapore: Heinemann Educational Books, 1979), pp. 133–143; and Umemura Yoshiyuki, "Rikyō no zenya," *Bungaku Geppō*, no. 54 (September 1939), pp. 73–77.

3. Wu Zuxiang, "On the Eve of Leaving Home," *West Willow*, pp. 3–4.

4. Cheng Peikai, "Zhandou de haojiao xiangle—Wu Zuxiang duanpian chuang-zuo de yishu chengjiu" [The Battle Trumpet Has Sounded—Artistic Achievements in the Short Fiction of Wu Zuxiang], *Dousou*, no. 8 (March 1975), p. 4.

5. "On the Eve of Leaving Home," *West Willow*, p. 13.

6. Cheng Peikai argues that the narrator's mother and wife are the two foci of conflict in "The Battle Trumpet Has Sounded," *Dousou*, p. 4.

7. "On the Eve of Leaving Home," *West Willow*, p. 15.

8. "On the Eve of Leaving Home," *West Willow*, p. 4.

9. "On the Eve of Leaving Home," *West Willow*, p. 14.

10. "On the Eve of Leaving Home," *West Willow*, p. 13. In a personal interview with Wu held on 23 March 1983, he said that maternal love was "the dominating fac-tor in Die's decision to stay in the village." Most critics also focus on maternal love at the expense of sufficient regard for the the subtle influence of conservative village norms of maternal duty. One such view is that of Gu Zhenbang, "Guihua de youxiang—tan Wu Zuxiang xiaoshuo de youdian he buzu" [The Delicate Fragrance of Cassia Blossoms—Virtues and Defects in Wu Zuxiang's Fiction], *Pan Gu*, no. 71 (July 1974), p. 26: "Originally a Chinese 'Nora,' Die nevertheless drops her studies when confronted with the cries of her child."

11. Shen Zhenyu claims that the *chi'ai* [infatuation] of mother for child "domi-nates the story" while the real obstacle to Die's independence, "the power of feudal-ism," does not come across; he seems to have overlooked the matron's incisive artic-ulation of archaic (or "feudal") norms of family responsibility. See "An Exploratory Essay on Wu Zuxiang's Fiction," *Zhongguo wenxue yanjiu* (Wuhan, 1981), p. 336.

12. Interview with Wu Zuxiang, 23 March 1983.

13. "On the Eve of Leaving Home," *West Willow*, p. 5.

14. William Lyell, *Lu Hsün's Vision of Reality* (Berkeley: Univ. of California Press, 1976), p. 184.

15. Lyell, *Lu Hsün's Vision of Reality*, p. 135.

16. Randall Oliver Chang, "Yü Ta-fu (1896–1945): the Alienated Artist in Modern Chinese Literature," Diss. Claremont 1973, p. 28.

17. When interviewed by Perry Link in August 1981, Wu Zuxiang sympatheti-cally described a Chinese-American couple's dissatisfaction about the decline of fil-ial piety: "Instead of answering the telephone themselves, their children would im-periously shout, 'Mother, the phone's ringing!' The parents were Chinese raised in the old country, and ruefully complained that the generation gap separating them from their children was even wider than the social distance between host and for-mal guest in China."

18. Lucian Pye, *The Spirit of Chinese Politics: A Psychocultural Study of Authority Crisis in Political Development* (Cambridge: M.I.T. Press, 1968), p. 113.

19. James Guetti, *Word-Music: the Aesthetic Aspect of Narrative Fiction* (New Brunswick: Rutgers Univ. Press, 1980), p. 62.

20. Théophile Ribot has classified onomatopoeic interjections as a type of non-cognitive aural expression. See his *Essay on the Creative Imagination*, trans. Arthur Allin (Chicago: Open Court, 1906), p. 204. Edward Gunn suggests something of the plenitude of interjections and final particles in Wu's stories in *Rewriting Chinese: Style and Innovation in Twentieth-century Chinese Prose* (Stanford: Stanford Univ. Press, 1991), p. 210.

21. "On the Eve of Leaving Home," *West Willow*, p. 7.

22. Wu Zuxiang, "Liangzhi xiao maque" [Two Young Sparrows], *Wenxue yuekan*, vol. 2, no. 1, pp. 37–49. I follow the version of this story as anthologized in *West Willow*, pp. 19–52. The story is framed in an epistolary format, but its extended passages of dialogue and interior monologue prevent the sense of actually reading a letter from taking hold; re the perfunctory use of the epistolary format in an ancient model of prose, see Diana Yu-shih Mei, "Han Yü as a Ku-wen Stylist," *Tsing-hua Journal of Chinese Studies*, vol. 7, no. 1 (1968), p. 147.

23. Wu Zuxiang seldom uses true place-names in his fiction, preferring instead a variation on an actual geographical location. For example, the imaginary place-name "Hekou" is probably a variation on the actual village of Xikou, which Wu also acknowledged to be the model for the village portrayed in his novel *Mountain Torrent* (according to an interview in May 1983).

24. "Two Young Sparrows," *West Willow*, p. 52. I depart from the conventions of *pinyin* romanization in separating the familiar term of address, *A*, from the given name, *Bao*, and spelling the former "Ah" instead of "A."

25. "Two Young Sparrows," *West Willow*, p. 32.

26. On p. 34 of "Two Young Sparrows," Jia grandiloquently addresses Ah Bao's father in the second-person plural: "You are the masters of the nation, the backbone elements of society."

27. "Two Young Sparrows," *West Willow*, p. 20.

28. "Two Young Sparrows," *West Willow*, p. 35. This jest about snakes may well contain some powerful personal associations for Wu: in one of the most "revolting" recurrent nightmares he had during the 1930s, he would see himself standing amidst writhing snakes "crammed together so thickly that there was no room for me to take a single step." See "Tan meng" [On My Dreams], *After-hours*, p. 69.

29. Wu quotes Masuda Wataru in the former's essay, "Youmo he fengci" [Humor and Satire], in Chen Wangdao, ed., *Xiaopinwen he manhua* [The Familiar Essay and the Cartoon Sketch] (1935; rpt. Shanghai: Shanghai shudian, 1981), p. 15. Displaying much imprecision in defining what he means by "humor," Wu associates it with social irresponsibility and escapism. Satire of a "constructive" sort, however, meets with his approval even in this defensive and owlishly solemn essay.

30. Sigmund Freud, *The Interpretation of Dreams*, tr. James Strachey (New York: Avon, 1965), p. 87.

31. "Two Young Sparrows," *West Willow*, pp. 50–51.

32. Freud, *Interpretation of Dreams*, p. 466. When the dreamer expresses no surprise or regret during an encounter with the dead person's return to the living, the

attitude revealed by the dreamer is one of ambivalence, according to Freud. Wu's dreams of his parents were precisely of this ambivalent type.

33. On the infantile factors involved in dreaming of the death of a loved one, see Freud, *The Interpretation of Dreams*, pp. 281–289. Freud notes that during dreaming, the barriers erected by the conscious side of the personality are inactive, thus allowing a torrent of repressed infantile urges to surface and find expression in dream imagery.

34. E. D. Edwards, tr., *Chinese Prose Literature of the T'ang Period*, vol. I (London: Arthur Probsthain, 1937), p. 144.

35. For an explanation of how local militia levies were established in the late Qing period to help stave off the Taiping rebels, see Frederic Wakeman, Jr., *The Fall of Imperial China* (New York: Free Press, 1975), p. 165.

36. Lu Xun, "Zhu fu" [The New Year's Sacrifice], *Panghuang* [Wandering] (1926, rpt; Beijing: Renmin wenxue chubanshe, 1976), pp. 1–25.

37. Three *jiao* (thirty cents) was by no means a petty expenditure for a middling-to-poor peasant during the 1930s. As an example of how prices ran back then, the hardback edition of *West Willow* sold for eighty cents in 1934.

38. "Two Young Sparrows," *West Willow*, pp. 33–35.

39. Although Wu was sufficiently acquainted with the life of the middling-to-poor to draw many of his most memorable fictional characters from their humble ranks, he would never attempt to create a narrative persona from the lower social strata.

40. "Xiao Hua de shengri" [Xiao Hua's birthday] first appeared in *Zhongguo shehui*, vol. 1, no. 1 (January 1932), pp. 17–26. It was reprinted without alterations in *Qinghua zhoukan*, vol. 39, nos. 5–6 (April 1933), pp. 451–459. I shall make citations from the *Qinghua zhoukan* version, since this journal is better known and less difficult to find than *Zhongguo shehui*.

41. The verification of Madame Wu's term of address is from an interview with Pan Tongshou in Xuancheng, 13 May 1983. Wu Zuxiang's fiction contains the exact names of real persons only in the case of children. The liking Wu's mother had for mahjongg was mentioned by Wu Zuxiang in an interview on 24 November 1982.

42. Economic subsistence for all is the fundamental social value for traditional peasant society, according to James C. Scott, in *The Moral Economy of the Peasant: Rebellion and Subsistence in Southeast Asia* (New Haven: Yale Univ. Press, 1976). As long as the local elite shares with the underclass during times of economic scarcity, class antagonisms are usually smoothed over before they reach the point of breaking out into violent conflict.

43. "Xiao Hua's Birthday," *Qinghua zhoukan*, p. 458.

44. Jaroslav Prušek, *Studies in Modern Chinese Literature* (Berlin: Akademie Verlag, 1964), p. 28.

45. Peter Brooks, *The Melodramatic Imagination* (New Haven: Yale Univ. Press, 1976), pp. 11–12.

46. The phrase from James comes from Richard Ellman and Charles Fiedelson, Jr., eds., *The Modern Tradition: Backgrounds of Modern Literature* (New York: Oxford Univ. Press, 1965), p. vi.

47. For a discussion of naturalism in Langxian's "A Single Copper Cash," see Patrick Hanan, *The Chinese Vernacular Story* (Cambridge: Harvard Univ. Press, 1981), p. 132.

48. "Xiao Hua's Birthday," *Qinghua zhoukan*, p. 456.

49. "Xiao Hua's Birthday," *Qinghua zhoukan*, p. 458.

50. "Xiao Hua's Birthday," *Qinghua zhoukan*, pp. 451, 453.

51. "Xiao Hua's Birthday," *Qinghua zhoukan*, p. 452.

52. On the rural labor surplus, see Walter Mallory, *China: Land of Famine* (New York: National Geographic Society, 1926).

53. On the role of crime in Wu Zuxiang's fiction, see Zhao Yuan, "Wu Zuxiang ji qi tongdai zuojia" [Wu Zuxiang and His Contemporaries], *Shiyue*, no. 1, 1984, p. 250.

54. "Xiao Hua's Birthday," *Qinghua zhoukan*, p. 453.

55. "The Flowering Gardenia" [*Zhizi hua*] originally appeared in *Wenxue yuekan*, vol. 2, no. 2 (January 1932), pp. 23–34. It was first anthologized in *West Willow*, pp. 53–85.

56. Interview of Wu Zuxiang, 23 March 1983.

57. Marston Anderson has suggested that an apocalyptic vision runs through many of Wu Zuxiang's stories. See Anderson's discussion in Leo Ou-fan Lee, ed., *Lu Xun and His Legacy* (Berkeley: Univ. of California Press, 1985), pp. 48–49.

58. "The Flowering Gardenia," *West Willow*, pp. 84–85.

59. "The Flowering Gardenia," *West Willow*, p. 55. This is the first of many stories in which a botanical image has close associations with the milieu and even the protagonists.

60. For a discussion of temporary motor paralysis in the state of sleep, see Freud's *The Interpretation of Dreams*, pp. 371–372.

61. "The Flowering Gardenia," *West Willow*, p. 55.

62. "The Flowering Gardenia," *West Willow*, pp. 59–60.

63. William Mallory, *China: Land of Famine*, p. 119; and Chiang Yee, *A Chinese Childhood*, p. 187.

64. Mallory, *China: Land of Famine*, p. 119.

65. "The Flowering Gardenia," *West Willow*, pp. 79–80.

66. The pun occurs when Xiangfa mistakes *xingyun* [fortunate] for *shiyun* [shift in the world's fortunes]. The second term is a pre-modern term without intellectual respectability among Wu and his Western-influenced peers.

67. The similarly devised pun here connects *diguozhuyizhe* [imperialists] with *dizhu* [monarch].

68. "The Flowering Gardenia," *West Willow*, pp. 67–68.

69. Frank O'Connor, *The Lonely Voice: A Study of the Short Story* (Cleveland: World Publishing Co., 1962), p. 28.

70. Cheng Peikai, *Dousou*, no. 8 (March 1975), p. 9. Like most Chinese critics of Wu's stories, Cheng overlooks the undercurrents of humor in many of Wu's symposia. In the above symposium, Cheng excerpts no more than the first two sentences of the dialogue, thereby giving the impression that the entire passage involved polemics of the strictly solemn variety.

71. "Miss Jin and the Xue Girl" [*Jin Xiaojie yu Xue Guniang*], *Qinghua zhoukan*, vol. 37, no. 1 (February 1932), pp. 87–101. First anthologized in *West Willow*, pp. 87–123. "Xue" is only half of the given name of one of the young women, Wang Xuezi, while "Jin" is the surname of Jin Jiafeng.

72. Zhao Yuan, "Wu Zuxiang and His Contemporaries," p. 250.

73. "Miss Jin and the Xue Girl," *West Willow*, p. 92.

74. "Miss Jin and the Xue Girl," *West Willow*, pp. 99–100.

75. "Miss Jin and the Xue Girl," *West Willow*, p. 111.

76. One of the most popular love romances of the 1930s was a novel scorned as lowbrow by most leading May Fourth writers of the day: Zhang Henshui's *Ti xiao yinyuan* [Fate in Tears and Laughter] (Shanghai: Sanyou shushe, 1930).

77. "Miss Jin and the Xue Girl," *West Willow*, pp. 110–111.

78. "Miss Jin and the Xue Girl," *West Willow*, p. 102.

79. Re the female characters mixed up in the famous Qing novel's triangular love affair, see Andrew J. Plaks, *Archetypes and Allegory in the Dream of the Red Chamber* (Princeton: Princeton Univ. Press, 1976), pp. 66–67.

80. "Miss Jin and the Xue Girl," *West Willow*, p. 118.

81. "Miss Jin and the Xue Girl," *West Willow*, pp. 103, 109. The Wu family dialectal expressions used in this story include *cidi* [here], *lena* [at], *lixiang* [inside], and *nai* [you].

82. Wu Zuxiang, "Xin shu jieshao—'Ziye'" [Review of a New Book—"Midnight"], *Wenyi yuebao*, vol. 1, no. 1 (June 1933), p. 106.

83. Wu Zuxiang, "Guanguan de bupin" [Little Lord Guanguan's Tonic], *Qinghua zhoukan*, vol. 37, no. 6 (April 1932), pp. 28–41. Anthologized in *West Willow*, pp. 125–162. First translated into English by Oldřich Král in highly abridged form: see *New Orient*, vol. 6, no. 4 (August 1967), pp. 107–111. Translated into French as "Les Fortifiants" by Martine Vallette-Hémery, *Récits Chinois, 1918–1942* (Paris: Éditions de l'Herne, 1970), pp. 212–237. Translated into English as "Young Master Gets His Tonic" by Cyril Birch in Joseph S. M. Lau, C. T. Hsia, and Leo Ou-fan Lee, eds., *Modern Chinese Stories and Novellas, 1918–1949* (New York: Columbia Univ. Press, 1981), pp. 372–381. The reader should be cautioned that both of these full-length translations follow the bowdlerized 1954 version of the original story. With regard to the anonymous short critique of "Guanguan," it acknowledges the story's heavily ironic presentation without registering much sensitivity or appreciation for the work as a whole. See *Qinghua zhoukan*, vol. 37, no. 6 (1934), p. 174. C. T. Hsia was the first scholar to write a critique of the story in recent decades; see *A History of Modern Chinese Fiction, 1917–1957* (New Haven: Yale Univ. Press, 1970), pp. 282–283. A genre-based analysis of the story may be consulted in Cyril Birch, "Teaching May Fourth Fiction," *Modern Chinese Literature Newsletter*, vol. 2, no. 1 (1978), p. 15. Critiques from the other side of the Pacific have increased in recent years: see Cheng Peikai, *Dousou*, no. 8, pp. 9–11; Yuan Liangjun, "Tempered Steel Pounded Into Flexible Wire—an Informal Look at Wu Zuxiang's Art," *Beijing Daxue xuebao*, no. 6, p. 51; and Zhao Yuan, "Wu Zuxiang and His Contemporaries," p. 253.

84. "A Modest Proposal" by Swift, "The Marquis de Fumerol" by Maupassant, and *A Clockwork Orange* by Anthony Burgess are each narrated by a persona who betrays his corrupt ethical standards and intellectual shallowness without seeming

aware of having done so. Lu Xun also uses a certain amount of this sort of presentational irony, but never employs a narrator whose values differ so strikingly from those of the implied reader. The closest Chinese equivalent to "Little Lord Guanguan's Tonic" or the above European writers may well be a story by the Shanghai author Mu Shiying, "Zamen de shijie" [Our World], *Nan bei ji* (Shanghai: Hu feng shuju, 1932), pp. 25–47; in 1989, Shanghai shudian reprinted this anthology in a facsimile edition.

85. Guanguan's footloose existence and roguish ways would seem to make him eligible for the status of a picaro, but in his failure to capture the sympathies of the typical reader, he is unable to become a "lovable rogue."

86. Sean O'Faolain, *The Short Story* (London: Collins, 1948), p. 125. Mau-sang Ng has noted that during the formative May Fourth years from 1919 to 1922, French literature was second only to Russian in translations to the Chinese, and Maupassant emerged as by far the most frequently translated French author. See *The Russian Hero in Modern Chinese Fiction* (Albany: State Univ. of New York, 1988), p. 19.

87. Robert Scholes and Robert Kellogg, *The Nature of Narrative* (New York: Oxford Univ. Press, 1966), p. 263.

88. For an example of how Jia of "Two Young Sparrows" is a forerunner of Guanguan, see the scene from "Sparrows" in which Jia sneers at a village wet-nurse who is too poor to keep herself clean and fresh-looking like the women from the local elite (*West Willow*, pp. 29–30).

89. C. T. Hsia, *A History of Modern Chinese Fiction*, p. 282.

90. Wu Zuxiang, "Little Lord Guanguan's Tonic," *West Willow*, pp. 131, 132, 133, 149.

91. "Little Lord Guanguan's Tonic," *West Willow*, pp. 132–133, 135. The use of human milk as a tonic for wealthy Chinese is attested in the Ming novel *Jin Ping Mei cihua* [Golden Lotus] (rpt. Hong Kong: Taiping shuju, 1982), chap. 79, p. 2b. Nevertheless, Chinese writers have more often than not frowned upon such unnatural uses of human milk. An anecdote about excesses and extravagances in *Shi shuo xin yu* relates how some eccentric 3rd-century noblemen invited the Emperor for a feast of suckling pig. Remarking upon the unusual aroma of the pork, the Emperor asked why the flavor was so delicate. The hosts replied that the pig had been nourished with human milk. The Emperor was so shocked that he immediately stood up from the table and took his leave without further ado. See Liu I-ching, *A New Account of Tales of the World*, trans. Richard Mather (Minneapolis: Univ. of Minnesota Press, 1976), p. 459.

92. "Little Lord Guanguan's Tonic," *West Willow*, pp. 140–141.

93. Critics for the most part have also strongly disapproved of writers like Zhang Ziping, who capitalized on providing a popular urban readership with captivating love romances, especially love-triangle novels. Leo Ou-fan Lee condemns Zhang as a "notorious exploiter" in *The Romantic Generation of Modern Chinese Writers* (Cambridge: Harvard Univ. Press, 1973), p. 269.

94. "Little Lord Guanguan's Tonic," *West Willow*, pp. 142–143.

95. "Little Lord Guanguan's Tonic," *West Willow*, pp. 159–160. The execution scene may well be the worst instance of bowdlerization in Wu's 1954 anthology. The 1954 version portrays Baldy, not the executioner, as the character whose fierce mien

strikes terror into the onlookers prior to the beheading; and the episode in which a group of peasants finish Baldy off by hurling rocks at his bloody head is cut in its entirety. The editor's rationale seems to have been that since Baldy is a member of the working classes, he must by definition remain more courageous than members of the reactionary militia in the face of the whole ordeal; moreover, the peasant onlookers would never finish off their own class brother. See Wu's *Fiction and Prose*, pp. 71–72. For a translation of the bowdlerized version, see Cyril Birch's rendition in Lau, Hsia, and Lee, eds., *Modern Chinese Stories and Novellas*, pp. 380–381.

96. C. T. Hsia, *A History of Modern Chinese Fiction*, p. 30.

97. Jaroslav Prušek, *Studies in Modern Chinese Literature*, p. 23.

98. Hua-ling Nieh, *Shen Ts'ung-wen*, pp. 59–60, 22.

99. Cited from an unpublished diary of Wu Zuxiang, 29 November 1942.

100. John Ching-yu Wang, *Chin Sheng-t'an* (Boston: Twayne, 1972), p. 36.

101. John Barrell and John Bull, eds., *A Book of English Pastoral Verse* (New York: Oxford Univ. Press, 1975), p. 423. I do not claim a direct influence on Wu Zuxiang here, but instead a strong affinity in subject matter, metaphor, and mood.

102. According to Frederic Wakeman, Jr., beginning in the nineteenth century, the Chinese upper elite had created a "cadre of rural tax and rent managers" whose services allowed the elite to get involved in urban politics. In the cities, "they discovered new roles . . . as investors and sponsors of the modern schools that were rapidly educating Chinese youths away from the world of their ancestors. " This urbanized elite no longer identified themselves as classical gentrymen, but focused instead on developments in commerce and education in the large cities. See *The Fall of Imperial China*, p. 254.

103. If China was not conquered by the modern industrialized powers as it once had been by the Mongols and the Manchus, its sovereignty was nevertheless compromised, particularly in economic terms. Resentment against Westerners and other foreigners as the instigators of China's socio-economic problems in the modern world cannot be dismissed as irrational xenophobia. However, if one compares the fate of China in the age of imperialism with that of many other countries in Asia and Africa, China retained a greater measure of independence from Western control than the norm. As Lucian Pye has noted, "Most European nations have had to endure a far more competitive existence and most of them have experienced more frequent conquests and more severe destruction of their material resources than have the Chinese; and most Asian and African peoples have had far more intimate experience with colonial rule. " See *The Spirit of Chinese Politics*, p. 73.

104. "Little Lord Guanguan's Tonic," *West Willow*, pp. 151–152.

105. The urbanized character in "Little Lord Guanguan's Tonic" who embodies many of the author's views is Guanguan's cousin, the young businessman on vacation from his shop in Shanghai.

106. Re Victor Shklovsky's theory of defamiliarization, see Raymond Tallis, *In Defense of Realism* (London: Edward Arnold, 1988), pp. 176, 178–179; Michael Boyd, *The Reflexive Novel: Fiction as Critique* (Toronto: Lewisburg Bucknell Univ. Press, 1983), p. 25; Douwe Fokkema and Elrud Ibsch, *Theories of Literature in the Twentieth Century* (New York: St. Martin's Press, 1978), pp. 15–16; and Boris Eichenbaum,

"The Theory of the 'Formal Method,'" in Hazard Adams, ed., *Critical Theory Since Plato* (New York: Harcourt and Brace, 1971), pp. 834–35.

107. Quoted in Boris Eichenbaum, "The Theory of the 'Formal Method,'" in *Critical Theory Since Plato*, p. 835.

## Notes to Chapter 3

1. Originally published in *Qinghua zhoukan*, vol. 38, no. 12 (January 1933), pp. 180–185. First anthologized in *West Willow*, pp. 163–181. English translation by Yu Fanqin in *Chinese Literature*, no. 1, 1964, pp. 66–74; reprinted in *Stories from the Thirties, vol.* 2 (Beijing: Panda, 1982), pp. 9–19, and *Green Bamboo Hermitage* (Beijing: Panda, 1989), pp. 13–23. Although Wu Zuxiang wrote prolifically as a graduate student, he lasted only one year in the graduate program. For an account of the incident that apparently hastened Wu's departure, see the interview of Wu by Shen Chengkuan and Wu Fuhui entitled "Wu Zuxiang tan Zhang Tianyi" [Wu Zuxiang Discusses Zhang Tianyi], *Xin wenxue shiliao*, no. 2, 1981, p. 122.

2. I here depart from the conventions of *pinyin* romanization that would make the wife's name "Ayuan" instead of "Ah Yuan."

3. Although the two characters for *yuan* in "Ah Yuan" and "Shuyuan" are not identical, they do share the same tone and radical.

4. In January 1941, Chiang Kai-shek's 40th Division stealthily occupied the forested mountains ringing Maolin in order to encircle the headquarters contingent of the Communist New Fourth Army that was camped within the village. The local terrain aided the Nationalist Division in wiping out most of the Communist contingent trapped there, and provided telling evidence of the speedy unraveling of the wartime United-Front coalition between the two rival parties.

5. This curious custom of wedding a living bride to a dead groom was not traditionally regarded as bizarre. According to Arthur H. Smith, "The motive on the part of the family of the deceased husband is to make the ancestral graves complete." See *Village Life in China: A Study in Sociology* (New York: Fleming H. Revell, 1899), p. 299.

6. Wu Zuxiang, "The Verdant Bamboo Hermitage," *West Willow*, p. 167.

7. "The Verdant Bamboo Hermitage," *West Willow*, p. 169.

8. "The Verdant Bamboo Hermitage," *West Willow*, p. 172.

9. "The Verdant Bamboo Hermitage," *West Willow*, pp. 173–174.

10. "The Verdant Bamboo Hermitage," *West Willow*, p. 170.

11. "On My Dreams," *After-hours*, p. 87.

12. "The Verdant Bamboo Hermitage," *West Willow*, p. 170. Cheng Peikai has captured part of the mood of Wu's story in comparing it to Poe's "The Fall of the House of Usher" and Hawthorne's "Rappaccini's Daughter." Yet the comic finale in the story makes it more akin to *Northanger Abbey*, as I argue below. See Cheng, *Dousou*, no. 8, p. 5.

13. C. T. Hsia notes that the Taoist nuns in *The Peony Pavilion*, a drama by the Ming playwright Tang Xianzu, have repressed their passions to the point where they cannot refrain from "parading their physical or mental deformity for our comic attention." See "Time and the Human Condition in the Plays of Tang Xianzu," in *Self and Society in Ming Thought*, ed. William Theodore DeBary (New York: Co-

lumbia Univ. Press, 1970), p. 277. For a work of Ming fiction that portrays monks as well as nuns in a similar satiric vein, see Langxian's "He Daqing yihen yuanyang tao" [He Daqing's Regrets for the Mandarin Duck Ribbon], *Xing shi heng yan* (Hong Kong: Zuojia chubanshe, 1958), pp. 278–305.

14. Wu Zuxiang, "The Verdant Bamboo Hermitage," *West Willow*, pp. 170–172.

15. "The Verdant Bamboo Hermitage," *West Willow*, pp. 174, 178, 180.

16. "The Verdant Bamboo Hermitage," *West Willow*, pp. 168, 171.

17. "The Verdant Bamboo Hermitage," *West Willow*, pp. 171–173, 175. "On My Dreams," *After-hours*, p. 85.

18. "The Verdant Bamboo Hermitage," *West Willow*, p. 171. This statement clarifies the author's conscious intention of using setting to enhance characterization.

19. "The Verdant Bamboo Hermitage," *West Willow*, pp. 164–165, 167–168, 177. The fictional term Wu uses most here is "story," which appears five times overall. For a detailed study of Li Yu, see Patrick Hanan, *The Invention of Li Yu* (Cambridge: Harvard Univ. Press, 1988). In *Zhongguo wenxue fazhan shi* [A History of the Development of Chinese Literature] (Taibei: Hua zheng shuju, 1976), Liu Dajie traces the scope of Tang *chuanqi* (pp. 370–382) and discusses the *Liaozhai zhi yi* (pp. 1057–1069).

20. Among the modern writers most fond of such self-conscious narratorial intrusions are Thomas Mann, Bertolt Brecht, and John Barth. For source material illuminating one of the origins of this interest in the "observer effect, " whereby the observer cannot help but alter what is being observed, see Werner Heisenberg, "Nonobjective Science and Uncertainty," in Ellman and Feidelson, eds., *The Modern Tradition*, pp. 444–450.

21. Todorov groups the Gothic horror tale under the broad category of the fantastic, in *The Fantastic: A Structural Approach to a Literary Genre* (Ithaca: Cornell Univ. Press, 1975). With regard to the appropriateness of dramatized narration for the fantastic, he states: "The repressed (or 'dramatized') narrator is suitable for the fantastic, for he facilitates the necessary identification of the reader with the characters" (p. 86).

22. Milena Doleželová-Velingerová, "Narrative Modes in Late Qing Novels, " in *The Chinese Novel at the Turn of the Century* (Toronto: Univ. of Toronto Press, 1980), p. 70. The novel by Wu Woyao to which Doleželová-Velingerová refers has been translated in an abridged version by Shih Shun Liu as *Vignettes from the Late Ch'ing: Bizarre Happenings Eyewitnessed over Two Decades* (Hong Kong: Chinese Univ. of Hong Kong Press, 1978).

23. Cheng Peikai, *Dousou*, no. 8, p. 5.

24. See Chapter 21 of Jane Austen's *Northanger Abbey* for a sardonic version of the chilling Gothic tale. For critical commentary on Austen's inversion of Gothic conventions, see F. B. Pinion, *A Jane Austen Companion* (London: MacMillan, 1973).

25. Shi Zhecun, "Modao" [Injurious Courses], *Mei yu zhi xi* (Shanghai: Xin Zhongguo shuju, 1933), pp. 42–72.

26. Yuan Liangjun, "Tempered Steel," p. 60.

27. Zhao Yuan, "Wu Zuxiang and His Contemporaries," pp. 253, 251.

28. In my interview with Wu Zuxiang on 23 March 1983, he elaborated on the autobiographical dimension of "The Verdant Bamboo Hermitage," mentioning that

the setting was based on a dwelling he had once visited in the vicinity of a village called Nanrong, which is approximately ten miles from Maolin and at a higher elevation.

29. Wu Zuxiang, "Huanghun" [Twilight], *Wenxue*, vol. 1, no. 5 (November 1933), pp. 708–713. First anthologized in *West Willow*, pp. 183–205. English translation by Susan Dewar in *Green Bamboo Hermitage*, pp. 208–218.

30. "Twilight," *West Willow*, p. 205.

31. "Twilight," *West Willow*, pp. 191, 192–193, 203–204.

32. James Hightower, *The Poetry of T'ao Ch'ien* (Oxford: Clarendon Press, 1970), p. 187.

33. Wu Zuxiang, "Twilight," *West Willow*, p. 184.

34. Note the pointed references to darkness in "Twilight," *West Willow*, pp. 198, 205.

35. "Twilight," *West Willow*, p. 189. At the time when the story was written, Chinese umbrellas could not be folded up as compactly as they can be today, and were often stored in a large hempen pouch.

36. Barrell and Bull, eds., *A Book of English Pastoral Verse*, p. 392. The author makes a direct borrowing from Oliver Goldsmith at the point where he mentions a clump of spindly grass growing atop the compound's enclosing wall ("Twilight," p. 184). Compare this with Goldsmith's "Sunk are thy bowers in shapeless ruin all, / And the long grass o'ertops the mouldering wall." (p. 392).

37. See David Hawkes's translation of "Summons of the Soul," in Cyril Birch, ed., *Anthology of Chinese Literature: From Early Times to the Fourteenth Century* (New York: Grove Press, 1965), pp. 73–78.

38. Wu Zuxiang, "Twilight," *West Willow*, p. 193.

39. The narrator's wife edges closer to his side, remarking, "Listen! It's enough to scare you to death!" (*West Willow*, p. 198).

40. "Twilight," *West Willow*, pp. 201–202.

41. "Twilight," *West Willow*, p. 205.

42. Mao Dun, "'Xi liu ji,'" *Wenxue*, vol. 3, no. 5 (November 1934), p. 1075. Wang Yao dutifully repeats Mao Dun's charge of "excessive objectivity" in *Zhongguo xin wenxue shi gao* [A Draft History of Modern Chinese Literature] (Hong Kong: Bowen shuju, 1972), p. 245.

43. Interview with Wu Zuxiang, 22 October 1982. Unfortunately, none of Wu's published writings from the 1930s confronts this issue, so one has little opportunity but to observe how Wu views this issue in retrospect.

44. Shen Zhenyu, "An Exploratory Essay on Wu Zuxiang's Fiction," *Zhongguo wenxue yanjiu*, p. 349.

45. Yuan Liangjun, "Tempered Steel," pp. 50–51. Note that Yuan chooses the Europeanized term *puluo* for "proletarian." His alternative would have been *wuchanjieji*, a Sinified political term that is not safe to treat in such a sceptical fashion, particularly for a party member like Yuan who is anxious to remain politically correct.

46. Yuan Liangjun, "Tempered Steel," p. 57.

47. Zhao Yuan, "Wu Zuxiang and His Contemporaries," p. 251.

48. Aside from the several onomatopoeic expressions rendered by characters, the story also uses romanization occasionally to couch highly aural figures of speech such as interjections and onomatopoeia.

49. Wu Zuxiang, "Wanzi jinyinhua" [Splay-petaled Honeysuckle], *Qinghua zhoukan*, vol. 40, nos. 3–4 (November 1933), pp. 80–86; first anthologized in *West Willow*, pp. 207–229. Translated by Yu Fanqin in *Chinese Literature*, no. 3 (Autumn) 1986, pp. 147–153; reprinted in *Green Bamboo Hermitage*, pp. 24–33. "Splay-petaled Honeysuckle" was the first work by Wu that Mao Dun reviewed, as can be consulted in Ti Ruo (pseud. for Mao Dun), "Shubao shuping: *Qinghua zhoukan* wenyi chuangzuo zhuanhao" [A Critique of the *Qinghua Weekly* Special Issue On Literature], *Wenxue*, vol. 2, no. 2 (January 1934), pp. 359–362. He remarks that "Splay-petaled Honeysuckle" is "touching in a natural way, without a trace of heavy-handedness" (p. 362). Even in Mao Dun's unexpectedly harsh review of *West Willow* in November of that same year, he found words of admiration for this story.

50. Two references from Wu's 1940s diaries refer to occasions in which he discussed his own works when teaching a course. On 26 August 1945 he read and discussed "Splay-petaled Honeysuckle," arguing that its mood of *dandan de bei'ai* [muted melancholy] has more evocative power than the more heightened and cathartic types of melancholy—a point that Gu Zhenbang overlooked even as he insightfully used a phrase equivalent to "muted melancholy" in describing the overall temper of Wu's fiction. A diary entry from 22 March 1946 also mentions reading one of his stories aloud in a classroom at Central University in Chongqing; this time the story was "The Verdant Bamboo Hermitage."

51. Lu Xun, "Guxiang" [My Old Home], *Nahan* [Outcry] (Beijing: Renmin wenxue chubanshe, 1973), p. 65. Here is what the fortyish narrator imagines just after his mother voices the two syllables in Runtu's name: "...A miraculous picture suddenly flashed into my mind: under the golden full moon hanging in a deep blue sky, the sandy seaside fields were planted with dark-green watermelons as far as the eye could see; in their midst was a lad of eleven or twelve wearing a necklace with a silver amulet and holding a steel trident, which he was thrusting with all his might at a *zha* critter. The *zha* actually wriggled to safety by slipping between the boy's legs." This passage comes across as conceptualized and vague not only because it is an idealized and romanticized image of a rural scene the narrator never saw first-hand, but also since the animal to which he refers, the *zha*, is simply a coined term without any concrete attributes: it is as if an author in English were to substitute a nonsense word like "schwuck" for "woodchuck. "

52. Sigmund Freud, *A General Introduction to Psychoanalysis*, trans. Joan Riviere (New York: Pocket Books, 1953), p. 210.

53. Freud, *A General Introduction to Psychoanalysis*, p. 211.

54. See the selections from Proust's *Remembrance of Things Past* quoted in Ellman and Feidelson, eds., *The Modern Tradition*, pp. 730–737.

55. Yuan Liangjun, "Tempered Steel," pp. 55–56.

56. Wu Zuxiang, "Splay-petaled Honeysuckle," *West Willow*, pp. 220–221.

57. "Splay-petaled Honeysuckle," *West Willow*, p. 222.

58. In his memorial eulogy on Zhu Ziqing published in *Wen xun yuekan*, vol. 9, no. 3 (1948), Wu compares his own experiences of sickness with those of Zhu Ziqing,

who had recently died from an acute intestinal malady. "My serious illness," noted Wu, "belonged to the psychosomatic type; when the pain intensified, all of the color drained from my face, and I temporarily found myself bereft of the ability to speak. In the grip of spasms, I could not keep from thrashing about on the bed" (p. 132).

59. "Splay-petaled Honeysuckle," *West Willow*, pp. 227–228.

60. The three stories alluded to are "Yiqianbabai dan" [1800 Bushels], "Tianxia taiping" [The World At Peace], and "Fan jia pu" [Fan Hamlet].

61. "The World At Peace" was first published in *Wenxue*, vol. 2, no. 4 (March 1934), pp. 660–675. First anthologized in *West Willow*, pp. 335–397. There are two English translations: one by James C. T. Shu in Lau, Hsia, and Lee, eds., *Modern Chinese Stories and Novellas, 1919–1949*, pp. 382–397; and the other by Linda Jaivin, in *Green Bamboo Hermitage*, pp. 81–119.

62. Wu Zuxiang, "The World At Peace," *West Willow*, p. 341.

63. The most strenuous manual labor jobs in the author's home region were usually handled by migrants from impoverished regions of Jiangsu and Anhui to the north of the Yangzi River. These migrants from "Jiangbei" [North-o'-the-River] are featured below in the stories "The Woodcutter" and "The Woman."

64. The landowner is using a paper spill to light his hookah.

65. "The World At Peace," *West Willow*, pp. 355–357.

66. "The World At Peace," *West Willow*, pp. 388, 395.

67. See Zhao Yuan, "Wu Zuxiang and His Contemporaries," p. 251.

68. The clan hall is looted in "1800 Bushels"; the three iconoclastic images appear in "1800 Bushels" (January), "The World At Peace" (March), and "Fan Hamlet" (April).

69. Mao Dun, "'Xi liu ji,'" *Wenxue*, vol. 3, no. 5 (November 1934), p. 1076.

70. Patrick Hanan, *The Chinese Vernacular Story* (Cambridge: Harvard Univ. Press, 1981), p. 160. See Ling Mengchu's satiric fiction in the four volumes of the seventeenth-century collection *Pai an jing qi* [Slapping the Table in Amazement], ed. Wang Gulu (Shanghai, 1957).

71. Wu Zuxiang, "On My Dreams," *After-Hours*, pp. 81–89.

72. "On My Dreams," *After-hours*, p. 82; "The World At Peace," *West Willow*, p. 297.

73. Mao Dun, *Wenxue*, p. 1076; Wang Hanzhuo, *Qinghua zhoukan*, p. 133. See also Ruo Ying, "Ping 'Wenxue' chuangzuo zhuanhao" [A Critique of the Special Issue on Creative Writing in "Literature"], *Wenxue*, vol. 3, no. 1 (July 1934), p. 490; and Su Fei, "Du 'Wenxue' chuangzuo zhuanhao" [On Reading the Special Issue on Creative Writing in "Literature"], *Wenxue*, vol. 3, no. 1, p. 489.

74. Zhao Yuan, "Wu Zuxiang and His Contemporaries," pp. 251–252.

75. Interview with Pan Tongshou, 13 May 1983. The temple was destroyed sometime between the late 1930s and recent years; nothing more than a pile of rubble marked the site when I visited it in 1983.

76. Arthur H. Smith, *Village Life in China*, p. 137.

77. Jeffrey Kinkley, "Shen Ts'ung-wen's Vision of Republican China," Diss. Harvard 1977, p. 35.

78. Interview with Wu Zuxiang, 24 November 1982.

79. Cheng Peikai, *Dousou*, no. 8, p. 17. Mao Dun claims that "Splay-petaled Honeysuckle" is an "essay" or "sketch," not a genuine piece of fiction. See *Wenxue*, vol. 2, no. 1 (January 1934), p. 203.

80. Interview with Wu Zuxiang, 7 March 1983.

81. Dong Meng, "'Wenxue' chuangzuo zhuanhao" [The Special Issue on Creative Writing in "Literature"], *Wenxue*, vol. 3, no. 1, p. 489.

82. Ruo Ying, *Wenxue*, vol. 3, no. 1, p. 490.

83. Wu Zuxiang, "Fan Hamlet," *Wenxue jikan*, vol. 1, no. 2 (April 1934), pp. 213–234; first anthologized in *After-hours*, pp. 1–62. There are two English translations: one by Russell McLeod and C. T. Hsia in Lau, Hsia, and Lee, eds., *Modern Chinese Stories and Novellas, 1919–1949*, pp. 398–415; and the second by Yu Fanqin in *Green Bamboo Hermitage*, pp. 120–155.

84. Mao Dun, "'Wenxue jikan' di'erqi nei de chuangzuo" [Fiction in the Second Number of the "Literature Quarterly"], *Wenxue*, vol. 3, no. 1 (July 1934), p. 450. C. T. Hsia, *A History of Modern Chinese Fiction*, p. 285.

85. G. M. A. Grube, tr., *Aristotle on Poetry and Style* (Indianapolis: Bobbs-Merrill, 1958), p. 27.

86. The original journal version of "Fan Hamlet" captures Xianzi's final ambivalence toward her mother more skillfully than his revised versions in either the 1935 or 1954 anthologies. Here are the three different versions of the story's closing scene in which Xianzi unexpectedly runs into Gouzi:

> "Is that you? Heavens, it *is* you! Then—the county seat really was—" As Xianzi gasped for breath, her legs seemed to turn to jelly. "Oh, Mama!" she cried, and then blacked out. [*Wenxue jikan*, 1934, p. 234]

> "Is that you? Heavens, it *is* you! Then—the county seat really was—" As Xianzi gasped for breath, she wondered whether the whole thing was but a dream. [*After-hours*, 1935, p. 61]

> "Is that you? Heavens, it *is* you! Then—the county seat really was–" As she gasped for breath, her legs seemed to turn to jelly; swaying on her feet, she had a vague feeling that she was dreaming. [*Fiction and Prose*, 1954, p. 177]

87. Cheng Peikai, *Dousou*, no. 9, p. 17.

88. Tzvetan Todorov, *The Fantastic: A Structural Approach to a Literary Genre*, pp. 143–144.

89. Grube, *Aristotle on Poetry and Style*, pp. 21–22. A reversal occurs when the outcome of an episode is the exact opposite of what one or more of the major characters have expected, and yet is reasonable within the context of the overall logic of the work.

90. Grube, *Aristotle on Poetry and Style*, pp. 21–22.

91. Suzanne K. Langer, *Feeling and Form: A Theory of Art* (New York: Scribner's, 1953), p. 357.

92. Murray Krieger, *The Tragic Vision* (Baltimore: Johns Hopkins Univ. Press, 1973), p. 5.

93. Wu Zuxiang, "Fan Hamlet," *After-hours*, p. 25.

94. Other stories by Wu in which main characters faint or collapse upon learning of a loved one's death are "Soaring Hawks and Plunging Fish," "Two Young Sparrows," "The Flowering Gardenia," "Miss Jin and the Xue Girl," and "Splay-petaled Honeysuckle."

95. "Fan Hamlet," *After-hours*, p. 55.

96. Quoted from Rudolph Kausen, "The Laius Complex and Mother-Child Symbiosis," *Journal of Individual Psychology*, vol. 28, no. 1 (May 1972), p. 34. See also Thomas S. Vernon, "The Laius Complex," *The Humanist*, Nov.-Dec. 1971, pp. 27–28.

97. Oedipus' act of gouging out his own eyes is generally thought to represent a self-imposed castration, or regression to a state of infantilism that precedes an awareness of the genitals. Similarly, the sensation of total powerlessness during a collapse from fainting amounts to an infantile dependence on others for even basic locomotion.

98. Mao Dun, "'Wenxue jikan' di'erqi nei de chuangzuo," *Wenxue*, vol. 3, no. 1, p. 450. C. T. Hsia, *A History of Modern Chinese Fiction*, pp. 285–286. Wang Yao represents the opinion of literal-minded economic determinists in his reduction of the motivations for murder to dire economic need. See his *Draft History of Modern Chinese Literature*, p. 245.

99. Mao Dun, *Wenxue*, vol. 3, no. 1, p. 450. See the story "Father and Son" in *Wang Tongzhao wenji* [Collected Writings of Wang Tongzhao], vol. 1 (Jinan: Shandong renmin chubanshe, 1980), pp. 485–505.

100. Mao Dun, *Wenxue*, vol. 3, no. 1, p. 450. Sister Lian complains of "great changes in people's hearts" in "Fan Hamlet," p. 13.

101. Wu Zuxiang, "Fan Hamlet," *After-hours*, p. 22.

102. Re the widespread *modus vivendi* existing between government armies and bandit gangs, see Jeffrey Kinkley, "Shen Ts'ung-wen's Vision of Republican China," p. 54.

103. Wu Zuxiang, "Fan Hamlet," *After-hours*, p. 48.

104. "Fan Hamlet," *After-hours*, p. 21.

105. C. A. S. Williams, *Outline of Chinese Symbolism and Art Motives*, 3rd edition (New York: Dover Publications, 1976), p. 408.

106. Derk Bodde, *Festivals in Classical China* (Princeton: Princeton Univ. Press, 1975), pp. 83, 294.

107. A cassia tree would normally represent constancy, but here it burns and perishes along with a whole social order; a Buddhist incense burner would normally enhance the pious ambiance of Buddhist prayer or meditation, but here it is used to murder a Buddhist devotee; a candleholder reserved for ancestral sacrifices would normally instill a feeling of awe and respect for one's ancestors, but here a daughter wields it to murder her mother. For an explanation of the psychological associations with what C. K. Yang calls "the mystical symbol of the ancestors' tablets, incense, and candles," see *The Chinese Family in the Communist Revolution*, p. 195.

108. If "Fan Hamlet" breaks new ground in Wu's canon with its thoroughgoing iconoclasm, its cast of characters owes a great deal to Wu's earliest story about rural family life, "Soaring Hawks and Plunging Fish" (1925). Xianzi is an outgrowth of

the assertive young woman in "Soaring Hawks" who dares to defy the wishes of a domineering old matron; the same matron is herself the forerunner of Xianzi's mother, as both of them complain without end about disrespect for elders among the young. Finally, the nun of "Soaring Hawks" who joins the matron in disapproving of unfilial youth is the model for Sister Lian and her complaints about "great changes in people's hearts."

109. Interview with Wu Jinglin, 14 May 1983.

110. Interview with Wu Zuxiang, 24 November 1982.

111. Wu Zuxiang, "The Woodcutter," *Wenxue*, vol. 3, no. 6 (December 1934), pp. 1179–1184. First anthologized in *After-hours*, pp. 89–104. Translated as "Maki" by Masuda Wataru in *Shina Endo tampenshū* [A Collection of Short Stories from China and India], ed. Satō Haruo (Tokyo, 1936). English translation by Denis Mair in *Green Bamboo Hermitage*, pp. 246–259.

112. Wu's only work prior to 1935 that presented a vision of rural recovery was "1800 Piculs" (1934).

113. "The Woodcutter," *After-hours*, p. 90.

114. "The Woodcutter," *After-hours*, p. 95. For a study of Jiangbei migrants to urban rather than rural areas to the south, see Emily Honig, "Pride and Prejudice: Subei People in Contemporary Shanghai," in *Unofficial China: Popular Culture and Thought in the People's Republic*, eds. Perry Link, Richard Madsen, and Paul G. Pickowicz (Boulder: Westview, 1989), pp. 138–155.

115. "The Woodcutter," *After-hours*, p. 99.

116. "The Woodcutter," *After-hours*, p. 102.

117. Northrop Frye, *The Well-tempered Critic* (Bloomington: Indiana Univ. Press, 1963), pp. 21–22.

118. Stuart H. Traub and Craig B. Little, eds., *Theories of Deviance*, 2nd ed. (Itasca, Ill.: F. E. Peacock Publishers, 1980), p. 64.

## Notes to Chapter 4

1. The suffering may be gender-related, as in the case of the young widow who violates patriarchal social mores in "Splay-petaled Honeysuckle," or else class-based, as the fate of the tenant farmer Baldy in "Little Lord Guanguan's Tonic" illustrates. At other times, the bitter lot of the characters stems from forces far too large for them to comprehend, as is the case with the Great Depression that catalyzes the ruin of both Wang Xiaofu of "Let There Be Peace" and Xiangfa of "The Flowering Gardenia."

2. Wu Zuxiang, "1800 Bushels," *Wenxue jikan*, vol. 1, no. 1 (January 1934), pp. 61–86; first anthologized in *West Willow*, pp. 231–334; English translation by Gladys Yang in *Stories From the Thirties, Vol. 2* (Beijing: Panda, 1982), pp. 20–69; reprinted in *Green Bamboo Hermitage* (Beijing: Panda, 1989), pp. 34–80.

3. For an account of the dwindling role of the family as a social unit in the decades prior to 1949, see C. K. Yang's section on the family revolution in Chapter One of *The Chinese Family in the Communist Revolution*, pp. 10–17. A fine study of the development of secret societies and peasant associations during this period is Elizabeth J. Perry's *Rebels and Revolutionaries in North China, 1845–1945* (Stanford: Stanford

Univ. Press, 1980). The features of the new local elite in transitional China are outlined by Philip A. Kuhn in "Local Self-government Under the Republic," in *Conflict and Control in Late Imperial China*, eds. Frederic Wakeman, Jr. and Carolyn Grant (Berkeley: Univ. of California Press, 1975), pp. 257–268.

4. C. T. Hsia, *A History of Modern Chinese Fiction*, p. 284.

5. See Cheng Peikai, "The Battle Trumpet Has Sounded," *Dousou*, no. 9, pp. 9–12, and Shen Zhenyu, *Studies in Chinese Literature*, p. 346.

6. Wu Zuxiang, "1800 Bushels," *West Willow*, p. 240.

7. "1800 Bushels," *West Willow*, pp. 273–274.

8. "1800 Bushels," *West Willow*, pp. 274–275.

9. "1800 Bushels," *Wenxue jikan*, vol. 1, no. 1, p. 86.

10. Interview with Wu Zuxiang, 22 October 1982.

11. Interviews with Wu Zuxiang on 7 March 1983 and with Wu Monong on 14 May 1983.

12. James C. Scott, *The Moral Economy of the Chinese Peasant*, p. 5.

13. See Lillian M. Li, "Food, Famine, and the Chinese State," *Journal of Asian Studies*, vol. XLI, no. 4, p. 700.

14. According to a personal interview on 14 May 1983 with Wu Baohua, a nephew of Wu Zuxiang who still resides in Maolin, beancurd proprietors had an especially low social status among shopkeepers in his locale.

15. C. T. Hsia, *A History of Modern Chinese Fiction*, p. 284. For questionable uses of the term, "landlord class," see Cheng Peikai, "Trumpet," *Dousou*, no. 9, p. 16; Shen Zhenyu, "Exploratory Essay, " p. 340; and Yuan Liangjun, "Tempered Steel," p. 54.

16. With regard to difficulties in disciplining the notoriously unscrupulous *shengyuan*, see Frederic Wakeman, Jr., *The Fall of Imperial China*, p. 32, and Chung-li Chang, *The Chinese Gentry*, pp. 36–37.

17. Frederic Wakeman, Jr., *The Fall of Imperial China*, p. 234.

18. Wu Zuxiang, "1800 Bushels," *West Willow*, p. 302.

19. Avrahm Yarmolinsky, ed., *The Portable Chekhov* (New York: The Viking Press, 1975), p. 575.

20. The diary entry is dated 8 February 1945. Women were allowed entry to the clan temple only on certain occasions like New Year's, and generally had to assume a position of inferiority to men of similar age and social station.

21. Interview with Pan Tongshou in Xuancheng, 13 May 1983.

22. The head of the Maolin Cultural Affairs Station, Wu Jinglin, showed me the most recent photograph (taken in 1950) of the missing votive tablets on 14 May 1983.

23. Wu mentioned his refusal to accept land from debtors in an interview on 23 March 1983.

24. "1800 Bushels," *West Willow*, pp. 322–323.

25. Y. C. Wang, *Chinese Intellectuals and the West*, p. 21.

26. On *ganqing*, see Wakeman, *The Fall of Imperial China*, p. 16.

27. Interview with Wu Zuxiang, 23 March 1983.

28. Mao Dun (pseud. Ti Ruo), "Shubao pingshu: 'Wenxue jikan' chuangkanhao" [A Critical Review of the Inaugural Issue of the "Literature Quarterly"], *Wenxue*, vol. 2, no. 2 (February 1934), p. 362.

29. Lü Ren, *Yi shi bao*, Tianjin, 23 January 1934, p. 14.

30. The only negative media review of "1800 Bushels" that I found was a diatribe on the entire issue of *Wenxue jikan* in the famous Shanghai "Unfettered Talk" [*Ziyou tan*] column in *Shen bao*. See Zhong Fang, "Du 'Wenxue jikan' chuangkanhao" [A Reading of the Inaugural Issue of the "Literature Quarterly"], 1 February 1934, p. 19. Since Zhong Fang's attack on the inaugural issue is so sweeping and incoherent, it does not merit further discussion.

31. Yi-tsi Feuerwerker argues that "Shui" fails to meet the standard set by many of Ding Ling's earlier stories in its unconvincing and incoherent portrayal of the sudden transformation of "an exhausted, starving crowd of wretched subhuman beings" into an efficient and fearless "fighting force"; see *Ding Ling's Fiction: Ideology and Narrative in Modern Chinese Literature* (Cambridge: Harvard Univ. Press, 1982), p. 67. Marston Anderson offers no reply to this argument in his interpretation of "Shui," in which he claims that the story is very "effective" in its use of the "water metaphor" for the new-found power of peasants who crowd together (*The Limits of Realism* [Berkeley: Univ. of California Press, 1990], pp. 185–186). Ding Ling's harping away at the marvelous unity between peasants and flood waters that supposedly reverberates through the minds of all the famished and uneducated farmers seems not to strike Anderson as the least bit contrived or improbable, for he argues that "the crowd has taken possession of the flood's power"; he also seems convinced by the narrator's giddy claim that the peasant crowd had become "even fiercer" than the raging flood waters themselves (p. 186). Unless one imagines that Ding Ling was a whimsical fabulist who cared little about portraying recognizable human motivations in a compelling way, Feuerwerker's criticisms of "Shui" cannot be so cavalierly ignored, even if Ding Ling's water metaphor shows some imaginative potential.

32. Information on Lu Xun's handling of "Yiqianbabai dan" and "Shui" comes from Ge Zhenghui, Kong Haizhu, and Lu Diaowen, eds., "Lu Xun, Mao Dun xuanbian 'Caoxie jiao' de wenxian" [Writings by Lu Xun and Mao Dun on the Editing of "Straw Sandals"], *Zhongguo xiandai wenyi ziliao congkan*, no. 5 (April 1980), pp. 187–188. Re the tendentious quality of Ding Ling's "Shui," Tani Barlow has noted that this work marks Ding Ling's "turn towards explicitly ideological left-wing fiction," and adopts a narrative approach "largely determined by revolutionary politics." See her introduction to Tani E. Barlow and Gary J. Bjorge, eds., *I Myself Am a Woman: Selected Writings of Ding Ling* (Boston: Beacon Press, 1989), p. 29.

33. Wendy Larson, *Literary Authority and the Modern Chinese Writer: Ambivalence and Autobiography* (Durham: Duke Univ. Press, 1991), pp. 92, 157.

34. Lu Xun's preface to *Straw Sandals* associates "progressive" writing with involvement in "social struggle." See the expanded reprint version in Chinese, *Caoxie jiao* (Changsha: Hunan renmin chubanshe, 1981), pp. 1–2.

35. Sima Changfeng persuasively argues that it was Lu Xun who was responsible for not including even a single work by Shen Congwen in the largest anthology of contemporary Chinese fiction, *Zhongguo xin wenxue da xi*, which was compiled in 1935. See Sima Changfeng's *Xin wenxue congtan* [Collected Discussions on Modern Literature] (Hong Kong: Shaoming chubanshe, 1975), pp. 181–182.

36. Lu Xun's friend, Masuda Wataru, wrote Chinese rather awkwardly, so when he wanted to contact a Chinese writer he would usually write the letter to Lu Xun, who would correct its Japanized grammar before forwarding it on to the Chinese

writer addressed. According to *Lu Xun quanji* [Collected Works of Lu Xun] (Beijing: Renmin wenxue, 1981, vol. 13, pp. 618–619), when Lu Xun read Wu Zuxiang's reply to Masuda's first letter, his reaction was harshly critical of Wu. Among other things, Lu Xun scoffed at Wu Zuxiang's statement that a humorous temperament was more common among urbanites than among country folk, even though Lu Xun himself had far less first-hand knowledge of country life than either Wu or Shen Congwen. Shen, incidentally, would not have accepted Lu Xun's dismissal of Wu's remark, for the Hunan writer once noted that the average countryman "is serious about every-thing, so much so that he appears almost idiotic" (quoted in Hua-ling Nieh, *Shen Ts'ung-wen* [Boston: Twayne, 1972], p. 66). Lu Xun's pejorative use of "petty bour-geois" in the quoted passage hardly differs from the oratorical habits of his arch-en-emy, Zhou Yang; see *Lu Xun quanji*, vol. 13, p. 619.

37. Marston Anderson has aptly noted the "theatrical" facet of the conclusion of "1800 Bushels," for the site to which the crowd drags the two most prominent clan leaders for pillorying is none other than an outdoor stage (*The Limits of Realism*, p. 188). However, the ritualistic significance of the pillorying comes across as more fundamental, in that the stage had been used most recently for ceremonial sacrifices to the rain god rather than secular performances. Moreover, the uproar of gongs and intimidating shouts served the same sort of ritualistic function as bagpipes in a Scottish military attack: to overawe the enemy with a show of power. For more in-formation on the significance of gong-beating and other ritualistic group intimida-tion tactics in local Chinese feuds, see Harry J. Lamley, "Lineage Feuding in South-ern Fujian and Eastern Guangdong Under Qing Rule," in *Violence in China: Essays in Culture and Counterculture*, eds. Jonathan N. Lipman and Stevan Harrell (Albany: State Univ. of New York Press, 1990), pp. 27–64, esp. p. 45.

38. C. T. Hsia, *A History of Modern Chinese Fiction*, pp. 283–284, 287; Yuan Liangjun, "Tempered Steel," p. 59; Zhao Yuan, "Contemporaries," *Shiyue*, no. 1, 1984, p. 253.

39. The inclination of Hemingway and Maupassant to a highly dramatic mode of narratorial presentation is mentioned by Frank O'Connor, *The Lonely Voice: A Study of the Short Story* (Cleveland: World Publishing Co., 1962), pp. 25–26, and Austin Warren and René Wellek, *Theory of Literature* (New York: Harcourt Brace, 1942), p. 218.

40. See Zhu Ziqing, *Jingdian chang tan* [An Informal Discussion of the Classics] (Beijing: Sanlian shudian, 1980), p. 18. Also see Burton Watson, *Early Chinese Litera-ture* (New York: Columbia Univ. Press, 1962), pp. 23, 50.

41. Watson, *Early Chinese Literature*, p. 50. While a few sections of interior mono-logue in "1800 Bushels" function in a manner foreign to an early work of narrative like the *Zuo zhuan*, such passages are both short and few in number. Yuan Liangjun has compared Wu's suggestiveness of narratorial presentation with that in the *Spring and Autumn Annals* in "Tempered Steel," p. 51.

42. Pu Liangpei (pseud. Lin Fei), *Xiandai liushi jia sanwen zhaji* [Notes on Reading Sixty Prose Writers] (Tianjin: Bai hua wenyi chubanshe, 1980), p. 158.

43. Wu Zuxiang, preface to *West Willow*, p. i.

44. Shen Chengkuan and Wu Fuhui, "Wu Zuxiang Discusses Zhang Tianyi," *Xin wenxue shiliao*, no. 2, 1981, p. 122.

45. Another factor involved with the sketchy nature of his writings in this period was the mid-1930s surge in popularity of the *xiaopinwen* [familiar essay]. Lin Yutang's journals that catered to *xiaopinwen* such as *Ren jian shi* [In the Human World] were soon rivalled by journals of similar format but of more serious social content, such as *Tai bai*. Three of Wu's pieces were published in *Tai bai* during 1935, but only one was strictly fictional in nature.

46. Wu Zuxiang, "In Memory of Lu'er," *After-hours*, pp. 114, 120.

47. Preface to *After-hours*, p. i.

48. Wu Zuxiang, "Nen huang zhi yi" [Memories of My Childhood Days], *Wenxue jikan*, vol. 1, no. 3 (July 1934), pp. 258–259.

49. "Recuperating from an Illness," in "Memories of My Childhood Days," p. 258.

50 "On the Grass Heap," in "Memories of My Childhood Days," p. 258.

51. "The Vegetable Garden," in "Memories of My Childhood Days," p. 259.

52. The favorable review, already mentioned in Chapter Two, is Wang Hanzhuo (pseud. Bai Pin), "Wu Zuxiang's 'Xi liu ji,'" *Qinghua zhoukan*, vol. 42, no. 1, pp. 131–134. Mao Dun's cantankerous review appeared in *Wenxue*, vol. 3, no. 5, pp. 1074–1080.

53. See Yuan Liangjun, "Tempered Steel, " pp. 50–51, and Mao Dun, *Wenxue*, vol. 3, no. 5, pp. 1075–1076. Wang Hanzhuo had made a value-free comment about a recurrent feature in plot structure—the tendency for the climax to appear at the very end of Wu's stories—before moving on to a gentle Marxist exhortation to not stop short at "exposing reality" but to press on, "directing and propelling reality forward" (p. 134). Mao Dun takes what might have been little more than an afterthought for Wang Hanzhuo and makes it the center of his attack on *West Willow* a month later. He lambastes Wu Zuxiang for passively reflecting reality without injecting the work with a moral standpoint based on social ideals; therefore, Wu's typical work of "out-and-out objectivist fiction" is a "failure" (p. 1075). Mao Dun's broadsides at a "bourgeois" writer like Wu Zuxiang become more comprehensible if we recall the elder's role since the 1920s as a "very high level [Communist] Party propagandist," to quote Yu-shih Chen in *Realism and Allegory in the Early Fiction of Mao Tun* (Bloomington: Indiana Univ. Press, 1986), p. 182.

54. I have seen no evidence that Lu Xun ever publicized his private views on Wu or "1800 Bushels," which have come down to us through his letters and correspondence. Most likely, Lu Xun harbored considerable antipathy for much of the Beijing literary scene at that time, and would have been no more severe or harshly dismissive to Wu Zuxiang than to Lao She or Shen Congwen.

55. Wang Yao, *A Draft History of Modern Chinese Literature*, p. 245.

56. Wu Zuxiang, Preface to *After-hours*, p. i. Ba Jin shared Wu's affinity for Turgenev, even going so far as to style the great Russian novelist his "first teacher" in the art of writing fiction. See Mau-sang Ng, *The Russian Hero in Modern Chinese Fiction* (Albany: State Univ. of New York Press, 1988), p. 193.

57. Wu Zuxiang, "The Woman," *Tai bai*, vol. 1, no. 8 (January 1935), pp. 342–344; first anthologized in *After-hours*, pp. 105–112; English translation by Paul Crescenzo and Vivian Hsu in Hsu, ed., *Born of the Same Roots* (Bloomington: Indiana Univ. Press, 1981), pp. 8–11.

58. In an interview with Wu Zuxiang on 24 November 1982, Wu mentioned that *dao meizi* is a Jiangbei dialectal obscenity which insinuates that the speaker has been sleeping with the listener's younger sister. It occurs nearly ten times in the Jiangbei maid's speech over the course of the story.

59. Interview with Wu Zuxiang, 24 November 1982.

60. Wu Zuxiang, "The Woman," *After-hours*, p. 105.

61. "The Woman," *After-hours*, pp. 105–106.

62. A string of cash was worth a tael, or roughly an ounce of silver. It was a sizeable sum indeed from the viewpoint of the rural poor.

63. "The Woman," *After-hours*, p. 111.

64. "The Woman," *After-hours*, p. 110.

65. "The Woman," *After-hours*, p. 112.

66. "The Woman," *After-hours*, p. 105.

67. Percy G. Adams, *Travel Literature and the Evolution of the Novel* (Lexington: Univ. of Kentucky Press, 1983). Adams argues that early picaresque and adventure novels were particularly indebted to the episodic and coincidental plot structure of the typical travel account (pp. 278–279). To be sure, the footloose quality of *Water Margin* and *Journey to the West* suggests the centrality of travel motifs in some of the classic Chinese novels.

68. Here is how Pu Liangpei frames the issue in *Xiandai liushi sanwen zhaji*, p. 158: "The essays that Wu Zuxiang has penned seldom directly reveal his beliefs and feelings, instead outlining scenes from life with detachment and intricacy as he depicts the personalities of his characters. If we say that Xiao Hong adopts some techniques of the essay when writing fiction, thereby increasing its lyrical and imagistic qualities, we can also say that Wu Zuxiang adopts some techniques of fiction when writing the essay."

69. Wu Zuxiang (pseud. Wu Di), "Yangzhou Jottings," *Qinghua zhoukan*, vol. 41, nos. 3–4 (April 1934), pp. 153–160. Though Wu wrote this piece a few months before moving back to the lower Yangzi Valley, he had already planned to leave Beijing and was preparing to move to the lower Yangzi. The one city in that region for which he felt a strong distaste was Shanghai, whose intrusive foreign presence irritated him. The pseudonym "Wu Di" is homonymous with Wu Zuxiang's nickname at Qinghua University, "Wu Di" [Wu the Younger]. His older brother, Wu Zuguang, was also a Qinghua alumnus, and was known as Wu Ge [Wu the Elder].

70. Wu Zuxiang, "Sights At Mount Tai, " *Wenxue*, vol. 5, no. 4 (November 1935), pp. 714–726; first anthologized in *After-hours*, pp. 125–159; recently anthologized in Ma Zhonglin et al., eds., *Zhongguo xiandai youji xuan* [A Collection of Modern Chinese Travel Accounts] (Beijing: Zhongguo luyou chubanshe, 1982), pp. 62–79. Translated into English by Geremie Barmé in *Green Bamboo Hermitage*, pp. 219–245.

71. "Yangzhou Jottings," p. 159.

72. The gradual eclipse of inland water transport by rail and oceangoing transport brought the fate of genteel decline to various old canal entrepots like Yangzhou, which even today is on the fringes of the Chinese transportation network.

73. "Yangzhou Jottings," p. 156.

74. "Yangzhou Jottings," p. 160. Hence Wu's strong aversion to China's most cosmopolitan city, Shanghai, as detailed in Chapter 2.

75. "Yangzhou Jottings," p. 157.

76. Feng Yuxiang was something of a conversation piece in Parisian literary salons during the 1920s. See Sinclair Lewis' novel of 1929, *Dodsworth* (New York: New American Library, 1972), p. 180.

77. James E. Sheridan, *Chinese Warlord: the Career of Feng Yü-hsiang* (Stanford: Stanford Univ. Press, 1966), p. 269.

78. See Feng Hongda and Yu Huaxin, *Feng Yuxiang Jiangjun hun gui Zhonghua* [General Feng Yuxiang's Return to China in Spirit] (Beijing: Wen shi ziliao chubanshe, 1981), p. 15, and Yu Zhigong, "Feng Yuxiang Xiansheng yu wenyi jie" [Mr. Feng Yuxiang and the Literary Scene], *Xin wenxue shiliao*, no. 2, 1983, p. 244.

79. Interview with Wu Zuxiang, 29 December 1982.

80. Shen Chengkuan and Wu Fuhui, "Wu Zuxiang Discusses Zhang Tianyi," p. 126. According to Wu's diaries of 1942, he stopped working for Feng in the early 1940s partly because he loathed the task of editing Feng's prolix and poorly written manuscripts.

81. Interview with Wu Zuxiang, 7 March 1983.

82. Wu Zuxiang, "Sights at Mount Tai, " *After-hours*, p. 131.

83. "Sights at Mount Tai," *After-hours*, p. 141.

84. "Sights at Mount Tai," *After-hours*, pp. 135–136.

85. "Sights at Mount Tai," *After-hours*, p. 137.

86. "Sights at Mount Tai," *After-hours*, pp. 157–158.

87. Sinclair Lewis' famous novel, *Babbitt*, has also been viewed primarily as social investigation.

88. Wu Zuxiang, "A Certain Day," in Xia Mianzun, ed., *Shinian* [A Decade] (Shanghai: Kaiming shudian, 1936), pp. 197–217. Later anthologized in *Fiction and Prose*, pp. 183–200. There are two English translations: one by David Kwan in *Green Bamboo Hermitage*, pp. 156–172, and the other by Marston Anderson in Helen F. Siu, ed., *Furrows: Peasants, Intellectuals, and the State: Stories and Histories from Modern China* (Stanford: Stanford Univ. Press, 1990), pp. 40–54.

89. "A Certain Day," *Fiction and Prose*, p. 196.

90. "A Certain Day," *Fiction and Prose*, p. 196.

91. The Dragon King is a rain god.

92. "A Certain Day," *Fiction and Prose*, p. 197.

93. For a glimpse of Huniu's self-indulgence near the end of her term of pregnancy in *Camel Xiangzi*, see *Lao She wenji*, vol. 3 (Beijing: Renmin wenxue chubanshe, 1982), pp. 176–177.

94. "A Certain Day," *Fiction and Prose*, p. 198.

95. "A Certain Day," *Fiction and Prose*, p. 196.

96. The son reviles his father as a "whore," thereby indicating that he has learned only the pejorative connotations, not the literal meanings, of such terms (*Fiction and Prose*, p. 188).

97. "A Certain Day," *Fiction and Prose*, pp. 183, 200.

98. "A Certain Day," *Fiction and Prose*, p. 200. Marston Anderson has also made reference to the "rosy" description of the land and clouds at story's end, though his

brief synopsis does not mention that the concluding cloud mass embodies a developing coalescence of the wispy clouds described at the outset. See *The Limits of Realism: Chinese Fiction in the Revolutionary Period* (Berkeley: Univ. of California Press, 1990), p. 198.

99. The *wujiu* tree had special significance for Wu, since his family had a large amount invested in small shops that pressed *wujiu* oil.

100. Cheng Peikai, *Dousou*, no. 9, p. 19.

101. "A Certain Day," *Fiction and Prose*, p. 200.

102. C. K. Yang, *A Chinese Village in Early Communist Transition*, p. 205.

103. James C. Scott, *The Moral Economy of the Peasant*, p. 28.

104. In Liu I-ching, *Shih-shuo Hsin-yü*, trans. Richard Mather, pp. 447–448, an anecdote describes how a country squire passes off his undesirable daughter to be the bride of a peasant eager to rise in the world.

105. "A Certain Day," *Fiction and Prose*, p. 189.

## Notes to Chapter 5

1. Wu Zuxiang, "The Requisitioned Boat," *Qiyue* [July], no. 11 (March 1938), pp. 342–345. Categorized as a *tongxun* [travel report], this work was first anthologized in *Fiction and Prose*, pp. 278–288.

2. Wu Zuxiang, "Wo duiyu wenyi jie tongyi zhanxian de jidian guanjian" [A Few Personal Views on the National United Front of Literary Circles], *Xinhua ribao*, 27 March 1938, p. 4. During the time Wu wrote this essay, and specifically from December 1937 to September 1938, he served as Secretary of the Nationwide Writers' War of Resistance Consultative Conference [*Zhonghua quanguo wenyi jie kangdi xiehui*] in Wuhan.

3. "A Few Personal Views," *Xinhua ribao*, 27 March 1938, p. 4.

4. One can perceive a similarly radical change in authorial attitudes to soldiery before and after 1937 in Lao She and Ba Jin, who also tend to portray Chinese soldiers as unscrupulous mercenary types before 1937, and upright patriots after that date. See Olga Lang, *Pa Chin and His Fiction* (Cambridge: Harvard Univ. Press, 1967), p. 202.

5. According to Wu Baohua during an interview on 15 May 1983, Baizi stayed with his grandmother in Maolin until her death in 1944. At that point he joined the Army.

6. Wu Zuxiang, "The Requisitioned Boat, " *Fiction and Prose*, p. 281.

7. "The Requisitioned Boat," *Fiction and Prose*, p. 282.

8. "The Requisitioned Boat," *Fiction and Prose*, p. 281. I follow the 1954 version of this passage except for its substitution of "spreading warmth" for "gushing" in the original version of 1938. "Spreading warmth" implies that the sight of patriotic soldiers and children merely comforted the narrator, whereas the original version suggests that this sight upset him even more than he had been before, due to its function of heightening the contrast between the grass-roots sense of national mission and elite profligacy and malfeasance.

9. Lin Huanping, "Duo chansheng xie 'Chai chuan'" [Let's Produce More "Requisitioned Boats"], *Kangzhan wenyi pinglun ji* [Collected Critical Essays on Resistance Literature] (Hong Kong: Min'ge chubanshe, 1939), pp. 153–155.

10. Wu Zuxiang, "Stuffy Ironsides," *Zhongguo qingnian* [Chinese Youth], vol. 7, nos. 4–5 (November 1942), pp. 55–71; first anthologized in *Fiction and Prose*, pp. 201–226. English translation by Jeff Book in *Green Bamboo Hermitage* (Beijing: Panda, 1989), pp. 173–207.

11. For a critical exposition of another story that embodies the sonata form, see Harold A. Basilins, "Thomas Mann's Use of Musical Structure and Technique in 'Tonio Kroger,'" *Germanic Review*, vol. 19 (1944), pp. 284–308.

12. "Stuffy Ironsides," *Fiction and Prose*, p. 204. The first sentence of this passage—about the way words of fulsome praise often have a hollow ring to them—was expurgated from the 1954 edition; see *Zhongguo qingnian*, November 1942, p. 57. After all, a regime which makes such heavy use of self-congratulatory rhetoric cannot countenance the open expression of skepticism toward empty platitudes.

13. "Stuffy Ironsides," *Fiction and Prose*, p. 220. The phrase "I exclaimed with a sneer" is from the original wording in *Zhongguo qingnian*, p. 68. The 1954 edition replaced this wording with "A chill shot through my body," thereby obscuring the speaker's darkly humorous overtones.

14. "Stuffy Ironsides," *Fiction and Prose*, p. 213.

15. "Stuffy Ironsides," *Fiction and Prose*, p. 226.

16. "Stuffy Ironsides," *Fiction and Prose*, p. 219.

17. For a satirical look at how the formula *yi shen zuo ze* has been disingenuously utilized by hypocritical officials, see Feng Jicai's "The Street-sweeping Show," in Susan W. Chen, tr., *Chrysanthemums and Other Stories* (San Diego: Harcourt Brace, 1985), pp. 244–250.

18. Chow Tse-tsung, *The May Fourth Movement*, pp. 16, 158.

19. While mentioning the self-dissolution of a pickpockets' ring, Lawrence R. Sullivan notes that "the 'dog-eat-dog' character of life in Beijing rapidly gave way [in May 1989] to a social graciousness and common concern for individual welfare that surprised Chinese and foreign observers alike." See "The Emergence of Civil Society in China, Spring 1989," in Tony Saich, ed., *The Chinese People's Movement: Perspectives on Spring 1989* (Armonk, N.Y.: M. E. Sharpe, 1990), pp. 126–144, esp. p. 130. During this month, Joseph W. Esherick noted a similar sudden increase in public-spiritedness at Xi'an: see "Xi'an Spring," *The Australian Journal of Chinese Affairs*, no. 24 (Jul. 1990), pp. 209–235, esp. p. 225.

20. Zhao Yuan, "Wu Zuxiang and His Contemporaries," p. 250.

21. "Stuffy Ironsides," *Fiction and Prose*, p. 215. The reference to bound feet was expurgated from the 1954 edition; see *Zhongguo qingnian*, November 1942, p. 64.

22. Interview with Wu Zuxiang, 7 November 1982. Pan Tongshou reiterated this point during an interview on 13 May 1983. Phil Billingsley also notes that bandits of that period often delighted in wearing brightly colored and fine-textured garb, including feminine undergarments taken from victims or hostages; see *Bandits in Republican China* (Stanford: Stanford Univ. Press, 1988), pp. 130–131.

23. Philip Thomson, *The Grotesque* (London: Methuen, 1972), pp. 20–21, 51.

24. "Stuffy Ironsides," *Fiction and Prose*, p. 212.

25. Philip Thomson, *The Grotesque*, p. 59.

26. Wu's diary entry of 8 December 1942 describes a conversation between Wu and Wang Zhongrong about Tolstoy's approach to characterization.

27. Yu Zhigong, "Feng Yuxiang and the Literary World," *Xin wenxue shiliao*, no. 2, 1983, p. 245. Yu Zhigong claims that the newspapers were confiscated for political reasons by Nationalist Party functionaries, but presents no solid corroborating evidence. This wasteful stockpiling of propaganda materials may have simply been due to the carelessness and inefficiency so widespread during those hectic months soon after the invasion.

28. Interview with Wu Zuxiang, 7 November 1982.

29. Cheng Peikai, *Dousou*, no. 10, pp. 33–34. Yao Xueyin's story was originally published in *Wenyi zhendi*, vol. 1, no. 3 (May 1938), and has been anthologized many times since.

30. Yuan Liangjun, "Tempered Steel," p. 56.

31. Wu Zuxiang, *Fiction and Prose*, p. 215. See also *Zhongguo Qingnian*, November 1942, p. 64, for portions of the passage which were altered in the 1954 edition.

32. Lu Xun, Preface to *Outcry* (Beijing: Renmin wenxue chubanshe, 1973), p. 5.

33. See Elizabeth Perry's thesis that regional ecological conditions played a major role in determining the likelihood of peasant rebellion, in *Rebels and Revolutionaries in North China, 1845–1945*, pp. 10–25, 261–262.

34. Elizabeth Perry, *Rebels and Revolutionaries*, pp. 43–44. The unwillingness of Chinese peasants to voice open dissent over extremely impractical production drives like the Great Leap Forward is illustrated in Gao Xiaosheng's story, "Li Shunda Builds a House" (tr. Ellen Klempner), in Lee Yee, ed., *The New Realism* (New York: Hippocrene Books, 1983), pp. 31–55.

35. Joseph R. Levenson, *Confucian China and Its Modern Fate*, vol. I (Berkeley: Univ. of California Press, 1968), pp. 103–108.

36. Chalmers Johnson, *Peasant Nationalism and Communist Power*, pp. 2–6, 31–70.

37. *Mountain Torrent* is the title as revised for the second edition of the novel in 1946 (Shanghai: Xing qun chubanshe); the title of the orignal 1943 edition was *Yazui lao* [Duckbill Deluge] (Chongqing: Shi yu chao yinshua suo).

38. The novel first appeared as *Duckbill Deluge* in *Kangzhan wenyi* [War of Resistance Literature], vol. 7, no. 1 (January 1941), pp. 58–65, 90 and vol. 7, nos. 2–3 (March 1941), pp. 131–151. The edition I shall follow unless specifically pointed out otherwise in the endnotes is *Shan hong* (Beijing: Renmin wenxue chubanshe, 1982).

39. William Mallory, *China: Land of Famine*, p. 77.

40. Hsi-sheng Ch'i, *Nationalist China at War: Military Defeats and Political Collapse, 1937–45* (Ann Arbor: Univ. of Michigan Press, 1982), p. 97.

41. James J. Y. Liu, *The Poetry of Li Shang-yin, Ninth-Century Baroque Chinese Poet* (Chicago: Univ. of Chicago Press, 1969), p. 177. While an important part of Li Shangyin's poetic canon, political satires are less representative of Li than of other Tang poets such as Bo Juyi and Yuan Zhen. See Liu Dajie, *A History of the Development of Chinese Literature*, pp. 481–486.

42. Wu Zuxiang, *Mountain Torrent*, p. 76.

43. *Mountain Torrent*, p. 84. The rumors circulating in the village about Japanese military brutality are mostly second or even third-hand, for the Japanese army never bothers to venture to the remote hills where the novel is set.

44. *Mountain Torrent*, p. 141.

45. Wang Ruowang, "Zhannian han" [The Indentured Fiancé], in *Yanbuzhu de guangmang* [Glory That Can't Be Concealed] (Beijing: Renmin wenxue chubanshe, 1983), p. 9. The handling of ideological work under the Nationalists resembled the situation under the Communists in a number of ways. A most striking similarity arose from the Nationalists' intensified use of the Leninist political commissar system during the War. See Hsi-sheng Ch'i, *Nationalist China At War*, pp. 94–96.

46. *Mountain Torrent*, p. 128.

47. *Mountain Torrent*, p. 194.

48. *Mountain Torrent*, p. 199.

49. *Mountain Torrent*, p. 8.

50. *Mountain Torrent*, pp. 198–199.

51. Li Changzhi, "'Yazui lao,'" *Shi yu chao wenyi*, vol. 4, no. 1 (September 1944), p. 142.

52. Interview with Wu Zuxiang, 7 March 1983. These relatives of Wu lived in a village about twenty miles from Maolin called Xikou, whose rustic and rugged environs provided the opportunities for hunting and fishing described in the novel.

53. Edward Gunn, *Rewriting Chinese: Style and Innovation in Twentieth-century Chinese Prose* (Stanford: Stanford Univ. Press, 1991), p. 109.

54. In Wu's earlier works, what few abstractions there were tended to be confined to short passages of dialogue, particularly symposiums about current social issues in China. Ordinary narrative passages and interior monologues tended to be concrete.

55. *Mountain Torrent*, pp. 82–83.

56. Ye Yiqun, "'Yazui lao' du hou" [On Reading "Duckbill Deluge"], *Kangzhan wenyi*, vol. 9, nos. 1–2 (February 1944). Marston Anderson, *The Limits of Realism* (Berkeley: Univ. of California Press, 1990), p. 199.

57. See Klöpsch's remarks in Milena Doleželová-Velingerová, ed., *A Selective Guide to Chinese Literature, 1900–1949, Vol. I: The Novel* (Leiden: E. J. Brill, 1988), p. 175.

58. Li Changzhi, *Shi yu chao wenyi*, pp. 141–142. In contrast to the interpretations of Klöpsch and Li Changzhi, Anderson argues that the quoted passage in which Zhang Sanguan's mind teems with abstractions is "as powerful an expression of lyric immersion in the crowd as can be found in modern Chinese fiction" (*The Limits of Realism*, p. 199). As if anxious about having overstated his point, Anderson at once deflates this supposedly "powerful lyric immersion" with the disclaimer that "such an experience remains inoperative"—inoperative because of what he presents as the inevitably stereotyped quality in the literary depiction of crowds *vis-à-vis* individuals (pp. 185, 188). Rather than pointing to the example of a peasant protagonist who ruminates like an urban intellectual and making categorical claims about the supposed "inoperativity" of *any* immersion in the crowd, one could more fruitfully call attention to what degree these various immersions may strike the reader as convincing. For example, are the protagonist's thoughts about the crowd recognizable, in that they tally with what one might likely encounter in a flesh-and-blood individual of similar socio-cultural background? This criterion would lead one to judge the protagonist's identification with the onshore crowd in "The Requisitioned Boat" as more compelling than Zhang Sanguan's musings upon the Chinese troops' depar-

ture. Contrary to post-structuralist caricatures of realism's goals, accomplished realist writers like Wu have not aimed at the mere substitution of linguistic constructs for the reality of the phenomenal world, but have instead self-consciously adopted literary conventions that foreground correspondences and connections—not a simple-minded identity—between the literary work and the phenomenal world (cf. Anderson's sweeping negation of realism's possibilities on p. 200: "Since a linguistic construct can never replace reality, the mimetic undertaking is destined to fail").

59. See the afterword to *Mountain Torrent*, p. 208, and Edward Seidensticker, *Kafū the Scribbler* (Stanford: Stanford Univ. Press, 1965), pp. 94–95.

60. Mention of this abstract quality of the novel may be found in the above-mentioned reviews by Ye Yiqun and Li Changzhi, as well as Qian Er, "Ping Wu Zuxiang de 'Yazui lao'" [A Critique of Wu Zuxiang's "Duckbill Deluge"], *Qunzhong* [The Masses], vol. 9, no. 18 (September 1944), pp. 812–813, and Lao She, "Du 'Yazui lao'" [Reading "Duckbill Deluge"], in *Lao She lun chuangzuo* [Lao She's Critical Essays on Literature] (Shanghai: Shanghai wenyi chubanshe, 1980), pp. 313–314.

61. Lao She, "A Reading of 'Duckbill Deluge,'" p. 314.

62. Sha Ting, *Tao jin ji* (Shanghai: Wenhua shenghuo chubanshe, 1943). For Helmut Martin's synopsis of the novel, see Milena Doleželová-Velingerová, ed., *A Selective Guide to Chinese Literature, 1900–1949, I: The Novel* (Leiden: E. J. Brill, 1988), pp. 145–146.

63. Wu Zuxiang, diary entry of early February 1944 (exact day of month not specified) . The novel cited is Yao Xueyin, *Xin miao* (Chongqing: Xiandai chubanshe, 1943).

64. See Lao She's complaint over the difficulties writers encountered at that time with patriotic wartime subject matter, in C. T. Hsia, *A History of Modern Chinese Fiction*, p. 367.

65. Wu Zuxiang, diary entry of early February 1944.

66. See the afterword to *Mountain Torrent*, p. 209.

67. *Mountain Torrent*, p. 212.

68. See Bonnie S. McDougall, *Mao Zedong's "Talks at the Yan'an Conference on Literature and Art": A Translation of the 1943 Text With Commentary*, Michigan Papers in Chinese Studies 39 (Ann Arbor: Michigan Center for Chinese Studies, 1981), pp. 80–81.

## Notes to Chapter 6

1. Wu Zuxiang, "Ruhe chuangzuo xiaoshuo zhong de renwu" [How to Create Characters in Fiction], *Kangzhan wenyi*, vol. 7, nos. 2–3 (1941), p. 159; "Jieshao duanpian xiaoshuo sipian" [A Brief on Four Short Stories], *Guowen yuekan*, no. 11 (December 1941), p. 18.

2. "How to Create Characters in Fiction," *Kangzhan wenyi*, p. 160.

3. "Twilight," *West Willow*, p. 183.

4. "Twilight," *West Willow*, p. 205.

5. See C. T. Hsia, *A History of Modern Chinese Fiction*, p. 287; Yuan Liangjun, "Tempered Steel," p. 59; and Zhao Yuan, "Wu Zuxiang and His Contemporaries," p. 253.

6. Mao Dun, "'Xi liu ji,'" *Wenxue*, vol. 3, no. 5 (November 1934), pp. 1174–1175.

7. Wang Yao, *Zhongguo xin wenxue shi gao*, p. 245.

8. Interview with Wang Yao, 19 April 1983.

9. Xing Tiehua briefly describes the important role of reader response in handling objective narration in "Wu Zuxiang jiqi zuopin" [Wu Zuxiang and His Works], *Yi tan* [Pool of Art], 1982, no. 2, p. 119.

10. Re Yan Yu's concept of *bu luo yan quan*, see Guo Shaoyu, *Zhongguo wenxue piping shi* [A History of Chinese Literary Criticism], 2nd ed. (Shanghai: Shanghai guji chubanshe, 1981), p. 275; and Yan Yu, *Canglang shi hua*, ed. Guo Shaoyu (Beijing: Renmin wenxue chubanshe, 1961), pp. 24, 35.

11. Interview with Wu Zuxiang, 2 October 1982.

12. Quoted in Sean O'Faolain, *The Short Story*, p. 83.

13. Douwe Fokkema and Elrud Ibsch, *Theories of Literature in the Twentieth Century*, 3rd ed. (New York: St. Martin's, 1986), p. 100.

14. Wu Zuxiang, "Briefs on Four Short Stories," *Guowen yuekan*, no. 11, p. 18.

15. Interview with Wu Zuxiang, 23 March 1983.

16. See C. T. Hsia, "Yen Fu and Liang Ch'i-ch'ao as Advocates of Modern Fiction," in *Chinese Approaches to Literature*, ed. Adele Rickett (Princeton: Princeton Univ. Press, 1978), pp. 243–257.

17. Frank O'Connor, *The Lonely Voice: A Study of the Short Story*, p. 28.

18. On the issue of typicality, see Terry Eagleton, *Marxism and Literary Criticism* (Berkeley: Univ. of California Press, 1976), pp. 28–29, 44–46; Raymond Williams, *Marxism and Literature* (Oxford: Oxford Univ. Press, 1977), pp. 101–103; and Lee Baxandall and Stefan Morawski, eds., *Marx and Engles On Literature and Art* (St. Louis: Telos Press, 1973), pp. 31, 114–116. A character's expression of forces in social history may either occur in an indirect manner through the unfolding of the story line, or else in a direct manner like the symposia's forthright give and take of opinions on a social issue.

19. Turgenev's concept of the intellectual as a "superfluous man" met with an eager reception among many modern Chinese literati. With *Rudin*, the protagonist of the same name stirred many a Chinese intellectual to regret the seeming ineffectuality of their high-flown meliorist theories. Wu Zuxiang once confessed his seeming resemblance to Turgenev's archetypal superfluous intellectual, Rudin, in the wartime essay "Dui deng" [Facing My Lamp], *Shi yu chao wenyi*, vol. 2, no. 5 (June 1943), pp. 47–48. For a sense of the considerable influence exerted by Turgenev on another prominent May Fourth intellectual, the Communist critic Qu Qiubai, see Ellen Widmer, "Qu Qiubai and Russian Literature," in Merle Goldman, ed., *Modern Chinese Literature in the May Fourth Era* (Cambridge: Harvard Univ. Press, 1977), pp. 103, 105–106, 124–125.

20. Ivan Turgenev, *The Hunting Sketches*, tr. Bernard Builbert Guerney (New York: New American Library, 1962), p. 75. I have made some minor alterations to various awkwardly rendered portions of the passage, particularly the final sentence quoted.

21. For more comments on the role played by Ziyu in "1800 Bushels," see the first section in Chapter Three.

22. Turgenev, *The Hunting Sketches*, p. 80.

23. Wu Zuxiang, "1800 Bushels," *West Willow*, p. 302.

24. "1800 Bushels," *West Willow*, p. 301.

25. "1800 Bushels," *West Willow*, pp. 320–321.

26. "Little Lord Guanguan's Tonic," *West Willow*, pp. 155–156.

27. "Fan Hamlet," *After-hours*, pp. 19–20.

28. In contrast to the concept of typicality upheld by Marxist critics with a sense of respect for literature as a demanding craft, "typicality" is sometimes used by Party apparatchiks as a high-sounding version of the idea of "Party-spiritedness" [*dangxing*], or a rigid conformity to whatever latest set of guidelines on proper characterization that Party authorities have seen fit to decree. On the problem of Party-spiritedness, see Fokkema and Ibsch, *Theories of Literature in the Twentieth Century*, pp. 105, 112–113, and Bonnie S. McDougall, ed., *Mao Zedong's "Talks at the Yan'an Conference on Literature and Art"*, p. 75.

29. Wu Zuxiang, "How To Create Characters in Fiction," *Kangzhan wenyi*, vol. 7, nos. 2–3, p. 161.

30. Robert Dessaix, tr., *The Mysterious Tales of Ivan Turgenev* (Canberra: The Australian National Univ. Faculty of Arts, 1979), pp. 1–48.

31. Dessaix, *The Mysterious Tales of Ivan Turgenev*, pp. 10, 11.

32. Dessaix, *The Mysterious Tales of Ivan Turgenev*, p. xxxi.

33. Wu Zuxiang, "On My Dreams," *After-hours*, pp. 81–88.

34. The diary entries are 4 July 1942 and 7 December 1942 for his father and mother, respectively. The dream of the return of Wu's father to the living is analyzed in detail in Chapter 1.

35. Wu Zuxiang, "Fan Hamlet," *After-hours*, p. 13.

36. "On Dreams," *After-hours*, p. 85.

37. J. A. Hadfield, *Dreams and Nightmares*, p. 168.

38. Wu Zuxiang, "On My Dreams," *After-hours*, p. 82.

39. Hadfield, *Dreams and Nightmares*, pp. 168–169; and Sigmund Freud, *The Interpretation of Dreams*, pp. 57–58, 71–72.

40. George Lakoff and Mark Johnson, *Metaphors We Live By* (Chicago: Univ. of Chicago Press, 1980), p. 14–15.

41. Freud, *The Interpretation of Dreams*, p. 430; and Hadfield, *Dreams and Nightmares*, p. 169.

## Notes to Chapter 7

1. Wu Zuxiang, "How to Create Characters in Fiction," *Kangzhan wenyi*, vol. 7, nos. 2–3, p. 159, and "Briefs on Four Short Stories," *Guowen yuekan*, vol. 11, p. 18.

2. The only exception to Wu's norm of minimalist plot structuration is "Little Lord Guanguan's Tonic," where the single-family source of the two tonics—human milk and blood—seems too coincidental to retain the necessary unobtrusiveness. However, this feature does not necessarily weaken the story's overall impact.

3. According to an interview with Wu Zuxiang on 7 March 1983, his two favorite Western authors were Maupassant and Tolstoy. Two prominent examples of the French writer's experimentation with unreliable narrators are "The Count de Fumerol" and "That Pig of a Morin," which may be found in English translation in

*The Complete Stories of Guy de Maupassant* (New York: P. F. Collier & Son, 1903), pp. 219–223, 172–179.

4. Susan Sniader Lanser, *The Narrative Act: Point of View in Prose Fiction* (Princeton: Princeton Univ. Press, 1981), pp. 141–147. Gérard Genette, *Narrative Discourse: An Essay in Method*, tr. Jane E. Levin (Ithaca: Cornell Univ. Press, 1980), pp. 189–191.

5. See Wayne Booth, *The Rhetoric of Fiction*, pp. 47–49.

6. Zola and Garland, for example, both closely adhere to the third-person mode in their novels featuring lower-class protagonists. Not until after the First World War did many writers turn to portraying underclass life with underclass narrators, as in some of the stories of Mu Shiying and most of Louis-Ferdinand Céline's novels.

7. Lanser, *The Narrative Act*, p. 220.

8. Only one of Wu's works departs from his norm of utilizing first-person narration in stories featuring the local elite, and third-person narration in works featuring the humbler social strata. It is "1800 Bushels," a piece whose uniqueness Wu mentioned in an interview on 7 March 1983. Of that story's six focalizers—characters whose private thoughts are entered by the omniscient narrator—only the temple caretaker Shuangxi hails from the humble classes.

9. Re Ba Jin's autobiographical leanings, see his *Random Thoughts*, tr. Geremie Barmé (Hong Kong: Joint Publications, 1984), pp. 61–62. As to Yu Dafu's, see Leo Ou-fan Lee, *The Romantic Generation of Modern Chinese Writers*, pp. 110–113. This is not to claim that any of Yu Dafu's or Ba Jin's fictional narrators could be identified *in toto* with the author; some distance between the two figures is inevitable.

10. Leo Ou-fan Lee, *Voices from the Iron House: A Study of Lu Xun* (Bloomington: Indiana Univ. Press, 1987), p. 59.

11. Wayne Booth, *A Rhetoric of Irony*, pp. 73–76.

12. Booth, *A Rhetoric of Irony*, pp. 67–73.

13. Wu Zuxiang, "Little Lord Guanguan's Tonic," *West Willow*, pp. 151–152.

14. Booth, *A Rhetoric of Irony*, pp. 57–67.

15. "Little Lord Guangguan's Tonic," *West Willow*, p. 127.

16. "Little Lord Guanguan's Tonic," *West Willow*, p. 159.

17. See Patrick Hanan, "The Technique of Lu Hsün's Fiction," *Harvard Journal of Asiatic Studies*, vol. 34, no. 1 (1974), pp. 55 –57, 74–75, 77, 80–81, 86, 96.

18. Mu Shiying, *Nan bei ji* (Shanghai: Hufeng shuju, 1932).

19. For Zhu Ziqing's views on Mu Shiying's facility with the northern vernacular, see "Lun baihua: du *Nan bei ji* (Mu Shiying zuo) yu 'Xiao Bide' (Zhang Tianyi zuo) de ganxiang" [An Essay on the Vernacular: Reactions from Reading Mu Shiying's *North and South Poles* and Zhang Tianyi's "Little Peter"], *Ni wo* [You and I] (1936; rpt. Hong Kong: Taiping shuju, 1963), pp. 155–160.

20. Booth discusses the sort of "deep" or investigative reading required for the appreciation of prose works riddled with irony generated by the narrator. See *The Rhetoric of Fiction*, pp. 364–374.

21. Booth, *A Rhetoric of Irony*, p. 58.

22. One can readily gather from Wu's 1940s diaries that Maupassant and Tolstoy were the two Western authors whose works fascinated him the most during at least the latter part of his writing career. Except for some of Maupassant's brief prose

sketches, the writings of these two authors rarely accentuate plot intricacies at the expense of well-crafted characterization.

23. Robert Scholes and Robert Kellogg, *The Nature of Narrative*, p. 232. In an interview on 2 October 1982, Wu Zuxiang noted that many of his stories embody the "slice of life" approach to plot construction.

24. For sample views of Edith Wharton and E. M. Forster on the secondary role of plot in realist narrative, see Elizabeth Dipple, *Plot* (London: Methuen, 1970), pp. 3–4, 37. The two authors' views may be directly consulted in Wharton, *The Writing of Fiction* (New Haven: Yale Univ. Press, 1925), and Forster, *Aspects of the Novel* (New York: Harcourt Brace, 1927).

25. According to Robert Caserio, "Flexibility in Melville means that the plotting author . . . yields the authority of articulated finish and fullness to the ambiguous authority of a draft." See *Plot, Story, and the Novel* (Princeton: Princeton Univ. Press, 1979), p. 137.

26. As literary realism has waned to some degree in Western fiction since the Second World War, many writers like Thomas Pynchon and John Barth have reverted to plot-centered writing. See Ihab Hassam, *Contemporary American Literature, 1945–1972* (New York: Frederick Ungar, 1973), pp. 24–25, 56–60, 84–85.

27. On the primacy of plotting in Chinese pre-modern vernacular fiction, see John Bishop, *The Colloquial Short Story in China: A Study of the San-Yen Collections* (Cambridge: Harvard Univ. Press, 1965), pp. 42–43.

28. V. I. Semanov, *Lu Hsün and His Predecessors*, tr. Charles J. Alber (White Plains, N.Y.: M. E. Sharpe, 1980), pp. 109–110.

29. V. I. Semanov, *Lu Hsün and His Predecessors*, p. 97; Theodore Huters, *Qian Zhongshu* (Boston: Twayne, 1982), p. 72.

30. See Wu Zuxiang's disparaging remarks about the plot-centered fiction of Conan Doyle and many of the Ming vernacular short story collections in "How to Create Characters in Fiction," *Kangzhan wenyi*, vol. 7, nos. 2–3, p. 159, and "Briefs on Four Short Stories," *Guowen yuekan*, vol. 11, p. 18.

31. Wu Zuxiang, "The World At Peace," *West Willow*, p. 339. This passage from "The World At Peace" is reminiscent of the terse report of a fugitive's death that commonly serves as the opening of a hard-boiled detective novel.

32. On the profligacy with which flashbacks have occasionally been used in post-Mao fiction, see Jeffrey Kinkley, review of Lee Yee's *The New Realism: Writings from China After the Cultural Revolution* in *The Journal of Asian Studies*, vol. XLIV, no. 3 (May 1985), p. 597, and Perry Link, *Roses and Thorns: The Second Blooming of the Hundred Flowers in Chinese Fiction, 1979–1980* (Berkeley: Univ. of California Press, 1984), p. 23.

## Notes to Chapter 8

1. Mark Schorer, "Fiction and the 'Analogical Matrix,'" in *Essays in Stylistic Analysis*, ed. Howard S. Babb (New York: Harcourt Brace, 1972), pp. 340–352.

2. Mark Schorer, "Fiction and the 'Analogical Matrix,'" pp. 340–352. Here are some of the representative metaphors which Schorer has highlighted in italics within quotes from the three novels analyzed in his essay: "Young Mr. Elliot has

'nothing to *gain* by being on *terms* with Sir Walter'" (p. 340, quoted from *Persuasion*); "Catherine had 'a suddenly *clouded* brow–her humor was a mere *vane* for constantly changing caprices'" (p. 343, quoted from *Wuthering Heights*); "'She was *looking forward* to *higher* initiation in ideas'" (p. 349, quoted from *Middlemarch*).

3. Mark Schorer, "Fiction and the 'Analogical Matrix,'" p. 351.

4. Mark Schorer, "Fiction and the 'Analogical Matrix,'" pp. 344–345.

5. Wu Zuxiang, "Little Lord Guanguan's Tonic," *West Willow*, p. 137.

6. Wu Zuxiang, "The World At Peace," *West Willow*, pp. 340, 361, 375, 393. Wang Xiaofu is also described as a "small beast of burden" on p. 340.

7. For occurrences of the term "parasitism" in "The World At Peace," see *West Willow*, pp. 339, 350, 368, 370.

8. Some scholars of peasant socio-economics like James C. Scott argue that even during times of rural prosperity, peasants generally avoid risk-taking economic behavior in favor of low-yielding but safe investments. For a look at how the peasant "ethic of subsistence" was intensified in eastern and southeastern parts of Asia during the Great Depression, see Scott's *The Moral Economy of the Peasant*, pp. 85–90.

9. Mark Schorer, "Fiction and the 'Analogical Matrix,'" p. 340.

10. Wu Zuxiang, "The World At Peace," *West Willow*, pp. 365, 366, 381.

11. Instead of rendering human phenomena in non-human or animalistic terms, Wu sometimes turns around and personifies non-human phenomena, particularly features of setting. In his earlier stories, personifications of inanimate objects or abstract forces usually impute unpleasant or even hostile qualities to these objects or forces. For example, in "The Verdant Bamboo Hermitage," the narrator remarks that "a gust of mildew *assailed* our nostrils" (*West Willow*, p. 171). Less connotative of threatening designs and yet highly suggestive of social decline is a description in "The World At Peace" of a tumbledown courtyard wall which had crumbled at the top and "bulged and *bellied* out part way to the ground" (*West Willow*, p. 384). These unsavory metaphorical personifications of non-human forces suggest that the characters in Wu's early works must cope with a material setting that seems somewhat forbidding and occasionally even hostile. Not until his later works of societal coalescence does the personified setting seem to change from foe to friend, as in this quote from "A Certain Day": "The clouds . . . *charmed* the eye with their unusual clarity of outline" (*Fiction and Prose*, p. 200).

12. Wu Zuxiang, "Miss Jin and the Xue Girl," *West Willow*, pp. 112–113.

13. Wu Zuxiang, "The World At Peace," *West Willow*, p. 385.

14. Wu Zuxiang, "The Verdant Bamboo Hermitage," *West Willow*, p. 180.

15. Wu Zuxiang, "Miss Jin and the Xue Girl," *West Willow*, p. 102.

16. "Miss Jin and the Xue Girl," *West Willow*, p. 96.

17. Wu Zuxiang, "On the Eve of Leaving Home," *West Willow*, p. 9.

18. Wu Zuxiang, "Twilight," *West Willow*, p. 184.

19. Wu Zuxiang, "On the Eve of Leaving Home," *West Willow*, p. 9.

20. Lu Xun and Guo Moruo gave up medical studies for literature, partly out of a conviction that saving souls through literature would bring about a greater impact on Chinese society than would saving bodies through medicine. See Leo Ou-fan Lee, *Voices from the Iron House* (Bloomington: Indiana Univ. Press, 1987), pp. 17–18, and *The Romantic Generation of Modern Chinese Writers*, pp. 177–200.

21. Wu Zuxiang, "Miss Jin and the Xue Girl," *West Willow*, p. 89.

22. Wu Zuxiang, "Splay-petaled Honeysuckle," *West Willow*, p. 228.

23. George Lakoff and Mark Johnson, *Metaphors We Live By*, p. 172.

24. Wu Zuxiang, "Miss Jin and the Xue Girl," *West Willow*, p. 111.

25. Wu Zuxiang, "The Verdant Bamboo Hermitage," *West Willow*, p. 186.

26. "The Verdant Bamboo Hermitage," *West Willow*, pp. 167–168.

27. "The Verdant Bamboo Hermitage," *West Willow*, p. 176.

28. "The Verdant Bamboo Hermitage," *West Willow*, pp. 164, 165, 166, 167, 177.

29. "The Verdant Bamboo Hermitage," *West Willow*, pp. 164, 177.

30. "The Verdant Bamboo Hermitage," *West Willow*, pp. 167, 165.

31. "The Verdant Bamboo Hermitage," *West Willow*, pp. 168, 164, 165.

32. Wayne Booth, *The Rhetoric of Fiction*, p. 155.

33. Wu Zuxiang, "Splay-petaled Honeysuckle," *West Willow*, p. 228.

34. Wu Zuxiang, "Miss Jin and the Xue Girl," *West Willow*, pp. 89, 92, 121.

35. John Fletcher and Malcolm Bradbury, "The Introverted Novel," in *Modernism*, ed. Malcolm Bradbury and James McFarlane (Harmondsworth: Penguin Books, 1976), p. 401.

36. Lakoff and Johnson, *Metaphors We Live By*, pp. 30–32.

37. Mao Dun, "'West Willow Anthology,'" *Wenxue*, vol. 3, no. 5, p. 1076.

38. Mark Schorer, "Fiction and the 'Analogical Matrix,'" p. 349.

39. What follows is a description of the growling stomach of Wang Xiaofu's famished son in "The World At Peace," *West Willow*, pp. 360–361: "He endured his hunger, no matter how much his stomach chattered, with its 'goolooloo,' no matter how much cold sweat seeped out all over his face and body."

40. The metaphor of barehandedness is not limited to Wu Zuxiang any more than upward-looking visions are limited to George Eliot. However, both writers use these respective types of metaphors far more often than the norm.

41. Wu Zuxiang, "Little Lord Guanguan's Tonic," *West Willow*, p. 155.

42. Wu Zuxiang, "1800 Bushels," *West Willow*, pp. 319, 322.

43. Wu Zuxiang, "The World At Peace," *West Willow*, p. 343, 346.

44. The concept of emptiness [*kong*] is also used in a more literal sense at times. For example, "One business after another was emptied out by debts" ("1800 Bushels," *West Willow*, p. 287). Also, Wang Xiaofu's hopes for a certain part-time job "came to nothing" ("The World At Peace," *West Willow*, p. 354).

45. Although "mouthful" usually functions as a metaphor for spoken phrases, it can on rare occasion take a literal reference. In "1800 Bushels," for example, "Chairman Song Zishou of the Chamber of Commerce was chewing a mouthful of pork fritter" (*West Willow*, p. 292); earlier in the same work, "A mouthful of saliva frothed over the corners" of the stuttering Jingyuan's mouth (*West Willow*, p. 275).

46. Wu Zuxiang, "Splay-petaled Honeysuckle," *West Willow*, p. 228.

47. Wu Zuxiang, "Little Lord Guanguan's Tonic," *West Willow*, p. 142.

48. Wu Zuxiang, "The Verdant Bamboo Hermitage," *West Willow*, p. 167.

49. Wu Zuxiang, "1800 Bushels," *West Willow*, pp. 290, 319.

50. Roland Barthes, *Mythologies*, tr. Annette Lavers (New York: Hill and Wang, 1975), pp. 148–149.

51. Yuen Ren Chao, *A Grammar of Spoken Chinese* (Berkeley: Univ. of California Press, 1968), p. 578.

52. Yuen Ren Chao, *A Grammar of Spoken Chinese*, pp. 578–579.

53. Wu Zuxiang, "1800 Bushels," *West Willow*, p. 331: the phrase referred to is "cheeks covered with beard"; "The World At Peace," *West Willow*, p. 354: the phrase referred to is "with a smile all over his face"; "1800 Bushels," *West Willow*, p. 326: the phrase referred to is "with a wry smile all over his face"; "Miss Jin and the Xue Girl," *West Willow*, p. 120: the phrase referred to is "tears flowed all over my cheeks"; "The World At Peace," *West Willow*, p. 351: the phrase referred to is "his whole face was bright red"; "The World At Peace," *West Willow*, p. 354: the phrase referred to is "something hot surged through his whole face."

54. Wu Zuxiang, "The World At Peace," *West Willow*, pp. 365, 382. Other examples of this usage of *man* include: "Her eyes were brimming with passion and love" ("Little Lord Guanguan's Tonic," *West Willow*, p. 140); "a gutful of pent-up enthusiasm" ("Miss Jin and the Xue Girl," *West Willow*, p. 102); and "My heart was chock full of a . . . feeling of distraction" ("Splay-petaled Honeysuckle," *West Willow*, p. 223).

55. Wu Zuxiang, "Little Lord Guanguan's Tonic," *West Willow*, pp. 160, 159, 138.

56. Wu Zuxiang, "The World At Peace," *West Willow*, p. 337.

57. Wu Zuxiang, "Two Young Sparrows," *West Willow*, p. 28.

58. Wu Zuxiang, "Miss Jin and the Xue Girl," *West Willow*, p. 87.

59. Wu Zuxiang, "1800 Bushels," *West Willow*, p. 330.

60. Wu Zuxiang, "Little Lord Guanguan's Tonic," *West Willow*, p. 160.

61. Wu Zuxiang, "1800 Bushels," *West Willow*, p. 330.

62. "1800 Bushels," *Wenxue jikan*, vol. 1, no. 1, pp. 85–86. Part of this section was excised from *West Willow* and later collections.

63. "1800 Bushels," *West Willow*, pp. 329, 333.

64. Wu Zuxiang, "A Certain Day," *Fiction and Prose*, pp. 199, 200. The father-in-law from the local elite is described as a weasel while he retreats from Da Mao's farmhouse. The weasel's reputation for rapacious cunning was surely one factor in the author's choice of this particular animal image.

65. Wu Zuxiang, "The Requisitioned Boat," *Fiction and Prose*, p. 281.

66. Wu Zuxiang, *Mountain Torrent* (1982 ed.), p. 82.

67. *Mountain Torrent*, p. 206.

68. *Mountain Torrent*, p. 155.

## Notes to Chapter 9

1. See Jeffrey Kinkley, *The Odyssey of Shen Congwen* (Stanford: Stanford Univ. Press, 1987), pp. 265–270.

2. Joseph Levenson, *Confucian China and Its Modern Fate*, vol. 3, p. 8.

3. In *The Odyssey of Shen Congwen*, Jeffrey Kinkley points out that quite a few of Shen's fellow writers who had assumed a front-line position of leadership on the contemporary P.R.C. literary scene, such as Ding Ling, had been purged as a result (p. 272).

4. Wu's essays of 1947–1948 are among the most personal and least socially engaged of any during his career. "Meiguo de dongtian" [Winter in America] revolves around the theme of Wu's homesickness, and does not even bring up the agent responsible for his presence in America, Feng Yuxiang–not to mention Feng's increasingly obvious political agenda (*Ren jian shi*, vol. 1, no. 2 [April 1947], pp. 47–51). "Tan shenghuo" [On Living] is a meditation on how Robert Browning's concept of "the beauty of imperfection" can be viewed as the striking of a balance between a Confucian attachment to society and a Daoist transcendence of the phenomenal world (*Jinling nüzi wenli xueyuan xiaokan*, no. 144 [October 1947], pp. 3–4). "Jingdao Peixian Xiansheng" [In Respectful Remembrance of Zhu Ziqing] is a low-key but moving elegy that emphasizes the personal and creative sides of Zhu Ziqing's character rather than his role as a meliorist writer (*Wen xun yuekan*, vol. 9, no. 3 [September 1948], pp. 131–135).

5. Wu's diary entry of 3 March 1946 describes some of Feng Yuxiang's wartime journals as "verbose and trivial." James E. Sheridan also notes the repetitious nature of Feng's diaries and journals in *Chinese Warlord: The Career of Feng Yü-hsiang*, p. 361. For a corroborating Chinese view, consult Zhang Yuanxi, "Ji Feng Yuxiang zai Meiguo de nei yi nian" [My Recollections of the Year Feng Yuxiang Was in America], *Zhuanji wenxue* [Biographical Literature], vol. 33, no. 3 (pp. 28–30), no. 4 (pp. 77–80), and no. 5 (pp. 55–59); see especially no. 5, p. 56.

6. The diary entry of 4 March 1946 discusses the journals of Feng that treat the early War years.

7. Diary entry of 23 February 1946.

8. Diary entry of 28 February 1946.

9. Diary entry of 27 February 1946. By way of contrast, Wu's classes in pre-modern Chinese literature were quite full.

10. Diary entry of 5 March 1946.

11. James Sheridan, *Chinese Warlord*, p. 277.

12. James Sheridan, *Chinese Warlord*, p. 278. Zhang Yuanxi, the member of Feng's entourage who did most of the chauffering, notes in "My Recollections of the Year Feng Yuxiang Was in America" that one of the first things Feng purchased in the U.S. was a movie camera and projector, which he made heavy use of during his stay (no. 5, p. 59).

13. Feng made this speech on 7 September 1947, according to Feng Hongda and Yu Huaxin, *The Soul of General Feng Yuxiang Returns to China*, p. 100.

14. James Sheridan, *Chinese Warlord*, p. 281. Sheridan accepts the Soviet account of Feng's death by accident as the most likely interpretation among many, and Zhang Yuanxi provides a more detailed version of this same general account in "My Recollections of the Year Feng Yuxiang Was in America," *Zhuanji wenxue*, vol. 33, no. 5, p. 59. Feng Yuxiang's nephew Feng Jifa, who served as an orderly to the General from 1946 to 1948, later told Zhang Yuanxi how both the General and his daughter Feng Xiaoda died as a result of having let one of their films get stuck in an operating projector and ignite: the projection room had quickly turned into an inferno.

15. Zhang Yuanxi, "My Recollections of the Year Feng Yuxiang Was in America," no. 5, 56–57.

16. Wu Zuxiang, "A Winter in America," *Ren jian shi*, vol. 1, no. 2, pp. 47–51.

17. Wu Zuxiang, "In Respectful Memory of Zhu Ziqing," *Wen xun yuekan*, vol. 9, no. 3, pp. 131–135.

18. The diary entry for 30 August 1945 enumerates three necessary conditions for democracy which Wu finds lacking in China: a tradition of rule by law, magnanimity and tolerance toward opposition views and parties, and a spirit in which the citizenry at large assumes their responsibilities in the public realm.

19. Wu's dismissal from Central University is mentioned in the anonymous preface to the Hong Kong anthology of his works, *Wu Zuxiang xuanji* (Hong Kong: Xianggang wenxue yanjiu she, 1978), p. 2.

20. Since 1949, Wu has prudently had nothing but denunciations for Chiang Kai-shek and the Nationalists. However, Chiang's reputation among a great many independent intellectuals of Wu's caliber was fairly intact at the end of the Second World War. In a diary entry from August 1945, Wu expresses his uneasiness over Mao Zedong's apparent eagerness to intensify the opposition power struggle against "Mr. Chiang," as Wu respectfully refers to the Generalissimo. Further along in the same diary entry, Wu has copied out the entire text of Mao's famous poem, "Snow," expressing his disapproval over how the poem was "full of the spirit of old-fashioned personal heroism." Clearly, even though Wu became disillusioned with the Nationalist regime by the late 1940s and has been unquestionably loyal to Beijing since 1949, in 1945 he had more trepidations about Mao Zedong than about Chiang Kai-shek.

21. Olga Lang notes that Ba Jin's decision to remain in China was representative of the vast majority of modern Chinese writers. See *Pa Chin and His Writings*, p. 217. Ranbir Vohra makes the same point with reference to Lao She in *Lao She and the Chinese Revolution* (Cambridge: Harvard Univ. Press, 1974), p. 148.

22. For background on the Hundred Flowers and Anti-Rightist Campaigns, see Merle Goldman, *Literary Dissent in Communist China* (1967; rpt. New York: Atheneum, 1971), pp. 158–242. A concise overview of these campaigns, along with the Cultural Revolution, may be obtained in John K. Fairbank, *The Great Chinese Revolution: 1800–1985* (New York: Harper and Row, 1986), pp. 286–295, 316–341.

23. Czeslaw Milosz has remarked that many writers under State Socialist regimes select college careers "because research into literary history offers a safe pretext for plunging into the past and for converse with works of great aesthetic value" (*The Captive Mind*, tr. Jane Zielonko [New York: Vintage, 1951], p. 64). Most of Wu's published research between the Anti-Rightist Campaign and the Cultural Revolution was on the 18th-century novel *Hong lou meng* [Dream of the Red Chamber].

24. Interview with Wu Zuxiang, 7 November 1982.

25. In April 1983, I learned of Shuyuan's serious psychological scars from a reliable Beijing source who prefers to remain anonymous.

26. One of Wu's manuscripts confiscated by the Red Guards, the original draft of *Mountain Torrent*, was returned to him after the Cultural Revolution. See the postscript to the novel (1982 edition), pp. 211–212.

27. Wu Zuxiang, "A Few Personal Views On the National United Front of Literary Circles," *Xinhua ribao*, 27 March 1938, p. 4.

28. For Mao's formulist imperative to write only for peasants, workers, and soldiers, see Bonnie McDougall, *Mao Zedong's "Talks at the Yan'an Conference on Literature and Art": A Translation of the 1943 Text with Commentary*, pp. 65–67.

29. Two examples of his memoirs in essay form are "Wu Zuxiang Discusses Zhang Tianyi," *Xin wenxue shiliao*, no. 2, 1981, and "Ganji he huainian—Lu Xun Xiansheng yibai zhounian huaiyi" [Gratitude and Remembrance—In Commemoration of Lu Xun's Hundredth Birthday], *Wenyi bao*, no. 2 (February), 1982, pp. 6–9.

30. C. T. Hsia, *A History of Modern Chinese Fiction*, p. 287; Yuan Liangjun, "Tempered Steel," p. 50.

31. Diary entry, 15 September 1945.

32. Bonnie McDougall, *Mao Zedong's "Talks at the Yan'an Conference"*, pp. 68–69.

33. Diary entry, 15 September 1945.

34. See, for example, his "*Ru lin wai shi* de sixiang yu yishu" [The Philosophy and Art of *The Scholars*], *Renmin wenxue*, no. 8 (August), 1953, pp. 82–99, and "Lun Jia Baoyu dianxing xingxiang" [Jia Baoyu as a Typical Character], *Beijing daxue xuebao*, no. 4 (November), 1956, pp. 1–32.

35. A representative article focusing on technique, in this case methods of characterization, is "Tan *Hong lou meng* jige peichen renwu de anpai" [Regarding Several Designs for Setting Off Characters in *Dream of the Red Chamber*], *Renmin wenxue*, no. 8 (August), 1959, pp. 112–119. For the class-analysis approach, an example which appears in English is "*Pilgrimage to the West* and Its Author," in Yang Xianyi and Gladys Yang, eds., *Excerpts from Three Classical Chinese Novels* (Beijing: Panda Books, 1981), pp. 200–212. Wu argues on p. 209 that the trio of protagonists in the latter novel consist of a well-intentioned but deluded disciple of "the orthodox thought of the ruling class" (Tripitaka), an "upholder of justice" in the struggle against "feudalism" (Monkey), and a small-scale peasant landholder who is extremely productive and resourceful, but also opportunistic, avaricious, and conservative (Pigsy).

36. Wu Zuxiang, "Gratitude and Remembrance—In Commemoration of Lu Xun's Hundredth Birthday, " p. 7.

37. Diary entry of 2 July 1942. Other notable figures who appeared in Wu's wartime diaries include Feng Yuxiang and Sha Ting, according to the above entry and that of 21 October 1945. This is not to say that Lu Xun could not have possibly appeared in Wu's dreams, only that he never appeared in the dozens of dreams described over a period of four years, while a few other literary figures among Wu's close associates did in fact so appear.

38. Wu Zuxiang, "Wode yige kanfa" [A View of Mine], *Wenyi bao*, no. 8 (May), 1957, p. 2.

39. For the list of the thirty-three prominent P.R.C. intellectuals, of whom Wu Zuxiang was one of the few from the older generation, see "Hai nei wai zhishifenzi de lianhe xingdong" [United Measures Taken by Intellectuals Within China and from Abroad], *Zhengming* [Contend], no. 3 (March), 1989, pp. 22–23.

40. Wu Zuxiang, "Chu jian jiefangjun" [My First Sight of the Liberation Army], *Xin guancha*, vol. 3, no. 1 (August 1951), pp. 8–9.

41. A social scientist who was present at the original Communist victory march through Beijing on 31 January 1949, observed that most of the civilians who lined the streets of Beijing were "unemotional and undemonstrative," expressing "neither antipathy nor enthusiasm, but rather a simple curiosity about their 'liberators,' their new rulers." See Doak Barnett's *China on the Eve of the Communist Takeover* (New York: Frederick A. Praeger, 1963), p. 339.

42. Czeslaw Milosz, *The Captive Mind*, p. 66.

43. Wu Zuxiang, "'Shengming zui hao de nianyue'" ["The Best Time in My Life"], *Xin guancha*, vol. 2, no. 2 (January 1951), pp. 16–17.

44. Wu Zuxiang, "Huang Demao," *Xin guancha*, no. 8 (April), 1954, pp. 5–6.

45. See the quoted portions attributed to Wu Zuxiang in the jointly authored newspaper articles: "Zhongguo zuojia xiehui gudian wenxue bu zhaokai de *Hong lou meng* yanjiu zuotanhui jilu" [Record of a Conference on *Dream of the Red Chamber* Research Convened by the Classical Literature Section of the Chinese Writers' Association], *Guangming ribao*, 14 November 1954, p. 5; and "Jianjue xiang Ding-Chen fandang jituan douzheng" [Resolutely Struggle With the Ding-Chen Anti-Party Clique], *Guangming ribao*, 23 August 1957, p. 3.

46. Wu was very willing to recount his victimization during the Cultural Revolution, as became clear during an interview on 7 November 1982. However, he was obviously uncomfortable when asked on 23 March 1983 about the nature of his role in the 1957 campaign of denunciation against Ding Ling and Feng Xuefeng; when shown the denunciatory article in the *Guangming ribao* that bore his name along with that of Feng Zhi and Bian Zhilin, Wu hastily averred that he had not written the article himself, and immediately changed the subject. There is nothing unusual about this technique of selective amnesia about past conformance to party calls to victimize fellow literati. What is truly remarkable is the rare courage of an individual like Zhou Yang, who in 1978 openly admitted and sincerely apologized for having denounced and punished innocent literati in the past. See Vera Schwarcz's afterword to Carol Hamrin and Timothy Cheek, eds., *China's Establishment Intellectuals* (Armonk, N.Y.: M. E. Sharpe, 1986), pp. 254–256.

47. Wu Zuxiang, "Tan *Shui hu*" [On *Water Margin*], *Wenyi bao*, no. 2, 1978, pp. 5–11. The quote about "capitulationism" to hegemonism (American and/or Soviet) comes from a *People's Daily* editorial entitled "Unfold Criticism of *Water Margin*," which was reprinted in the *Peking Review*, no. 37 (September), 1975, pp. 7–8. For further interpretations of the numerous Thaw essays that "exonerated" Song Jiang, see Michelle Loi, "Reevaluations of Political and Literary Trends in the People's Republic of China During the Last Two Years," in *Essays in Modern Chinese Literature and Literary Criticism*, eds. Wolfgang Kubin and Rudolph G. Wagner (Bochum: Studio Brockmeyer, 1982), p. 417.

48. James C. F. Wang, *Contemporary Chinese Politics* (Englewood Cliffs, N.J.: Prentice-Hall, 1980), p. 180.

49. Wu Zuxiang, "On *Water Margin*," p. 11.

50. See Roger Garside, *Coming Alive: China After Mao* (New York: McGraw-Hill, 1981), p. 79.

51. For more information on the efforts within Chinese universities to help middle-aged scholars catch up for time lost during the Cultural Revolution and before, see Vera Schwarcz, *Long Road Home: A China Journal* (New Haven: Yale Univ. Press, 1984).

52. See Wu Zuxiang's preface to *Zhongguo xin wenxue da xi, 1927–1937* [Anthology of Modern Chinese Literature, 1927–1937], vol. 10 (Shanghai: Shanghai wenyi chubanshe, 1985), pp. 1–7.

53. Wu Zuxiang, "The Verdant Bamboo Hermitage," rpt. in *Shiyue*, no. 1, 1984, pp. 254–256.

## Notes to the Conclusion

1. Patrick Hanan has pointed out that the pre-modern Chinese vernacular story "is vastly unrepresentative, with its concentration on cities and towns." See *The Chinese Vernacular Story* (Cambridge: Harvard Univ. Press, 1981), p. 127.

2. Although a minority of readers would hail from the countryside rather than the town, the most literate among these would aspire to the urban lifestyle of the scholar-official status group.

3. See Lu Xun's disparagement of the idealized, offhand way the rural "toiling masses" were portrayed by pre-modern Chinese writers in V. I. Semanov, *Lu Hsün and His Predecessors*, trans. Charles J. Alber (Armonk, NY: M.E. Sharpe, 1980), p. 121. In objecting to the sweeping quality of Lu Xun's comment, Semanov overlooks how the context of Lu Xun's statement implies that his focus is on rural toilers, not simply toilers in general.

4. According to Tanigawa Michio, when community relations were working smoothly, they tended to bring about a "blurring of class relations." For example, "organs of mutual aid within a single-clan village—such as relief offered by rich families or the system of manorial or ceremonial loans—stressed one's place as a 'community' member over class relations within the clan." See *Medieval Chinese Society and the Local "Community"*, tr. Joshua A. Fogel (Berkeley: Univ. of California Press, 1985), p. 7.

5. For example, modern agricultural cooperatives do not owe their genesis wholly to abstract blueprints, but were based at least partly on the traditional informal pooling of scarce draught animals and tools among farmers in a given locale.

# Western-Language Works Cited

Adams, Percy G. *Travel Literature and the Evolution of the Novel*. Lexington: Univ. of Kentucky Press, 1983.

Anderson, Marston. *The Limits of Realism: Chinese Fiction in the Revolutionary Period*. Berkeley: Univ. of California Press, 1990.

Ba Jin. *Random Thoughts*. Trans. Geremie Barmé. Hong Kong: Joint Publishing, 1984.

Barlow, Tani E. and Bjorge, Gary J., eds. *I Myself Am a Woman: Selected Writings of Ding Ling*. Boston: Beacon Press, 1989.

Barnett, A. Doak. *China on the Eve of the Communist Takeover*. New York: Frederick A. Praeger, 1963.

Barrell, John and Bull, John, eds. *A Book of English Pastoral Verse*. New York: Oxford Univ. Press, 1975.

Barthes, Roland. *Mythologies*. Trans. Annette Lavers. New York: Hill and Wang, 1975.

Basilins, Harold A. "Thomas Mann's Use of Musical Structure and Technique in 'Tonio Kroger.'" *Germanic Review*. Vol. 19 (1944). Pp. 284–308.

Baxandall, Lee and Morawski, Stefan, eds. *Marx and Engels on Literature and Art*. St. Louis: Telos Press, 1973.

Billingsley, Phil. *Bandits in Republican China*. Stanford: Stanford Univ. Press, 1988.

Birch, Cyril. "Teaching May Fourth Fiction." *Modern Chinese Literature Newsletter*. Vol. 2, no. 1 (1978). Pp. 1–16.

Bishop, John. *The Colloquial Short Story in China: a Study of the San-Yen Collections*. Cambridge: Harvard Univ. Press, 1965.

Bodde, Derk. *Festivals in Classical China*. Princeton: Princeton Univ. Press, 1975.

Booth, Wayne. *The Rhetoric of Fiction*. Chicago: Univ. of Chicago Press, 1961.

_____ . *A Rhetoric of Irony*. Chicago: Univ. of Chicago Press, 1974.

Boyd, Michael. *The Reflexive Novel: Fiction as Critique*. Toronto: Lewisburg Bucknell Univ. Press, 1983.

Brooks, Peter. *The Melodramatic Imagination*. New Haven: Yale Univ. Press, 1976.

Brown, Edward J. *Russian Literature Since the Revolution*. New York: Collier Books, 1963.

Caserio, Robert L. *Plot, Story, and the Novel*. Princeton: Princeton Univ. Press, 1979.

Chang, Chung-li. *The Chinese Gentry: Studies on Their Role in Nineteenth-century Chinese Society*. Seattle: Univ. of Washington Press, 1955.

Chang, K.C. *Food in Chinese Culture*. New Haven: Yale Univ. Press, 1972.

Chang, Randall Oliver. "Yü Ta-fu (1896–1945): the Alienated Artist in Modern Chinese Literature." Diss. Claremont 1973.

Chao, Yuan Ren. *A Grammar of Spoken Chinese*. Berkeley: Univ. of California Press, 1968.

Chen, Yu-shih (formerly Mei, Diana Yu-shih). "Han Yü as a Ku-wen Stylist." *Tsing Hua Journal of Chinese Studies*. Vol. 7, no. 1 (1968). Pp. 143–208.

———. *Realism and Allegory in the Early Fiction of Mao Tun*. Bloomington: Indiana Univ. Press, 1986.

Ch'i, Hsi-sheng. *Nationalist China at War: Military Defeats and Political Collapse, 1937–45*. Ann Arbor: Univ. of Michigan Press, 1982.

Chou, Chih-p'ing. *Yuan Hung-tao and the Kung-an School*. Princeton: Princeton Univ. Press, 1988.

Chow, Tse-tsung. *The May Fourth Movement: Intellectual Revolution in Modern China*. Stanford: Stanford Univ. Press, 1967.

Davidson, Jeremy H. C. S. and Cordell, Helen, eds. *The Short Story in South East Asia: Aspects of a Genre*. London: School of Oriental and African Studies, 1982.

Dessaix, Robert, trans. *The Mysterious Tales of Ivan Turgenev*. Canberra: The Australian National Univ. Faculty of Arts, 1979.

Dipple, Elizabeth. *Plot*. London: Methuen, 1970.

Doleželová-Velingerová, Milena. "Narrative Modes in Late Qing Novels." In Doleželová-Veligerová, ed., *The Chinese Novel at the Turn of the Century*. Toronto: Univ. of Toronto Press, 1980. Pp. 38–56.

———. ed. *A Selective Guide to Chinese Literature, 1900–1949*, Vol. I: The Novel. Leiden: E. J. Brill, 1988.

Dorsch, T. S., trans. *Classical Literary Criticism: Aristotle, Horace, and Longinus*. Baltimore: Penguin, 1965.

Eagleton, Terry. *Marxism and Literary Criticism*. Berkeley: Univ. of California Press, 1976.

Edwards, E. D. *Chinese Prose Literature of the T'ang Period*. Vol. I. London: Arthur Probsthain, 1937.

Eichenbaum, Boris. "The Theory of the Formal Method." In *Critical Theory Since Plato*. Ed. Hazard Adams. New York: Harcourt Brace, 1971. Pp. 828–846.

Ellman, Richard and Feidelson, Charles, Jr., eds. *The Modern Tradition: Backgrounds of Modern Literature*. New York: Oxford Univ. Press, 1965.

Elvin, Mark. *The Pattern of the Chinese Past*. Oxford: Oxford Univ. Press, 1973.

Empson, William. "Proletarian Literature." In *Some Versions of Pastoral*. New York: New Directions, 1974. Pp. 3–23.

Esherick, Joseph W. "Xi'an Spring," *The Australian Journal of Chinese Affairs*. No. 24 (Jul. 1990). Pp. 209–235.

Fairbank, John K. *The Great Chinese Revolution, 1800–1985*. New York: Harper and Row, 1986.

Fei, Hsiao-tung. *China's Gentry*. Chicago: Univ. of Chicago Press, 1953.

Feng Jicai. *Chrysanthemums and Other Stories*. Ed. Susan W. Chen. San Diego: Harcourt Brace, 1985.

Feuerwerker, Yi-tsi Mei. *Ding Ling's Fiction: Ideology and Narrative in Modern Chinese Literature*. Cambridge: Harvard Univ. Press, 1982.

Fletcher, John and Bradbury, Malcolm. "The Introverted Novel." In *Modernism*. Eds. Malcolm Bradbury and James McFarlane. Harmondsworth: Penguin Books, 1976. Pp. 394–415.

Fokkema, Douwe and Ibsch, Elrud. *Theories of Literature in the Twentieth Century*. New York: St. Martin's Press, 1978.

Forster, E.M. *Aspects of the Novel.* New York: Harcourt Brace, 1927.

Frazer, Sir James George. *The Golden Bough.* New York: MacMillan, 1922.

Freud, Sigmund. *A General Introduction to Psychoanalysis.* Trans. Joan Riviere. New York: Pocket Books, 1953.

_____ . *The Interpretation of Dreams.* Trans. James Strachey. New York: Avon Books, 1965.

Frye, Northrop. *The Anatomy of Criticism.* Princeton: Princeton Univ. Press, 1957.

_____ . *The Well-tempered Critic.* Bloomington: Indiana Univ. Press, 1963.

Garside, Roger. *Coming Alive: China After Mao.* New York: McGraw-Hill, 1981.

Gide, André. "Second Notebook on *The Counterfeiters,*" trans. Justin O'Brien. In *The Counterfeiters.* Trans. Dorothy Bussy. New York: Vintage, 1973. Pp. 373–432.

Glicksberg, Charles I. *The Literature of Commitment.* Lewisburg: Bucknell Univ. Press, 1976.

Goldblatt, Howard, ed. *Chinese Literature for the 1980s: The Fourth Congress of Writers and Artists.* Armonk: M. E. Sharpe, 1982.

Goldman, Merle. *Literary Dissent in Communist China.* 1967; rpt. New York: Atheneum, 1971.

_____ . ed. *Modern Chinese Literature in the May Fourth Era.* Cambridge: Harvard Univ. Press, 1977.

Grube, G. M. A., trans. *Aristotle On Poetry and Style.* Indianapolis: Bobbs-Merrill, 1958.

Guetti, James. *Word-Music: the Aesthetic Aspect of Narrative Fiction.* New Brunswick: Rutgers Univ. Press, 1980.

Gunn, Edward. *Rewriting Chinese: Style and Innovation in Twentieth-century Chinese Prose.* Stanford: Stanford Univ. Press, 1991.

Hadfield, J. A. *Dreams and Nightmares.* Baltimore: Penguin, 1954.

Hamrin, Carol Lee and Cheek, Timothy, eds. *China's Establishment Intellectuals.* Armonk: M. E. Sharpe, 1986.

Hanan, Patrick. "The Technique of Lu Hsün's Fiction." *Harvard Journal of Asiatic Studies.* Vol. 34, no. 1 (1974). Pp. 53–96.

_____ . *The Chinese Vernacular Story.* Cambridge: Harvard Univ. Press, 1981.

_____ . *The Invention of Li Yu.* Cambridge: Harvard Univ. Press, 1988.

Hassam, Ihab. *Contemporary American Literature, 1945–1972.* New York: Frederick Ungar, 1973.

Hemingway, Ernest. "The Big Two-hearted River." In A. Walton Litz, ed., *Major American Short Stories.* Oxford: Oxford Univ. Press, 1980. Pp. 454–470.

Hightower, James. *The Poetry of T'ao Ch'ien.* Oxford: Clarendon Press, 1970.

Ho, Ping-ti. *The Ladder of Success in Imperial China: Aspects of Social Mobility, 1368–1911.* New York: Columbia Univ. Press, 1962.

Honig, Emily. "Pride and Prejudice: Subei People in Contemporary Shanghai." In *Unofficial China: Popular Culture and Thought in the People's Republic.* Perry Link, Richard Madsen, and Paul Pickowicz, eds. Boulder: Westview, 1989. Pp. 138–155.

Hsia, C. T. *The Classic Chinese Novel.* New York: Columbia Univ. Press, 1968.

_____ . *A History of Modern Chinese Fiction, 1917–1957.* 2nd ed. New Haven: Yale Univ. Press, 1970.

_____ . "Time and the Human Condition in the Plays of T'ang Hsien-tsu." In *Self and Society in Ming Thought*, ed. William Theodore DeBary. New York: Columbia Univ. Press, 1970. Pp. 249–290.

_____ . "Yen Fu and Liang Ch'i-ch'ao as Advocates of Modern Fiction." In *Chinese Approaches to Literature*, ed. Adele Rickett. Princeton: Princeton Univ. Press, 1978. Pp. 243–257.

Hsia, T. A. *The Gate of Darkness: Studies on the Leftist Literary Movement in China.* Seattle: Univ. of Washington Press, 1968.

Hsu, Immanuel C. Y. *The Rise of Modern China.* 3rd ed. New York: Oxford Univ. Press, 1983.

Hsu, Vivian Ling, ed. *Born of the Same Roots: Stories of Modern Chinese Women.* Bloomington: Indiana Univ. Press, 1981.

Hummel, Arthur W. *Eminent Chinese of the Ch'ing Period.* Vol. 1.Washington, D.C.: U.S. Government Printing Office, 1943.

Huters, Theodore. *Qian Zhongshu.* Boston: Twayne Publishers, 1982.

Jackson, Helen Hunt. *Ramona.* Boston: Little, Brown, & Co., 1884.

James, Henry. *Partial Portraits.* London: n.p., 1905.

_____ . *The Ambassadors.* New York: New American Library, 1960.

James, Jean M. Introduction to *Rickshaw*. Honolulu: The Univ. Press of Hawaii, 1979.

Johnson, Chalmers A. *Peasant Nationalism and Communist Power: the Emergence of Revolutionary China, 1937–1945.* Stanford: Stanford Univ. Press, 1962.

Kausen, Rudolph. "The Laius Complex and Mother-Child Symbiosis." *Journal of Individual Psychology.* Vol. 28, no. 1 (May 1972). Pp. 33–37.

Kinkley, Jeffrey C. "Shen Ts'ung-wen's Vision of Republican China." Diss. Harvard 1977.

_____ . "Shen Congwen and the Uses of Regionalism in Modern Chinese Literature." *Modern Chinese Literature.* Vol. 1, no. 2 (Spring 1985). Pp. 157–183.

_____ . *The Odyssey of Shen Congwen.* Stanford: Stanford Univ. Press, 1987.

Král, Oldřich. "Wu Tsu-hsiang." In Jaroslav Prušek, ed., *Dictionary of Oriental Literatures.* New York: Basic Books, 1974. Vol. I, p. 205.

Krieger, Murray. *The Tragic Vision.* Baltimore: Johns Hopkins Univ. Press, 1973.

Kubin, Wolfgang and Wagner, Rudolph G., eds. *Essays in Modern Chinese Literature and Literary Criticism.* Bochum: Studio Brockmeyer, 1982.

Kuhn, Philip A. "Local Self-Government Under the Republic." In *Conflict and Control in Late Imperial China.* Eds. Frederic Wakeman, Jr. and Carolyn Grant. Berkeley: Univ. of California Press, 1975. Pp. 257–298.

Lai, D. C. *Chinese Couplets.* Hong Kong: Kelly and Walsh, 1969.

Lakoff, George and Johnson, Mark. *Metaphors We Live By.* Chicago:Univ. of Chicago Press, 1980.

Lang, Olga. *Pa Chin and His Writings.* Cambridge: Harvard Univ. Press, 1967.

Langer, Suzanne K. *Feeling and Form: A Theory of Art.* New York: Scribner's, 1953.

Lanser, Susan Sniader. *The Narrative Act: Point of View in Prose Fiction.* Princeton: Princeton Univ. Press, 1981.

Larson, Wendy. *Literary Authority and the Modern Chinese Writer: Ambivalence and Autobiography.* Durham: Duke Univ. Press, 1991.

Lau, Joseph S. M., Hsia, C. T. and Lee, Leo Ou-fan, eds. *Modern Chinese Stories and Novellas, 1919–1949.* New York: Columbia Univ. Press, 1981.

Lee, Leo Ou-fan. *The Romantic Generation of Modern Chinese Writers*. Cambridge: Harvard Univ. Press, 1973.

———. ed. *Lu Xun and His Legacy*. Berkeley: Univ. of California Press, 1985.

———. *Voices from the Iron House: A Study of Lu Xun*. Bloomington: Indiana Univ. Press, 1987.

Lee Yee, ed. *The New Realism*. New York: Hippocrene Books, 1983.

Legge, James, trans. *The Book of Poetry*. The Chinese Classics, vol. 4. Hong Kong: London Missionary Society's Printing Office, 1939.

Levenson, Joseph R. *Confucian China and Its Modern Fate*. Berkeley: Univ. of California Press, 1968.

Lewald, H. Ernest. *The Cry of Home: Cultural Nationalism and the Modern Writer*. Knoxville: Univ. of Tennessee Press, 1972.

Lewis, Sinclair. *Dodsworth*. New York: New American Library, 1972.

Li, Lillian M. "Food, Famine, and the Chinese State." *Journal of Asian Studies*. Vol. XLI, no. 4 (1982). Pp. 687–707.

Link, E. Perry. *Mandarin Ducks and Butterflies: Popular Fiction in Early Twentieth-century Chinese Cities*. Berkeley: Univ. of California Press, 1981.

Liu E. *The Travels of Lao Ts'an*. Trans. Harold Shadick. Ithaca: Cornell Univ. Press, 1952.

Liu I-ching. *Shih shuo Hsin-yü: A New Account of Tales of the World*. Trans. Richard Mather. Minneapolis: Univ. of Minnesota Press, 1976.

Liu, James J. Y. *The Poetry of Li Shang-yin, Ninth-Century Baroque Chinese Poet*. Chicago: Univ. of Chicago Press, 1969.

Liu, Shih Shun, trans. *Vignettes from the Late Ch'ing: Bizarre Happenings Eyewitnessed Over Two Decades, by Wu Woyao*. HongKong: The Chinese Univ. of Hong Kong Press, 1975.

Lu Xun. *A Brief History of Chinese Fiction*. Trans. Yang Xianyi and Gladys Yang. Beijing: Foreign Languages Press, 1976.

Lyell, William. *Lu Hsün's Vision of Reality*. Berkeley: Univ. of California Press, 1976.

McCaskey, Michael Joseph. "Chu Tzu-ch'ing as Essayist and Critic." Diss. Yale 1965.

McDougall, Bonnie S. *The Introduction of Western Literary Theories Into Modern China, 1919–1925*. Tokyo: Centre for East Asian Cultural Studies, 1971.

———. *Mao Zedong's "Talks at the Yan'an Conference on Literature and Art:" A Translation of the 1943 Text with Commentary*. Michigan Papers in Chinese Studies, no. 39. Ann Arbor: Univ. of Michigan Center for Chinese Studies, 1980.

———. ed. *Popular Chinese Literature and Performing Arts in the People's Republic of China, 1949–1979*. Berkeley: Univ. of California Press, 1984.

Mallory, William. *China: Land of Famine*. New York: National Geographic Society, 1926.

Mann, Thomas. *Death in Venice and Seven Other Stories*. Trans. H. T. Lowe-Porter. New York: Vintage, 1958.

Maupassant, Guy de. *The Complete Stories of Guy de Maupassant*. New York: P. F. Collier & Son, 1903.

Mills, Harriet. "Lu Hsün: 1927–1936, the Years on the Left." Diss. Columbia 1964.

Milosz, Czeslaw. *The Captive Mind*. Trans. Jane Zielonko. New York: Vintage, 1951.

Munro, S. R. *Genesis of a Revolution: An Anthology of Short Stories*. Singapore: Heinemann Educational Books, 1979.

Ng, Mau-sang. *The Russian Hero in Modern Chinese Fiction*. Albany: State Univ. of New York Press, 1988.

Nieh, Hua-ling. *Shen Ts'ung-wen*. Boston: Twayne, 1972.

O'Connor, Frank. *The Lonely Voice: A Study of the Short Story*. Cleveland: World Publishing Co., 1962.

O'Faolain, Sean. *The Short Story*. London: Collins, 1948.

Perry, Elizabeth J. *Rebels and Revolutionaries in North China, 1845–1945*. Stanford: Stanford Univ. Press, 1980.

Pickowicz, Paul G. *Marxist Literary Thought in Contemporary China: The Influence of Ch'ü Ch'iu-pai*. Berkeley: Univ. of California Press, 1981.

Pinion, F. B. *A Jane Austen Companion*. London: MacMillan, 1973.

Plaks, Andrew H. *Archetypes and Allegory in the Dream of the Red Chamber*. Princeton: Princeton Univ. Press, 1976.

Pollard, David. *A Chinese Look at Literature: the Literary Values of Chou Tso-jen in Relation to the Tradition*. Berkeley: Univ. of California Press, 1973.

Prušek, Jaroslav. *Studies in Modern Chinese Literature*. Berlin: Akademie Verlag, 1964.

——— . *The Lyrical and the Epic: Studies of Modern Chinese Literature*. Ed. Leo Ou-fan Lee. Bloomington: Indiana Univ. Press, 1980.

Pye, Lucian. *The Spirit of Chinese Politics: A Psychocultural Study of Authority Crisis in Political Development*. Cambridge: M.I.T. Press, 1968.

Qu Yuan. "Summons of the Soul." Trans. David Hawkes. In *Anthology of Chinese Literature: From Early Times to the Fourteenth Century*, ed. Cyril Birch. New York: Grove Press, 1965. Pp. 73–78.

*Renmin ribao* Editorial Staff. "Unfold Criticism of *Water Margin*." In *Beijing Review*. No. 37 (September), 1975. Pp. 7–8.

Ribot, Théophile. *Essay On the Creative Imagination*. Trans. Arthur Allin. Chicago: Open Court, 1906.

Scholes, Robert and Kellogg, Robert. *The Nature of Narrative*. New York: Oxford Univ. Press, 1966.

Schorer, Mark. "Fiction and the 'Analogical Matrix.'" In *Essays in Stylistic Analysis*, ed. Howard S. Babb. New York: Harcourt Brace, 1972. Pp. 340–352.

Schwarcz, Vera. *Long Road Home: A China Journal*. New Haven: Yale Univ. Press, 1984.

Scott, James C. *The Moral Economy of the Peasant: Rebellion and Subsistence in Southeast Asia*. New Haven: Yale Univ. Press, 1976.

Seidensticker, Edward. *Kafū the Scribbler*. Stanford: Stanford Univ. Press, 1965.

Semanov, V. I. *Lu Hsün and His Predecessors*. Trans. Charles J. Alber. White Plains, N.Y.: M. E. Sharpe, 1980.

Sheridan, James E. *Chinese Warlord: The Career of Feng Yü-hsiang*. Stanford: Stanford Univ. Press, 1966.

Siu, Helen F., ed., *Furrows: Peasants, Intellectuals, and the State: Stories and Histories from Modern China*. Stanford: Stanford Univ. Press, 1990.

Smith, Arthur H. *Village Life in China: A Study in Sociology*. New York: Fleming H. Revell, 1899.

Stewart, John. *The Flaming Years, 1920–1929*. Filmarama, vol. 2. Metuchen, N.J.: Scarecrow Press, 1977.

*Stories from the Thirties, Vol.* 2. Beijing: Panda, 1982.

Su Hsüeh-lin. "Present-Day Fiction and Drama in China." In *1500 Modern Chinese Novels and Plays*, ed. Joseph Schyns. 1948; rpt. Hong Kong: Lung Men Bookstore, 1966. Pp. iii–lviii.

Sullivan, Lawrence K. "The Emergence of Civil Society in China, Spring 1989." In Tony Saich, ed., *The Chinese People's Movement: Perspectives on Spring 1989*. Armonk, N.Y.: M. E. Sharpe, 1990. Pp. 126–144.

Tallis, Raymond. *In Defense of Realism*. London: Edward Arnold, 1988.

Tanigawa Michio. *Medieval Chinese Society and the Local "Community"*. Trans. Joshua A. Fogel. Berkeley: Univ. of California Press, 1985.

Thomson, Philip. *The Grotesque*. London: Methuen, 1972.

Tidemann, R.G. "The Persistence of Banditry: Incidents in Border Districts of the North China Plain." *Modern China*. Vol. 8, no. 4 (October 1982). Pp. 395–433.

Todorov, Tsvetan. *The Fantastic: A Structural Approach to a Literary Genre*. Trans. Richard Howard. Ithaca: Cornell Univ. Press, 1975.

Traub, Stuart H. and Little, Craig B., eds. *Theories of Deviance*. 2nd ed. Itasca: F. E. Peacock Publishers, 1980.

Trilling, Lionel. "On the Teaching of Modern Literature," *Beyond Culture: Essays on Literature and Learning*. New York: Viking Press, 1965. Pp. 3–30.

Turgenev, Ivan. *The Hunting Sketches*. Trans. Bernard Builbert Guerney. New York: New American Library, 1962.

Vallette-Hémery, Martine, trans. *Récits Chinois, 1918–1942*. Paris: Éditions de l'Herne, 1970.

Vernon, Thomas S. "The Laius Complex." *The Humanist*. Nov./Dec. 1971. Pp. 27–28.

Vohra, Ranbir. *Lao She and the Chinese Revolution*. Cambridge: Harvard Univ. Press, 1974.

Wakeman, Frederic, Jr. *The Fall of Imperial China*. New York: Free Press, 1975.

Wang, James C. F. *Contemporary Chinese Politics*. Englewood Cliffs: Prentice-Hall, 1980.

Wang, John Ching-yu. *Chin Sheng-t'an*. Boston: Twayne, 1972.

Wang, Y. C. *Chinese Intellectuals and the West, 1872–1949*. Chapel Hill: Univ. of North Carolina Press, 1966.

Warren, Austin and Wellek, René. *Theory of Literature*. 2nd ed. New York: Harcourt Brace, 1956.

Watson, Burton. *Early Chinese Literature*. New York: Columbia Univ. Press, 1962.

Wharton, Edith. *The Writing of Fiction*. New Haven: Yale Univ. Press, 1925.

Widmer, Ellen. "Qu Qiubai and Russian Literature." In Merle Goldman, ed., *Modern Chinese Literature in the May Fourth Era*. Cambridge: Harvard Univ. Press, 1977. Pp. 103–125.

Williams, C. A. S. *Outlines of Chinese Symbolism and Art Motives*. 3rd ed. New York: Dover Publications, 1976.

Williams, Philip F. "Wu Zuxiang and His Meliorist Rural Fiction in China From the Twenties to the Forties." Diss. U.C.L.A. 1985.

Williams, Raymond. *Marxism and Literature*. Oxford: Oxford Univ. Press, 1977.

Wixted, John Timothy. "The Literary Criticism of Yuan Hao-wen (1190–1257)." Diss. Oxford 1976.

Wu Zuxiang. *Green Bamboo Hermitage*. Beijing: Panda, 1989.

Yang, C. K. *The Chinese Family in the Communist Revolution*. 1959; rpt. Cambridge: M.I.T. Press, 1965.

————. *A Chinese Village in Early Communist Transition*. 1959; rpt. Cambridge: M.I.T. Press, 1965.

Yang, Winston L. Y. and Mao, Nathan K., eds. *Modern Chinese Fiction—a Guide to Its History and Appreciation*. Boston: G.K. Hall, 1981.

Yarmolinsky, Avrahm, ed. *The Portable Chekhov*. New York: Viking Press, 1975.

Yu, Pauline. *The Poetry of Wang Wei: New Translations and Commentary*. Bloomington: Indiana Univ. Press, 1980.

# Chronological List
# of Wu's Creative Works

"Buxing de xiao cao" [The Ill-fated Little Plant]. *Min'guo*
ribao. 7 Oct. 1923. Pp. 3-4. 不幸的小草, 民國日報

"Yuan fei yu yue" [Soaring Hawks and Plunging Fish]. *Funü zazhi*
[The Women's Magazine]. Vol. 11, no. 3 (Mar. 1925).
Pp. 542-545. 鳶飛魚躍, 婦女雜誌

"Wo yao tazhe yun feiteng" [I'll Step Up to the Clouds and Soar].
*Qinghua zhoukan* [The Qinghua Weekly]. Vol. 32, no. 5 (Nov.
1929). P. 45. 我要踏著雲飛騰, 清華週刊

"Ge Leimengna zhe" [He Sings of Ramona]. *Qinghua zhoukan*. Vol.
32, no. 8 (Dec. 1929). Pp. 63-66. 歌蕾蒙娜者, 清華週刊

"Li jia de qianye" [On the Eve of Leaving Home]. *Funü zazhi*.
Vol. 17, no. 7 (Jul. 1931). Pp. 119-123. Rpt. *Xi liu ji*
[West Willow Anthology], pp. 1-18. 離家的前夜, 婦女雜誌

"Huang mei shijie" [The Plum-ripening Season]. *Qinghua zhoukan*.
Vol. 39, nos. 5-6 (Nov. 1931). Pp. 535-536.
黃梅時節, 清華週刊

"Liangzhi xiao maque" [Two Young Sparrows]. *Wenxue yuekan* [The
Literary Monthly]. Vol. 2, no. 1 (Dec. 1931). Pp. 37-49.
Rpt. *Xi liu ji*, pp. 19-52. 兩隻小麻雀, 文學月刊

"Xiao Hua de shengri" [Xiao Hua's Birthday]. *Zhongguo shehui*
[Chinese Society]. Vol. 1, no. 1 (Jan. 1932). Pp. 17-26.
Rpt. *Qinghua zhoukan*, vol. 39, nos. 5-6 (Apr. 1933),
pp. 451-459. 小花的生日, 中國社會

"Zhizi hua" [The Flowering Gardenia]. *Wenxue yuekan*. Vol. 2,
no. 2 (Jan. 1932). Pp. 23-34. Rpt. *Xi liu ji*, pp. 53-85.
梔子花, 文學月刊

"Jin Xiaojie yu Xue Guniang" [Miss Jin and the Xue Girl].

    *Qinghua zhoukan.*  Vol. 37, no. 1 (Feb. 1932).  Pp. 87-101.

    Rpt. *Xi liu ji*, pp. 87-123. 金小姐與雪姑娘, 清華週刊

"Guanguan de bupin" [Little Lord Guanguan's Tonic].  *Qinghua*

    *zhoukan.*  Vol. 37, no. 6 (Apr. 1932).  Pp. 28-41.  Rpt. *Xi*

    *liu ji*, pp. 125-162. 官官的補品, 清華週刊

"Lu zhu shanfang" [The Verdant Bamboo Hermitage].  *Qinghua*

    *zhoukan.*  Vol. 38, no. 12 (Jan. 1933).  Pp. 180-185.  Rpt.

    *Xi liu ji*, pp. 163-181. 菉竹山房, 清華週刊

"Huanghun" [Twilight].  *Wenxue* [Literature].  Vol. 1, no. 5 (Nov.

    1933).  Pp. 708-713.  Rpt. *Xi liu ji*, pp. 183-205. 黃昏, 文學

"Wanzi jinyinhua" [Splay-petaled Honeysuckle].  *Qinghua zhoukan.*

    Vol. 40, nos. 3-4 (Nov. 1933).  Pp. 80-86.  Rpt. *Xi liu ji*,

    pp. 207-229. 卍字金銀花, 清華週刊

"Yiqianbabai dan" [1800 Bushels].  *Wenxue jikan* [Literature

    Quarterly].  Vol. 1, no. 1 (Jan. 1934).  Pp. 61-86.  Rpt. *Xi*

    *liu ji*, pp. 231-334. 一千八百擔, 文學季刊

"Tianxia taiping" [The World At Peace].  *Wenxue.*  Vol. 2, no. 4

    (Mar. 1934).  Pp. 660-675.  Rpt. *Xi liu ji*, pp. 335-397.

    天下太平, 文學

"Fan jia pu" [Fan Hamlet].  *Wenxue jikan.*  Vol. 1, no. 2 (Apr.

    1934).  Pp. 213-234.  Rpt. *Fan yu ji* [After-hours], pp.

    1-62. 樊家舖, 文學季刊

"Yangzhou zaji" [Yangzhou Jottings].  *Qinghua zhoukan.*  Vol. 41,

    nos. 3-4 (Apr. 1934).  Pp. 153-160. 揚州雜記, 清華週刊

"Nen huang zhi yi" [Memories of Childhood Days].  *Wenxue jikan.*

    Vol. 1, no. 3 (Jul. 1934).  Pp. 258-259. 嫩黃之憶, 文學季刊

"Cun ju jishi er ze" [Two Extracts from My Records of Living in
the Countryside]. *Wenxue.* Vol. 3, no. 1 (Jul. 1934). Pp.
414-420. Rpt. *Fan yu ji*, pp. 63-80. 村居記事二則, 文學

*Xi liu ji.* Shanghai: Shenghuo shudian, Aug. 1934. Rpt.
Shanghai: Shanghai shudian, 1987. 西柳集

"Tan meng" [On My Dreams]. *Tai bai.* Vol. 1, no. 4 (Nov. 1934).
Pp. 175-177. Rpt. *Fan yu ji*, pp. 81-88. 談夢, 太白

"Chai" [The Woodcutter]. *Wenxue.* Vol. 3, no. 6 (Dec. 1934).
Pp. 1179-1184. Rpt. *Fan yu ji*, pp. 89-104. 柴, 文學

"You he" [Voyage Along the River]. *Qinghua zhoukan.* Vol. 42,
nos. 9-10 (Dec. 1934). P. 153. 遊河, 清華週刊

"Nüren" [The Woman]. *Tai bai.* Vol. 1, no. 8 (Jan. 1935). Pp.
342-344. Rpt. *Fan yu ji*, pp. 105-112. 女人, 太白

"Dao Lu'er" [In Memory of Lu'er]. *Tai bai.* Vol. 2, no. 4 (May
1935). Pp. 167-170. Rpt. *Fan yu ji*, pp. 113-124.
悼鹿兒, 太白

"Taishan fengguang" [Sights at Mount Tai]. *Wenxue.* Vol. 5, no.
4 (Nov. 1935). Pp. 714-726. Rpt. *Fan yu ji*, pp. 125-159.
泰山風光, 文學

*Fan yu ji.* Shanghai: Wenhua shenghuo chubanshe, Dec. 1935. 飯餘集

"Mouri" [A Certain Day"]. in *Shi nian* [A Decade], ed. Xia
Mianzun. Shanghai: Kaiming shudian, 1936. Pp. 197-217.
Rpt. *Wu Zuxiang xiaoshuo sanwen ji* [Anthology of Wu
Zuxiang's Fiction and Prose], pp. 183-200. 某日, 十年

"Chai chuan" [The Requisitioned Boat]. *Qiyue* [July]. No. 11
(Mar. 1938). Pp. 342-345. Rpt. *Wu Zuxiang xiaoshuo sanwen
ji*, pp. 278-288. 差船, 七月

"Fuguan ji qita" [The Aide-de-camp and Others].  *Kangzhan wenyi*
    [Literature of the War of Resistance].  Vol. 6, no. 4 (Dec.
    1940).  Pp. 250-258.  Rpt. *Wu Zuxiang xiaoshuo sanwen ji*,
    pp. 289-310. 副官及其他, 抗戰文藝

"Tie menzi" [Stuffy Ironsides].  *Zhongguo qingnian*.  Vol. 7, nos.
    4-5 (Nov. 1942).  Pp. 55-71.  Rpt. *Wu Zuxiang xiaoshuo
    sanwen ji*, pp. 201-226. 鐵悶子, 中國青年

"'Bai' gushi" ["Contriving" a Story].  *Kangzhan wenyi*.  Vol. 8,
    nos. 1-2 (Nov. 1942).  P. 84. "擺" 故事, 抗戰文藝

"Hou jie" [The Back Street].  *Kangzhan wenyi*.  Vol. 8, nos. 1-2
    (Nov. 1942).  P. 84. 後街, 抗戰文藝

*Yazui lao* [Duckbill Deluge].  Chongqing: Shi yu chao yinshau suo,
    Mar. 1943.  Rept. as *Shan hong* [Mountain Torrent].
    Shanghai: Xingqun chubanshe, 1946;  Beijing: Renmin wenxue
    chubanshe, 1982. 鴨嘴澇, 山洪

"Dui deng" [Facing My Lamp].  *Shi yu chao wenyi* [Literature of
    the Age and Its Trends].  Vol. 2, no. 5 (Jun. 1943).  Pp.
    47-48. 對燈, 時與潮文藝

"Yan" [Tobacco].  *Shi yu chao wenyi*.  Vol. 4, no. 3 (Nov. 1944).
    Pp. 13-16. 煙, 時與潮文藝

*Wu Zuxiang xiaoshuo sanwen ji*.  Beijing: Renmin wenxue chubanshe,
    1954. 吳組緗小說散文集

*Wu Zuxiang xuanji* [Anthology of Wu Zuxiang].  Hong Kong:
    Xianggang wenxue yanjiu she, 1978. 吳組緗選集

*Su cao ji* [Grass of Yore].  Beijing: Beijing daxue chubanshe,
    1988.  Collection of previously published fiction, based on
    expurgated versions in the 1954 anthology;  partial
    citations of original sources. 宿草集

# Selected Bibliography
## of Other Writings by Wu

"He dajia tantan keneng ba" [I Suppose It's Possible to Discuss
    This with Everyone].  *Funü zazhi*.  Vol. 11, no. 11 (Nov.
    1925).  Pp. 1722-1724. 和大家談談可能吧, 婦女雜誌
"Tantan Qinghua de wen feng" [The Literary Climate at Qinghua].
    *Qinghua zhoukan*.  Vol. 36, no. 3 (Nov. 1931).  Pp. 2-5.
    談談清華的文風, 清華週刊
"Xin shu jieshao--Ziye" [Review of a New Book--*Midnight*].  *Wenyi
    yuebao*.  Vol. 1, no. 1 (Jun. 1933).  Pp. 105-107.
    新書介紹子夜, 文藝月報
"Youmo he fengci" [Humor and Satire].  In Chen Wangdao, ed.,
    *Xiaopinwen he manhua* [The Familiar Essay and the Cartoon].
    1935; rpt. Shanghai shudian, 1981.  Pp. 15-17. 幽默和諷刺
"Shuo Zhao Wangyun Xiansheng de hua" [On the Paintings of Zhao
    Wangyun].  *Zhongyang ribao* [Central Daily News].  4 Feb.
    1936.  P. 6. 說趙望雲先生的畫, 中央日報
"Wen Lu Xun Xiansheng de si hao" [Upon Hearing the News of Lu
    Xun's Death].  *Zhong liu* [Central Current].  Vol. 1, no. 5
    (Nov. 1936).  Pp. 265-266. 聞魯迅先生死耗, 中流
"Wo duiyu wenyijie tongyi zhanxian de jidian guanjian" [A Few
    Personal Views On the National United Front of Literary
    Circles].  *Xinhua ribao* [New China Daily].  27 Mar. 1938.
    P. 4. 我對於文藝界統一戰線的幾點管見, 新華日報
"Yiwei songyang shi bu gou de" [A Chorus of Yea Is Not Enough].
    *Xin shu bao* [New Sichuan Daily].  22 Jan. 1940.  P. 4.
    一味頌揚是不夠的, 新蜀報
"Ruhe chuangzuo xiaoshuo zhong de renwu" [How to Create

Characters in Fiction]. *Kangzhan wenyi*. Vol. 7, nos. 2-3
(Mar. 1941). Pp. 159-161. 如何創作小説中的人物,
抗戰文藝

"Jieshao duanpian xiaoshuo sipian" [A Brief on Four Short
Stories]. *Guowen yuekan* [The National Language Monthly].
No. 11 (Dec. 1941). Pp. 18-20. 介紹短篇小説四篇, 國文月刊

Diary MS. 1942-1946. Private collection of Wu Zuxiang.

"Tan *Shi nian shi xuan*" [On *An Anthology of a Decade's Worth of
Poetry*]. *Wen xiao* [The Literary Whistle]. Vol. 1, no. 1
(May 1945). Pp. 65-66. 談十年詩選, 文嘯

"Wei Zhongguo xianshizhuyi wenxue zhuhe" [Congratulations Are Due
to Realist Literature in China]. *Xinhua ribao*. 24 Jun.
1945. 為中國現實主義文學祝賀, 新華日報

"Meiguo de dongtian" [Winter in America]. *Ren jian shi* [In the
Human World]. Vol. 1, no. 2 (Apr. 1947). Pp. 47-51.
美國的冬天, 人間世

"Tan shenghuo" [On Living]. *Jinling nüzi wenli xueyuan xiaokan*
[Journal of the Jinling Women's Academy of Arts and
Sciences]. No. 144 (Oct. 1947). Pp. 3-4. 談生活,
金陵女子文理學院校刊

"Jingdao Peixian Xiansheng" [In Respectful Remembrance of Zhu
Ziqing]. *Wen xun yuekan* [Literary News Monthly]. Vol. 9,
no. 3 (Sep. 1948). Pp. 131-135. 敬悼佩弦先生, 文訊月刊

"*Shengming zhong zui hao de nianyue*" [*The Best Time in My Life*].
*Xin guancha* [New Observer]. Vol. 2, no. 2 (Jan. 1951). Pp.
16-17. 生命中最好的年月, 新觀察

"Chu jian jiefangjun" [My First Sight of the People's Liberation

Army"]. *Xin guancha*. Vol. 3, no. 1 (Aug. 1951). Pp. 8-9.
初見解放軍, 新觀察

"*Rulin waishi* de sixiang yu yishu" [The Philosophy and Art of *The
Scholars*]. *Renmin wenxue* [People's Literature]. No. 8
(Aug.), 1953. Pp. 82-99. Translated in abridged form in
*Chinese Literature*, no. 4 (April), 1954, pp. 155-165.
儒林外史的思想與藝術, 人民文學

"Tan Andongnuofu de duanpian xiaoshuo" [On the Short Stories of
Aldonov]. *Guangming ribao* [Brightness Daily]. 21 Mar.
1954. P. 3. 談安東諸夫的短篇小說, 光明日報

"Huang Demao." *Xin guancha*. No. 8 (Apr.), 1954. Pp. 5-6.
黃德茂, 新觀察

"Zhongguo zuojia xiehui gudian wenxuebu zhaokai de *Hong lou meng*
yanjiu zuotanhui jilu" [Record of a Conference on *Dream of
the Red Chamber* Research; Convened by the Classical
Literature Section of the Chinese Writers' Association].
*Guangming ribao*. 14 Nov. 1954. Pp. 5-6. (Criticism of Yu
Pingbo俞平伯). 中國作家協會古典文學部召開的
紅樓夢研究座談會記錄, 光明日報

"Zai Zhongguo zuojia xiehui di'erci lishi huiyi shang de fayan"
[Speeches at the Second Meeting of the Secretariat of the
Chinese Writers' Association]. *Wenyi bao* [Literary
Gazette]. No. 7 (April), 1956. Pp. 13-18. 在中國作家
協會第二次理事會議上的發言, 文藝報

"Kan *Tian xian pei*" [Watching *A Match for the Beauty*]. *Beijing
ribao* [Beijing Daily]. 1956: 3 Oct., p. 6, and 4 Oct.,
p. 3. 看天仙配, 北京日報

"Lun Jia Baoyu dianxing xingxiang" [Jia Baoyu As a Typical
    Character].  *Beijing daxue xuebao* [Journal of Beijing
    University].  No. 4 (Nov.), 1956.  Pp. 1-32.
    論賈寶玉典型形象，北京大學學報
"Wode yige kanfa" [A View of Mine].  *Wenyi bao*.  No. 8 (May),
    1957.  Pp. 2-3.  我的一個看法，文藝報
"Jianjue xiang Ding-Chen fandang jituan douzheng" [Resolutely
    Struggle With the Ding-Chen Anti-Party Clique].  *Guangming
    ribao*.  23 Aug. 1957.  P. 3.  Jointly authored with Feng Zhi
    馮至 and Bian Zhilin 卞之琳．   堅決向丁陳反黨
    集團鬥爭，光明日報
"Guanyu gudian zuojia de shijie guan" [Concerning the World
    Outlook of Classical Writers].  *Renmin wenxue*.  Vol. 4
    (Apr.), 1958.  Pp. 79-82.  關於古典作家的
    世界觀，人民文學
"Tan *Hong lou meng* li jige peichen renwu de anpai" [Regarding
    Several Designs of Setting Off Characters in *Dream of the
    Red Chamber*].  *Renmin wenxue*.  No. 8 (Aug.), 1959.  Pp. 112-
    119. 談紅樓夢裡幾個陪襯人物的安排，人民文學
"Da hu de gushi" [A Story About Fighting with Tigers].  *Renmin
    ribao* [People's Daily].  7 Mar. 1961.  P. 8.
    打虎的故事，人民日報
"Shenghuo, xiezuo, du shu" [Living, Writing, and Reading].
    *Jiefangjun wenyi* [P.L.A. Literature].  Vol. 2 (Feb.), 1962.
    Pp. 22-28.  生活寫作讀書，解放軍文藝
"Jia Baoyu de xingge tedian he tade lian'ai hunyin beiju"
    [Features of Jia Baoyu's Personality and the Tragedy of His

Romance and Marriage]. *Ningxia wenyi.* No. 4 (Aug.), 1963.

    Pp. 43-51. 賈寶玉的性格特點和他的戀愛
婚姻悲劇，寧夏文藝

"Tan *Shui hu*" [On *Water Margin*]. *Wenyi bao.* No. 2 (Feb.), 1978.

    Pp. 5-11. 談水滸，文藝報

"Song--jingzeng Beijing Yiyuan Zhang Hong deng qiwei hushi

    tongzhi" [And Ode Presented to Beijing Hospital's Seven

    Nurses Led by Zhang Hong]. *Renmin ribao.* 11 Apr. 1980. P.

    8. 頌敬贈北京醫院張紅等七位護士同志，人民日報

"Duanpian he changpian xiaoshuo chuangzuo mantan" [An Informal

    Discussion of Short Vs. Full-length Fiction]. *Wenyi yanjiu.*

    No. 3 (June), 1980. Pp. 41-47. 短篇和長篇小說
創作漫談，文藝研究

"Wei Shaocheng *Hong lou meng banben xiao kao* daixu" [Preface to

    Wei Shaocheng's *Brief Investigations Into the Editions of*

    *Dream of the Red Chamber*]. *Hong lou meng xuekan.* No. 3

    (Aug.), 1981. Pp. 23-32. 魏紹昌紅樓夢版本
小考代序，紅樓夢學刊

"Tan sanwen" [A Discussion of the Essay]. *Wenyi bao.* No. 18

    (Sep.), 1981. Pp. 60-62. 談散文，文藝報

"*Pilgrimage to the West* and Its Author." In Yang Xianyi and

    Gladys Yang, eds., *Excerpts From Three Classical Novels.*

    Beijing: Panda, 1981. Pp. 200-212.

"Ganji he huainian--Lu Xun Xiansheng yibai zhounian huaiyi"

    [Gratitude and Remembrance--In Commemoration of Lu Xun's

    Hundredth Birthday]. *Wenyi bao.* No. 2 (Feb.), 1982. Pp.

    6-9. 感激和懷念魯迅先生一百週年懷憶，文藝報

*Shuo bai ji* [Discussions of Fiction]. Beijing: Beijing daxue
    chubanshe, 1987. Collection of previously published essays
    on classical fiction; most selections include partial
    citations of original sources. 說稗集

*Shi huang ji* [Prose Gleanings]. Beijing: Beijing daxue
    chubanshe, 1988. Collection of previously published
    essays on miscellaneous topics; most selections include
    partial citations of original sources. 拾荒集

*Yuan wai ji* [Outside the Literary Garden]. Beijing: Beijing
    daxue chubanshe, 1988. Collection of previously published
    essays and speeches about literature; few selections contain
    information on original sources. 苑外集

# Selected Bibliography of Other
East Asian Source Materials

Ai Gan. "'Gui gong tan' he 'Tianxia taiping'" ["Gui Gong Pond" and "The World At Peace"]. *Chun guang* [Spring Brightness]. Vol. I, no. 3 (May 1934). Pp. 540-543. 艾淦, 桂公塘和天下太平, 春光

Ai Wu. "Qiu shou" [Autumn Harvest]. *Ai Wu xuanji* [An Anthology of Ai Wu]. Hong Kong: Xianggang wenxue yanjiushe, 1979. Pp. 98-113. 艾蕪, 秋收, 艾蕪選集

"Bian hou" [Editorial Afterword]. *Qinghua zhoukan*. Vol. 37, no. 6 (Apr. 1932). Pp. 173-174. The first published review of Wu's works: an anonymous critique of "Little Lord Guanguan's Tonic." 編後, 清華週刊

Chen Wangdao, ed. *Xiaopinwen he manhua* [The Familiar Essay and the Cartoon]. 1935; rpt. Shanghai: Shanghai shudian, 1981. 陳望道, 小品文和漫畫

Cheng Peikai (pseud. Cheng Bukui). "Zhandou de haojiao xiangle-- Wu Zuxiang duanpian chuangzuo de yishu chengjiu" [The Battle Trumpet Has Sounded--the Artistic Achievement of Wu Zuxiang's Short Fiction]. *Dousou*. Mar., May, and Jul. 1975: no. 8 (pp. 1-11). no. 9 (pp. 7-19), and no. 10 (pp. 25-37). 鄭培凱 (筆名程步奎), 戰鬥的號角響了 吳組緗短篇創作的藝術成就, 抖擻

Dong Meng. "*Wenxue* chuangzuo zhuanhao" [The Special Issue on Creative Writing in *Literature*]. *Wenxue*. Vol. 3, no. 1 (July 1934). P. 488. 東萌, 文學創作專號, 文學

Feng Hongda and Yu Huaxin.  *Feng Yuxiang Jiangjun hun gui Zhonghua*
[General Feng Yuxiang's Return to China in Spirit].  Beijing:
Wen shi ziliao chubanshe, 1981. 馮洪達, 余華心
馮玉祥將軍魂歸中華

Fukagawa Kenji, trans.  "Tenka taihei" [The World At Peace].
*Bungaku annai* [Literature Guide].  Vol. 2, no. 1 (Jan. 1936).
深川賢二, 天下太平, 文學案內

Ge Zhenghui, Kong Haizhu, and Lu Diaowen, eds.  "Lu Xun, Mao Dun
xuanbian *Caoxie jiao* de wenxian" [Writings By Lu Xun and Mao
Dun on Editing *Straw Sandals*].  *Zhongguo xiandai wenyi ziliao
congkan* [Series on Materials in Modern Chinese Literature].
No. 5 (Apr. 1980).  Pp. 186-199. 葛正慧, 孔海珠, 盧調
文, 魯迅, 茅盾選編草鞋腳的文獻, 中國現代文藝資料叢刊

Gu Zhenbang.  "Guihua de youxiang--tan Wu Zuxiang xiaoshuo de
youdian he buzu" [The Delicate Fragrance of Cassia Blossoms--
Virtues and Defects of Wu Zuxiang's Fiction].  *Pan Gu*.  No.
71 (July 1974).  Pp. 26-27. 谷震邦, 桂花的幽香談
吳組緗小說的優點和不足, 盤古

Guo Shaoyu.  *Zhongguo wenxue piping shi* [A History of Chinese
Literary Criticism].  2nd ed.  Shanghai: Shanghai guji
chubanshe, 1981. 郭紹虞, 中國文學批評史

Huang Chengzhu, ed.  *Jingxian zhi* [Jingxian Gazetteer].  Vol. 231.
1806; rpt. Taibei: Chengwen chubanshe, 1975. 黃成助,
涇縣誌

Jiang Guangci.  *Jiang Guangci xuanji* [An Anthology of Jiang
Guangci].  Hong Kong: Gang qing chubanshe, 1979.
蔣光慈, 蔣光慈選集

*Jin Ping Mei cihua* [Golden Lotus]. Rpt. Hong Kong: Taiping shuju, 1982. 金瓶梅詞話

Langxian. "He Daqing yihen yuanyang tao" [He Daqing's Regrets for the Mandarin Duck Ribbon]. In *Xingshi hengyan* [Tales to Awaken the World]. Rpt. Hong Kong: Zuojia chubanshe, 1958. Pp. 278-305. 浪仙，赫大卿遺恨鴛鴦縧，醒世恆言

Lao She. "Du *Yazui lao*" [Reading *Duckbill Deluge*]. In *Lao She lun chuangzuo* [Lao She's Essays on Creative Writing]. Shanghai: Shanghai wenyi chubanshe, 1980). Pp. 313-314. Originally published in the Chongqing newspaper *Shi shi xin bao*, 18 June 1943. 老舍,讀鴨嘴澇, 老舍論創作, 時事新報

------. *Lao She wenji* [Collected Works of Lao She]. Vol. 3. Beijing: Renmin wenxue chubanshe, 1982. 老舍文集

Li Bangnong, ed. *Huangshan de chuanshuo* [Legends of the Yellow Mountains]. Beijing: Zhongguo minjian wenyi chubanshe, 1982. 黎邦農，黄山的傳説

Li Changzhi. "*Yazui lao.*" *Shi yu chao wenyi*. Vol. 4, no. 1 (Sept. 1944). Pp. 139-142. 李長之，鴨嘴澇, 時與潮文藝

Lin Huanping. "Duo chansheng xie 'Chai chuan'" [Let Us Produce More "Requisitioned Boats"]. *Kangzhan wenyi pinglun ji* [Collected Essays on War of Resistance Literature]. Hong Kong: Min'ge chubanshe, 1939. Pp. 153-155. 林煥平，多產生些差船，抗戰文藝評論集

Liu Dajie. *Zhongguo wenxue fazhan shi* [A History of the

Development of Chinese Literature]. Rpt. Taibei: Hua zheng
    shuju, 1976. 劉大杰，中國文學發展史

Liu Shousong. *Zhongguo xin wenxue shi chu gao* [A Preliminary
    Draft History of Modern Chinese Literature]. 2 vols.
    Beijing: Zuojia chubanshe, 1956. 劉綬松，中國
    新文學史初稿

Lü Ren. Review of the Inaugural Issue of *Wenxue jikan*. *Yi shi*
    *bao* (Tianjin). 23 Jan. 1934. P. 14. 呂人，益世報

Lu Xun. *Nahan* [Outcry]. 1923; rpt. Beijing: Renmin wenxue
    chubanshe, 1973. 魯迅，吶喊．

------. *Panghuang* [Wandering]. 1926; rpt. Beijing: Renmin wenxue
    chubanshe, 1976. 彷徨

------. *Lu Xun quanji* [Complete Works of Lu Xun]. Vol. 8.
    Beijing: Renmin wenxue chubanshe, 1981. 魯迅全集

------, ed. *Caoxie jiao* [Straw Sandals]. Changsha: Hunan renmin
    chubanshe, 1981. 草鞋腳

Ma Zhonglin, ed. *Zhongguo xiandai youji xuan* [A Collection of
    Modern Chinese Travel Accounts]. Beijing: Zhongguo luyou
    chubanshe, 1982. 馬忠林，中國現代游記選

Mao Dun (pseud. Ti Ruo). "Shubao shuping: *Qinghua zhoukan* wenyi
    chuangkanhao" [A Critical Review of the *Qinghua Weekly*
    Inaugural Issue on Literature]. *Wenxue*. Vol. 2, no. 1 (Jan.
    1934). Pp. 202-203. 茅盾（筆名惕若），書報述評
    清華週刊文藝創刊號，文學

------. "Shubao shuping: *Wenxue jikan* chuangkanhao" [A Critical
    Review of the Inaugural Issue of the *Literature Quarterly*].
    *Wenxue*. Vol. 2, no. 2 (Feb. 1934). Pp. 359-362. 書報

述評, 文學季刊創刊號, 文學

------. "*Wenxue jikan* di'erqi nei de chuangzuo" [Fiction in the
Second Number of *Literature Quarterly*]. *Wenxue*. Vol. 3, no.
1 (Jul. 1934). Pp. 447-452. Rpt. in *Mao Dun lun chuangzuo*
[Mao Dun's Essays on Creative Writing]. Shanghai: Shanghai
wenyi chubanshe, 1981, pp. 287-296. 文學季刊第二期內
的創作, 文學, 茅盾論創作

------. "*Xi liu ji*" [*West Willow*]. *Wenxue*. Vol. 3, no. 5 (Nov.
1934). Pp. 1074-1080. Rpt. in *Mao Dun lun chuangzuo*, pp.
297-307. 西柳集, 文學, 茅盾論
創作

Masuda Wataru, trans. "Maki" [The Wood{cutter}]. In *Shina Endo
tampenshū* [A Collection of Short Stories from China and
India. Ed. Satō Haruo. Tokyo, 1936. 增田涉, 薪,
支那印度短篇集, 佐藤春夫主編

Mu Shiying. "Zamen de shijie" [Our World]. In *Nan bei ji* [Poles
North and South]. Shanghai: Hufeng shuju, 1932. Pp. 25-47.
穆時英, 咱們的世界, 南北極

Pan Songshou. Personal interview. 14 May 1983. 潘松壽

Pan Tongshou. Personal interview. 13 May 1983. 潘桐壽

Pu Liangpei (pseud. Lin Fei). *Xiandai liushi jia sanwen zhaji*
[Notes on Reading Sixty Prose Writers]. Tianjin: Baihua
wenyi chubanshe, 1980. 浦良培 (筆名林非),
現代六十家散文札記

------. *Zhongguo xiandai sanwen shi gao* [A Draft History of
Modern Chinese Prose]. Beijing: Zhongguo shehui kexue
chubanshe, 1981. 中國現代散文史稿

Qian Er.  "Ping Wu Zuxiang de *Yazui lao*" [A Critique of Wu
     Zuxiang's *Duckbill Deluge*].  *Qunzhong* [The Masses].  Vol. 9,
     no. 18 (Sep. 1944).  Pp. 812-813.  鉗耳，評吳組緗
     的鴨嘴澇，群眾

Ruo Ying.  "Ping *Wenxue* chuangzuo zhuanhao" [A Critique of the
     Special Issue on Creative Writing in *Literature*].  *Wenxue*.
     Vol. 3, no. 1 (Jul. 1934).  P. 490.  弱纓，評文學
     創作專號， 文學

Sha Ting.  *Tao jin ji* [A Tale of Gold Prospecting].  Shanghai:
     Wenhua shenghuo chubanshe, 1943.  沙汀，淘金記

Shao Wencui.  "Anhui Yixian de funü" [Women of Yixian County in
     Anhui Province].  *Funü zazhi*.  Vol. 15, no. 3 (Mar. 1929).
     Pp. 8-10.  邵文萃，安徽黟縣的婦女，婦女雜誌

Shen Chengkuan and Wu Fuhui.  "Wu Zuxiang tan Zhang Tianyi" [Wu
     Zuxiang Discusses Zhang Tianyi].  *Xin wenxue shiliao*
     [Historical Materials on Modern Literature].  No. 2, 1981.
     Pp. 122-128.  沈承寬，吳福輝，吳組緗談
     張天翼，新文學史料

Shen Zhenyu.  "Shilun Wu Zuxiang de xiaoshuo chuangzuo" [A
     Tentative Essay on Wu Zuxiang's Fiction].  In *Zhongguo wenxue
     yanjiu* [Research on Chinese Literature], eds. Lu Yaodong,
     Huang Manjun, and Zhou Bo.  Wuhan: Hubei sheng wenxue xuehui,
     1981.  Pp. 333-351.  沈振煜，試論吳組緗的小說
     創作，中國文學研究，陸耀東，黃曼君，周勃

Shi Zhecun.  "Modao" [Injurious Courses].  *Mei yu zhi xi* [Spring
     Showers at Dusk].  Shanghai: Xin Zhongguo shuju, 1933.  Pp.
     47-72.  施蟄存，魔道．梅雨之夕

Sima Changfeng. *Xin wenxue congtan* [Collected Discussions on Modern Literature]. Hong Kong: Shaoming chubanshe, 1975.
司馬長風, 新文學叢談

------. *Zhongguo xin wenxue shi* [A History of Modern Chinese Literature]. 3 vols. Hong Kong: Zhao ming chubanshe, 1978.
中國新文學史

Su Fei. "Du *Wenxue* chuangzuo zhuanhao" [On Reading the Special Issue on Creative Writing in *Literature*]. *Wenxue*. Vol. 3, no. 1 (Jul. 1934). P. 489. 蘇韮, 讀文學創作 專號, 文學

Tang Yuan. *Wu Zuxiang zuopin xinshang* [Wu Zuxiang's Works: An Appreciation]. Nanning: Guangxi renmin chubanshe, 1986. Eight-story anthology. 唐沅, 吳組緗作品欣賞

Umemura Yoshiyuki, trans. "Rikyō no zenya" [On the Eve of Leaving Home]. *Bungaku Geppō* [Literature Monthly]. No. 54 (Sep. 1939), pp. 73-77. 梅村良之, 離鄉の前夜, 文學月報

Wang Hanzhuo (pseud. Bai Pin). "Wu Zuxiang de *Xi liu ji*" [Wu Zuxiang's *West Willow*]. *Qinghua zhoukan*. Vol. 42, no. 1 (Oct. 1934). Pp. 131-134. 王漢倬 (筆名白蘋), 吳組緗的西柳集

Wang Jiayu. "Du *Wenxue* chuangzuo zhuanhao hou" [After Reading the Special Issue on Creative Writing in *Literature*]. *Wenxue*. Vol. 3, no. 1, p. 489. 王家瑜, 讀文學創作 專號後, 文學

Wang Ruowang. "Zhannian han" [The Indentured Fiancé]. In *Yanbuzhu de guangmang* [Glory That Can't Be Covered Up].

Beijing: Renmin wenxue chubanshe, 1983. 王若望,
站年漢, 掩不住的光芒

Wang Tongzhao. "Fu zi" [Father and Son]. In *Wang Tongzhao wenji*
[Collected Writings of Wang Tongzhao]. Vol. 1. Ji'nan:
Shandong renmin chubanshe, 1980). 王統照, 父子,
王統照文集

Wang Yao. *Zhongguo xin wenxue shi gao* [A Draft History of Modern
Chinese Literature]. 1951; rpt. Hong Kong: Bowen shuju,
1972. 王瑤, 中國新文學史稿

------. Personal interview. 19 April 1983.

Wei Chaoran. "Lun Wu Zuxiang kangzhan qian de duanpian xiaoshuo"
[The Pre-war Short Stories of Wu Zuxiang]. *Anhui daxue
xuebao* [Anhui University Journal]. No. 1, 1985. Pp. 81-86.
魏超然, 論吳組緗抗戰前的短篇
小說, 安徽大學學報

Wu Baohua. Personal interview. 14 May 1983. 吳報華

Wu Fengnian. Personal interview. 14 May 1983. 吳奉年

Wu Jinglin. Personal interview. 14 May 1983. 吳景琳

Wu Monong. Personal interview. 14 May 1983. 吳沫濃

Wu Xiaohan. Personal interview. 15 May 1983. 吳效韓

Wu Zuxiang. Interview by Perry Link. August 1981.

Wu Zuxiang. Personal interviews. *1982:* 18 Sep., 2 Oct., 22
Oct., 7 Nov., 24 Nov., 7 December, and 29 December.
*1983:* 7 March, 23 March, and 7 May.

Xia Mianzun, ed. *Shinian* [A Decade]. Shanghai: Kaiming shudian,
1936. 夏丏尊, 十年

Xing Tiehua. "Wu Zuxiang ji qi zuopin" [Wu Zuxiang and His

Writings]. *Yi tan* [The Pool of Art]. No. 1, 1982.
Pp. 117-119. 邢鐵華，吳組緗及其作品，
藝潭

Xu Dishan. "Yuguan." In *Wei chao zhui jian* [Missives From an
Imperilled Nest]. 1947; rpt. Hong Kong: Zhaoli chubanshe,
1977. Pp. 172-232. 許地山，玉官，危巢墜簡

Yan Yu. *Canglang shi hua* [Canglang's Comments on Poetry].
Beijing: Renmin wenxue chubanshe, 1961. 嚴羽，
滄浪詩話

Yao Xueyin. "Cha ban che maijie" [Off By Half a Cartload of
Wheatstraw]. *Wenyi zhendi* [The Literature Front]. Vol. 1,
no. 3 (May 1938). 姚雪垠，差半車麥稭，
文藝陣地

Ye Yiqun. "*Yazui lao* du hou" [After Reading *Duckbill Deluge*].
*Kangzhan wenyi*. Vol. 9, nos. 1-2 (Feb. 1944).
葉以群，鴨嘴澇讀後，抗戰文藝

Yu Zhigong. "Feng Yuxiang Xiansheng yu wenyi jie" [Feng Yuxiang
and Literary Circles]. *Xin wenxue shiliao*. No. 2 (May),
1983. Pp. 244-249. 于志恭，馮玉祥與
文藝界，新文學史料

Yuan Liangjun. "Bai lian gang huawei rao zhi rou--Wu Zuxiang
xiaoshuo yishu manbi" [Tempered Steel Pounded Into Flexible
Wire--an Informal Look at Wu Zuxiang's Fictional Art].
*Beijing daxue xuebao*. No. 6 (Dec.), 1982. Pp. 50-60.
袁良駿，百煉鋼化為繞指柔吳組緗小說
藝術漫筆，北京大學學報

Zeng Zhennan. "Shan xiang min hun de xiezhen--du *Shan hong*"

[Reading *Mountain Torrent*--a portrait of the Soul of Countryside Hill Folk]. *Shu lin* [Forest of Books]. No. 3, 1983. Pp. 35-36. 曾鎮南，山鄉民魂的寫真讀山洪，書林

Zhang Henshui. *Ti xiao yinyuan* [Fate in Tears and Laughter]. Shanghai: Sanyou shushe, 1930. 張恨水，啼笑因緣

Zhang Yuanxi. "Ji Feng Yuxiang zai Meiguo de nei yi nian" [My Recollections of the Year Feng Yuxiang Was in America]. *Zhuanji wenxue* [Biographical Literature]. Vol. 38 (1978): no. 3 (Sep./pp. 28-30), no. 4 (Oct./pp. 77-80), and no. 5 (Nov./pp. 55-59). 章元義，記馮玉祥在美國的那一年，傳記文學

Zhao Yuan. "Wu Zuxiang ji qi tongdai zuojia" [Wu Zuxiang and His Contemporaries]. *Shiyue*. No. 1, 1984. 趙園，吳組緗及其同代作家，十月

Zheng Zhenduo. *Zhongguo wenxue yanjiu* [Studies in Chinese Literature]. 3 vols. Beijing: Zuojia chubanshe, 1957. 鄭振鐸，中國文學研究

Zhong Fang. "Du *Wenxue jikan* chuangkanhao" [A Reading of the Inaugural Issue of *Literature Quarterly*]. *Shen bao*. 1 Feb. 1934. P. 19. 仲方，讀文學季刊創刊號，申報

*Zhongguo wenxue jia cidian* [A Dictionary of Chinese Writers]. Ed. Beijing Language Institute Editorial Group. Vol. 1 (moderns). Chengdu: Sichuan renmin chubanshe, 1979. 中國文學家辭典

*Zhongguo xin wenxue da xi, 1927-37* [The Great Series in Modern Chinese Literature, 1927-37]. Vol. 10: Prose. Shanghai:

Shanghai wenyi chubanshe, 1986. 中國新文學大系

Zhou Zuoren. "Wenyi de tongyi" [The Unification of Literature].
*Zhou Zuoren xuanji* [An Anthology of Zhou Zuoren]. Hong Kong:
Xianggang wenxue yanjiushe, n.d. Pp. 11-13. 周作人,

文藝的統一, 周作人選集

Zhu Ziqing. "Lun baihua: du *Nan bei ji* (Mu Shiying zuo) yu *Xiao
Bide* (Zhang Tianyi zuo) de ganxiang" [An Essay On the
Vernacular: Reactions to Reading Mu Shiying's *North and South
Poles* and Zhang Tianyi's *Little Peter*]. *Ni wo* [You and Me].
1936; rpt. Hong Kong: Taiping shuju, 1963. Pp. 155-160.

朱自清. 論白話讀南北極 (穆時英作)
與小彼德 (張天翼作), 你我

------. *Jingdian chang tan* [An Ordinary Discussion of the
Classics]. 1946; rpt. Beijing: Sanlian shudian, 1980.

經典常談

# Glossary

| | | | |
|---|---|---|---|
| Ah Bao | 阿寶 | cu | 粗 |
| Ah Yuan | 阿圓 | Da Boniang | 大伯娘 |
| An'gang | 鞍鋼 | da hu renjia | 大戶人家 |
| Anqing | 安慶 | Da Hua | 大花 |
| "Aoyu tuo jin gui" | 鰲魚馱金龜 | Da Mao | 大毛 |
| Ba Jin | 巴金 | da tang shu | 大堂叔 |
| Baizi | 白子 | dandan de bei'ai | 淡淡的悲哀 |
| bian | 扁 | dao meizi | 搗妹子 |
| "Bing yu" | 病愈 | Deng Chumin | 鄧初民 |
| Bo Juyi | 白居易 | Deng Xiaoping | 鄧小平 |
| Botang | 柏堂 | Die | 蝶 |
| bu luo yan quan | 不落言筌 | diguozhuyizhe | 帝國主義者 |
| Buqing | 步青 | dizhu | 帝主 |
| "Caiyuan" | 菜園 | Ding Ling | 丁玲 |
| "Cao dun shang" | 草墩上 | Dong Laodie | 東老爹 |
| Cao Xueqin | 曹雪芹 | Donglin | 東林 |
| Cao Yu | 曹禺 | Dong Zhicheng | 董志誠 |
| Chen | 陳 | Er Gugu | 二姑姑 |
| chenchen | 沈沈 | er ke | 二刻 |
| Chizhi daxue | 持志大學 | er tang shu | 二堂叔 |
| "    " fushu zhongxue | 附屬中學 | fei sha | 飛沙 |
| <u>Chu ci</u> | 楚辭 | Fengcun | 鳳村 |
| chu ke | 初刻 | Feng Jifa | 馮紀發 |
| chuanqi | 傳奇 | fengjian | 封建 |
| cidi | 此地 | Feng Suzhu | 馮素珠 |

---

*This glossary omits authors and titles that have their own
listings in the bibliographical sections above.

| | | | | |
|---|---|---|---|---|
| Feng Xiaoda | 馮 小 達 | | huang mei xi | 黃 梅 戲 |
| Feng Xuefeng | 馮 雪 峰 | | Huang Xiaodou | 黃 小 斗 |
| Fengyuan | 豐 垣 | | Huizhou | 徽 州 |
| Fu Baozi | 福 寶 子 | | Ji'nan | 濟 南 |
| Fu qun xiaoxue | 福 群 小 學 | | ji shi | 記 事 |
| gainianhua | 概 念 化 | | ji yan | 記 言 |
| ganqing | 感 情 | | Jia | 佳 |
| ge jiu qu | 歌 舊 曲 | | Jiaqing | 嘉 慶 |
| geng du renjia | 耕 讀 人 家 | | Jia Zheng | 賈 政 |
| Gongan | 公 安 | | Jiangbei | 江 北 |
| Gouzi | 狗 子 | | jiao | 角 |
| "Guxiang" | 故 鄉 | | Jin Jiafeng | 金 家 鳳 |
| Guan Di | 關 帝 | | Jin Shengtan | 金 聖 嘆 |
| Guihua Saozi | 桂 花 嫂 子 | | jinshi | 進 士 |
| Guo Moruo | 郭 沫 若 | | Jingyuan | 景 元 |
| guowen jiaoyuan | 國 文 教 員 | | Jiu | 鳩 |
| Hadai | 哈 代 | | jiuguo | 救 國 |
| Hanlin | 翰 林 | | juren | 舉 人 |
| "Han lu" | 旱 麓 | | Juewu | 覺 悟 |
| Han Yu | 韓 愈 | | Kang Youwei | 康 有 為 |
| Hanzhi | 翰 芝 | | Kangri zaobao | 抗 日 早 報 |
| haohaodangdang | 浩 浩 蕩 蕩 | | kong | 空 |
| Hekou | 河 口 | | "Kong Yiji" | 孔 乙 己 |
| He Shaoji | 何 紹 基 | | Lai Yali | 賴 亞 力 |
| heidong | 黑 洞 | | Lan Hua | 蘭 花 |
| henhen | 狠 狠 | | lao | 老 |
| Huniu | 虎 妞 | | Lao Bage | 老 八 哥 |

| | | | | |
|---|---|---|---|---|
| Laorui | 勞瑞 | Meirong | 美容 |
| Lao Tongbao | 老通寶 | men | 們 |
| Lao Yi | 老易 | Minzhai | 敏齋 |
| Lao Zhu | 老朱 | ming'an | 明暗 |
| lena | 勒吶 | minghuan | 名宦 |
| Li Da | 李達 | Ming-Qing | 明清 |
| lixiang | 裡廂 | Nahan | 吶喊 |
| Li Yu | 李漁 | nai | 倷 |
| Lian Shifu | 蓮師傅 | Nanrong | 南容 |
| Liang Qichao | 梁啓超 | niang xin pei | 釀新醅 |
| Liao zhai zhi yi | 聊齋志異 | niaormen | 鳥兒們 |
| Lin Yutang | 林語堂 | Pai an jingqi | 拍案驚奇 |
| Ling Mengchu | 凌濛初 | Pancun | 潘村 |
| ling zhi cao | 靈芝草 | Pei ying | 培英 |
| Ling Ziyan | 凌子彥 | puluo | 普羅 |
| Liu Dakai | 劉大開 | qi | 奇 |
| Liu Dequan | 劉德全 | qifang | 七房 |
| Liu Jiahua | 劉甲華 | Qiye | 七爺 |
| Liu Wendian | 劉文典 | Qianlong | 乾隆 |
| Liu Xiping | 劉希平 | Qinghong bang | 青紅幫 |
| Liu Zongyuan | 柳宗元 | Qinghua zhoukan | 清華週刊 |
| Lu Rouji | 陸柔姬 | fukan | 副刊 |
| Luotuo Xiangzi | 駱駝祥子 | qingxiang | 傾向 |
| man | 滿 | quan | 全 |
| Maolin | 茂林 | ren xin da bian | 人心大變 |
| Mao Zedong | 毛澤東 | Runtu | 閏土 |
| Meihua jiao | 梅花腳 | san chi jian | 三尺劍 |

| | | | |
|---|---|---|---|
| San Taitai | 三太太 | suxie | 速寫 |
| Shaoxuan | 紹軒 | Tian Han | 田漢 |
| she hui[snake society] | 蛇會 | Tie Bajiao saozi | 鐵芭蕉嫂子 |
| shehui | 社會 | ting xi | 聽戲 |
| Shen Congwen | 沈從文 | tongxun | 通訊 |
| Shen Hanpu | 沈漢朴 | tufei | 土匪 |
| Shen Shuyuan | 沈菽園 | Wan'an | 皖安 |
| shengyuan | 生員 | Wang Gulu | 王古魯 |
| Shi jing | 詩經 | Wang Mian | 王冕 |
| Shi shuo xin yu | 世說新語 | Wang Xiaofu | 王小福 |
| Shiyue | 十月 | Wang Xuezi | 王雪姿 |
| shiyun | 世運 | Wang Zhongrong | 王仲榮 |
| Shuhong | 叔鴻 | Wei Jingsheng | 魏京生 |
| Shu jing | 書經 | Weisheng(character) | 渭生 |
| Shuangxi | 雙喜 | Weisheng(cousin) | 畏生 |
| "Shui" | 水 | Wei Zhongxian | 魏忠賢 |
| Shuihu zhuan | 水滸傳 | wenhua zhan | 文化站 |
| Shuyuan[bean garden] | 菽園 | wenming | 文明 |
| Shuyuan[graceful maiden] | 淑媛 | wen yuan | 文苑 |
| Si Gouzi | 四狗子 | wuchanjieji | 無產階級 |
| sima di | 司馬第 | wu che shu | 五車書 |
| sishu | 私塾 | Wu Dashen | 吳大紳 |
| Si Taitai | 四太太 | Wu Di(nickname) | 吳弟 |
| Song | 宋 | Wu Di(pen name) | 蕪帝 |
| Song Jiang | 宋江 | Wu Fangpei | 吳芳培 |
| Songling | 松齡 | Wu Gang | 吳剛 |
| Songshou | 松壽 | Wu Ge | 吳哥 |

| | | | |
|---|---|---|---|
| Wuhan | 武漢 | xingyun | 幸運 |
| Wuhu | 蕪湖 | Xu Zhenya | 徐枕亞 |
| Wu Jixin | 吳季莘 | Xuzhou | 徐州 |
| Wu Jianzi | 吳鑒字 | Xuancheng | 宣城 |
| Wu Jingzi | 吳敬梓 | yanjiu shi | 研究室 |
| wujiu | 烏桕 | Yang Bojun | 楊伯峻 |
| Wu Qingyu | 吳慶餘 | Yang zheng xiaoxue | 養正小學 |
| Wu Runbao | 吳潤寶 | yecaomen | 野草們 |
| Wu Shangmo | 吳尚默 | ye haizi | 野孩子 |
| Wu Shaolie | 吳紹烈 | Ye Mingchen | 葉銘琛 |
| Wu Shifan | 吳世蕃 | yi | 一 |
| Wu Shiji | 吳士驥 | Yishan lizuan | 義山離纂 |
| Wu Weijun | 吳維駿 | yi shen zuo ze | 以身作則 |
| Wu Xiaohan | 吳效韓 | yinshi | 隱士 |
| Wu Yanglie | 吳楊烈 | Yu Dafu | 郁達夫 |
| Xikou | 溪口 | Yu Huaxin | 余華心 |
| Xianzi | 線子 | Yu ying xiaoxue | 育英小學 |
| Xiangfa | 祥發 | yu yue yu yuan | 魚躍于淵 |
| Xianglin sao | 祥林嫂 | yuan fei li tian | 鳶飛戾天 |
| Xiao Hong | 蕭紅 | Yuan fei yu yue | 鳶飛魚躍 |
| Xiao Hua | 小花 | zhai | 齋 |
| Xiao Huaizi | 小槐子 | Yuan Zhen | 元稹 |
| Xiao Tanzi | 小炭子 | Zeng Guofan | 曾國藩 |
| xiaoxiao | 小小 | zha | 猹 |
| Xin miao | 新苗 | zhanlong | 站籠 |
| Xin min zhongxue | 新民中學 | Zhang Huasuo | 張華索 |
| Xinqiao | 鑫橋 | Zhang Sanguan | 章三官 |

| | |
|---|---|
| Zhang Ziping | 張資平 |
| <u>Zhe shan</u> | 赭山 |
| zheng | 整 |
| Zhonghua quanguo wenyijie kangdi xiehui | 中華全國文藝界抗敵協會 |
| Zhong Kui | 鍾馗 |
| Zhongyang daxue | 中央大學 |
| Zhou Enlai | 周恩來 |
| Zhou Yang | 周陽 |
| Zhou Zuoren | 周作人 |
| "Zhu fu" | 祝福 |
| Zhutang | 竹堂 |
| Zishou | 子壽 |
| "Ziyou tan" | 自由談 |
| zongpu | 宗譜 |
| Zuxiang[ancestral scroll sheath] | 祖紺 |
| Zuxiang[organized scroll sheath] | 組紺 |
| <u>Zuo zhuan</u> | 左傳 |

# About the Book
# and Author

This ground-breaking book is the first in-depth study of Wu Zuxiang, one of modern China's most distinguished writers on rural life. Philip Williams surveys Wu's literary career, provides a critical examination of his *oeuvre,* and traces his life after the establishment of the People's Republic of China—a time when Wu no longer wrote fiction. The author's jargon-free literary analysis, combined with his meticulous biographical and historical research, illuminates Wu's development as both writer and social critic.

Tracing Wu's increasing emphasis on peasant solidarity in China, Williams explores how this Beijing-educated writer was able to avoid the common leftist pitfall of presenting biased and oversimplified portrayals of problems faced by clan elites. The author discusses the subsequent charges of "petty bourgeois objectivism" leveled against Wu by influential leaders in Shanghai's powerful League of Left-wing Writers, providing a fascinating case study of the challenges faced by *engagé* writers outside the League.

Drawing on interviews and previously unavailable, unpublished diaries, Williams provides an intimate exploration of the issues and ideas animating Wu's fiction. A selection of the writer's dream accounts sheds new light on the motif of the uncanny within his essentially realist *oeuvre.* Wu's writing departed from that of his contemporaries when he began to explore in depth the possibilities for ironic and unreliable narration, adeptly raising it to a new level of complexity. "The Verdant Bamboo Hermitage" is an example of stories in which Wu presaged such works of "metafiction" as Nabokov's *Pale Fire.* Wu's view of the writer as social critic blended both with novelists such as Turgenev, Eliot, and Tolstoy and with the traditional Chinese view that moral insights typically inform serious writing. It is within this larger literary context that Williams fully reveals the originality of Wu's psychological acuity and unique auditory techniques.

Philip F. Williams is assistant professor of Chinese and Asian languages coordinator at Arizona State University.

# Index

Abstractions, 137, 138, 139, 146, 174, 234(n54)
Adams, Percy, 110, 229(n67)
*After-hours Anthology, An,* 104, 106
Agriculture, 13, 247(n5)
Ai Wu, 6
Alienation, 30–31, 42
Ambivalence, 22
Ancestors/elders, 24
Anderson, Marston, 137, 213(n57), 226(n31), 227(n37), 230(n98), 234(n58)
Andreyev, Leonid, 3
Anomie. *See under* Rural issues
Anqing, 122
*Anthology of Fiction and Prose by Wu Zuxiang,* 30
Anti-Rightist Purge of 1957–1958, 189
Aristotle, 80, 82, 163, 222(n89)
Aural qualities. *See* Description, aural vs. visual; Dialogue
Austen, Jane, 66, 167, 169
Authoritarianism, 188
Authority issues, 3, 27, 36, 84, 93, 118, 132
Autobiographical elements, 51, 79, 86, 87, 98–100, 104–105, 113, 122, 130, 155, 160, 170, 205(n16), 211(n23), 218(n28). *See also* Diaries, entries; Memoirs; Wu Zuxiang, relationship between life and works

"Back Street, The," 7
Ba Jin, 106, 140, 160, 228(n56), 231(n4)
Barlow, Tani, 226(n32)
Barnett, Doak, 193

Barth, John, 3, 239(n26)
Barthes, Roland, 175
Beggars, 114–115
Beijing, 2, 101, 183, 188, 193, 232(n19), 245(n41)
  Beijing University, 189, 194
  pro-democracy demonstrations (1989), 129
  *See also* Qinghua University
Benevolence, 30, 113, 130, 196
Bodde, Derk, 85
*Book of Odes, The,* 23
Booth, Wayne, 161, 173
Bowdlerizations, 214(n83), 215(n95)
Bradbury, Malcolm, 173
Bronte, Emily, 167
Brooks, Peter, 44

Calligraphy, 16, 19
*Canglang shi hua* (Yan Yu), 147
Cao Xueqin, 157
Cao Yu, 44
Capitalism, 194
Caserio, Robert, 239(n25)
Cassia trees, 81, 85–86
Central University, 125, 140, 184, 185, 188
"Certain Day, A," 5, 6, 116–120, 133, 136, 164, 178, 179, 230(n88)
Chambers of commerce, 96
Chang, Randall, 36
Chao, Yuen Ren, 176
Characterization, 145–157, 163
Chastity, 66
Chekhov, Anton, 9, 97, 147–148
Cheng Peikai, 65, 79, 81, 94, 119, 131, 213(n70)

*Cherry Orchard, The* (Chekhov), 97

Chiang Kai-shek, 1, 3, 104, 185, 186–187, 188, 217(n4), 244(n20)

Chiang Yee, 49

Chinese Writer's Association, 189

Chongqing, 26, 122, 136. *See also* Central University

Chou Chih-p'ing, 203(n29)

Chow Tse-tsung, 128–129

Christians, 84

Civil War, 187, 188, 190, 193

Classical Chinese, 21

Class issues, 37–42, 96, 196, 197, 198, 212(n42), 247(n4). *See also* Elites; Upperclass

Climaxes, 47, 228(n53)

Communist Party, 1, 3, 128, 141, 184, 185, 189, 217(n4), 237(n38)

Compensatory, relation between life and works, 90, 91–92

Confucianism, 14, 16, 17, 205(n17)

Corruption, 119, 123, 124–125

Crowds, 137, 177–179, 234(n58)

Cultural Revolution, 184, 189–190, 194, 246(n46). *See also* Red Guards

Democracy, 188, 244(n18)

Deng Chumin, 112

Deng Xiaoping, 192, 193, 194, 195

Denunciation campaigns, 101, 193–194, 246(n46)

Description, aural vs. visual, 36, 71, 89, 197

"Deserted Village, The" (Goldsmith), 67–68, 69, 85

Dialects, 54

Dialogue, 29, 30, 36, 44, 79–80, 92, 102, 106, 109, 110, 139, 145, 197. *See also* Symposia

Diaries, 189
    entries, 71, 98, 130, 139, 140, 154, 155, 184, 188, 191, 192, 220(n50), 230(n80), 244(nn 18, 20)
    of Feng Yuxiang, 187

Didacticism, 71, 140, 147, 190, 192

Ding Ling, 10, 193, 226(nn 31, 32), 242(n3), 246(n46)

Disillusionment, 29, 72

Doleželová-Velingerová, Milena, 65

Dong Meng, 80

Dong Zhicheng, 112

Doubles, 81–82

*Dream of the Red Chamber,* 21–22, 53, 170, 205(n17), 244(n23)

Dreams, 7, 26–27, 39–40, 48, 58, 63, 64, 74, 79, 82, 98, 156, 157, 192, 208(n63), 211–212(nn 32, 33), 245(n37). *See also* Nightmares

Duty, 8, 35, 91, 100, 120

*Dwarf Bamboo* (Nagai Kafū), 139

Economic issues. *See* Great Depression; Poverty; *under* Rural issues

Education, 13, 16, 191. *See also under* Wu Zuxiang

"1800 Bushels," 3–4, 5, 24, 75, 92–102, 133, 149, 150, 151, 156, 159, 160, 165, 166, 175, 176, 177, 179, 197, 224(n2), 227(n37), 238(n8)

Eliot, George, 3, 167, 174, 176

Elites, 2, 3, 5, 6, 8, 38–39, 43, 93, 95, 96, 97, 100, 102, 116, 119, 120, 124, 125, 132, 133, 151, 159, 160, 177, 178, 179, 196, 216(n102). *See also* Upperclass

Elliot, Ebenezer, 59

Ellman, Richard, 9

Emotions, 169–171, 180

*Engagé* literature, 3, 8–9, 101

Essays, 7, 8, 27, 40, 79, 121, 183, 187, 188, 192, 195, 243(n4)
    fictionalized travel, 110–116, 229(n68)
    *See also* Memoirs

Examinations, 13, 15, 26, 204(n14), 209(n71)

Exclamations, 23, 29, 46

Executions, 5, 57–58, 177

Exile, 91, 122, 138

Exposé elements, 123, 124, 125

Fables, 22, 105, 206(n41)

"Facing My Lamp," 7

"Fall of the House of Usher" (Poe), 65–66

Family issues, 35–36, 42–46, 82, 83, 102–103, 139, 210(nn 11, 17)

Famine relief, 100

"Fan Hamlet," 80–87, 105, 152, 155, 160, 164, 197, 222(nn 83, 86)

Fate, 151–152

*Fate in Tears and Laughter* (Zhang Henshui), 171

"Father and Son" (Wang Tongzhao), 84

"Faust: A Story in Nine Letters" (Turgenev), 153–154, 157

Feidelson, Charles, Jr., 9

Fei Xiaotong, 209(n76)

Feng Suzhu (mother), 16, 17, 27, 43–44, 122, 155, 205(n23), 208(n63)

Feng Xiaoda, 187, 243(n14)

Feng Xuefeng, 193, 246(n46)

Feng Yuxiang, 103–104, 112, 122, 125, 130, 184–188, 186(photo), 230(n80), 243(nn 12, 14)

Feudalism, 35, 210(n11)

Feuerwerker, Yi-tsi, 100, 226(n31)

"Few Personal Views on the National United Front of Literary Circles, A," 121, 231(n2)

Fiction writing, role of, 65

Fire symbolism, 85

Flashbacks, 73, 104, 164–165, 166

Flaubert, Gustave, 9, 202(n25)

Fletcher, John, 173

"Flowering Gardenia, The," 47–51, 60, 61, 79, 155, 159, 165, 177

Foreigners, 59, 174

Foreshadowing, 45–46, 63, 93, 118, 165–166

Forster, E. M., 163

Freud, Sigmund, 26, 39, 40, 48, 73, 83, 156, 211–212(nn 32, 33)

Frye, Northrop, 89

Garland, Hamlin, 159, 238(n6)

Generalizations, 146. *See also* Abstractions

Genette, Gérard, 159

Ghost stories, 19, 172

Glicksberg, Charles I., 202(n18)

"Golden Tortoise Straddles a Sea Turtle, The" (folk tale), 22

Goldsmith, Oliver, 67–68, 69, 85, 219(n36)

Goncharov, Ivan, 139

*Gongan* school of writing, 8

Gothic horror stories, 65, 218(n21)

Grassroots solidarity. *See* Rural issues, solidarity among masses

Great Depression, 7, 8, 46, 49, 59, 76, 79, 94, 98, 174

Grotesque elements, 129–130

Guerrillas, 133, 134, 179. *See also* Soldiers

Guetti, James, 36

Guilt, 7

Gunn, Edward, 137

Guo Moruo, 170, 240(n20)

Hadfield, J. A., 155, 156

Hanan, Patrick, 79, 162, 247(n1)

Hawthorne, Nathaniel, 65

Hemingway, Ernest, 102

"He Sings of Ramona," 28, 29, 30, 52

Hightower, James, 67

Historical change, 61. *See also* Rural issues, past vs. present

Homer, 164

Hsia, C. T., 55, 80, 84, 93, 96, 191

Hsia, T. A., 6

Hsi-sheng Ch'i, 134

Humor, 39, 56, 66, 102, 126, 129–130, 135, 136, 211(n29), 213(n70), 227(n36)

Hundred Flowers Campaign, 189, 192, 194

*Hunting Sketches* (Turgenev), 149, 150

Huters, Theodore, 164

Iconoclasm, 78, 80, 81, 86

Idealism, 15, 114, 150

Ideology, 184, 192, 234(n45)

"Ill-fated Little Plant, The," 20–21

"Injurious Courses" (Shi Zhecun), 66

Injustice, 37–42, 58, 97, 107–108, 129

"In Memory of Lu'er," 104

Insanity, 67, 69
Irony, 3, 25, 54, 63, 66, 158, 161–162,
    163, 215(n84)
Irrationality, 40, 62, 79, 153–156, 157
Isaacs, Harold, 100
Isolation, 30. *See also* Alienation

James, Henry, 9, 45, 159
Japanese invasion of 1937, 3, 91, 113,
    116, 120, 121, 140, 190, 233(n43).
    *See also* War of Resistance
Jiangbei, 107
Jiang Guangci, 2
Jingxian, 87, 206(n32)
Jin Shengtan, 59
Johnson, Chalmers, 132
Johnson, Mark, 156, 171, 174

*Kangri zao bao*, 130
Kang Youwei, 15, 204(n14)
Kinkley, Jeffrey, 242(n3)
Klöpsch, Volker, 138
KMT. *See* Nationalists
"Kong Yiji" (Lu Xun), 162
Krieger, Murray, 82

Lai Yali, 112, 130
Lakoff, George, 156, 171, 174
Langer, Suzanne, 82
Lanser, Susan, 159
Lao She, 54, 101, 117, 139, 148, 189, 198,
    231(n4)
Larson, Wendy, 101
League of Left-wing Writers, 4, 101,
    190
Lee, Leo Ou-fan, 160, 215(n93)
Levenson, Joseph, 184
Lewald, H. Ernest, 6
Liang Qichao, 15, 148
*Liao zhai zhi yi*, 172
Li Changzhi, 136
Li Da, 112
Ling Mengchu, 79
Lin Huanping, 124
Li Shangyin, 41, 134, 233(n41)
Literary controls, 141, 188, 190–191,
    197, 237(n28)

Literary research, 183, 194, 244(n23)
"Little Lord Guanguan's Tonic," 3, 5,
    54–60, 78, 152, 158, 160, 161–162,
    164, 166, 168, 174, 175, 177, 179,
    214(n83), 237(n2)
Liu Jiahua, 140
Liu Wendian, 33(photo), 103
Liu Xiping, 20
*Lost in the Funhouse* (Barth), 3
Love, 51, 52, 56, 82, 170, 171–172, 173,
    214(n76), 215(n93)
    maternal, 35, 210(n10)
Lowdermilk, Walter, 186
*Luotuo Xiangzi* (Lao She), 117
Lu Xun, 2, 3, 4, 36, 41, 42, 58, 72, 100–
    101, 106, 132, 152, 160, 162, 163–
    164, 166, 170, 192, 195, 197,
    215(n84), 226(nn 34, 35, 36),
    228(n54), 240(n20), 247(n3)
Lyell, William, 36

McDougall, Bonnie, 9, 202(n25)
Mahjongg, 43, 44
Malaria, 16, 75, 205(n20)
Mallory, William, 49, 133–134
Mao Dun, 4, 9, 70–71, 78, 79, 80, 84,
    100, 105–106, 146–147, 174,
    220(n49), 228(n53)
Maolin village, 1–2, 4, 13, 17–19, 24, 26,
    32, 85, 86, 95, 98, 102, 122, 132,
    206(n32)
Mao Zedong, 4, 141, 184, 188, 190, 191,
    194, 197, 244(n20)
Marriage, 36, 52, 217(n5)
Marx, Karl, 132. *See also* Marxist
    critics/theory
Marxist critics/theory, 149, 153, 192
Masuda Wataru, 39, 101, 226(n36)
Matricide. *See* Parricide
Maupassant, Guy de, 65, 81, 102, 158,
    162, 163, 215(n86), 237(n3)
May Fourth writers, 166, 170, 190, 191,
    196, 203(n29). *See also* New Culture
    Movement
Melancholy, 220(n50)

Meliorism, 7–8, 46, 56, 66, 70, 75, 101–
102, 120, 121, 125, 132, 148, 157,
171, 197, 198, 236(n19)
and injustice, 58
and metaphors, 180
and piquancy, 10, 114, 115, 131
and realism, 9
use of term, 202(n24)
Melodrama, 44–45, 57
Melville, Herman, 163, 239(n25)
Memoirs, 191, 192, 245(n29)
"Memories of My Childhood Days,"
104
Memory, 5, 17, 72–73
Meta-fiction, 3
Metaphors, 167–180, 239(n2). *See also*
Personification
Metonymy, 109
*Middlemarch* (Eliot), 167, 174
Migrants, 88, 89, 221(n63)
Milosz, Czeslaw, 193, 244(n23)
*Minguo ribao*, 20
*Miscellanea of Yishan* (Li Shangyin), 41
"Miss Jin and the Xue Girl," 51–54, 60,
155, 169, 170, 171, 173, 177, 198
*Mountain Torrent (Shan hong)*, 5, 6, 121,
132–140, 159, 166, 178–179, 190,
195, 197, 233(nn 37, 38)
Mount Tai, 110
Mu Shiying, 162–163, 238(n6)
"My Old Home" (Lu Xun), 3, 4, 72, 197
*Mythologies* (Barthes), 175

Nabokov, Vladimir, 3
Nagai Kafū, 139
*Nan bei ji* (Mu Shiying), 162–163
Nanjing, 23, 107, 110, 116, 193
Central Research Institute, 103
Renovate-the-People Middle School,
23, 207(n44)
Women's Academy of Arts and
Sciences, 188
Narrators, 42, 65, 72, 126, 137, 158–166,
214(n84), 218(n21), 238(nn 6, 8)
Nationalism, 126, 132, 138, 141

Nationalists (KMT), 1, 59, 122, 140, 190,
233(n27), 234(n45). *See also* Chiang
Kai-shek; Feng Yuxiang
Naturalism, 45, 46, 57, 159
New Culture Movement, 19, 20, 196,
202(n25)
New Fourth Army Incident, 1
*New Observer* (journal), 193
"New Year's Sacrifice, The" (Lu Xun),
41, 42, 162
Ng, Mau-sang, 215(n86)
Nightmares, 40, 48, 60, 82, 154–155,
211(n28). *See also* Dreams
*Northanger Abbey* (Austen), 66
Nostalgia, 72, 104

Objectivism/objectivity, 9, 70–71, 106,
147, 203(n26), 219(n42), 228(n53)
O'Connor, Frank, 50
Oedipus complex, 83–84
"Off by a Cartload of Wheatstraw"
(Yao Xueyin), 131
"On My Dreams," 40
Onomatopoeia, 37
"On the Eve of Leaving Home," 28, 30,
33–37, 60, 62, 71, 160, 168, 170, 177,
205(n23), 210(nn 10, 11)
"On the Grass Heap," 105
"On *Water Margin*," 194
Optimism, 5, 7, 120, 125, 126, 130–131,
141, 180, 185, 190
*Outcry* (Lu Xun), 163
"Ovsianikov, the Freeholder"
(Turgenev), 149, 150, 156

*Pale Fire* (Nabokov), 3
Pan clan, 18
Pan Village, 18, 79
Pan Xiaosong, 98
Parallelism, 19, 21, 22, 206(n37)
Parasitism, 168–169
Parricide, 80, 84
Patriarchy, 3, 75, 110, 180
Peasants, 4, 6, 41, 55, 69, 70, 92, 95, 119,
129, 132, 133–134, 136–137, 138,
161, 198, 233(nn 33, 34). *See also*
Rural issues

People's Liberation Army, 193
People's Republic of China (P.R.C.),
    191–195. *See also* Cultural
    Revolution; Mao Zedong
Perseverance College (Shanghai), 25
Personification, 207(n56), 240(n11)
*Persuasion* (Austen), 167
Pessimism, 9, 120, 188
Piquancy, 39, 50, 66, 71, 102, 120, 127,
    153, 171, 180, 203(n28). *See also
    under* Meliorism
Playscripts, 148
Plot structure, 158, 163–166, 228(n53),
    237(n2), 239(n23)
Poe, Edgar Allen, 65
Poems, 104–105
Populism, 30, 70, 124, 150, 153, 161,
    178, 184, 190, 196
Poverty, 7, 37, 69, 85, 89, 112, 167
Power, 30
P.R.C. *See* People's Republic of China
Proust, Marcel, 73
Prušek, Jaroslav, 44, 58, 201(n3)
Pu Liangpei, 102, 110, 229(n68)
Pye, Lucian, 36, 216(n103)

Qinghua University, 2, 8, 18, 25, 26, 28–
    29, 32, 89–90, 102, 103, 189
    Chinese Literature Association
    members, 33(photo)
Qing period, 148
*Qui shou* (Ai Wu), 6
Qu Qiubai, 7, 202(n16)
*Quwei. See* Piquancy

"Rappaccini's Daughter"
    (Hawthorne), 65–66
Realism, 3, 9, 79, 135, 148, 159, 163,
    202(n25), 235(n58)
Rebelliousness, 21, 23, 24, 36, 96, 100,
    107–108, 132, 152, 153
"Recuperating from an Illness," 104–
    105
Red Guards, 148, 189, 244(n26). *See also*
    Cultural Revolution
Refugees, 85, 122
*Renmin wenxue* (journal), 183, 189

"Requisitioned Boat, The," 121, 122–
    125, 178
Reversals, 82, 222(n89)
Reviews/reviewers, 79–80, 105–106,
    138, 146–147, 166, 174, 220(n49),
    226(n30)
*Romance of the Western Chamber,* 170
*Rulin waishi,* 76
Ruo Ying, 80
Rural issues, 30, 59, 196
    anomie, 8, 43, 67–71
    economic issues, 42–46, 67, 84–85,
        99–100, 102–103, 133, 156, 169, 198,
        204(n12), 212(nn 37, 42), 240(n8).
        *See also* Great Depression; Poverty
    elderly people, 150–151, 153
    norms/values, 35, 212(n42)
    past vs. present, 61–90, 197
    recovery at grassroots level, 91–120,
        167, 180
    rural/urban issues, 2, 30–31, 32–60,
        61, 72, 96, 174, 209(n76), 227(n36),
        247(n2)
    social dislocation, 84, 85, 87. *See also*
        Social decline
    solidarity among masses, 4–5, 7, 75,
        109–110, 116, 118, 119, 120, 160, 167,
        177–179, 180
    vulnerability to predators, 131–132
    women's role, 60, 66, 225(n20)
    *See also* Peasants

Satire, 78–79, 110, 111, 211(n29)
Schorer, Mark, 167, 168, 172, 174,
    239(n2)
Scott, James C., 95, 119, 212(n42),
    240(n8)
Secret societies, 94
Semanov, V. I., 163, 247(n3)
Sentence structure. *See* Parallelism
Sentimentalism, 28, 147
Sex, 51, 66, 129
Shanghai, 4, 23, 25, 26, 54, 56, 101, 112,
    128, 140, 161, 170, 175, 229(n69)
*Shan hong. See Mountain Torrent*
Sha Ting, 139
Shaw, George Bernard, 9

Shen Congwen, 4, 5, 30, 58, 79, 101, 105, 131, 184, 198, 226(n35)
Shen Shuyuan (wife), 25, 35, 98, 185, 189, 208(n57)
Shen Zhenyu, 35, 70, 94, 210(n11)
Sheridan, James, 112, 185, 243(n14)
*Shi shuo xin yu*, 215(n91)
Shi Zhecun, 66
Shklovsky, Victor, 60
"Shui" (Ding Ling), 100–101, 226(nn 31, 32)
*Shu jing*, 102
*Sienna Mountain* (journal), 20
"Sights at Mount Tai," 110, 112–116
Sima Changfeng, 226(n35)
Sisyphus, 85
Sketches, 80
Smith, Arthur H., 217(n5)
"Soaring Hawks and Plunging Fish," 23–25, 29, 30, 207(n56), 223(n108)
Social decline, 67–68, 126, 176. *See also* Rural issues, anomie; Rural issues, social dislocation
Soldiers, 6, 121–122, 123, 133–134, 179, 193, 231(n4)
Sophocles, 83
Sovereignty, 216(n103)
"Splay-petaled Honeysuckle," 3, 71–75, 78, 104, 164–165, 171, 173, 175, 177, 220(nn 49, 50)
"Splendid Village, The" (Elliot), 59
"Spring Silkworms" (Mao Dun), 4
Stalinist-Maoist literary policy, 141. *See also* Literary controls
*Straw Sandals* (anthology), 100–101
Student protests, 128–129
"Stuffy Ironsides," 125–132, 160, 232(nn 12, 13)
Style, 45, 46, 79–80, 102, 158, 161. *See also* Description, aural vs. visual; Dialogue; Piquancy
Suicides, 23, 24, 69, 79, 189
Sullivan, Lawrence R., 232(n19)
Supernatural elements, 64, 66, 153
Superstition, 41, 42, 49, 63, 112
Symposia, 50, 59–60, 99–100, 148–153

*Tai bai* (journal), 106, 228(n45)
Taiping Rebellion, 14
Taiwan, 188
Tanigawa Michio, 196–197, 247(n4)
*Tao jin ji* (Sha Ting), 139
Temples, 79, 85, 95, 112, 113, 151
Theatre, 148
Thomson, Philip, 129
Tian Han, 44
Todorov, Tsvetan, 65, 81, 218(n21)
Tolstoy, Count Lev, 3, 9, 163
Tragedy, 80, 82
Travel essays, 110–116
*Travel Literature and the Evolution of the Novel* (Adams), 110
Trilling, Lionel, 30
Turgenev, Ivan, 3, 7, 9, 149, 150, 153–154, 156–157, 198, 228(n56), 236(n19)
"Twilight," 66, 67–71, 145–146, 160, 164, 170
"Two Young Sparrows," 37–42, 50, 60, 61, 62, 152, 155, 168, 177, 211(n22)
Typicality, 148–153, 237(n28)

United States. *See* Wu Zuxiang, visits to America
Upperclass, 96, 153. *See also* Elites
Uprisings, 95, 132. *See also* Rebelliousness
Urban issues, 49–50, 60, 161, 216(n102). *See also* Rural issues, rural/urban issues; Shanghai

Values, 8, 151, 156, 159, 163, 191. *See also* Rural issues, norms/values
"Vegetable Garden, The," 105
"Verdant Bamboo Hermitage, The," 3, 19, 61–66, 78, 153, 154, 155, 157, 160, 164, 165, 170, 171–173, 175, 177, 183, 195, 197
Vernacular writing, 19, 21–22, 25, 148, 183, 189, 195, 196, 247(n1)
"View of Mine, A," 194
Violence, 46, 57, 98
Virtue(s), 76, 119, 124, 125, 130

Wakeman, Frederic, Jr., 216(n102)
Wang, John, 59
Wang Hanzhuo, 79, 228(n53)
Wang Jiayu, 80
Wang Meng, 164
Wang Ruowang, 135
Wang Tongzhao, 84
Wang Yao, 106, 147, 219(n42), 223(n98)
War of Resistance, 128, 131, 132, 133,
    178, 184. *See also* Japanese invasion
    of 1937
*Water Margin*, 194
Watson, Burton, 102
Wei Jingsheng, 193
*Wenxue* (journal), 80
*Wenxue jikan* (journal), 92
West Hunan, 5
*West Willow* (anthology), 5, 78, 103,
    105–106, 146, 174, 176
Wharton, Edith, 163
"Woman, The," 106–110
Women, 6, 17, 60, 107, 108, 122,
    207(n56), 225(n20)
    widows, 66
"Woodcutter, The," 27–28, 87–89, 104,
    160, 177, 183, 205(n23), 224(n111)
"World at Peace, The," 76–80, 105, 156,
    160, 164, 168–169, 174, 177,
    221(n61)
World War II, 5
Wu Fangpei, 14
Wu Gang (mythical figure), 85
Wuhan, 122, 184
Wuhu, 87, 206(n32)
    Number Five Provincial Middle
        School, 19–20
Wu Jingzi, 15
Wu Jixin, 15, 204(n10)
Wu Qingyu (father), 15–16, 17, 19, 26,
    28, 155, 204(n14), 205(n23),
    207(n45)
Wu Runbao (sister), 17, 66
Wu Shangmo, 13–14, 203(n3)
Wu Shaolie, 15, 204(n7)
Wu Shifan, 14–15
*Wuthering Heights* (Bronte), 167, 168
Wu Woyao, 65

Wu Yanglie, 15, 204(nn 8, 10)
Wu Zuguang (brother), 18, 26, 47, 98,
    207(n45)
Wu Zuxiang, 33(photo), 186(photo)
    birth/childhood, 17–19
    children of, 25
    clan ancestry, 13–14, 15, 203(nn3, 5),
        204(nn 6, 7)
    education, 19–20, 23, 25, 26, 28–29,
        98, 103
    employment, 102–104, 140, 188,
        208(n60). *See also* Central
        University; Feng Yuxiang
    exile, 122
    family background, 14–17
    and fatherhood, 27–28, 104, 205(n17)
    health, 139, 140, 220(n58). *See also*
        Malaria
    marriage, 25
    relationship between life and works,
        90, 91–92, 120. *See also*
        Autobiographical elements
    as typical/unique writer, 3–4
    visits to America, 36, 184–188, 193,
        195

Xiao Hong, 110
"Xiao Hua's Birthday," 42–46, 79, 159,
    165, 205(n23)
*Xinhua ribao*, 121
*Xin miao* (Yao Xueyin), 140
Xuancheng, 19
Xu Dishan, 6, 201(n9)

Yang, C. K., 119
Yang Bojun, 130
"Yangzhou Jottings," 110, 111–112,
    229(n69)
Yan Yu, 147
Yao Xueyin, 131, 140
Ye Yiqun, 137
Ye Zi, 196
Yuan Hung-tao, 203(n29)
Yuan Liangjun, 66, 70–71, 106, 131, 191,
    203(n26), 219(n45), 227(n41)
Yu Dafu, 36, 160
"Yuguan" (Xu Dishan), 6, 201(n9)

Yu Guanying, 28, 103, 139
Yu Pingbo, 193
Yu Zhigong, 233(n27)

Zeng Guofan, 15
Zhang Henshui, 171, 214(n76)
Zhang Huasuo, 140
Zhang Tianyi, 140, 192
Zhang Yuanxi, 187, 243(nn 12, 14)
Zhang Ziping, 215(n93)
Zhao Shuli, 198

Zhao Yuan, 52, 66, 71, 79, 129
Zheng Zhenduo, 33(photo), 206(n41)
Zhong Kui (mythical figure), 64
Zhou Enlai, 194
Zhou Yang, 246(n46)
Zhou Zuoren, 8, 10
Zhu Ziqing, 32, 90, 102, 103, 162, 187,
    192, 220(n58)
Zola, Emile, 3, 139, 159, 238(n6)
*Zuo zhuan*, 102